WESTERN CIVILIZATION

Sources, Images, and Interpretations

FIFTH EDITION / VOLUME I: TO 1700

Dennis Sherman

JOHN JAY COLLEGE OF CRIMINAL JUSTICE, CITY UNIVERSITY OF NEW YORK

Boston   Burr Ridge, IL   Dubuque, IA   Madison, WI
New York   San Francisco   St. Louis
Bangkok   Bogotá   Caracas   Lisbon   London   Madrid   Mexico City
Milan   New Delhi   Seoul   Singapore   Sydney   Taipei   Toronto

McGraw-Hill Higher Education

A Division of The **McGraw-Hill** Companies

WESTERN CIVILIZATION: SOURCES, IMAGES, AND INTERPRETATIONS
VOLUME I: TO 1700, FIFTH EDITION

This book is printed on acid-free paper.

1 2 3 4 5 6 7 8 9 0 DOC/DOC 0 9 8 7 6 5 4 3 2 1 0

ISBN 0–07–233573–4

Editorial director: *Jane E. Vaicunas*
Senior sponsoring editor: *Lyn Uhl*
Developmental editor: *Donata Dettbarn*
Senior marketing manager: *Suzanne Daghlian*
Project manager: *Jill R. Peter*
Production supervisor: *Laura Fuller*
Design director: *Keith J. McPherson*
Senior photo research coordinator: *Lori Hancock*
Supplement coordinator: *Brenda A. Ernzen*
Compositor: *GAC—Indianapolis*
Typeface: *10/12 Caledonia*
Printer: *R. R. Donnelley & Sons Company/Crawfordsville, IN*

Cover designer: *Trudi Gershenov Design*
Cover image: *Su concessione del Castello del Buonconsiglio. Monumenti e collezioni provinciali. Trento*
Photo research: *Barbara Salz*

Library of Congress Catalog Card Number: 99–64527

www.mhhe.com

ABOUT THE AUTHOR

Dennis Sherman is Professor of History at John Jay College of Criminal Justice, the City University of New York. He received his B.A. (1962) and J.D. (1965) degrees from the University of California at Berkeley and his Ph.D. (1970) from the University of Michigan. He was Visiting Professor at the University of Paris (1978–1979; 1985). He received the Ford Foundation Prize Fellowship (1968–1969, 1969–1970), a fellowship from the Council for Research on Economic History (1971–1972), and fellowships from the National Endowment for the Humanities (1973–1976). His publications include *A Short History of Western Civilization,* Eighth Edition (co-author); *World Civilizations: Sources, Images, and Interpretations* (co-author); *The West in the World: A Mid-Length Narrative History;* a series of introductions in the Garland Library of War and Peace; several articles and reviews on nineteenth-century French economic and social history in American and European journals; and short stories in literary reviews.

ADVISORY EDITOR

Raymond Grew, University of Michigan

To Pat, Joe, Darryl, Vera, and Raymond

In time choice, change, and obligation merge;
How quietly we listen to ourselves.

CONTENTS

PART II THE MIDDLE AGES

PART III RENAISSANCE, REFORMATION, AND EXPANSION

VISUAL SOURCES

SECONDARY SOURCES

Chapter Fourteen: Overseas Expansion and New Politics

PRIMARY SOURCES

VISUAL SOURCES

SECONDARY SOURCES

PART IV THE EARLY MODERN PERIOD

°Note: *Volume II: Since 1660* of this work begins with chapter 16, and overlaps Volume I. Thus, chapters 16 and 17 are found in both volumes.

PREFACE

This book provides a broad introduction to the sources historians use, the kinds of interpretations historians make, and the evolution of Western civilization over the past six thousand years. A large selection of documents, photographs, and maps is presented along with introductions, commentaries, and questions designed to place each selection in a meaningful context and facilitate an understanding of its historical significance. Each selection has been carefully edited to keep the length of the book down while providing a wide variety of materials.

The sources have been organized to introduce Western civilization and the discipline of history in several ways. First, the sources provide insights into the major developments in each era. Second, the selections reveal the wide range of historical developments and interpretations: political and intellectual history are balanced with social, economic, and cultural history. Third, the sources indicate how historians apply input from other disciplines, such as psychology or sociology. Finally, the types of sources selected in this book demonstrate the kinds of materials used by historians—not just traditional written documents, but paintings, maps, and artifacts that also can tell a story, provide evidence, or serve as interpretive tools.

A brief look at the task facing historians of Western civilization will supply a background to what will be covered in this book. To discover what people thought and did and to organize this into a chronological record of the human past, historians must search for evidence—for the sources of history. Most sources are written materials, ranging from government records to gravestone inscriptions, memoirs, and poetry. Other sources include paintings, photographs, sculpture, buildings, maps, pottery, and oral traditions. In searching for sources, historians usually have something in mind—some tentative goals or conclusions that guide their search. Thus, in the process of working with sources, historians must decide which ones to emphasize. What historians ultimately write is a synthesis of the questions posed, the sources used, and their own ideas.

Historians of Western civilization consider their subject to be what is today Europe, along with those offshoots of Europe that have become established in various parts of the world. As they look back into the past, they focus on the origins of today's Western civilization in the Mediterranean basin, a cultural region that includes parts of North Africa and the Near East as well as Europe itself.

STRUCTURE OF THE BOOK

The basic organization of this book is chronological, beginning with the origins of Western civilization in the ancient Near East and gradually moving up to the present. From time to time this chronological approach is modified and certain important developments such as the Renaissance are pulled out of the chapter covering their period of occurrence and are discussed separately. All the chapters, however, are organized the same way. Each chapter is broken into sections consisting of the following features:

Each chapter opens with a **chapter introduction,** in which the period of history and the general topics to be dealt with in the chapter are described. The introduction provides a brief sketch of some of the most important developments, but no effort is made to cover the period. Instead, the purpose is to introduce the topics, issues, and questions that the sources in the chapter focus on and to place these sources in the historical context of Western civilization.

The introduction is followed by a **time line,** showing the relevant dates, people, events, and developments of the period, to provide a historical context for the selections in the chapter. In addition, a time line at the beginning of each of the six parts in the book puts the developments covered in each chapter into a broader perspective.

The chapter time line is followed by the **primary sources.** These are documents written by individuals involved in the matter under investigation. Historians consider these documents their main building blocks for learning about and interpreting the past. They are pieces of evidence that show what people thought, how they acted, and what they accomplished. At the same time historians must criticize these sources both externally—to attempt to uncover forgeries and errors—and internally—to find the authors' motives, inconsistencies within the documents, and different meanings of words and phrases.

Each document is preceded by a **headnote.** The headnote provides some information on the nature of the source, places it in a specific historical context, and indicates its particular focus.

The headnotes end with suggestions of **points to consider.** These points are not simply facts to be searched for in the selection. Rather, they are designed to stimulate analytical thought about the selections and to indicate some of the uses of each source.

The primary sources are followed by visual sources, including maps, and then by **secondary sources.**

Secondary sources are documents written by scholars about the time in question. Usually, they are interpretations of what occurred based on examination of numerous primary documents and other sources. They reflect choices the authors have made and their own particular understandings of what has happened. Often there are important differences of opinion among scholars about how to understand significant historical developments. Secondary sources should therefore be read with these questions in mind: What sort of evidence does the author use? Does the author's argument make sense? What political or ideological preferences are revealed in the author's interpretation? How might one argue against the interpretation presented by the author? At times the distinction between primary and secondary documents becomes blurred, as when the author is a contemporary of the events he or she is interpreting. If a document by that author is read as an interpretation of what occurred, it would be a secondary source. As evidence for the assumptions and attitudes of the author's times, however, the document would be a primary source.

Like the primary documents, all the secondary documents are preceded by headnotes and suggestions for points to consider.

Visual sources are paintings, drawings, sculpture, ceramics, photographs, buildings, monuments, coins, and so forth, that can provide valuable historical insights or information. Although they often include characteristics of secondary documents, they are usually most valuable when used in the same way as primary documents. In this book their purpose is not merely to supplement the documents or provide examples of the great pieces of art throughout history. It is to show how these visual materials can be used as sources of history and to provide insights difficult to gain solely through written documents. To this end, each visual source is accompanied by a relatively extensive interpretive description. Care should be taken in viewing these sources and using these descriptions. By their very nature, visual sources usually have a less clear meaning than written documents. Scholars differ greatly over how sources such as paintings, ceramics, and coins should be interpreted. Therefore, the descriptions accompanying the visual sources are open to debate. They are designed to show how it is possible for historians to use visual materials as sources of history—as unwritten evidence for what people thought and did in the past.

Maps often combine elements of primary documents, secondary documents, and visual sources. However, here they are usually used to help establish relationships, such as the connections between geographic factors and political developments, thereby enabling us to interpret what occurred differently than we could have if we had relied on written sources alone. As is the case with visual sources, each map is accompanied by an interpretive description. These descriptions indicate some of the ways maps might be used by historians.

Each chapter ends with **chapter questions.** These are designed to draw major themes of the chapter together in a challenging way. Answers to these questions require some analytical thought and the use of several of the selections in the chapter.

In the first chapter of each volume there are three special sections: **Using Primary Sources, Using Visual Sources,** and **Using Secondary Sources.** They are designed as guides to specific ways these three different kinds of sources can be used and analyzed.

Finally, for teachers there is **A Guide to Classroom Discussion** for this book. The **Guide** is designed to show some of the ways in which the materials in this book can be used for classroom discussion.

NEW IN THIS EDITION

In the fifth edition of *Western Civilization: Sources, Images, and Interpretations,* some important changes have been made. Chapter order has been reorganized to fit better with the way most textbooks survey Western civilization. In response to the popularity of illustrations and maps, several new visual sources have been added. In addition to several new primary documents, many secondary sources reflecting historical scholarship over the past fifteen years have been added, replacing older sources. The last two chapters in particular have been extensively revised to account for changing developments and perceptions over the past two decades.

CONTEXT AND ACKNOWLEDGMENTS

Since a book of this size can only sample what is available and outline what has occurred, this book is truly an introduction to Western civilization and its sources. Indeed, it is my hope that the materials presented here will reveal the range of sources that can be used to deepen our understanding of Western civilization and serve as a jumping-off point for further exploration into history and the historian's discipline.

McGraw-Hill and the author would like to thank the following reviewers for their many helpful comments and suggestions: Dr. Narasingha Sil, Western Oregon University; Professor Glenn S. Sunshine, Central Connecticut State University; Professor Charlie Steen, University of New Mexico; Professor Robert S. Babcock, Hasting College; Professor Paul B. Goodwin, University of Connecticut; Professor Alison Williams Lewin, St. Joseph's University; Professor Andrew Harris, Bridgewater State College; Professor Thomas Melton, Brewton Parker College; Professor Alice Bullard, Georgia Institute of Technology; Professor Marjorie Beale, University of California, Irvine; Professor Pamela Beattie, University of Louisville.

Dennis Sherman

Schematic of Evolution of Western Civilization

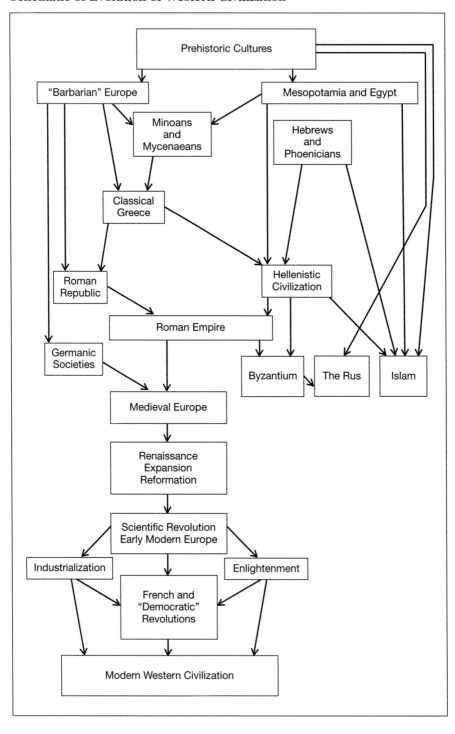

THE EVOLUTION OF
WESTERN CIVILIZATION

This chart is a schematic illustration of the development of Western civilization up to modern times. Caution should be exercised when reading such a chart. The connections made are a matter more of judgment than of fact. Moreover, what is missing—the how and why of the connections—is of great importance. Nevertheless, the chart can make it easier to see some of the broadest connections between societies and civilizations, connections that are often lost when a single period or society is examined in detail.

Consider:
Possible reasons for the various connections within the chart; what might be added to this chart to make it more useful.

I

CIVILIZATIONS OF THE ANCIENT WORLD

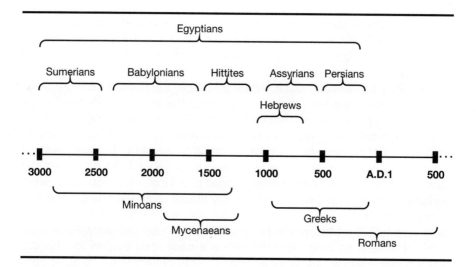

CHAPTER ONE

Civilizations of the Ancient Near East

What historians call *civilization* arose some five to six thousand years ago out of small agricultural villages in the river valleys of the ancient Near East, first in Mesopotamia near the Tigris and Euphrates rivers and shortly thereafter in Egypt around the Nile. In the delta of the Tigris-Euphrates river system, the Sumerians organized into city-states such as Ur. About 2340 B.C. the Sumerians were overwhelmed by the Akkadians from the north, and over the next two thousand years this area, a meeting point between Asia, Africa, and Europe, experienced great instability as in their turn the Babylonians, Hittites, Assyrians, Chaldeans, Medes, and Persians gained dominance. Egyptian civilization developed toward the end of the fourth millennium B.C. and is usually dated from about 3000 B.C., when the upper and lower Nile areas were unified under one king. Although there were some periods of change, this was a remarkably stable civilization, lasting almost three thousand years.

In many respects the Mesopotamian and Egyptian civilizations were similar. Both were dependent on rivers and the rich soil deposited by periodic floods; both had to develop and maintain organized systems of irrigation and flood control. Both eventually had powerful kings and a priestly caste. Both believed in all-powerful gods who played an active role in the world. But there were also important differences between these two civilizations. Mesopotamia was not as well protected geographically as Egypt and was thus more open to attack. Her rivers were not as navigable, nor were the floods as regular as the Nile's. Her culture and religion reflected a sense of instability and pessimism in comparison to the stability and optimism that characterized Egyptian civilization.

Between these two areas there arose a number of smaller and politically less significant states, the most important of which were the Phoenician and the Hebrew states. The Phoenicians, a mercantile people, facilitated trade, established colonies, and spread Near Eastern culture. The Hebrews developed religious and ethical ideas that would be a foundation for both Christian and Islamic civilizations.

A number of sources in this chapter deal with the origins, nature, and spread of the earliest civilizations. How should one define "civilization"? Why did civilizations arise where and when they did? What were the main characteristics of these ancient civilizations? Through what processes did civilizations spread? The rest of the documents concern each of the three main civilizations: the Mesopotamians, the Egyptians, and the Hebrews. For Mesopotamia, most of the sources center on the culture, the legal system, and the insights they provide into the nature of civilization there. Other documents focus on the position of women in Mesopotamian societies. For Egypt, what was the relation between the Nile and religion? What were some of Egypt's main economic and social characteristics? What was the significance of the pharaoh? How did the Egyptians view death and the afterlife? For the Hebrews, how did their religion, which became so important in the development of Western civilization, compare to others?

In sum, the sources in this chapter provide an introduction to the nature of civilization and its deep roots in the ancient Near East. The more direct foundations of Western civilization in ancient Greece will be examined in the next chapter.

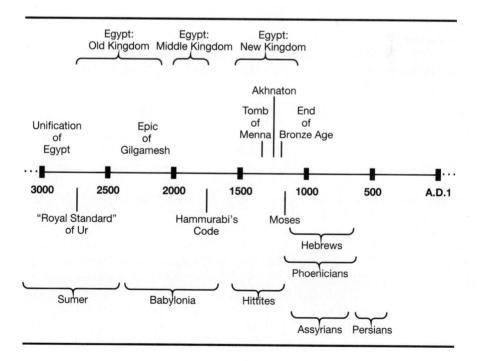

The sources in this and all chapters are divided into three sections: Primary Sources, Visual Sources, and Secondary Sources. In this chapter, each one of these three sections begins with a guide containing suggestions on how to use the sources, focusing on the first source within the section.

PRIMARY SOURCES

Using Primary Sources: The Laws of Hammurabi

Primary sources are briefly defined and discussed in the Preface. What follows is a more specific guide to the use of primary sources. It focuses on the first primary source in this book, the *Laws of Hammurabi*, which immediately follows as an example.

1.   When reading primary sources such as the following selections from the *Laws of Hammurabi*, try to think of every line as evidence. Assume that you are a historian who knows very little about the history of Mesopotamia and that this document falls into your hands. Your job is to use this document as evidence to support some conclusions about Babylonian civilization.

Actually, you have a head start. You already know something about the peoples of Mesopotamia from the chapter introduction, the time line, and the headnote preceding the source. You can use this information to better place the source in a historical context and to gain a sense of how the evidence in the source can be used. You also can use information from the headnote to identify the general nature of the source, where it came from, and when it was written.

2.   Think of questions as you read the source. These can keep you focused on how words and lines and sections of the source might be used as evidence. A general question to keep in mind is, "What does this tell me about this civilization, about how people behaved, how they thought, what they believed?" Try reading each line as a piece of evidence to answer part of this general question. More specific questions can be derived from the "consider" points in italics just before the beginning of the document. These points indicate that the source might be particularly useful for providing evidence about the Babylonian legal system, about Babylonian social divisions, and about Babylonian politics and economics.

3.   There are several ways almost any of these selections might be used as evidence. Read Article 1, the first section of the *Laws of Hammurabi*. It might be argued that the fact that a Babylonian could bring "a charge" of murder against someone, that this charge had to be "proved," and that consequences flowed from the outcome of the process (if the accuser does not prove it he shall be put to death) constitutes evidence that the Babylonians had a formal legal system. You may further infer that this legal system was based on some principles of fairness (having to "prove" an accusation) and

justice (death to those whose accusations are "not proved"). On the other hand, we must be careful not to read too much into this article—above all, not to read our own assumptions into the past. For example, this article does not tell us what constitutes proof or whether there is a jury system, although Article 3 might provide some evidence here (testimony is used and the truth of that testimony is at least open to challenge).

Read Articles 17, 18, and 19. Clearly they reveal that there were slaves within Babylonian society. They also imply that there was a problem with slaves attempting to escape, for rewards were offered to those who caught and returned slaves to their owners (Article 17) and penalties were imposed on those who hid escaped slaves (Article 19). Article 18 can be used as evidence for the existence of an organized bureaucracy of officials who kept written records ("take him to the palace in order that his record may be investigated").

Read Articles 53 and 54. They require landowners to keep dikes against water in repair (Article 53) and impose stiff penalties against those who do not (Articles 53 and 54). Together, the articles provide evidence for the existence of extensive water control systems for agriculture that required the cooperation (voluntary or imposed) of landowners and the government (by creating and enforcing these laws). Article 54 also reveals more about slavery in Babylonia, for since a landowner could be sold into slavery ("they shall sell him") we now have evidence that the source of slaves was not only external—from other societies through war, raids, or trade—but also internal.

Read Articles 141 and 142. How can the information in these articles be used to provide evidence for marriage, family life, and the relative positions of men and women in Babylonian society?

4.   After working on various parts of the source, pull back and consider the source as a whole. It can be used to provide evidence for conclusions about Babylonia's system and principles of justice (the existence of laws, what the laws were, judgment and enforcement of laws, what crimes are more serious than others), its society (the importance and sources of slavery, the existence of different social classes, relations between men and women, the institution of marriage), its government (the king, the bureaucracy or core of governmental officials), and its economy (agriculture with a flood control system, a monetary system).

The Laws of Hammurabi

Much information about the peoples of Mesopotamia comes from compilations of laws, prescriptions, and decisions that were written as early as the twenty-third century B.C. The best known of these are the Laws of Hammurabi (often referred to as the Code of Hammurabi), issued by an eighteenth-century B.C. Babylonian king who probably used older Sumerian and Akkadian laws. The laws refer to almost all aspects of life in Babylonia. The following selections are taken from

SOURCE: From Pritchard, James B., *Ancient Near Eastern Texts Relating to the Old Testament*, copyright 1951 by Princeton University Press. Reprinted by permission of Princeton University Press.

this code, which originally had about 282 articles and included a long prologue and epilogue that traced Hammurabi's authority to the gods.

> **Consider:** *The principles of justice reflected by these laws; the social divisions in Babylonian society disclosed in these laws; the political and economic characteristics of Babylonia revealed in this document.*

1: If a seignior[39] accused a(nother) seignior and brought a charge of murder against him, but has not proved it, his accuser shall be put to death.

✿

3: If a seignior came forward with false testimony in a case, and has not proved the word which he spoke, if that case was a case involving life, that seignior shall be put to death.

4: If he came forward with (false) testimony concerning grain or money, he shall bear the penalty of that case.

✿

6: If a seignior stole the property of church or state, that seignior shall be put to death; also the one who received the stolen goods from his hand shall be put to death.

✿

17: If a seignior caught a fugitive male or female slave in the open and has taken him to his owner, the owner of the slave shall pay him two shekels[48] of silver.

18: If that slave will not name his owner, he shall take him to the palace in order that his record may be investigated, and they shall return him to his owner.

19: If he has kept that slave in his house (and) later the slave has been found in his possession, that seignior shall be put to death.

✿

22: If a seignior committed robbery and has been caught, that seignior shall be put to death.

23: If the robber has not been caught, the robbed seignior shall set forth the particulars regarding his lost property in the presence of god, and the city and governor, in whose territory and district the robbery was committed, shall make good to him his lost property.

✿

48: If a debt is outstanding against a seignior and Adad has inundated his field or a flood has ravaged (it) or through lack of water grain has not been produced in the field,

---

[39]The word *awēlum*, used here, is literally "man," but in the legal literature it seems to be used in at least three senses: (1) sometimes to indicate a man of the higher class, a noble; (2) sometimes a free man of any class, high or low; and (3) occasionally a man of any class, from king to slave. For the last I use the inclusive word "man," but for the first two, since it is seldom clear which of the two is intended in a given context, I follow the ambiguity of the original and use the rather general term "seignior," which I employ as the term is employed in Italian and Spanish, to indicate any free man of standing, and not in the strict feudal sense, although the ancient Near East did have something approximating the feudal system, and that is another reason for using "seignior."

[48]A weight of about 8 gr.

he shall not make any return of grain to his creditor in that year; he shall cancel his contract-tablet and he shall pay no interest for that year.

✿

53: If a seignior was too lazy to make [the dike of] his field strong and did not make his dike strong and a break has opened up in his dike and he has accordingly let the water ravage the farmland, the seignior in whose dike the break was opened shall make good the grain that he let get destroyed.

54: If he is not able to make good the grain, they shall sell him and his goods, and the farmers whose grain the water carried off shall divide (the proceeds).

✿

141: If a seignior's wife, who was living in the house of the seignior, has made up her mind to leave in order that she may engage in business, thus neglecting her house (and) humiliating her husband, they shall prove it against her; and if her husband has then decided on her divorce, he may divorce her, with nothing to be given her as her divorce-settlement upon her departure. If her husband has not decided on her divorce, her husband may marry another woman, with the former woman living in the house of her husband like a maidservant.

142: If a woman so hated her husband that she has declared, "You may not have me," her record shall be investigated at her city council, and if she was careful and was not at fault, even though her husband has been going out and disparaging her greatly, that woman, without incurring any blame at all, may take her dowry and go off to her father's house.

✿

195: If a son has struck his father, they shall cut off his hand.

196: If a seignior has destroyed the eye of a member of the aristocracy, they shall destroy his eye.

197: If he has broken a(nother) seignior's bone, they shall break his bone.

198: If he has destroyed the eye of a commoner or broken the bone of a commoner, he shall pay one mina of silver.

199: If he has destroyed the eye of a seignior's slave or broken the bone of a seignior's slave, he shall pay one-half his value.

200: If a seignior has knocked out a tooth of a seignior of his own rank, they shall knock out his tooth.

201: If he has knocked out a commoner's tooth, he shall pay one-third mina of silver.

202: If a seignior has struck the cheek of a seignior who is superior to him, he shall be beaten sixty (times) with an oxtail whip in the assembly.

✿

209: If a seignior struck a(nother) seignior's daughter and has caused her to have a miscarriage, he shall pay ten shekels of silver for her fetus.

210: If that woman has died, they shall put his daughter to death.

211: If by a blow he has caused a commoner's daughter to have a miscarriage, he shall pay five shekels of silver.

212: If that woman has died, he shall pay one-half mina of silver.

The Epic of Gilgamesh

Insight into a people's ideas about life and death can be gained by examining their myths and their literature. The Epic of Gilgamesh, *probably written in the latter part of the third millennium (2000s)* B.C., *was the great epic poem of Mesopotamia. Its hero, Gilgamesh, ruled the Sumerian city-state of Uruk around 2700* B.C. *The poem is about the mythical adventures this king, part god himself, has struggling with life, the gods, and death. In one adventure, Gilgamesh faces death by embarking on a search for immortality. As part of that search he descends into the Netherworld to find Utnapishtim, a human who has been granted immortality by the gods. In the following selection, Gilgamesh questions Utnapishtim, who tells him the story of the flood.*

> **Consider:** *The nature of the gods and their relations with humans; conclusions about life Mesopotamians might have come to reading or listening to this story; connections between this story and the biblical story of Noah and the flood.*

"Oh, father Utnapishtim, you who have entered the assembly of the gods, I wish to question you concerning the living and the dead, how shall I find the life for which I am searching?"

Utnapishtim said, "There is no permanence. Do we build a house to stand for ever, do we seal a contract to hold for all time? Do brothers divide an inheritance to keep for ever, does the flood-time of rivers endure? It is only the nymph of the dragon-fly who sheds her larva and sees the sun in his glory. From the days of old there is no permanence. The sleeping and the dead, how alike they are, they are like a painted death. What is there between the master and the servant when both have fulfilled their doom? When the Annunaki,[1] the judges, come together, and Mammetun the mother of destinies, together they decree the fates of men. Life and death they allot but the day of death they do not disclose."

Then Gilgamesh said to Utnapishtim the Faraway, "I look at you now, Utnapishtim, and your appearance is no different from mine; there is nothing strange in your features. I thought I should find you like a hero prepared for battle, but you lie here taking your ease on your back. Tell me truly, how was it that you came to enter the company of the gods and to possess everlasting life?" Utnapishtim said to Gilgamesh, "I will reveal to you a mystery, I will tell you a secret of the gods."

"You know the city Shurrupak, it stands on the banks of Euphrates? That city grew old and the gods that were in it were old. There was Anu, lord of the firmament, their father, and warrior Enlil their counsellor, Ninurta the helper, and Ennugi watcher over canals; and with them also was Ea.[2] In those days the world teemed, the people multiplied, the world bellowed like a wild bull, and the great god was aroused by the clamour. Enlil heard the clamour and he said to the gods in council, 'The uproar of mankind is intolerable and

---

SOURCE: N. K. Sandars, trans., *The Epic of Gilgamesh*, 2d rev. ed. (London: Penguin Books, 1972), copyright © N. K. Sandars, 1960, 1964, 1972.

[1]Gods.

[2]God of wisdom and good fortune.

sleep is no longer possible by reason of the babel.' So the gods in their hearts were moved to let loose the deluge; but my lord Ea warned me in a dream. He whispered their words to my house of reeds, 'Reed-house, reed-house! Wall, O wall, hearken reed-house, wall reflect; O man of Shurrupak, son of Ubara-Tutu; tear down your house and build a boat, abandon possessions and look for life, despise worldly goods and save your soul alive. Tear down your house, I say, and build a boat.'

"When I had understood I said to my lord, 'Behold, what you have commanded I will honour and perform, but how shall I answer the people, the city, the elders?' Then Ea opened his mouth and said to me, his servant, 'Tell them this: I have learnt that Enlil is wrathful against me, I dare no longer walk in his land nor live in his city; I will go down to the Gulf to dwell with Ea my lord. But on you he will rain down abundance, rare fish and shy wild-fowl, a rich harvest-tide. In the evening the rider of the storm will bring you wheat in torrents.'" . . .

"On the seventh day the boat was complete. . . .

"I loaded into her all that I had of gold and of living things, my family, my kin, the beasts of the field both wild and tame, and all the craftsmen. . . .

"For six days and six nights the winds blew, torrent and tempest and flood over-whelmed the world, tempest and flood raged together like warring hosts. When the seventh day dawned the storm from the south subsided, the sea grew calm, the flood was stilled; I looked at the face of the world and there was silence, all mankind was turned to clay. The surface of the sea stretched as flat as a rooftop; I opened a hatch and the light fell on my face. Then I bowed low, I sat down and I wept, the tears streamed down my face, for on every side was the waste of water. I looked for land in vain, but fourteen leagues distant there appeared a mountain, and there the boat grounded; on the mountain of Nisir the boat held fast, she held fast and did not budge. . . . When the seventh day dawned I loosed a dove and let her go. She flew away, but finding no resting-place she returned. Then I loosed a swallow, and she flew away but finding no resting-place she returned. I loosed a raven, she saw that the waters had retreated, she ate, she flew around, she cawed, and she did not come back. Then I threw everything open to the four winds, I made a sacrifice and poured out a libation on the mountain top. Seven and again seven cauldrons I set up on their stands, I heaped up wood and cane and cedar and myr-tle. When the gods smelled the sweet savour, they gathered like flies over the sacrifice. Then, at last, Ishtar also came, she lifted her necklace with the jewels of heaven that once Anu had made to please her. 'O you gods here present, by the lapis lazuli round my neck I shall remember these days as I remember the jewels of my throat; these last days I shall not forget. Let all the gods gather round the sacrifice, except Enlil. He shall not ap-proach this offering, for without reflection he brought the flood; he consigned my peo-ple to destruction.'

"When Enlil had come, when he saw the boat, he was wrath and swelled with anger at the gods, the host of heaven, 'Has any of these mortals escaped? Not one was to have sur-vived the destruction.' Then the god of the wells and canals Ninurta opened his mouth and said to the warrior Enlil, 'Who is there of the gods that can devise without Ea? It is Ea alone who knows all things.' Then Ea opened his mouth and spoke to warrior Enlil, 'Wis-est of gods, hero Enlil, how could you so senselessly bring down the flood?' . . .

"Then Enlil went up into the boat, he took me by the hand and my wife and made us enter the boat and kneel down on either side, he standing between us. He touched our foreheads to bless us saying, 'In time past Utnapishtim was a mortal man; henceforth he and his wife shall live in the distance at the mouth of the rivers.' Thus it was that the gods took me and placed me here to live in the distance, at the mouth of the rivers."

Hymn to the Nile

Most of the earliest civilizations were located in major river valleys. The Nile River provided the Egyptians with a strip of fertile land in an area otherwise relatively arid and hostile to large long-term settlement. Moreover, its predictable annual flooding ensured the continued fertility of the land and enabled the Egyptians to irrigate the crops that supported this long-lasting civilization. Understandably, the Nile became a focus for Egyptian religious beliefs and one of the Egyptians' chief deities. In the following selection from a hymn to the Nile, probably originating in an early period in Egyptian history, the Nile is praised for its power and deeds that have enabled the Egyptians to live in a relatively ordered, prosperous world.

> **Consider:** *The Egyptian view of the proper relationship between themselves and this deity; the Egyptian perception of this deity and its characteristics; the information this document provides concerning Egyptian economic, social, and political life.*

When he[1] is sluggish noses clog,
Everyone is poor;
As the sacred loaves are pared,
A million perish among men.
When he plunders, the whole land rages,
Great and small roar;
People change according to his coming,
When Khnum has fashioned him.
When he floods, earth rejoices,
Every belly jubilates,
Every jawbone takes on laughter,
Every tooth is bared.

Food provider, bounty maker,
Who creates all that is good!
Lord of awe, sweetly fragrant,
Gracious when he comes.
Who makes herbage for the herds,
Gives sacrifice for every god.
Dwelling in the netherworld,

Source: Miriam Lichtheim, *Ancient Egyptian Literature*, 3 vols., pp. 199, 206, 208–209. Copyright © 1973–1980 Regents of the University of California.

[1]The Nile.

He controls both sky and earth.
Conqueror of the Two Lands,
He fills the stores,
Makes bulge the barns,
Gives bounty to the poor.

      °

When you overflow, O Hapy,[2]
Sacrifice is made for you;
Oxen are slaughtered for you,
A great oblation is made to you.
Fowl is fattened for you,
Desert game snared for you,
As one repays your bounty.

One offers to all the gods
Of that which Hapy has provided,
Choice incense, oxen, goats,
And birds in holocaust.

Hymn to the Pharaoh

The history of Egypt and the instruction of kingship have been traced back to the end of the fourth millennium B.C., *when Upper and Lower Egypt were unified apparently under one great conquering king. The Egyptian king, or pharaoh, was considered both a god and the absolute ruler of his country. These beliefs are reflected in laudatory hymns addressed to pharaohs. The following selection is from one of those hymns, dating from the reign of Sesostris III, who ruled from about 1880 to 1840* B.C.

> **Consider:** *The Egyptian perception of the pharaoh; what deeds or powers of the pharaoh seemed most important to the Egyptians; similarities and differences between the Egyptian perceptions of the pharaoh and of the Nile.*

How [the gods] rejoice:
  you have strengthened their offerings!
How your [people] rejoice:
  you have made their frontiers!
How your forbears rejoice:
  you have enriched their portions!
How Egypt rejoices in your strength:
  you have protected its customs!

SOURCE: Miriam Lichtheim, *Ancient Egyptian Literature*, vol. I, pp. 199, 206, 208–209. Copyright © 1973–1980 Regents of the University of California.
[2]The Nile.

How the people rejoice in your guidance:
　　your might has won increase [for them]!
How the Two Shores rejoice in your dreadedness:
　　You have enlarged their holdings!
How the youths whom you levied rejoice:
　　you have made them prosper!
How your elders rejoice:
　　you have made them youthful!
How the Two Lands rejoice in your power:
　　you have protected their walls!

The Old Testament— Genesis and Exodus

Squeezed between the larger kingdoms of Mesopotamia and Egypt were a number of small states. For the development of Western civilization, the most important of these states was in Palestine, where the Hebrews formed Israel and Judah. Although their roots extend further into the past, the Hebrews were originally led out of northeastern Egypt toward Palestine by Moses near the end of the second millennium B.C. The power of the Hebrew nation reached its height during the tenth and ninth centuries B.C., but the nation's importance rests primarily in the religion developed by the Hebrews. Judaism differed in many ways from other Near Eastern religions, particularly in its monotheism, its contractual nature, and its ethical mandates. These characteristics of Judaism are illustrated in the following selections from Genesis and Exodus.

> **Consider:** *The relationship between God and people illustrated in these selections; how these Hebrew beliefs compare with Egyptian beliefs; as a set of laws, how these selections compare with Hammurabi's Code.*

12: The LORD had said to Abram, "Leave your country, your people and your father's household and go to the land I will show you.

"I will make you into a great nation and I will bless you;
I will make your name great, and you will be a blessing.
I will bless those who bless you, and whoever curses you I will curse;
and all peoples on earth will be blessed through you."

*

19: In the third month after the Israelites left Egypt—on the very day—they came to the Desert of Sinai. After they set out from Rephidim, they entered the Desert of Sinai, and Israel camped there in the desert in front of the mountain.

SOURCE: Scripture taken from the *Holy Bible, New International Version®*. NIV®. Copyright© 1973, 1978, 1984 by International Bible Society. Used by permission of Zondervan Publishing House. All rights reserved.

Then Moses went up to God, and the LORD called to him from the mountain and said, "This is what you are to say to the house of Jacob and what you are to tell the people of Israel: 'You yourselves have seen what I did to Egypt, and how I carried you on eagles' wings and brought you to myself. Now if you obey me fully and keep my covenant, then out of all nations you will be my treasured possession. Although the whole earth is mine, you will be for me a kingdom of priests and a holy nation.' These are the words you are to speak to the Israelites."

So Moses went back and summoned the elders of the people and set before them all the words the LORD had commanded him to speak. The people all responded together, "We will do everything the LORD has said." So Moses brought their answer back to the LORD.

20: And God spoke all these words:

"I am the LORD your God, who brought you out of Egypt, out of the land of slavery.

"You shall have no other gods before me.

"You shall not make for yourself an idol in the form of anything in heaven above or on the earth beneath or in the waters below. You shall not bow down to them or worship them; for I, the LORD your God, am a jealous God, punishing the children for the sin of the fathers to the third and fourth generation of those who hate me, but showing love to a thousand generations of those who love me and keep my commandments.

"You shall not misuse the name of the LORD your God, for the LORD will not hold anyone guiltless who misuses his name.

"Remember the Sabbath day by keeping it holy. Six days you shall labor and do all your work, but the seventh day is a Sabbath to the LORD your God. On it you shall not do any work, neither you, nor your son or daughter, nor your manservant or maidservant, nor your animals, nor the alien within your gates. For in six days the LORD made the heavens and the earth, the sea, and all that is in them, but he rested on the seventh day. Therefore the LORD blessed the Sabbath day and made it holy.

"Honor your father and your mother, so that you may live long in the land the LORD your God is giving you.

"You shall not murder.

"You shall not commit adultery.

"You shall not steal.

"You shall not give false testimony against your neighbor.

"You shall not covet your neighbor's house. You shall not covet your neighbor's wife, or his manservant or maidservant, his ox or donkey, or anything that belongs to your neighbor."

When the people saw the thunder and lightning and heard the trumpet and saw the mountain in smoke, they trembled with fear. They stayed at a distance and said to Moses, "Speak to us yourself and we will listen. But do not have God speak to us or we will die."

Moses said to the people, "Do not be afraid. God has come to test you, so that the fear of God will be with you to keep you from sinning."

The Aton Hymn and Psalm 104: The Egyptians and the Hebrews

Despite characteristics that made them unique in the ancient Near East, Hebrews were connected to and influenced by the Egyptians in many ways. Geographically, Palestine served as a buffer zone between Egypt and the large kingdoms of Mesopotamia. Historically, the formative ordeal of Moses and the Exodus stemmed from Egypt. Less apparent but of great importance were connections between Hebrew and Egyptian religious concepts and forms of expression. The following comparison of selections from the Egyptian Aton Hymn, composed in the fourteenth century B.C. during the rule of Akhenaten, who attempted to change some traditional religious views, and Psalm 104 from the Old Testament, written six or seven centuries later, illustrates striking parallels between the two documents.

Consider: *How the similarities between these two excerpts might be explained.*

THE ATON HYMN

When thou settest in the western horizon,
The land is in darkness like death . . .
Every lion comes forth from his den;

All creeping things, they sting.

At daybreak, when thou arisest in the
    horizon . . .
Thou drivest away the darkness . . .
Men awake and stand upon their feet . . .
All the world, they do their labor.
How manifold are thy works!
They are hidden from man's sight.
O sole god, like whom there is no other,
Thou hast made the earth according to
    thy desire.

PSALM 104

Thou makest darkness and it is night,
Wherein all the beasts of the forest
    creep forth.
The young lions roar after their prey.

The sun ariseth, they get them away . . .

Man goeth forth unto his work,

And to his labor until the evening.
O Jahweh, how manifold are thy works!
In wisdom has thou made them all;
The earth is full of thy riches.

VISUAL SOURCES

Using Visual Sources: The "Royal Standard" of Ur

Visual sources are briefly defined and discussed in the Preface. What follows is a more specific guide to the use of visual sources, focusing on our first visual source, *The "Royal Standard" of Ur,* which immediately follows as an example (photos 1–1 and 1–2).

SOURCE: Reprinted in *The Burden of Egypt* by John A. Wilson, by permission of The Chicago Press. Copyright © 1951, p. 227.

1.   Try to look at visual sources as if they were written, primary documents. As with primary documents, assume that you are a historian who knows very little about the history of Sumer and discovers this visual source, *The "Royal Standard" of Ur.* Your goal is to try to "read" it as evidence to support some conclusions about Sumerian civilization.

Without some guidance, "reading" a visual source as historical evidence is more difficult than using a written source. The reproduction makes the details harder to see and most people are not used to looking at a picture in this analytical way. Therefore in the first paragraph of the headnote to *The "Royal Standard" of Ur* there is a description that puts into words what appears in the visual source. In the second paragraph there is an analysis of the evidence drawn from the photo. Here, as with most visual sources, it is useful to go back and forth between the photo and the written description and analysis that accompany the photo.

2.   As with primary documents, think of questions as you look at the visual source and as you read the written guide to it. The general question to keep in mind is, "What does this tell me about this civilization, about how people behaved, how they thought, or what they believed?" Other questions are suggested in the "consider" points, such as what information the artist might have been attempting to convey to the viewer.

3.   Here the first panel shows the Sumerians at war. The headnote alerts us to "read" this three-line panel from bottom to top, for that is how the Sumerian artist intended it to be viewed. With the aid of the headnote we can see the chariot charging the enemy, then the infantry, and finally the captives being led to the victorious king.

The second panel shows the Sumerians at peace. Again reading from bottom to top, we can see this society organizing in preparation for a banquet and then the banquet itself.

The second paragraph suggests some of the ways the information derived from *The "Royal Standard" of Ur* can be used as historical evidence that Ur in Sumer was a well-organized society with centralized political control, a society that at least by 2700 B.C. had mastered the use of various domesticated animals, tools, and instruments.

4.   Now pull back and consider the source as a whole. Why might the artist have chosen to depict these scenes? What might be made of the lack of individualized differences in the figures? In what ways might a similar sort of decoration be made today and what might such a set of scenes depict?

Sumer: The "Royal Standard" of Ur

This piece of art—made of shell, lapis lazuli, and red stone inlaid on the sides of a wooden box and found in a grave dating around 2700 B.C.—illustrates two aspects of Sumerian life: war and peace. In the bottom line of the first panel, reading from left to right, a wooden chariot charges the enemy and knocks him over. In the second line the infantry, with protective cloaks, helmets,

Photo 1-1

Royal Standard of Ur, "War" side, from the Sumerian Royal Graves of Ur, Early Dynastic Period, 2750 BC (mosaic), The British Museum, London, UK/Bridgeman Art Library, London/New York

Photo 1-2

Royal Standard of Ur, "Peace" side, from the Sumerian Royal Graves of Ur, Early Dynastic Period, 2750 BC (mosaic), The British Museum, London, UK/Bridgeman Art Library, London/New York

and short spears, captures and leads off the enemy. In the third line soldiers on the right lead captives to the king in the center. The king, who has just alighted from his attended chariot on the left, towers over the rest. In the second panel the fruits of victory or of peace are enjoyed, at least by the court. In the bottom and middle lines produce, manufactured goods, and livestock are brought to a banquet by bearers and menials. In the top line the king on the left and his soldiers drink wine while attended by servants and serenaded by a harpist and female singer on the right.

Clearly, this offers evidence for what historians consider a civilized society. Agricultural products are shown. Various animals have been domesticated for specialized purposes. Important inventions such as the wheel are in use. Leisure activities have been cultivated, as revealed by the harp, the rather formal banquet, and the existence of this piece of art itself (which may have been a box for a lyre). The society has been organized and displays some discipline, as indicated by the use of chariots, the infantry, the porters, the musicians, the servants, and the banquet itself. Finally, the king represents centralized political authority that is directly tied to military prowess. Note that the sole female figure here is the singer.

> **Consider:** *Why there is a lack of individual differences in the people portrayed in this picture; bases for social distinction in Sumerian society revealed in this scene; things or scenes missing from this that you might have expected to find; reasons the artist chose to portray these particular scenes and to include only the things you see here.*

Egyptian Wall Paintings from the Tomb of Menna

This wall painting from the tomb of an Egyptian scribe, Menna, dating from the late fifteenth century B.C., illustrates the basis of Egyptian economic life (photo 1–3). This pictorial record of a harvest should be read from bottom to top. In the bottom row, from left to right, commoners are harvesting wheat with sickles. The wheat is then carried in rope baskets past two girls fighting over remaining bits of wheat and past two laborers (one of whom is playing a flute) who are taking a break under a date tree, to where the wheat is being threshed and raked out by laborers. In the second row, from right to left, oxen tread on the wheat, separating the kernels from the husks, and laborers remove the chaff by scooping up the wheat and allowing it to fall in the wind. The grain is then brought to the supervising scribe, Menna, standing in a kiosk. Menna is aided by subordinate recording scribes. In the top row, from left to right, the fields are being measured by ropes as a basis for assessing taxes. In the center Menna watches as subordinates line up and whip those who have apparently failed to pay their taxes or adequately perform their duties. Finally, the grain is stacked for shipment and carried off in a boat.

The harvest seems plentiful, and Egyptian society is tightly organized around it—from the gathering, processing, and shipping of the wheat to the assessing of taxes and enforcement of laws. Menna's authority is denoted by his size, by his placement in a kiosk, and by the symbols of power placed in his hand and immediately around him. The importance of writing in early societies is also demonstrated: Menna and his immediate subordinates are in an authoritative position in part because they can write, a skill connected here to the ability of the central authority to organize the economy and exact taxes. Finally, this wall painting reveals part of the nature of Egyptian religious beliefs. The scene is painted on the inside of a tomb. Thus the paintings were not for the living public, as the tombs were not to be visited, but for the dead or the world of the

Photo 1-3

©Elliott Erwitt/Magnum

dead. *This implies a belief that there were strong connections between this world, what one did in it, and the afterlife.*

   Consider: *The evidence for the existence of a civilized society here; the similarities and differences between this and The "Royal Standard" of Ur.*

The Environment and the Rise of Civilization in the Ancient Near East

These three maps relate weather, vegetation, agricultural sites, and civilizations in the ancient Near East. Map 1–1 shows the average annual rainfall in modern times (although weather patterns may have changed over the last five thousand years, it is likely that they have not changed greatly). Map 1–2 shows some of the vegetation patterns and a number of the earliest agricultural sites that have been discovered in the same area. Map 1–3 shows patterns of civilization in this part of the world.

Map 1-1   Rainfall

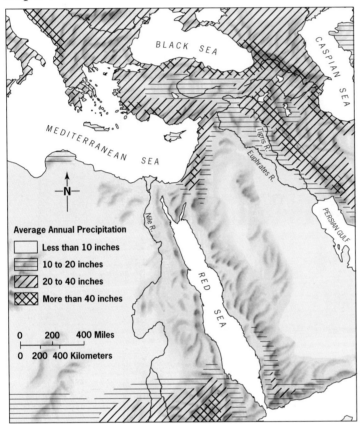

Together, these maps indicate a tendency for early agricultural sites to locate in areas of substantial rainfall and subtropical woodland, both appropriate for cereal farming. These areas often eventually supported the development of civilizations. Yet the earliest civilizations generally do not fall in these areas, but rather in areas of low rainfall that have a narrow strip of subtropical woodland along riverbanks. The rivers could compensate for the lack of rain, but low rainfall presented the challenge of developing irrigation systems along with corresponding social and political organizations. This is what happened in the earliest civilizations of Mesopotamia and Egypt.

Map 1-2   Vegetation and Agricultural Sites

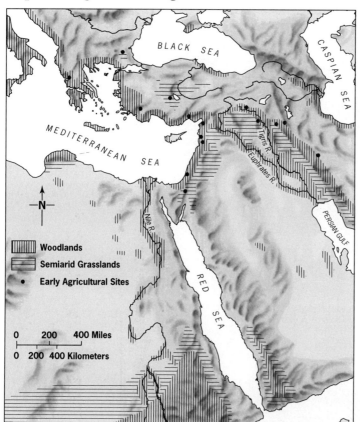

Consider: *How geographic and climatic factors help explain the rise of civilization in Mesopotamia and Egypt; how geographic and climatic factors facilitated the growth of settlements in some areas but not the blossoming of those settlements into large, organized societies.*

Map 1-3   Civilization

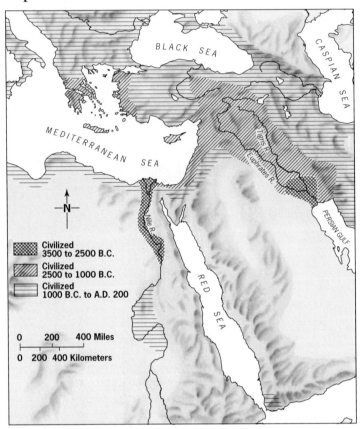

SECONDARY SOURCES

Using Secondary Sources: The Agricultural Revolution

Secondary sources are briefly defined and discussed in the Preface. What follows is a more specific guide to the use of secondary sources, focusing on our first secondary source, *The Agricultural Revolution*, which immediately follows as an example.

1.   Try to read a secondary source like *The Agricultural Revolution* by Robert J. Braidwood not as historical evidence (as you would for a primary source), but as a set of conclusions—an interpretation of the evidence from primary sources—by a scholar

(usually a historian). Your job is to try to understand what the writer's interpretation is, evaluate whether any arguments or evidence the writer presents seems to support it adequately, and decide in what ways you agree or disagree with that interpretation.

2.   Try to think of questions as you read a secondary source. This process can keep you alert to why the author selects and presents only certain information and what conclusions the author is trying to convey to the reader. Perhaps the two most important questions to keep in mind are, "What question is this author trying to answer?" and "What does all of what the author has written add up to?" For each secondary source, guidance for these two questions and related questions is provided in the headnote to the source and in the "consider" points.

Here the headnote to this secondary source tells us that the author, Robert J. Braidwood, is trying to interpret the agricultural revolution, particularly its spread and significance. The "consider" section alerts us to more specific aspects of what the author is trying to convince us of, such as his interpretation for the causes of the agricultural revolution and his rejection of alternative explanations (environmental determinism) for the agricultural revolution presented by other scholars.

3.   Try reading and summarizing in a few words what Braidwood is trying to say or argue in each paragraph. What conclusion is he reaching?

One could summarize the first paragraph by saying that Braidwood is trying to convince us that the agricultural revolution was an extremely important achievement of our species. He also defines the agricultural revolution ("the domestication of plants and animals" and "the achievement of an effective food-producing technology") and suggests why it was so important (the "subsequent developments" that "followed swiftly"—urban societies and later industrial civilization).

In the second paragraph Braidwood concludes that the agricultural revolution was caused ("the origin") by cultural evolution ("the record of culture"). He argues that the several independent inventions ("multiple occurrence") of agriculture support ("suggests that") his conclusion.

In the third paragraph Braidwood presents a contrary interpretation for the causes of the agricultural revolution ("environmental determinism"). He then presents an argument showing why he believes this opposing interpretation is wrong (what did and did not happen in reaction to climate change).

In the following three paragraphs Braidwood presents his interpretation and the arguments to support it in greater detail. In a few words, try to summarize what he is saying in each paragraph.

In the final paragraph, he, like many other authors, again tries to convince the reader that the topic he is writing about (the agricultural revolution) is important or of great significance. How does he do this?

4.   Finally, pull back and consider a secondary source as a whole. Try to formulate the author's arguments and conclusions in a nutshell.

Here you might say that Braidwood argues two things. First, the agricultural revolution was extremely important for human history because it directly led to the creation of urban civilizations. Second, the causes for the agricultural revolution were cultural differentiation and specialization (or the record of culture), not environmental determinism (circumstances).

The Agricultural Revolution

Robert J. Braidwood

Human beings populated parts of the earth for thousands of years before the first civilizations rise five or six thousand years ago in the ancient Near East. The causes for this relatively rapid transformation in the condition of human beings have been interpreted in a variety of ways. However, most historians and anthropologists point to the agricultural revolution of the Neolithic Age, in which—through the domestication of plants and animals—human beings became food producers rather than hunters and food gatherers, as the central development in this transformation to civilization. In the following selection, Robert J. Braidwood, an archaeologist and anthropologist, analyzes the agricultural revolution, its spread, and its significance.

> **Consider:** *The origins or causes of the agricultural revolution; Braidwood's rejection of environmental determinism and his acceptance of cultural differentiation and specialization; connections between agriculture and the beginnings of cities.*

Tool-making was initiated by pre-*sapiens* man. The first comparable achievement of our species was the agricultural revolution. No doubt a small human population could have persisted on the sustenance secured by the hunting and food-gathering technology that had been handed down and slowly improved upon over the 500 to 1,000 millennia of pre-human and pre-*sapiens* experience. With the domestication of plants and animals, however, vast new dimensions for cultural evolution suddenly became possible. The achievement of an effective food-producing technology did not, perhaps, predetermine subsequent developments, but they followed swiftly: the first urban societies in a few thousand years and contemporary industrial civilization in less than 10,000 years.

The first successful experiment in food production took place in southwestern Asia, on the hilly flanks of the "fertile crescent." Later experiments in agriculture occurred (possibly independently) in China and (certainly independently) in the New World. The multiple occurrence of the agricultural revolution suggests that it was a highly probable outcome of the prior cultural evolution of mankind and a peculiar combination of environmental circumstances. It is in the record of culture, therefore, that the origin of agriculture must be sought.

Not long ago the proponents of environmental determinism argued that the agricultural revolution was a response to the great changes in climate which accompanied the retreat of the last glaciation about 10,000 years ago. However, the climate had altered in equally dramatic fashion on other occasions in the past 75,000 years, and the potentially domesticable plants and animals were surely available to the bands of food-gatherers who lived in southwestern Asia and similar habitats in various parts of the globe. Moreover, recent studies have revealed that the climate did not change radically where farming began in the hills that flank the fertile crescent. Environmental determinists have

SOURCE: From *Hunters, Farmers, and Civilizations: Old World Archaeology* by C. C. Lamberg Karlovsky. Copyright © 1979 by W. H. Freeman and Company. Reprinted with permission.

also argued from the "theory of propinquity" that the isolation of men along with appropriate plants and animals in desert oases started the process of domestication.

In my opinion there is no need to complicate the story with extraneous "causes." The food-producing revolution seems to have occurred as the culmination of the ever increasing cultural differentiation and specialization of human communities. Around 8000 B.C. the inhabitants of the hills around the fertile crescent had come to know their habitat so well that they were beginning to domesticate the plants and animals they had been collecting and hunting. At slightly later times human cultures reached the corresponding level in Central America and perhaps in the Andes, in southeastern Asia and in China. From these "nuclear" zones cultural diffusion spread the new way of life to the rest of the world.

As the agricultural revolution began to spread, the trend toward ever increasing specialization of the intensified food-collecting way of life began to reverse itself. The new techniques were capable of wide application, given suitable adaptation, in diverse environments. Archeological remains at Hassuna, a site near the Tigris River somewhat later than Jarmo, show that the people were exchanging ideas on the manufacture of pottery and of flint and obsidian projectile points with people in the region of the Amouq in Syro-Cilicia. The basic elements of the food-producing complex—wheat, barley, sheep, goats and probably cattle—in this period moved west beyond the bounds of their native habitat to occupy the whole eastern end of the Mediterranean. They also traveled as far east as Anau, east of the Caspian Sea. Localized cultural differences still existed, but people were adopting and adapting more and more cultural traits from other areas. Eventually the new way of life traveled to the Aegean and beyond into Europe, moving slowly up such great river valley systems as the Dnieper, the Danube and the Rhone, as well as along the coasts. The intensified food-gatherers of Europe accepted the new way of life, but, as V. Gordon Childe has pointed out, they "were not slavish imitators: they adapted the gifts from the East . . . into a new and organic whole capable of developing on its own original lines." Among other things, the Europeans appear to have domesticated rye and oats that were first imported to the European continent as weed plants contaminating the seed of wheat and barley. In the comparable diffusion of agriculture from Central America, some of the peoples to the north appear to have rejected the new ways, at least temporarily.

By about 5000 B.C. the village-farming way of life seems to have been fingering down the valleys toward the alluvial bottom lands of the Tigris and Euphrates. Robert M. Adams believes that there may have been people living in the lowlands who were expert in collecting food from the rivers. They would have taken up the idea of farming from people who came down from the higher areas. In the bottom lands a very different climate, seasonal flooding of the land and small-scale irrigation led agriculture through a significant new technological transformation. By about 4000 B.C. the people of southern Mesopotamia had achieved such increases in productivity that their farms were beginning to support an urban civilization. The ancient site at Ubaid is typical of this period.

Thus in 3,000 or 4,000 years the life of man had changed more radically than in all of the preceding 250,000 years. Before the agricultural revolution most men must have spent their waking moments seeking their next meal, except when they could gorge following a great kill. As man learned to produce food, instead of gathering, hunting or collecting it, and to store it in the grain bin and on the hoof, he was compelled as well as enabled to settle in larger communities. With human energy released for a whole spectrum of new activities, there came the development of specialized nonagricultural crafts. It is no accident that such innovations as the discovery of the basic mechanical principles, weaving, the plow, the wheel and metallurgy soon appeared.

Freedom in the Ancient World: Civilization in Sumer

Herbert J. Muller

Historians generally see the development of cities as a sign of transformation into a civilized state and indeed an essential component of being civilized. Some of the earliest cities were formed by the Sumerians in the valley of the Tigris and Euphrates rivers, where settlers had already developed irrigation systems. In the following selection Herbert J. Muller analyzes the social, political, and religious significance of cities and irrigation systems for the Sumerians, and focuses particularly on the problems that civilization brought.

> **Consider:** *Why cities and irrigation systems require new systems of legal and political control; why Muller believes that the increased wealth and opportunity created by civilization was not an unmitigated benefit to the Sumerians; how political, economic, and social decisions made by the Sumerians were reflected in their religion.*

We must now consider the problems that came with civilization—problems due not so much to the sinful nature of man as to the nature of the city. "Friendship lasts a day" ran a Sumerian proverb; "kinship endures forever." The heterogeneous city was no longer held together by the bonds of kinship. Even the family was unstable. "For his pleasure: marriage," ran another proverb; "on his thinking it over: divorce." Hence the Sumerians could no longer depend on the informal controls of custom or common understanding that had sufficed to maintain order in the village. They had to supplement custom by political controls, a system of laws, backed by both force and moral persuasion. In this sense the city created the problem of evil. Here, not in Eden, occurred the Fall.

More specifically, the rise of civilization forced the social question that is still with us. By their great drainage and irrigation system the Sumerians were able to produce an increasing surplus of material wealth. The question is: Who was to possess and enjoy this wealth? The answer in Sumer was to be the invariable one: Chiefly a privileged few. The god who in theory owned it all in fact required the services of priestly bailiffs, and before long these were doing more than their share in assisting him to enjoy it, at the expense of the many menials beneath them. Class divisions grew more pronounced in the divine household, as in the city at large. The skilled artisans of Sumer, whose work in metals and

---

SOURCE: Excerpts from *Freedom in the Ancient World* by Herbert J. Muller. Copyright © 1961 by Harper & Row, Publishers, Inc. Reprinted by permission of HarperCollins Publishers, Inc.

gems has hardly ever been surpassed, became a proletariat, unable to afford their own products. "The valet always wears dirty clothes" noted the Sumerian scribe. Other proverbs dwelt on the troubles of the poor:

The poor man is better dead than alive;
If he has bread, he has no salt,
If he has salt, he has no bread.

The poor have not always been with us. As a class, they came with civilization. There was also the new type of the slave: victors in war had discovered that it was even more profitable to domesticate human captives than other types of animals. And outside its walls the city created still another type of man—the peasant. The villager had been pre-literate, on a cultural par with his fellows; the peasant was illiterate, aware of the writing he did not know, aware of his dependence on the powers of the city, and liable to exploitation by them. Altogether, the urban revolution produced the anomaly that would become more glaring with the Industrial Revolution. As the collective wealth increased, many men were worse off, and many more felt worse off, than the neolithic villager had been.

Similarly the great irrigation system posed a political problem: Who would control the organization it required, exercise the power it gave? The answer was the same—a privileged few. As the temple estate grew into a city, the priesthood needed more secular help, especially in time of war. Sumerian legend retained memories of some sort of democratic assembly in the early cities, but it emphasized that after the Flood "kingship descended from heaven." The gods had sent kings to maintain order and to assure the proper service of them upon which the city's welfare depended. This was not a pure heavenly boon, judging by the Sumerian myth of a Golden Age before the Flood: an Eden of peace and plenty in which there was no snake, scorpion, hyena, lion, wild dog, wolf—"There was no fear, no terror. Man had no rival." At any rate, the divinely appointed king ruled as an absolute monarch, and might be a terror. With him descended a plague of locusts—the tax collectors. Again civilization meant an anomaly: as the collective achieved much more effective freedom, many individuals enjoyed less freedom than prehistoric villagers had.

In Sumer these problems were aggravated by a profounder paradox. All along, we have seen, man had come to depend more and more on supernatural means of power as he extended his own power over nature. Now, with the most triumphant demonstration of his creative powers, he became convinced of his utter dependence upon the gods, his utter powerlessness without them. The monumental architecture of the Sumerians exemplifies this crowning paradox. The ziggurat, which inspired the Hebrew myth of the Tower of Babel, was by no means the symbol of human presumption that Jehovah mistook it for—it was a symbol of abject subservience. Sumerian myth taught that man had been created simply to be the slave of the gods; he did all the dirty work, that they might rest and freely enjoy. They got the credit for all the highest achievements of the Sumerians. They also got the prime benefits, since the works of the city were dedicated to the promotion of their welfare, not man's welfare.

The Intellectual Adventure
of Ancient Man

Henri Frankfort and H. A. Frankfort

One of the most difficult tasks of the historian is to understand ancient peoples' assumptions and attitudes about the world and their place in it. It is much easier to gather political or social information about ancient peoples, for this is often recorded in a manner understandable to us. To come to conclusions about how individuals perceived the world when those perceptions may have been quite different from our own requires a subtler use of evidence and imaginative interpretation. In the following selection Henri Frankfort, an archaeologist and cultural historian, and H. A. Frankfort attempt to describe one of the most fundamental differences in outlook between ancient and modern peoples: the ancients' perception of the physical world not as made up of inanimate things or natural forces (each one of which modern peoples refer to as "it") but as living, dynamic, individual beings (each one of which the ancients referred to as "thou").

> **Consider:** *The religious implications of this distinction of attitudes between modern and ancient peoples; the evidence that might be used to support or attack this interpretation; the role these attitudes might play in explaining the nature of science in the ancient world.*

The ancients, like the modern savages, saw man always as part of society, and society as imbedded in nature and dependent upon cosmic forces. For them nature and man did not stand in opposition and did not, therefore, have to be apprehended by different modes of cognition. We shall see, in fact, in the course of this book, that natural phenomena were regularly conceived in terms of human experience and that human experience was conceived in terms of cosmic events. We touch here upon a distinction between the ancients and us which is of the utmost significance for our inquiry.

The fundamental difference between the attitudes of modern and ancient man as regards the surrounding world is this: for modern, scientific man the phenomenal world is primarily an "It"; for ancient—and also for primitive—man it is a "Thou." . . .

The world appears to primitive man neither inanimate nor empty but redundant with life; and life has individuality, in man and beast and plant, and in every phenomenon which confronts man—the thunderclap, the sudden shadow, the eerie and unknown clearing in the wood, the stone which suddenly hurts him when he stumbles while on a hunting trip. Any phenomenon may at any time face him, not as "It," but as "Thou." In this confrontation, "Thou" reveals its individuality, its qualities, its will. "Thou" is not contemplated with intellectual detachment; it is experienced as life confronting life, involving every faculty of man in a reciprocal relationship. Thoughts, no less than acts and feelings, are subordinated to this experience. . . .

The whole man confronts a living "Thou" in nature; and the whole man—emotional and imaginative as well as intellectual—gives expression to the experience. All experience

SOURCE: Reprinted from *The Intellectual Adventure of Ancient Man,* by Henri Frankfort and H. A. Frankfort, by permission of The University of Chicago Press. Copyright © 1946, pp. 4–6.

of "Thou" is highly individual; and early man does, in fact, view happenings as individual events. An account of such events and also their explanation can be conceived only as action and necessarily take the form of a story. In other words, the ancients told myths instead of presenting an analysis or conclusions. We would explain, for instance, that certain atmospheric changes broke a drought and brought about rain. The Babylonians observed the same facts but experienced them as the intervention of the gigantic bird Imdugud which came to their rescue. It covered the sky with the black storm clouds of its wings and devoured the Bull of Heaven, whose hot breath had scorched the crops.

Daily Life in Ancient Egypt: The Afterlife

Lionel Casson

Conceptions about the afterlife can reveal much about a civilization, for these conceptions often reflect the moods, struggles, problems, and attitudes of a people. The Egyptians were greatly concerned with the afterlife, as indicated by their construction of large, elaborate pyramid-tombs. In the following selection, Lionel Casson analyzes the Egyptians' attitudes toward death and the afterlife, noting broad changes in those attitudes.

> **Consider:** *Exactly how the Egyptian view of the afterlife reflects the nature of the Egyptians; evidence for change after 1200 B.C.; how Sinuhe's account reflects a great concern with the afterlife.*

The Egyptians, as we have several times observed, were by nature buoyant, optimistic, and confident, and their view of the afterlife reflects this: throughout most of their history they conceived of it as something to be enjoyed, certainly not to be looked on with foreboding. Being at the same time pragmatic and material minded, they indulged in no fancies about its being a better world. As they saw it, death meant a continuation of one's life on earth, a continuation that, with the appropriate precautions of proper burial, prayer, and ritual, would include only the best parts of life on earth—nothing to fear, but on the other hand, nothing to want to hurry out of this world for. This attitude lasted from Old Kingdom times right up to the end of the Nineteenth Dynasty, about 1200 B.C., when change becomes noticeable. Pictures and texts in tombs from this time on no longer concern themselves with life on earth. The pictures cease portraying the deceased serenely contemplating the bustling life on his estates, and concentrate morbidly on the making of the mummy, the funeral, the judgment before Osiris, the demons the dead will see, and other aspects of death. The texts give up autobiography in favor of magical recipes for getting along in the life beyond the grave. This shift of emphasis is one of the distinctive features that mark Egypt's descent toward the religion-haunted, superstitious,

---

Source: Lionel Casson, "Daily Life in Ancient Egypt," *American Heritage*, pp. 107–108. Reprinted by permission of *American Heritage* magazine, a division of Forbes Inc., 1975.

ritualistic nation it was to become by the time Herodotus and other Greek and Roman authors wrote down their impressions.

But the shift did not occur until the very end of the period we are concerned with. Throughout most of the New Kingdom the Egyptians prepared for their entry into the next world with calm and confidence. It was an occupation that absorbed a man's time and resources for most of his life, since no one was able to rest easy until he was assured that the place of his final repose and its furnishings were ready. In *The Story of Sinuhe*, a Middle Kingdom tale of an official who went into exile but in his old age was recalled by the pharaoh in time to end his days happily in the fatherland, Sinuhe recounts the crowning joy of his homecoming:

> There was constructed for me a pyramid-tomb of stone in the midst of the pyramid-tombs. The stonemasons who hew a pyramid-tomb took over its ground-area. The outline-draftsmen designed in it; the chief sculptors carved in it; and the overseers of works who are in the necropolis made it their concern. Its necessary materials were made from all the outfittings which are placed at a tomb-shaft. Mortuary priests were given to me. There was made for me a necropolis garden, with fields in it formerly (extending) as far as the town, like that which is done for a chief courtier. My statue was overlaid with gold, and its skirt was of fine gold. It was his majesty who had it made.

Women of Egypt and the Ancient Near East

Barbara S. Lesko

In the early Egyptian and Mesopotamian civilizations, women had greater access to valued political, religious, and economic positions than in civilizations that followed. What explains the changes that would make societies in the Near East more dominated by men and more oppressive to women? Barbara S. Lesko, an Egyptologist, addresses this question in the following excerpt. Here her focus is on the centuries toward the end of the third millennium and the beginning of the second millennium.

> **Consider:** *What three factors explain the decline of women's status and freedoms; how Egypt and early Sumer differed from later societies such as Assyria; other possible explanations for the decline of women's status and freedoms.*

What was the real cause of the rise of patriarchy, which became increasingly oppressive to women in the Near East after Sumerian civilization waned? Several reasons suggest themselves. The first is militarism. In an early agrarian society like Egypt where internal disputes were effectively handled by the strong, centralized government, where wars

Source: Barbara S. Lesko, "Women of Egypt and the Ancient Near East," in Renate Bridenthal, Claudia Koonz, and Susan Stuard, *Becoming Visible: Women in European History*, 2d ed. (Boston: Houghton Mifflin Co., 1987), p. 74.

usually took place beyond the borders, where no standing army existed during the first 1500 years of recorded history, and where invasion seldom affected the country, women continually shared the burdens, full rights, and obligations of citizens. However, in the newer societies, founded by the sons of ever-vigilant and suspicious desert nomads, where warfare between cities was frequent and invasion by outside hostile forces familiar, militarism developed, excluding women and rendering them dependents. Second, where commercialism held sway at the same time—as in Assyria—the worst examples of patriarchy were found. Commerce based on private initiative first appears on a well developed scale in the Old Babylonian period where the first concerted effort by men to control women for financial gain is also documented. This is seen not only in the laws of Hammurabi but in institutions like that of the cloistered *Naditu* women. Coupled with virulent militarism, as in Assyria, the rise of commercialism had a devastating effect on women's rights. In Egypt large scale commerce long remained a virtual monopoly of the state, so its impact on society remained less significant.

We might further point out that, even during the somewhat militaristic Egyptian empire of the New Kingdom, women's status and freedoms did not diminish significantly. This introduces a third factor: confidence. A supremely confident nation can afford tolerance. Egypt had confidence in its gods, in the eternity of life, and in the bounty of its land. Sumer, in its early formative years, shared these advantages too. Not so the subsequent societies. It is the threatened male and the threatened society—like Assyria, surrounded on three sides by deadly enemies, and weak impoverished Israel—which created such a restricted role for their women.

A History of the Jews

Paul Johnson

A major task of the historian is to delineate what distinguished a people, an era, or a development from others. In analyzing the Jews, most historians emphasize that the Jewish religion was monotheistic, recognizing only one god, and that major elements of Judaism would later be directly related to and incorporated into two other major religions founded in that area of the world: Christianity and Islam. In the following selection, Paul Johnson goes beyond the monotheism of the Jewish religion to focus on the ways the Jews were unique as ancient writers.

> **Consider:** *Whether Johnson's interpretation is supported by the primary documents on religion in the ancient Near East; why these two characteristics of ancient Jewish literature are so important; how this interpretation of ancient Jewish literature compares with Frankfort's interpretation of ancient peoples' mentality.*

The Jews had two unique characteristics as ancient writers. They were the first to create consequential, substantial and interpretative history. It has been argued that they learned

SOURCE: Excerpt from *A History of the Jews* by Paul Johnson. Copyright © 1987 by Paul Johnson. Reprinted by permission of HarperCollins Publishers, Inc. and George Weidenfeld & Nicolson, Limited.

the art of history from the Hittites, another historically minded people, but it is obvious that they were fascinated by their past from very early times. They knew they were a special people who had not simply evolved from an unrecorded past but had been brought into existence, for certain definite purposes, by a specific series of divine acts. They saw it as their collective business to determine, record, comment and reflect upon these acts. No other people has ever shown, particularly at that remote time, so strong a compulsion to explore their origins. The Bible gives constant examples of the probing historical spirit: why, for instance, was there a heap of stones before the city gate at Ai? What was the meaning of the twelve stones at Gilgal? This passion for aetiology, the quest for explanations, broadened into a more general habit of seeing the present and future in terms of the past. The Jews wanted to know about themselves and their destiny. They wanted to know about God and his intentions and wishes. Since God, in their theology, was the sole cause of all events—as Amos put it, 'Does evil befall a city unless Yahweh wills it?'—and thus the author of history, and since they were the chosen actors in his vast dramas, the record and study of historical events was the key to the understanding of both God and man.

Hence the Jews were above all historians, and the Bible is essentially a historical work from start to finish. . . .

Ancient Jewish history is both intensely divine and intensely humanist. History was made by God, operating independently or through man. The Jews were not interested and did not believe in impersonal forces. They were less curious about the physics of creation than any other literate race of antiquity. They turned their back on nature and discounted its manifestations except in so far as they reflected the divine-human drama. The notion of vast geographical or economic forces determining history was quite alien to them. There is much natural description in the Bible, some of astonishing beauty, but it is stage-scenery for the historical play, a mere backdrop for the characters. The Bible is vibrant because it is entirely about living creatures; and since God, though living, cannot be described or even imagined, the attention is directed relentlessly on man and woman.

Hence the second unique characteristic of ancient Jewish literature: the verbal presentation of the human personality in all its range and complexity. The Jews were the first race to find words to express the deepest human emotions, especially the feelings produced by bodily or mental suffering, anxiety, spiritual despair and desolation, and the remedies for these evils produced by human ingenuity—hope, resolution, confidence in divine assistance, the consciousness of innocence, of righteousness, penitence, sorrow and humility.

Chapter Questions

1. What characteristics of the societies discussed in this chapter fit with what we usually consider as civilized?

2. How would you explain the rise of these civilizations and particularly the similarities between them?

3. Evaluate the relative importance of geographic, economic, and other factors in explaining the differing natures of these early civilizations.

4. Drawing from both primary and secondary documents, describe some of the most likely of ancient peoples' assumptions and attitudes about the world, about their societies, and about women. How might some of these assumptions and attitudes differ in the various societies of the ancient Near East?

CHAPTER TWO

The Emergence of Greek Civilization

Although Western civilization was born in the ancient Near East, we can more easily recognize our own roots in Greek civilization. Before reaching its apex during the fifth and fourth centuries B.C., Greek civilization has a long developmental history. Two related civilizations preceded the Greeks: the Minoans, who developed a sophisticated maritime civilization based on the island of Crete during the third and second millennia, and the Mycenaeans (Achaeons), a militaristic Indo-European people who rose to prominence on the Greek mainland during the second millennium. Both of these Bronze Age peoples fell before the invading Dorians between 1200 and 1000 B.C. After three centuries of cultural decline, the Greeks emerged and entered into a period of vigorous growth. Commerce expanded and the Greeks colonized lands from the Black Sea to the western Mediterranean. At the same time the city-states entered into a period of political evolution and cultural development.

Two city-states in particular became prominent toward the end of this period: Sparta and Athens. Each represents an extreme of developments other city-states would also experience. The Spartans developed a tightly organized, militaristic, land-based state, dominating the Peloponnesian Peninsula. Athens developed a relatively open, democratic, maritime state, dominating Attica and supporting commercial and cultural expansion. During the first decades of the fifth century B.C., these rivals managed to ally in face of the greater Persian threat; thereafter, they were competitors in struggles that involved most of the Greek world.

The selections in this chapter address five major questions. First, how do we explain the end of the Bronze Age civilizations of the Mycenaeans and Minoans and the decline into the succeeding "Dark Age"? Interpretations ranging from invasions to civil wars are examined. Second, what is the historical significance of the Homeric epics? What historical information about Mycenaean times and the Dark Ages do the Homeric epics provide? What was their significance for the Greeks and for Greek culture in general? Third, how did the Greek city-state evolve in the period between 800 and 500 B.C.? The focus here is on early Sparta and early Athens. Some of the social divisions reflected by political changes are also explored here. Fourth, what was the significance of Greek colonization between about 750 and 550 B.C.? How was colonization related to Greek economy and society? What role did colonization play in the spread of Greek civilization? Finally, what was the nature of Greek societies and ideals in this early period?

The sources in this chapter take us to the end of the sixth century B.C. At that point the Classical Age, which will be examined in the next chapter, began.

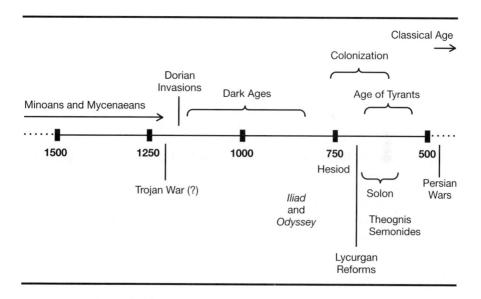

PRIMARY SOURCES

The Iliad

Homer

Homer's Iliad, a work of literature and an important cultural, religious, and social source on Greek civilization, is one of our few historical documents from the early period of Greek history. Most likely orally composed or assembled during the ninth or eighth century B.C., it refers to the great war between the Achaeans (Greeks of the Mycenaean Age) and the Trojans (occupants of a city in Asia Minor near the mouth of the Hellespont), probably fought in the thirteenth century B.C. The social and political conditions described in the Iliad are a mixture of traditions during Mycenaean times and typical practices during the ensuing "Dark Ages." The following selection refers to a shield being forged by Hephaistos, the Greek god of metalworking. The shield is decorated with scenes of two cities. In the first city, which is at peace, a trial is taking place. Around the second one, which is being besieged, are signs of a prosperous economy.

> **Consider:** *The political characteristics of these cities; the basis upon which this trial will be decided; the economic characteristics of the second city.*

On it he wrought in all their beauty two cities of mortal men. And there were marriages in one, and festivals.

They were leading the brides along the city from their maiden chambers under the flaring of torches, and the loud bride song was arising.

The young men followed the circles of the dance, and among them the flutes and lyres kept up their clamour as in the meantime the women standing each at the door of her court admired them.

The people were assembled in the market place, where a quarrel had arisen, and two men were disputing over the blood price for a man who had been killed. One man promised full restitution in a public statement, but the other refused and would accept nothing.

Both then made for an arbitrator, to have a decision; and people were speaking up on either side, to help both men.

But the heralds kept the people in hand, as meanwhile the elders were in session on benches of polished stone in the sacred circle and held in their hands the staves of the heralds who lift their voices.

The two men rushed before these, and took turns speaking their cases, and between them lay on the ground two talents of gold, to be given to that judge who in this case spoke the straightest opinion.

SOURCE: Reprinted from Homer, *The Iliad,* trans. by Richmond Lattimore, by permission of The University of Chicago Press. Copyright © 1977, pp. 388–390.

But around the other city were lying two forces of armed men shining in their war gear. For one side counsel was divided whether to storm and sack, or share between both sides the property and all the possessions the lovely citadel held hard within it.

But the city's people were not giving way, and armed for an ambush.

Their beloved wives and their little children stood on the rampart to hold it, and with them the men with age upon them, but meanwhile the others went out. And Ares led them, and Pallas Athene.

These were gold, both, and golden raiment upon them, and they were beautiful and huge in their armour, being divinities, and conspicuous from afar, but the people around them were smaller.

These, when they were come to the place that was set for their ambush, in a river, where there was a watering place for all animals, there they sat down in place shrouding themselves in the bright bronze.

But apart from these were sitting two men to watch for the rest of them and waiting until they could see the sheep and the shambling cattle, who appeared presently, and two herdsmen went along with them playing happily on pipes, and took no thought of the treachery.

Those others saw them, and made a rush, and quickly thereafter cut off on both sides the herds of cattle and the beautiful flocks of shining sheep, and killed the shepherds upon them. . . .

He made upon it a soft field, the pride of the tilled land, wide and triple-ploughed, with many ploughmen upon it who wheeled their teams at the turn and drove them in either direction. . . .

He made on it the precinct of a king, where the labourers were reaping, with the sharp reaping hooks in their hands. Of the cut swathes some fell along the lines of reaping, one after another, while the sheaf-binders caught up others and tied them with bind-ropes.

There were three sheaf-binders who stood by, and behind them were children picking up the cut swathes, and filled their arms with them and carried and gave them always; and by them the king in silence and holding his staff stood near the line of the reapers, happily.

And apart and under a tree the heralds made a feast ready and trimmed a great ox they had slaughtered. Meanwhile the women scattered, for the workman to eat, abundant white barley.

He made on it a great vineyard heavy with clusters, lovely in gold, but grapes upon it were darkened and the vines themselves stood out through poles of silver. About them he made a field-ditch of dark metal, and drove all around this a fence of tin; and there was only one path to the vineyard, and along it ran the grape-bearers for the vineyard's stripping.

Young girls and young men, in all their light-hearted innocence, carried the kind, sweet fruit away in their woven baskets, and in their midst a youth with a singing lyre played charmingly upon it for them, and sang the beautiful song for Linos in a light voice, and they followed him, and with singing and whistling and light dance-steps of their feet kept time to the music.

Works and Days

Hesiod

While the Homeric epics reflected many of the heroic values of the early Greeks, most Greeks faced the everyday realities of work. One of the earliest sources that describes these concerns with work and wealth was written by the Greek poet Hesiod, who lived in the eighth century B.C. In Works and Days, he includes thoughts about his own life and labor in the fields as well as fables and allegories. In the following excerpt, Hesiod discusses the importance of hard work and how wealth should be gained.

Consider: *The values Hesiod supports; the problems within Greek society that concern Hesiod; how, according to Hesiod, wealth is best obtained and guarded.*

Both gods and men are angry with a man who lives idle, for in nature he is like the stingless drones who waste the labour of the bees, eating without working; but let it be your care to order your work properly, that in the right season your barns may be full of victual. Through work men grow rich in flocks and substance, and working they are much better loved by the immortals. Work is no disgrace: it is idleness which is a disgrace. But if you work, the idle will soon envy you as you grow rich, for fame and renown attend on wealth. And whatever be your lot, work is best for you, if you turn your misguided mind away from other men's property to your work and attend to your livelihood as I bid you. An evil shame is the needy man's companion, shame which both greatly harms and prospers men: shame is with poverty, but confidence with wealth.

Wealth should not be seized: god-given wealth is much better; for if a man take great wealth violently and perforce, or if he steal it through his tongue, as often happens when gain deceives men's sense and dishonour tramples down honour, the gods soon blot him out and make that man's house low, and wealth attends him only for a little time. . . . He who adds to what he has, will keep off bright-eyed hunger; for if you add only a little to a little and do this often, soon that little will become great. What a man has by him at home does not trouble him: it is better to have your stuff at home, for whatever is abroad may mean loss. It is a good thing to draw on what you have; but it grieves your heart to need something and not to have it, and I bid you mark this. Take your fill when the cask is first opened and when it is nearly spent, but midways be sparing: it is poor saving when you come to the lees.

Let the wage promised to a friend be fixed; even with your brother smile—and get a witness; for trust and mistrust, alike ruin men.

Do not let a flaunting woman coax and cozen and deceive you: she is after your barn. The man who trusts womankind trusts deceivers.

There should be an only son, to feed his father's house, for so wealth will increase in the home; but if you leave a second son you should die old. Yet Zeus can easily give great wealth to a greater number. More hands mean more work and more increase.

If your heart within you desires wealth, do these things and work with work upon work.

SOURCE: Hugh G. Evelyn-White, trans., *Hesiod, the Homeric Hymns and Homerica.* New York: The Macmillan Co., 1914, pp. 25–31.

A Colonization Agreement

From about 750 to 550 B.C. Greeks from the mainland, the Aegean islands, and Asia Minor founded colonies throughout the Mediterranean region and as far east as the shores of the Black Sea. Historians speculate that this was one way for the Greeks to solve various social, political, and economic pressures, particularly resulting from population growth. In any case, the spread of colonies facilitated the growth of Greek commerce and laid the foundations for long-lasting Greek cultural influence throughout the Classical world. The following is a colonization agreement made around 630 B.C. by settlers sailing from Thera, an Aegean island, to Cyrene in North Africa.

> **Consider:** *The evidence for a sense of urgency or necessity in gaining support for this expedition; the kind of penalties considered legitimate and effective to enforce the will of the Assembly.*

OATH (AGREEMENT?) OF THE FOUNDERS

It was resolved by the Assembly [at Thera]. Since Apollo spontaneously ordered Battus and the Theraeans to colonize Cyrene, the Theraeans are determined to send to Libya Battus as leader and king; and the Theraeans shall sail as his companions. They shall sail on equal terms from each household, one son from each. Men in the prime of youth are to be enlisted from all the districts. Of the other Theraeans any free man may sail if he wishes. If the colonists occupy the settlement, men from the same households who later land in Libya shall share in citizenship, shall be eligible for office, and shall be allotted unoccupied land. But if they fail to occupy the settlement and if the people of Thera are unable to help them and if for five years they are beset by privation, then they may without fear leave the land [and return] to Thera, [receive back] their property and be citizens. He who refuses to sail when the city sends him shall be liable to the death penalty and his property shall be confiscated. Any father who gives refuge or asylum (?) to his son or any brother who [does the same] for his brothers shall suffer the same penalty as the person refusing to sail.

Poem on Women

Semonides of Amorgos

There are few sources in this early period of Greek history that tell us about Greek attitudes toward women. Most of the sources available were written by men, usually mentioning women only in passing. However there is evidence that abuse of women was a common theme in early Greek literature. The following selection is an example of this theme. The selection is an excerpt from a

SOURCE: *The Ancient World to A.D. 300*, 2d ed., edited by Paul J. Alexander. Copyright © 1963 by Macmillan Publishing Co., Inc. Reprinted by permission.

SOURCE: Hugh Lloyd-Jones, *Females of the Species: Semonides on Women* (Park Ridge, N.J.: Noyes Press, 1975), pp. 30, 32, 34, 38.

poem about women by Semonides of Amorgos, who lived on the island of Amorgos during the seventh century. The poem emphasizes how different females are from men, describing nine negative types of women and one positive type.

> **Consider:** *What this indicates about Greek men's attitudes toward women; the ways in which the good woman differs from the bad woman according to Semonides.*

In the beginning the god made the female mind separately. One he made from a long-bristled sow. In her house everything lies in disorder, smeared with mud, and rolls about the floor; and she herself unwashed, in clothes unlaundered, sits by the dungheap and grows fat.

⚬

Another he made from a wicked vixen; a woman who knows everything. No bad thing and no better kind of thing is lost on her; for she often calls a good thing bad and a bad thing good. Her attitude is never the same.

⚬

Another he made from a bitch, vicious, own daughter of her mother, who wants to hear everything and know everything. She peers everywhere and strays everywhere, always yapping, even if she sees no human being. A man cannot stop her by threatening, nor by losing his temper and knocking out her teeth with a stone, nor with honeyed words, not even if she is sitting with friends, but ceaselessly she keeps up a barking you can do nothing with.

⚬

Another is from a bee; the man who gets her is fortunate, for on her alone blame does not settle. She causes his property to grow and increase, and she grows old with a husband whom she loves and who loves her, the mother of a handsome and reputable family. She stands out among all women, and a godlike beauty plays about her. She takes no pleasure in sitting among women in places where they tell stories about love. Women like her are the best and most sensible whom Zeus bestows on men.

⚬

Zeus has contrived that all these tribes of women are with men and remain with them. Yes, this is the worst plague Zeus has made—women; if they seem to be some use to him who has them, it is to him especially that they prove a plague. The man who lives with a woman never goes through all his day in cheerfulness; he will not be quick to push out of his house Starvation, a housemate who is an enemy, a god who is against us. Just when a man most wishes to enjoy himself at home, through the dispensation of a god or the kindness of a man, she finds a way of finding fault with him and lifts her crest for battle. Yes, where there is a woman, men cannot even give hearty entertainment to a guest who has come to the house; and the very woman who seems most respectable is the one who turns out guilty of the worst atrocity; because while her husband is not looking . . . and the neighbours get pleasure in seeing how he too is mistaken. Each man will take care to praise his own wife and find fault with the other's; we do not realise that the fate of all of us is alike. Yes, this is the greatest plague that Zeus has made, and he has bound us to them with a fetter that cannot be broken. Because of this some have gone to Hades fighting for a woman. . . .

Aristocrats and Tyrants
Theognis of Megara

Between the seventh and fifth centuries B.C. there was a trend in most city-states away from aristocratic political and social dominance. Often part of that trend involved the rise of tyrants who professed to be leaders of the lower classes and who succeeded, if only temporarily, against the aristocrats. The rise of tyrants was particularly common during the sixth century and the results were painful to aristocrats. This is illustrated in the following selection from the bitter poems of Theognis of Megara, a sixth-century aristocrat who lost his property and was exiled upon the rise of a tyrant in his state.

> **Consider:** *How Theognis compares commoners and aristocrats; how a commoner might respond to Theognis; how a tyrant might respond to Theognis.*

Our commonwealth preserves its former frame,
Our common people are no more the same:
They that in skins and hides were rudely dress'd
Nor dreamt of law, nor sought to be redress'd
By rules of right, but in the days of old
Flock'd to the town, like cattle to the fold,
Are now the brave and wise; and we, the rest,
(Their betters nominally, once the best)
Degenerate, debasèd, timid, mean!
Who can endure to witness such a scene?
Their easy courtesies, the ready smile,
Prompt to deride, to flatter, and beguile!
Their utter disregard of right or wrong,
Or truth or honour!—Out of such a throng
(For any difficulties, any need,
For any bold design or manly deed)
Never imagine you can choose a just
Or steady friend, or faithful in his trust.
    But change your habits! Let them go their way!
Be condescending, affable, and gay! . . .
Court not a tyrant's favour, nor combine

SOURCE: George Howe and Gustave A. Harrer, eds., *Greek Literature in Translation*, J. H. Frere, trans., rev. ed., Preston H. Epps, ed. (New York: Harper and Brothers, 1948), pp. 139–140. Reprinted by permission of the Estates of George Howe and Gustave A. Harrer.

To further his iniquitous design;
But, if your faith is pledg'd, though late and loth,
If covenants have pass'd between you both,
Never assassinate him! keep your oath!
But should he still misuse his lawless power
To trample on the people, and devour,
Depose or overturn him; anyhow!
Your oath permits it, and the gods allow. . . .
    Yet much I fear the faction and the strife,
Throughout our Grecian cities, raging rife,
And their wild councils. But do thou defend
This town of ours, our founder and our friend! . . .

Early Athens

Solon

Between the eighth and fifth centuries B.C. *Athenian society became more complex. This affected Athens' political structure, which evolved from monarchical and aristocratic forms to more democratic institutions. A central struggle throughout this period took place between the wealthy aristocracy and the poorer classes. In the late seventh and early sixth centuries this struggle threatened to break out into civil war. In 594 Solon, a poet and wealthy aristocrat of recognized integrity, was called on to mediate and effect decisions to end this struggle. In the following document Aristotle quotes Solon and describes how Solon managed to find just solutions that recognized the issues on both sides without completely satisfying anyone.*

> **Consider:** *The principal social divisions within Athenian society according to Solon; Solon's justifications for his decisions; the political and social significance of Solon's decisions.*

The truth of this view of Solon's policy is established alike by the common consent of all, and by the mention which he has himself made of it in his poems. Thus:—

> I gave to the mass of the people such rank as befitted their need,
> I took not away their honour, and I granted naught to their greed;
> But those who were rich in power, who in wealth were glorious and great,
> I bethought me that naught should befall them unworthy their splendour and state;
> And I stood with my shield outstretched, and both were safe in its sight,
> And I would not that either should triumph, when the triumph was not with right.

Again he declares how the mass of the people ought to be treated:—

SOURCE: Aristotle, *The Athenian Constitution*, trans. F. G. Kenyon (London: George Bell and Sons, 1891), pp. 18–20.

But thus will the people best the voice of their leaders obey,
When neither too slack is the rein, nor violence holdeth the sway:
For satiety breedeth a child, the presumption that spurns control,
When riches too great are poured upon men of unbalanced soul.

And again elsewhere he speaks about the persons who wished to redistribute the land:—

So they came in search of plunder, and their cravings knew no bound,
Every one among them deeming endless wealth would here be found,
And that I with glozing[1] smoothness hid a cruel mind within.
Fondly then and vainly dreamt they; now they raise an angry din,
And they glare askance in anger, and the light within their eyes
Burns with hostile flames upon me. Yet therein no justice lies.
All I promised, fully wrought I with the gods at hand to cheer,
Naught beyond of folly ventured. Never to my soul was dear
With a tyrant's force to govern, nor to see the good and base
Side by side in equal portion share the rich home of our race.

Once more he speaks of the destitution of the poorer classes and of those who before
were in servitude, but were released owing to the Seisachtheia[2]:—

Wherefore I freed the racked and tortured crowd
From all the evils that beset their lot,
Thou, when slow time brings justice in its train,
O mighty mother of the Olympian gods,
Dark Earth, thou best canst witness, from whose breast
I swept the pillars[3] broad-cast planted there,
And made thee free, who hadst been slave of yore.
And many a man whom fraud or law had sold
Far from his god-built land, and outcast slave,
I brought again to Athens; yea, and some,
Exiles from home through debt's oppressive load,
Speaking no more the dear Athenian tongue,
But wandering far and wide, I brought again;
And those that here in vilest slavery
Crouched 'neath a master's frown, I set them free.
Thus might and right were yoked in harmony,
Since by the force of law I won my ends
And kept my promise. Equal laws I gave
To evil and to good, with even hand
Drawing straight justice for the lot of each.
But had another held the goad as I,
One in whose heart was guile and greediness,

---

[1]Explaining away.

[2]"Shaking off of burdens"—Solon's reform of the law of debt.

[3]These were the pillars set up on mortgaged lands, to record the fact of the encumbrance.

He had not kept the people back from strife.
For had I granted, now what pleased the one,
Then what their foes devised within their hearts,
Of many a man this state had been bereft.
Therefore I took me strength from every side
And turned at bay like wolf among the hounds.

And again he reviles both parties for their grumblings in the times that followed:—

Nay, if one must lay blame where blame is due,
Wer't not for me, the people ne'er had set
Their eyes upon these blessings e'en in dreams:—
But greater men, the men of wealthier life,
Should praise me and should court me as their friend.
For had any other man, he says, received this exalted post,—
He had not kept the people back, nor ceased
Till he had robbed the richness of the milk.
But I stood forth, a landmark in the midst,
And barred the foes from battle.

Constitution of the Lacedaemonians

Xenophon

Sparta was one of the most powerful and well-known Greek city-states. Located on the Pelopon-nesian Peninsula, it developed a reputation during the seventh and sixth centuries B.C. for being conservative, disciplined, inward-looking, and devoted to military pursuits and strength. Much of this reputation derived from events during the middle of the seventh century when the helots, for-merly the neighboring Messenians who had been conquered by the Spartans and subjected to serfdom, revolted against the far outnumbered Spartans. With great difficulty the revolt was put down, but from that point on the Spartans committed themselves to preserving their dominance at all costs. Various constitutional reforms were instituted to ensure Spartan unity and military strength. Traditionally, these reforms were attributed to a perhaps legendary lawgiver, Lycurgus. Direct primary sources for these reforms are thin. The best evidence we have comes from Xenophon (434?–355?), an Athenian admirer of Sparta who wrote some two centuries after these occurrences. The following is a selection from his Constitution of the Lacedaemonians.

> **Consider:** *Xenophon's explanation for the extraordinary power and prestige of Sparta; the nature and purposes of Sparta's education system; how Sparta differed from other Greek city-states.*

SOURCE: Francis R. B. Godolphin, ed., *The Greek Historians*, vol. II, trans. Henry G. Dakyns (New York: Random House, 1942), pp. 658–661, 666–669. Reprinted by permission.

I recall the astonishment with which I first noted the unique position of Sparta among the states of Hellas, the relatively sparse population, and at the same time the extraordinary power and prestige of the community. I was puzzled to account for the fact. It was only when I came to consider the peculiar institutions of the Spartans that my wonderment ceased. Or rather, it is transferred to the legislator who gave them those laws, obedience to which has been the secret of their prosperity. This legislator, Lycurgus, I admire, and hold him to have been one of the wisest of mankind. . . .

He insisted on the training of the body as incumbent no less on the female than the male; and in pursuit of the same idea instituted rival contests in running and feats of strength for women as for men. His belief was that where both parents were strong their progeny would be found to be more vigorous. . . .

Marriage, as he ordained it, must only take place in the prime of bodily vigour, this too being, as he believed, a condition conducive to the production of healthy offspring. . . .

But when we turn to Lycurgus, instead of leaving it to each member of the state privately to appoint a slave to be his son's tutor, he set over the young Spartans a public guardian, the Paidonomos, to give him his proper title, with complete authority over them. . . .

Instead of softening their feet with shoe or sandal, his rule was to make them hardy through going barefoot. This habit, if practised, would, as he believed, enable them to scale heights more easily and clamber down precipices with less danger. . . .

Instead of making them effeminate with a variety of clothes, his rule was to habituate them to a single garment the whole year through, thinking that so they would be better prepared to withstand the variations of heat and cold.

Again, as regards food, according to his regulation the prefect, or head of the flock, must see that his messmates gathered to the club meal, with such moderate food as to avoid that heaviness which is engendered by repletion, and yet not to remain altogether unacquainted with the pains of penurious living. His belief was that by such training in boyhood they would be better able when occasion demanded to continue toiling on an empty stomach. . . .

On the other hand, in order to guard against a too great pinch of starvation, though he did not actually allow the boys to help themselves without further trouble to what they needed more, he did give them permission to steal this thing or that in the effort to alleviate their hunger. . . .

It is obvious, I say, that the whole of this education was intended to make the boys craftier and more inventive in getting in supplies, while at the same time it cultivated their warlike instincts. . . .

Furthermore, and in order that the boys should not want a ruler, even in case the guardian himself were absent, he gave to any citizen who chanced to be present authority to lay upon them injunctions for their good, and to chastise them for any trespass committed. . . .

We all know that in the generality of states ever one devotes his full energy to the business of making money: one man as a tiller of the soil, another as a mariner, a third as a merchant, whilst others depend on various arts to earn a living. But at Sparta Lycurgus forbade his freeborn citizens to have anything whatsoever to do with the concerns of moneymaking. As freeman, he enjoined upon them to regard as their concern exclusively those activities upon which the foundations of civic liberty are based. . . .

In Sparta, on the contrary, the stronger a man is the more readily does he bow before constituted authority. And indeed, they pride themselves on their humility, and on a prompt obedience, running, or at any rate not crawling with laggard step, at the word of command. Such an example of eager discipline, they are persuaded, set by themselves, will not fail to be followed by the rest.

Accordingly the ephors[1] are competent to punish whomsoever they cloose: they have power to exact fines on the spur of the moment; they have power to depose magistrates in mid career, nay, actually to imprison and bring them to trial on the capital charge. Entrusted with these vast powers, they do not, as do the rest of states, allow the magistrates elected to exercise authority as they like, right through the year of office; but, in the style rather of despotic monarchs, or presidents of the games, at the first symptom of an offence against the law they inflict chastisement without warning and without hesitation. . . .

And yet another point may well excite our admiration for Lycurgus largely. It had not escaped his observation that communities exist where those who are willing to make virtue their study and delight fail somehow in ability to add to the glory of their fatherland. That lesson the legislator laid to heart, and in Sparta he enforced, as a matter of public duty, the practice of every virtue by every citizen. And so it is that, just as man differs from man in some excellence, according as he cultivates or neglects to cultivate it, this city of Sparta, with good reason, outshines all other states in virtue; since she, and she alone, has made the attainment of a high standard of noble living a public duty.

VISUAL SOURCES

Trade, Culture, and Colonization

This scene (photo 2–1) is from the inside of a Laconian cup dating from about 560 B.C. It shows King Arcesilas II of the Greek North African colony of Cyrene (a Dorian Greek colony originally founded by Thera around 630 B.C.) supervising the weighing and loading of a shipment of what is probably silphium, a medicinal plant exported from the area. On the left Arcesilas is sitting on the deck of a ship underneath a canopy, apparently arguing with his steward. On the right workers carry on the silphium and call out the weight while below workers fill the hold with it. Around are animals of the area: a lizard, a monkey, and birds.

This cup reflects the importance of trade for the Greeks and the role Greek colonies played in this trade. It also indicates a growing interconnectedness based on the Mediterranean—a

---

[1]Elected magistrates.

Photo 2-1

Bibliothèque Nationale, Paris

familiarity with the shoreland areas in which Greeks had settled and contact with the cultures and environment they found there, as might be surmised by the use of a North African plant for medicinal purposes in the Greek homeland and by the large number of cups similar to these that were being exported from Laconia. The words on the cup provide evidence for the spread of literacy among Greeks.

> **Consider:** *Connections between this cup and the colonization agreement; how this cup can be used as evidence for the importance of commerce and colonization in the Greek world.*

Migration and Colonization

These two maps reveal a number of relationships between history and geography in the Greek world. Map 2–1 shows some of the dialects of the Greeks; the arrows indicate some of the probable directions of Greek migrations as traced by these dialects in the aftermath of the Dorian invasions between the thirteenth and tenth centuries B.C. *Map 2–2 shows the extent of Greek settlement around the Mediterranean and Black seas between 750 and 550* B.C. *in comparison with the previously colonized or colonizing areas originating from Phoenicia and the relatively stable Etruscans in northern Italy. This map also distinguishes the Ionian, Dorian, and Aeolian origins of some of those Greek colonies.*

Map 2-1   Dialects

Comparison of these two maps shows that there is a trend for colonies to be located near, or be logical geographic extensions of, the earlier migrations of Greeks. For example, as Dorians spread south and southeast to Thera, Crete, and Rhodes, so would future colonies extend further south, such as those in North Africa (Cyrenaica), and southeast, to, for example, Aspendus. Generally, the Ionians were the most mobile in face of the Dorian invasions and fled across the islands of the Aegean to the east and to the coast of Asia Minor. They were the most prolific colonizers in num-ber and extent, stretching from Spain in the West to the extremes of the Black Sea in the North and East. Although colonies became independent city-states, some of the history of migrations and colonization affected future military alliances. For example, Greeks of the Ionic dialect tended to support each other in the Persian and Peloponnesian wars.

The extent of Greek colonization suggests the importance of colonies for diffusing culture throughout the Mediterranean. Greeks often came into contact (at times through war) with the competing Phoenicians as well as with the established Etruscans and later the Romans in the western Mediterranean. All this helps explain how Greek and Greco-Roman civilization came to

Map 2-2   Colonies

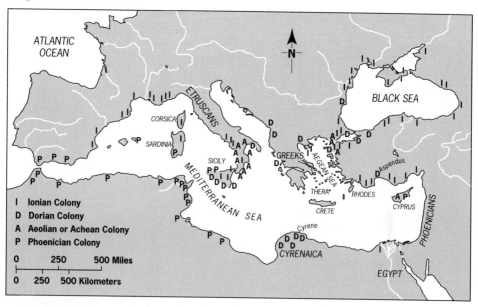

dominate most of the Mediterranean basin even when the Greeks were no longer a great military-political force and their colonies were no longer independent.

> **Consider:** How the history and geography of Greek migrations and colonization helped diffuse culture in the ancient world; how a geographic analysis of dialects can shed light on the history of a civilization.

SECONDARY SOURCES

The End of the Mycenaean World

Frank J. Frost

The highly developed Bronze Age civilizations of the Minoans and Mycenaeans seem to have collapsed suddenly between the thirteenth and twelfth centuries B.C. Indeed, the collapse was so

SOURCE: From Frank J. Frost, *Greek Society*, 3d ed., pp. 11–13. Copyright © 1987 DC Heath and Company.

complete that few records remain. This has forced historians and archaeologists to offer rather speculative interpretations for the fall. Some of these interpretations are evaluated in the following selection by Frank Frost.

> **Consider:** *The problems with the Dorian invasion interpretation; why Frost supports the civil wars interpretation.*

The return of the Greeks from Troy after such a long time caused many changes; in general, there was civil strife in the cities, and exiles from these founded other cities. . . . And eighty years after the War, the Dorians occupied the Peloponnesus with the Sons of Heracles.

Thucydides 1.12

Thus the historian Thucydides described the end of the Mycenaean world, but his brief words do little to describe the true picture: nearly every Mycenaean citadel and settlement destroyed or abandoned, an almost complete end to overseas trade, and the disappearance of a sophisticated town economy. There followed a 300-year period that may with every justification be called the "Dark Ages" of Greece.

Anyone interested in a given society must also be concerned with the reasons for the disintegration of that society. There is still disagreement about the end of the Mycenaean world: epic tradition and archaeology combined can only hint at the great disturbances that seem to have overtaken the entire eastern Mediterranean in the twelfth century B.C. For many years, scholars were content to assume that the great palaces were destroyed and the surrounding lands taken over by the Dorians led by the descendants of Heracles, as tradition suggested. There can be no doubt that the Dorians occupied lands once ruled by the Mycenaeans, because in classical times, the people of these areas spoke Doric and related dialects and were proud of their tribal heritage. The difficulty comes from analyzing the archaeological evidence, which indicates only that the old society had broken down. There was no replacement of Mycenaean hardware with Dorian counterparts.

Today many scholars concentrate on the first part of Thucydides' statement, which focuses attention on internal strife. There is widespread literary tradition to support this theory because even before the war, Thebes had been destroyed by returning exiles. Furthermore, all the heroes who returned from Troy found unrest at home. Agamemnon was butchered in his bathtub; Odysseus survived only by the skin of his teeth through a bloody massacre of his rivals. In city after city new dynasties had taken over, and refugees filled the eastern Mediterranean. In 1191 B.C., Rameses III repelled a great invasion of "sea peoples" from the coasts of Egypt, and it is often assumed that these marauders were a product of the contemporary disturbances in Greece. We are told by tradition that only Nestor returned to safety and prosperity at Pylos. Unfortunately, the archaeological record challenges tradition at this point, showing that the palace at Pylos was one of the first to be destroyed and its destruction was awful and complete.

Civil war, therefore, may have been responsible for the destruction of many citadels, for depopulation and abandonment of other sites, and finally, for a breakdown in the Mycenaean economy. Such an elaborate social and economic structure must always depend for survival on relatively peaceful conditions: the crops must be sown and harvested at the right times, goods must exchange hands, ships must arrive at their destinations, taxes must be paid, and clerks must keep records. A generation of war can easily upset the delicate balance of such an economy. Once foreign trade ends, domestic prosperity begins to decline. Towns become isolated, driving artisans and merchants who have no more markets back to the soil as farmers—for farmers at least eat during hard times.

Greek Realities:
The Homeric Epics

Finley Hooper

While the Homeric epics are significant in themselves as literature, they are doubly important for the historian. First, they supply us with much information about Greece during the late Bronze Age and the Dark Ages, periods we would otherwise know little about. Second, since the epics were of tremendous educational, religious, and cultural significance to the Greeks for centuries after the Dark Ages, they provide insight into Greek civilization during the Classical and Hellenistic ages. In the following selections Finley Hooper explains the importance of the Iliad *and the* Odyssey.

> **Consider:** *How Hooper compares the Homeric epics and the Bible; the ways in which it is useful to think of the epics as religious documents.*

The Homeric epics were as important to ancient Greek society as the Bible is to our own. Perhaps more so, for the *Iliad* and the *Odyssey* were the primers of Greek education. They still are. To the credit of the Greeks, their children have always learned to read and write by examples from the very best in native literature. A child may not go far with his schooling, but if he learns to read and write he knows Homer. When Socrates made his famous appeal to a large jury in Athens in 399 B.C. he quoted from the *Iliad*. Here at least was common ground.

Homer's writings did not comprise scripture in the sense that they were the "revealed word of God." Yet, as in the Bible, there were woven into these epics three persistent themes of human interest: the nature of the supernatural, the intervention of the supernatural in human events, and acute observations about the behavior of men toward one another.

The epics describe the province of each of the twelve Olympian gods. Nearly all of them were named in the Linear B tablets. Homer writes about the same deities as the Mycenaeans had actually worshipped. Yet the tablets mention other gods and not all of them have been clearly identified. Perhaps some of these represent the cruder aspects of religious practices, snake cults and fertility rites which Homer ignores. When the poet limited the number of gods to be given preference, he introduced order and a degree of sophistication into a highly confusing, often interchangeable, list of deities.

SOURCE: Reprinted from *Greek Realities* by Finley Hooper, by permission of the Wayne State University Press. Copyright © 1967, pp. 58–60.

In the remote past, sticks and stones had been considered divine, but Homer spoke for an age when supernatural powers were personified as men and women, larger than life, living forever on special food. They acted according to the same passions and prejudices of men, even as the Hebrew Yahweh who walked and talked in the cool of the evening, and described himself as a jealous God.

The nature of God is not a matter which historians need to decide for others, but the various ways in which men have conceived of the divine is a matter of historical interest. It may be observed that although a few Greek philosophers spoke of a single creative principle, the overwhelming majority of the Greeks throughout ancient times accounted for events according to the wishes of these anthropomorphic gods which Homer describes. . . .

Homer's epics do not offer an evolutionary development toward a higher concept of God, nor any single set of answers to life's major questions. As such, these "teachings" gave the religion common to all the Greeks a totally undogmatic character. The gods of course aided men and they must be worshipped, flattered, and obeyed. The welfare of the state could depend on this. To deny the gods was dangerous, even unpatriotic. But there was no creed or set of tenets to which a man must subscribe. Although the Greeks often quarreled over the physical control of their shrines, they never fought a religious war over faith. Ironically, the adherents of the later higher religions have suffered the embarrassment of bloodshed in the name of sacred books. Homer's writings actually united the Greeks by reconciling them to the common dilemma of human existence.

The Greek Experience: The Heroic Outlook

C. M. Bowra

The Homeric epics exemplify a theme that runs throughout Greek history: the heroic outlook. This outlook characterized Greek images of the Mycenaeans as well as Greek ideals expressed in various cultural productions. In the following selection C. M. Bowra, an Oxford scholar who has written extensively on Greek literature and thought and who lauds Greek values and achievements, analyzes the essence of the heroic outlook and its historical significance.

Consider: *Ways the heroic outlook reflects particular characteristics of Greek society, especially in comparison with other societies; how this analysis compares with Hooper's interpretation.*

The essence of the heroic outlook is the pursuit of honour through action. The great man is he who, being endowed with superior qualities of body and mind, uses them to the utmost and wins the applause of his fellows because he spares no effort and shirks no risk in his desire to make the most of his gifts and to surpass other men in his exercise of them. His honour is the centre of his being, and any affront to it calls for immediate

---

SOURCE: C. M. Bowra, *The Greek Experience* (New York: Praeger, 1957), pp. 20–21, 40–41.

amends. He courts danger gladly because it gives him the best opportunity of showing of what stuff he is made. Such a conviction and its system of behaviour are built on a man's conception of himself and of what he owes to it, and if it has any further sanctions, they are to be found in what other men like himself think of him. By prowess and renown he gains an enlarged sense of personality and well-being; through them he has a second existence on the lips of men, which assures him that he has not failed in what matters most. Fame is the reward of honour, and the hero seeks it before everything else. This outlook runs through Greek history from Homer's Achilles to the historical Alexander. It is countered and modified and altered, but it persists and even extends its field from an individual to a national outlook. It is a creed suited to men of action, and through it the Greeks justified their passionate desire to vary the pattern of their lives by resourceful and unflagging enterprise. Though in its early stages, as we see it in Homer, it has much in common with similar ideals in other heroic societies, it is more resilient in Greece than elsewhere and endures with unexpected vitality when the city-state is established with all its demands and obligations on its members, and when the new conception of the citizens might seem to exclude an ideal which sets so high a value on the single man and his notion of what is due to him. . . .

The heroic outlook, which the Greeks inherited from a distant past, shaped much of their thinking and their action. They fitted it into the frame of the city-state and its demands, and, when occasion called, into the larger pattern of Hellenism, of which they were never quite oblivious. When they claimed that they were superior to barbarians because they pursued a higher type of virtue, they were not wrong. In comparison with the herded multitudes of Egypt and Asia, or with the more primitive peoples on their own frontiers, the Greeks had found a principle which gave meaning to life and inspired them to astonishing achievements. Because they felt that they were different from other men, that they must always excel and surpass them, that a man wins his manhood through unflagging effort and unflinching risk, they broke away from the static patterns of society which elsewhere dominated their age, and inaugurated a way of life in which the prizes went to the eager and the bold, and action in all its forms was sought and honoured as the natural end of man.

Chapter Questions

1. How should the historical usefulness of the various primary documents, particularly those that are usually considered pieces of literature, be evaluated? What problems might arise for historians who rely on literary documents for their interpretations of early Greek civilization?

2. In what ways do the primary documents support interpretations of various ideals and outlooks, such as the "heroic outlook," as particularly Greek?

3. Considering historical, geographic, and cultural factors, in what ways did the Greeks differ from the earlier civilizations of the ancient Near East? How would you explain some of these differences?

CHAPTER THREE

Classical and Hellenistic Greece

During the fifth and fourth centuries B.C. Greek civilization reached its apex. Historians have been fascinated with this period of Greek history for several reasons. First, Classical Greece is considered the most direct foundation of Western civilization, more so than the civilizations of the ancient Near East that preceded it. Second, many Greeks took a rationalistic and naturalistic approach to almost all fundamental questions; thus they developed scientific explanations for the world around them and applied reason to questions of politics, ethics, history, and philosophy. Third, the Greeks explored and experienced the range of human emotions, above all in their literature and in the triumphant and tragic wars they fought. Fourth, they produced stunning aesthetic creations, particularly in their sculpture, architecture, and drama. Fifth, Greeks strongly believed in the dignity and power of human beings and in balance and control as a human ideal. Sixth, the Greeks experienced and experimented with a large variety of political forms. In short, we often recognize ourselves and our own concerns when we study Classical Greece.

This chapter surveys Greek civilization as it evolved from the Classical Age (500–323 B.C.) to the Hellenistic Age (323–31 B.C.). Three overlapping topics are discussed. The first concerns the nature of the polis, of central importance to the ancient Greeks. Greeks perceived the polis as the appropriate political and geographic context for the good life, as well as the center of social, economic, religious, and cultural life. How should it be ruled? How strong was the obligation to one's own polis compared to an allegiance to the Greek world as a whole? What was the proper balance between the individual and the state? To explore these questions, it is useful to look at divisions between rival poleis of different political and social forms, as exemplified by the Peloponnesian War. It is also helpful to examine Greek ideas about the political nature of humans and in particular Greek ideas about democracy—one of the many forms of government experimented with by the Greeks. And finally, the student of Greek civilization can learn a great deal by investigating the tension between the individual and his or her obligation as a citizen of the polis.

The second topic is the nature of Greek thought. Historians have traditionally been impressed by the "modernity" of Greek thought. This is particularly the case with the scientific and rationalistic nature of Greek thought and the Greek tendency to generalize and abstract their ideas without resort to religious or supernatural assumptions. A number of questions are examined to demonstrate these traits. What was the nature of scientific thought for the Greeks? How did they apply such thought to medicine, history, and politics? What methodological differences were within this rationalistic thought? In what ways did they tend to abstract and generalize their ideas? What was the role of irrational thought and belief in the supernatural among large portions of Greek society?

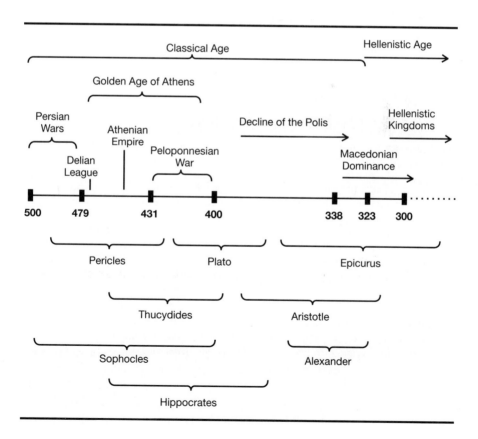

The third topic questions the validity of the traditional view of Greece during the Classical and Hellenistic ages. We usually think of the Greeks, and especially the Athenians, as being balanced, democratic, just, individualistic, rational, naturalistic, liberal, and open. Their great fault, supposedly, was in their inability to unify politically: thus the fratricidal tragedy of the Peloponnesian War, the decline of the fourth century B.C., the conquest of the Macedonians, the shift of a center of gravity away from the polis to the eastern Hellenistic kingdoms, and the end of the Classical Age. How true is this perception? To address this question it is necessary to examine a number of related questions: What were Greek ideals during the Classical Age, particularly in Athens, the epitome of Greek culture at its height? What was the position of women in Greek society? What was the significance of slavery for Greece? How democratic were the Greeks, and how did their greatest thinkers evaluate this democracy? How can the "decline" of the fourth century be explained, and indeed should it be considered a "decline" or simply a change?

PRIMARY SOURCES

The History of the Peloponnesian War: The Historical Method

Thucydides

The first of the great historians lived in Greece during the Classical Age. They provide us with the most useful material we have to trace events of the period. The greatest of these was Thucydides (471?–400?), a high-ranking and wealthy Athenian who was a general early in the war and who was later banished from Athens for twenty years for losing a campaign against the Spartans. In The History of the Peloponnesian War *Thucydides traces the origins of the war, its course, and its consequences for the participants and for the Greek world in general. In the following selection Thucydides outlines his approach and method as a historian and analyzes the origins of the conflict, distinguishing the immediate from the underlying causes.*

Consider: *Thucydides' assumptions and reasoning; what modern historians might point to as evidence for questionable practices of historical writing or a lack of a scientific approach; how Thucydides distinguishes the "immediate" from the "real" causes of the Peloponnesian War.*

SOURCE: From Francis R. B. Godolphin, ed., *The Greek Historians*, vol. I (New York: Random House, 1942), pp. 576–577. Reprinted by permission.

Yet any one who upon the grounds which I have given arrives at some such conclusion as my own about those ancient times, would not be far wrong. He must not be misled by the exaggerated fancies of the poets, or by the tales of chroniclers who seek to please the ear rather than to speak the truth. Their accounts cannot be tested by him; and most of the facts in the lapse of ages have passed into the region of romance. At such a distance of time he must make up his mind to be satisfied with conclusions resting upon the clearest evidence which can be had. And, though men will always judge any war in which they are actually fighting to be the greatest at the time, but, after it is over, revert to their admiration of some other which has preceded, still the Peloponnesian, if estimated by the actual facts, will certainly prove to have been the greatest ever known.

As to the speeches which were made either before or during the war, it was hard for me, and for others who reported them to me, to recollect the exact words. I have therefore put into the mouth of each speaker the sentiments proper to the occasion, expressed as I thought he would be likely to express them, while at the same time I endeavoured, as nearly as I could, to give the general purport of what was actually said. Of the events of the war I have not ventured to speak from any chance information, nor according to any notion of my own; I have described nothing but what I either saw myself, or learned from others of whom I made the most careful and particular enquiry. The task was a laborious one, because eye-witnesses of the same occurrences gave different accounts of them, as they remembered or were interested in the actions of one side or the other. And very likely the strictly historical character of my narrative may be disappointing to the ear. But if he who desires to have before his eyes a true picture of the events which have happened, and of the like events which may be expected to happen hereafter in the order of human things, shall pronounce what I have written to be useful, then I shall be satisfied. My history is an everlasting possession, not a prize composition which is heard and forgotten.

The greatest achievement of former times was the Persian War; yet even this was speedily decided in two battles by sea and two by land. But the Peloponnesian War was a protracted struggle, and attended by calamities such as Hellas had never known within a like period of time. Never were so many cities captured and depopulated—some by barbarians, others by Hellenes themselves fighting against one another; and several of them after their capture were repeopled by strangers. Never were exile and slaughter more frequent, whether in the war or brought about by civil strife. And rumours, of which the like had often been current before, but rarely verified by fact, now appeared to be well grounded. There are earthquakes unparalleled in their extent and fury, and eclipses of the sun more numerous than are recorded to have happened in any former age; there were also in some places great droughts causing famines, and lastly the plague which did immense harm and destroyed numbers of the people. All these calamities fell upon Hellas simultaneously with the war, which began when the Athenians and Peloponnesians violated the thirty years' truce concluded by them after the recapture of Euboea. Why they broke it and what were the grounds of quarrel I will first set forth, that in time to come no man may be at a loss to know what was the origin of this great war. The real though unavowed cause I believe to have been the growth of the Athenian power, which terrified the Lacedaemonians and forced them into war; but the reasons publicly alleged on either side were as follows.

The History of the Peloponnesian War: Athens During the Golden Age

Thucydides

The most famous "speech" presented by Thucydides in his History of the Peloponnesian War *is a eulogy delivered by the Athenian leader Pericles (490?–429 B.C.) during the winter of 431–430 B.C. for the Athenians killed during the first campaigns. In it Pericles compares the life and institutions of Athens with those of the enemy, Sparta. He explains to his fellow Athenians what made Athens so great. This funeral oration provides a superb idealized description of the Athenian city-state at its height.*

Consider: *The reliability of this report of Pericles' speech, especially considering Thucydides' description of his methods in the previous document; the description of Athens, its institutions, and its people in this document; how Pericles compares Athens and Sparta and how a Spartan leader might reply; how Pericles defines the proper balance between Athenians' freedom as individuals and their commitments as citizens.*

"I will speak first of our ancestors, for it is right and becoming that now, when we are lamenting the dead, a tribute should be paid to their memory. There has never been a time when they did not inhabit this land, which by their valour they have handed down from generation to generation, and we have received from them a free state. But if they were worthy of praise, still more were our fathers, who added to their inheritance, and after many a struggle transmitted to us their sons this great empire. And we ourselves assembled here to-day, who are still most of us in the vigour of life, have chiefly done the work of improvement, and have richly endowed our city with all things, so that she is sufficient for herself both in peace and war. Of the military exploits by which our various possessions were acquired, or of the energy with which we or our fathers drove back the tide of war, Hellenic or barbarian, I will not speak; for the tale would be long and is familiar to you. But before I praise the dead, I should like to point out by what principles of action we rose to power, and under what institutions and through what manner of life our empire became great. For I conceive that such thoughts are not unsuited to the occasion, and that this numerous assembly of citizens and strangers may profitably listen to them.

"Our form of government does not enter into rivalry with the institutions of others. We do not copy our neighbours, but are an example to them. It is true that we are called a democracy, for the administration is in the hands of the many and not of the few. But while the law secures equal justice to all alike in their private disputes, the claim of excellence is also recognised; and when a citizen is in any way distinguished, he is preferred to the public service, not as a matter of privilege, but as the reward of merit. Neither is

SOURCE: From Francis R. B. Godolphin, ed., *The Greek Historians*, vol. I (New York: Random House, 1942), pp. 648–651. Reprinted by permission.

poverty a bar, but a man may benefit his country whatever be the obscurity of his condition. There is no exclusiveness in our public life, and in our private intercourse we are not suspicious of one another, nor angry with our neighbour if he does what he likes; we do not put on sour looks at him which, though harmless, are not pleasant. While we are thus unconstrained in our private intercourse, a spirit of reverence pervades our public acts; we are prevented from doing wrong by respect for authority and for the laws, having an especial regard to those which are ordained for the protection of the injured as well as to those unwritten laws which bring upon the transgressor of them the reprobation of the general sentiment.

"And we have not forgotten to provide for our weary spirits many relaxations from toil; we have regular games and sacrifices throughout the year; at home the style of our life is refined; and the delight which we daily feel in all these things helps to banish melancholy. Because of the greatness of our city the fruits of the whole earth flow in upon us; so that we enjoy the goods of other countries as freely as of our own.

"Then, again, our military training is in many respects superior to that of our adversaries. Our city is thrown open to the world, and we never expel a foreigner or prevent him from seeing or learning anything of which the secret if revealed to an enemy might profit him. We rely not upon management or trickery, but upon our own hearts and hands. And in the matter of education, whereas they from early youth are always undergoing laborious exercises which are to make them brave, we live at ease, and yet are equally ready to face the perils which they face. And here is the proof. The Lacedaemonians come into Attica not by themselves, but with their whole confederacy following; we go alone into a neighbour's country; and although our opponents are fighting for their homes and we are on a foreign soil, we have seldom any difficulty in overcoming them. Our enemies have never yet felt our united strength; the care of a navy divides our attention, and on land we are obliged to send our own citizens everywhere. But they, if they meet and defeat a part of our army, are as proud as if they had routed us all, and when defeated they pretend to have been vanquished by us all.

"If then we prefer to meet danger with a light heart but without laborious training, and with a courage which is gained by habit and not enforced by law, are we not greatly the gainers? Since we do not anticipate the pain, although, when the hour comes, we can be as brave as those who never allow themselves to rest; and thus too our city is equally admirable in peace and in war.

"For we are lovers of the beautiful, yet with economy, and we cultivate the mind without loss of manliness. Wealth we employ, not for talk and ostentation, but when there is a real use for it. To avow poverty with us is no disgrace; the true disgrace is in doing nothing to avoid it. An Athenian citizen does not neglect the state because he takes care of his own household; and even those of us who are engaged in business have a very fair idea of politics. We alone regard a man who takes no interest in public affairs, not as a harmless, but as a useless character; and if few of us are originators, we are all sound judges of a policy. The great impediment to action is, in our opinion, not discussion, but the want of that knowledge which is gained by discussion preparatory to action. For we have a peculiar power of thinking before we act and of acting too, whereas other men are courageous from ignorance but hesitate upon reflection. And they are surely to be esteemed the bravest spirits who, having the clearest sense both of the pains and pleasures of life, do not on that account shrink from danger. In doing good, again, we are unlike others; we make our friends by conferring, not by receiving favours. Now he who confers a favour is the firmer friend, because he would fain by kindness keep alive the memory of an obligation; but the recipient is colder in his feelings, because he knows that in requiting another's generosity he will not be winning gratitude but only paying a debt. We alone do good to our neighbours not upon a calculation of interest, but in the confidence of freedom and in a frank and fearless spirit.

"To sum up: I say that Athens is the school of Hellas, and that the individual Athenian in his own person seems to have the power of adapting himself to the most varied forms of action with the utmost versatility and grace."

Antigone
Sophocles

Much of our information about Greece comes from dramas, which played such an important educational, religious, and cultural role in Greek life. Sophocles (496?–406 B.C.), an Athenian of aristocratic birth and an important public official, was one of the greatest dramatists of the Classical Age. In Antigone, which was first staged in 441, he focused on the conflicts between social obligations and individual convictions, between political and moral conscience. The first excerpt is a speech by Creon, King of Thebes, to his counselors. He refers to the recent strife in Thebes between the two sons of the tragically fallen King Oedipus. One of the sons, Polyneices, gathered Greek enemies of Thebes and attacked the city, which was defended by the other son, Eteocles. Both were killed in battle, and thus Creon, the brother of Oedipus, assumed the throne. A struggle arose between the strong-willed Antigone, Polyneices' sister, who felt compelled by dictates of blood and religion to give her brother a proper burial, and Creon, who felt that as ruler he had to uphold the authority of the state and punish rebellion. Here Creon justifies his decision to bury Eteocles honorably but to leave Polyneices unburied. In the second excerpt, Antigone justifies her burial of Polyneices and her disobeying the laws of the state.

> **Consider:** *The attitudes and ideals revealed in this selection; Creon's view of the duties of the ruler and how these duties conflict with obligations of conscience and religion; how Antigone replies to Creon; how the relation between the individual and the state presented in this document compares with the same relation presented in Pericles' funeral oration.*

CREON. My lords: for what concerns the state, the gods
Who tossed it on the angry surge of strife
Have righted it again; and therefore you
By royal edict I have summoned here,
Chosen from all our number. I know well
How you revered the throne of Laius;

SOURCE: *Sophocles: Three Tragedies,* trans. H. D. F. Kitto (© Oxford University Press, London, 1962), pp. 8–9, 16–17, by permission of Oxford University Press.

And then, when Oedipus maintained our state,
And when he perished, round his sons you rallied,
Still firm and steadfast in your loyalty.
Since they have fallen by a double doom
Upon a single day, two brothers each
Killing the other with polluted sword,
I now possess the throne and royal power
By right of nearest kinship with the dead.
   There is no art that teaches us to know
The temper, mind or spirit of any man
Until he has been proved by government
And lawgiving. A man who rules a state
And will not ever steer the wisest course,
But is afraid, and says not what he thinks,
That man is worthless; and if any holds
A friend of more account than his own city,
I scorn him; for if I should see destruction
Threatening the safety of my citizens,
I would not hold my peace, nor would I count
That man my friend who was my country's foe,
Zeus be my witness. For be sure of this:
It is the city that protects us all;
She bears us through the storm; only when she
Rides safe and sound can we make loyal friends.
   This I believe, and thus will I maintain
Our city's greatness.—Now, conformably,
Of Oedipus' two sons I have proclaimed
This edict: he who in his country's cause
Fought gloriously and so laid down his life,
Shall be entombed and graced with every rite
That men can pay to those who die with honour;
But for his brother, him called Polyneices,
Who came from exile to lay waste his land,
To burn the temples of his native gods,
To drink his kindred blood, and to enslave
The rest, I have proclaimed to Thebes that none
Shall give him funeral honours or lament him,
But leave him there unburied, to be devoured
By dogs and birds, mangled most hideously.
Such is my will; never shall I allow
The villain to win more honour than the upright;
But any who show love to this our city
In life and death alike shall win my praise.

CREON. You: tell me briefly—I want no long speech:
Did you not know that this had been forbidden?
ANTIGONE. Of course I knew. There was a proclamation.
CREON. And so you dared to disobey the law?
ANTIGONE. It was not Zeus who published this decree,
Nor have the Powers who rule among the dead
Imposed such laws as this upon mankind;
Nor could I think that a decree of yours—
A man—could override the laws of Heaven
Unwritten and unchanging. Not of today
Or yesterday is their authority;
They are eternal; no man saw their birth.
Was I to stand before the gods' tribunal
For disobeying *them,* because I feared
A man? I knew that I should have to die,
Even without your edict; if I die
Before my time, why then, I count it gain;
To one who lives as I do, ringed about
With countless miseries, why, death is welcome.
For me to meet this doom is little grief;
But when my mother's son lay dead, had I
Neglected him and left him there unburied,
That would have caused me grief; this causes none.
And if you think it folly, then perhaps
I am accused of folly by the fool.

The Republic

Plato

Various city-states in Classical Greece, and particularly Athens, have been admired for their democratic institutions and practices. Yet Plato (427?–347 B.C.), the greatest political theorist of the time, was a harsh critic of democracy. An aristocratic Athenian who grew up during the Peloponnesian War, Plato became embittered by the trial and death of his teacher, Socrates, in 399. After an extended absence from Athens, Plato returned in 386 and founded a school, the Academy, where he hoped to train philosopher-statesmen in accordance with his ideals as expounded in The Republic. *In the following selection from that work, Plato employs the dialogue form to examine democracy and its perils. This represents more than abstract thoughts, for at the time that it was written, there was a rivalry between democratic forms of government, best represented by Athens, and more structured authoritarian forms, represented by Sparta.*

Consider: *The strengths and weaknesses of Plato's argument; how Plato's view of (Athenian) democracy compares with the view of Pericles.*

SOURCE: M. J. Knight, ed., and B. Jowett, trans., *A Selection of Passages from Plato for English Readers* (Oxford, England: The Clarendon Press, 1895), pp. 80–82.

And then democracy comes into being after the poor have conquered their opponents, slaughtering some and banishing some, while to the remainder they give an equal share of freedom and power; and this is the form of government in which the magistrates are commonly elected by lot.

Yes, he said, that is the nature of democracy, whether the revolution has been effected by arms, or whether fear has caused the opposite party to withdraw.

And now what is their manner of life, and what sort of a government have they? For as the government is, such will be the man.

Clearly, he said.

In the first place, are they not free; and is not the city full of freedom and frankness— a man may say and do what he likes?

'Tis said so, he replied.

And where freedom is, the individual is clearly able to order for himself his own life as he pleases?

Clearly.

Then in this kind of State there will be the greatest variety of human natures?

There will.

This, then, seems likely to be the fairest of States, being like an embroidered robe which is spangled with every sort of flower. And just as women and children think a variety of colours to be of all things most charming, so there are many men to whom this State, which is spangled with the manners and characters of mankind, will appear to be the fairest of States.

Yes.

Yes, my good Sir, and there will be no better in which to look for a government.

Why?

Because of the liberty which reigns there—they have a complete assortment of constitutions; and he who has a mind to establish a State, as we have been doing, must go to a democracy as he would to a bazaar at which they sell them, and pick out the one that suits him; then, when he has made his choice, he may found his State.

He will be sure to have patterns enough.

And there being no necessity, I said, for you to govern in this State, even if you have the capacity, or to be governed, unless you like, or to go to war when the rest go to war, or to be at peace when others are at peace, unless you are so disposed—there being no necessity also, because some law forbids you to hold office or be a dicast, that you should not hold office or be a dicast, if you have a fancy—is not this a way of life which for the moment is supremely delightful?

For the moment, yes.

And is not their humanity to the condemned in some cases quite charming? Have you not observed how, in a democracy, many persons, although they have been sentenced to death or exile, just stay where they are and walk about the world—the gentleman parades like a hero, and nobody sees or cares?

Yes, he replied, many and many a one.

See too, I said, the forgiving spirit of democracy, and the 'don't care' about trifles, and the disregard which she shows of all the fine principles which we solemnly laid down at the foundation of the city—as when we said that, except in the case of some rarely gifted nature, there never will be a good man who has not from his childhood been used to play amid things of beauty and make of them a joy and a study—how grandly does she trample all these fine notions of ours under her feet, never giving a thought to the pursuits which make a statesman, and promoting to honour any one who professes to be the people's friend.

Yes, she is of a noble spirit.

These and other kindred characteristics are proper to democracy, which is a charming form of government, full of variety and disorder, and dispensing a sort of equality to equals and unequals alike.

We know her well.

Politics

Aristotle

Aristotle (384–322 B.C.), a student of Plato, the tutor of Alexander the Great, and the founder of the Lyceum (a school rivaling Plato's Academy), had a different approach to politics. Aristotle emphasized the collection and classification of facts, as in the biological and physical sciences. Although Aristotle believed that democracy was a deterioration of a more balanced, high-minded polis, his approach was more descriptive and thus seems less condemning of democracy than Plato's. This is reflected in the following selections from Politics. *In the first passage Aristotle examines the political and social nature of humans, revealing the typically Greek assumption that it is part of human nature to be organized into a polis. In the second passage Aristotle analyzes democracy.*

> **Consider:** *How the arguments of Aristotle and Plato compare in style and form; how Aristotle's description of democracy compares with Pericles' description of Athenian institutions; the characteristics of democracy listed by Aristotle that are generally not practiced today.*

Every state is a community of some kind, and every community is established with a view of some good; for mankind always act in order to obtain that which they think good. But, if all communities aim at some good, the state or political community, which is the highest of all, and which embraces all the rest, aims, and in a greater degree than any other, at the highest good. . . .

For governments differ in kind, as will be evident to any one who considers the matter according to the method which has hitherto guided us. As in other departments of science, so in politics, the compound should always be resolved into the simple elements or least parts of the whole. We must therefore look at the elements of which the state is composed, in order that we may see in what they differ from one another, and whether any scientific distinction can be drawn between the different kinds of rule.

He who thus considers things in their first growth and origin, whether a state or anything else, will obtain the clearest view of them. In the first place (1) there must be a union of those who cannot exist without each other; for example, of male and female,

SOURCE: Aristotle, *Politics*, trans. Benjamin Jowett (Oxford, England: The Clarendon Press, 1905), pp. 25–28, 239–241.

that the race may continue; and this is a union which is formed, not of deliberate purpose, but because, in common with other animals and with plants, mankind have a natural desire to leave behind them an image of themselves. And (2) there must be a union of natural ruler and subject, that both may be preserved. For he who can foresee with his mind is by nature intended to be lord and master, and he who can work with his body is a subject, and by nature a slave; hence master and slave have the same interest. Nature, however, has distinguished between the female and the slave For she is not niggardly, like the smith who fashions the Delphian knife for many uses; she makes each thing for a single use, and every instrument is best made when intended for one and not for many uses. But among barbarians no distinction is made between women and slaves, because there is no natural ruler among them: they are a community of slaves, male and female. Wherefore the poets say,—

'It is meet that Hellenes should rule over barbarians;' as if they thought that the barbarian and the slave were by nature one.

Out of these two relationships between man and woman, master and slave, the family first arises. . . .

The family is the association by nature for the supply of men's everyday wants, and the members of it are called by Charondas 'companions of the cupboard' and by Epimenides the Cretan, 'companions of the manger.' But when several families are united, and the association aims at something more than the supply of daily needs, then comes into existence the village. And the most natural form of the village appears to be that of a colony from the family, composed of the children and grandchildren, who are said to be 'suckled with the same milk.' And this is the reason why Hellenic states were originally governed by kings; because the Hellenes were under royal rule before they came together, as the barbarians still are. Every family is ruled by the eldest, and therefore in the colonies of the family the kingly form of government prevailed because they were of the same blood. . . .

When several villages are united in a single community, perfect and large enough to be nearly or quite self-sufficing, the state comes into existence, originating in the bare needs of life, and continuing in existence for the sake of a good life. And therefore, if the earlier forms of society are natural, so is the state, for it is the end of them, and the [completed] nature is the end. For what each thing is when fully developed, we call its nature, whether we are speaking of a man, a horse, or a family. Besides, the final cause and end of a thing is the best, and to be self-sufficing is the end and the best.

Hence it is evident that the state is a creation of nature, and that man is by nature a political animal. And he who by nature and not by mere accident is without a state, is either above humanity, or below it. . . .

⁂

The basis of a democratic state is liberty; which, according to the common opinion of men, can only be enjoyed in such a state—this they affirm to be the great end of every democracy. One principle of liberty is for all to rule and be ruled in turn, and indeed democratic justice is the application of numerical not proportionate equality; whence it follows that the majority must be supreme, and that whatever the majority approve must be the end and the just. Every citizen, it is said, must have equality, and therefore in a democracy the poor have more power than the rich, because there are more of them, and the will of the majority is supreme. This, then, is one note of liberty which all democrats affirm to be the principle of their state. Another is that a man should live as he likes. This, they say, is the privilege of a freeman; and, on the other hand, not to live as a man likes is the mark of a slave. This is the second characteristic of democracy, whence has arisen the claim of men to be ruled by none, if possible, or, if this is impossible, to rule and be ruled in turns; and so it coincides with the freedom based upon equality.

Such being our foundation and such the nature of democracy, its characteristics are as follows:—the election of officers by all out of all; and that all should rule over each, and each in his turn over all; that the appointment to all offices, or to all but those which require experience and skill, should be made by lot; that no property qualification should be required for offices, or only a very low one; that no one should hold the same office twice, or not often, except in the case of military offices; that the tenure of all offices, or of as many as possible, should be brief; that all men should sit in judgment, or that judges selected out of all should judge in all matters, or in most, or in the greatest and most important—such as the scrutiny of accounts, the constitution, and private contracts; that the assembly should be supreme over all causes, or at any rate over the most important, and the magistrates over none or only over a very few. Of all institutions, a council is the most democratic when there is not the means of paying all the citizens, but when they are paid even this is robbed of its power; for the people then draw all cases to themselves, as I said in the previous discussion. The next characteristic of democracy is payment for services; assembly, law-courts, magistrates, everybody receives pay, when it is to be had; or when it is not to be had for all, then it is given to the law-courts and to the stated assemblies, to the council and to the magistrates, or at least to any of them who are compelled to have their meals together. And whereas oligarchy is characterized by birth, wealth, and education, the notes of democracy appear to be the opposite of these—low birth, poverty, mean employment. Another note is that no magistracy is perpetual, but if any such have survived some ancient change in the constitution it should be stripped of its power, and the holders should be elected by lot and no longer by vote. These are points common to all democracies; but democracy and demos in their truest form are based upon the recognized principle of democratic justice, that all should count equally; for equality implies that the rich should have no more share in the government than the poor, and should not be the only rulers, but that all should rule equally according to their numbers. And in this way men think that they will secure equality and freedom in their state.

Household Management

Xenophon

Public life in Greece was dominated by men. Everyday life for women, even upper-class women in Athens, rarely extended beyond the bounds of the household. An image of this life for women, from a man's point of view, is provided by the Athenian historian and essayist Xenophon

---

SOURCE: Excerpts from *Not in God's Image: Women in History from Greeks to the Victorians* by Julia O'Faolain and Lauro Martines. Copyright © 1973 by Julia O'Faolain and Lauro Martines. Reprinted by permission of HarperCollins Publishers, Inc.

(434?–355 B.C.). In this excerpt from Oeconomicus (Household Management), *Ischomachus and Socrates discuss marriage, women, and domestic life.*

Consider: *How women are perceived; the relationship of husband and wife; the differing roles of men and women.*

'Here's another thing I'd like to ask you,' said I. 'Did you train your wife yourself or did she already know how to run a house when you got her from her father and mother?'

'What could she have known, Socrates,' said he, 'when I took her from her family? She wasn't yet fifteen. Until then she had been under careful supervision and meant to see, hear, and ask as little as possible. Don't you think it was already a lot that she should have known how to make a cloak of the wool she was given and how to dole out spinning to the servants? She had been taught to moderate her appetites, which, to my mind, is basic for both men's and women's education.'

'So, apart from that,' I asked, 'it was you, Ischomachus, who had to train and teach her her household duties?'

'Yes,' said Ischomachus, 'but not before sacrificing to the gods. . . . And she solemnly swore before heaven that she would behave as I wanted, and it was clear that she would neglect none of my lessons.'

'Tell me what you taught her first. . . .'

'Well, Socrates, as soon as I had tamed her and she was relaxed enough to talk, I asked her the following question: "Tell me, my dear," said I, "do you understand why I married you and why your parents gave you to me? You know as well as I do that neither of us would have had trouble finding someone else to share our beds. But, after thinking about it carefully, it was you I chose and me your parents chose as the best partners we could find for our home and children. Now, if God sends us children, we shall think about how best to raise them, for we share an interest in securing the best allies and support for our old age. For the moment we only share our home. . . ."'

'My wife answered, "But how can I help? What am I capable of doing? It is on you that everything depends. My duty, my mother said, is to be well behaved."'

'"Oh, by Zeus," said I, "my father said the same to me. But the best behavior in a man and woman is that which will keep up their property and increase it as far as may be done by honest and legal means."'

'"And do you see some way," asked my wife, "in which I can help in this?"'

❖

'" . . . it seems to me that God adapted women's nature to indoor and man's to outdoor work. . . . As Nature has entrusted woman with guarding the household supplies, and a timid nature is no disadvantage in such a job, it has endowed woman with more fear than man. . . . It is more proper for a woman to stay in the house than out of doors and less so for a man to be indoors instead of out. If anyone goes against the nature given him by God and leaves his appointed post . . . he will be punished. . . . You must stay indoors and send out the servants whose work is outside and supervise those who work indoors, receive what is brought in, give out what is to be spent, plan ahead what should be stored and ensure that provisions for a year are not used up in a month. When the wool is brought in, you must see to it that clothes are made from it for whoever needs them and see to it that the corn is still edible. . . . Many of your duties will give you pleasure: for instance, if you teach spinning and weaving to a slave who did not know how to do this when you got her, you double her usefulness to yourself, or if you make a good housekeeper of one who didn't know how to do anything . . ." Then I took her around the family living rooms, which are pleasantly decorated, cool in summer and warm in winter. I pointed out how the whole house faces south so as to enjoy the winter sun. . . . I showed her the women's quarters which are separated from the men's by a bolted door to prevent anything being improperly removed and also to ensure that the slaves should not have children without our permission. For good slaves are usually even more devoted once they have a family; but good-for-nothings, once they begin to cohabit, have extra chances to get up to mischief.'

Medicine and Magic

Hippocrates

By the fifth century B.C. the Greeks had developed a scientific approach to knowledge. One of the many subjects reflecting this development was medicine. Hippocrates of Cos (460?–377 B.C.) founded a medical school that stressed careful observation and natural causes for disease. This method involved abandoning many religious or supernatural assumptions about diseases and rejecting various forms of divine healing. In the following selection attributed to Hippocrates, or at least his school, this approach is applied to the "sacred disease," the common term for epilepsy.

> **Consider:** *How scientific the assumptions in this document are; the points that might be rejected or applauded by modern doctors.*

I do not believe that the 'Sacred Disease' is any more divine or sacred than any other disease but, on the contrary, has specific characteristics and a definite cause. Nevertheless, because it is completely different from other diseases, it has been regarded as a divine visitation by those who, being only human, view it with ignorance and astonishment. This theory of divine origin, though supported by the difficulty of understanding the malady, is weakened by the simplicity of the cure consisting merely of ritual purification and incantation. If remarkable features in a malady were evidence of divine visitation, then there would be many 'sacred diseases.' Quotidian, tertian and quartan fevers are among other diseases no less remarkable and portentous and yet no one regards them as having a divine origin. I do not believe that these diseases have any less claim to be caused by a god than the so-called 'sacred' disease but they are not the objects of popular wonder. Again, no less remarkably, I have seen men go mad and become delirious for no obvious reason and do many strange things. I have seen many cases of people groaning and shouting in their sleep, some who choke; others jump from their bed and run outside and remain out of their mind till they wake, when they are as healthy and sane as they were before, although perhaps rather pale and weak. These things are not isolated events but

SOURCE: From Hippocrates, *The Medical Works of Hippocrates*, trans. John Chadwick and W. N. Mann, 1950. Courtesy of Charles C. Thomas, Publisher, Springfield, Illinois, and Basil Blackwell, Publisher, Oxford, England.

frequent occurrences. There are many other remarkable afflictions of various sorts, but it would take too long to describe them in detail.

It is my opinion that those who first called this disease 'sacred' were the sort of people we now call witch-doctors, faith-healers, quacks and charlatans. These are exactly the people who pretend to be very pious and to be particularly wise. By invoking a divine element they were able to screen their own failure to give suitable treatment and so called this a 'sacred' malady to conceal their ignorance of its nature. . . .

They also employ other pretexts so that, if the patient be cured, their reputation for cleverness is enhanced while, if he dies, they can excuse themselves by explaining that the gods are to blame while they themselves did nothing wrong; that they did not prescribe the taking of any medicine whether liquid or solid, nor any baths which might have been responsible. . . .

It seems, then, that those who attempt to cure disease by this sort of treatment do not really consider the maladies thus treated of sacred or of divine origin. If the disease can be cured by purification and similar treatment then what is to prevent its being brought on by like devices? The man who can get rid of a disease by his magic could equally well bring it on; again there is nothing divine about this but a human element is involved. By such claims and trickery, these practitioners pretend a deeper knowledge than is given to others; with their prescriptions of 'sanctifications' and 'purifications', their patter about divine visitation and possession by devils, they seek to deceive. And yet I believe that all these professions of piety are really more like impiety and a denial of the existence of the gods, and all their religion and talk of divine visitation is an impious fraud which I shall proceed to expose. . . .

I believe that this disease is not in the least more divine than any other but has the same nature as other diseases and a similar cause. Moreover, it can be cured no less than other diseases so long as it has not become inveterate and too powerful for the drugs which are given.

Like other diseases it is hereditary. If a phlegmatic child is born of a phlegmatic parent, a bilious child of a bilious parent, a consumptive child of a consumptive parent and a splenetic child of a splenetic parent, why should the children of a father or mother who is afflicted with this disease not suffer similarly? The seed comes from all parts of the body; it is healthy when it comes from healthy parts, diseased when it comes from diseased parts. Another important proof that this disease is no more divine than any other lies in the fact that the phlegmatic are constitutionally liable to it while the bilious escape. If its origin were divine, all types would be affected alike without this particular distinction.

Individual Happiness

Epicurus

The Hellenistic Age's greater concern for individual happiness distinguished it from the preceding Classical Age. This concern is reflected in the teachings of Epicurus (342–268 B.C.), who founded

SOURCE: From *Epicurus: The Extant Remains,* trans. Cyril Bailey (1926), pp. 89–91, 95–97, 103, by permission of Oxford University Press.

a school in Athens and was a very influential Hellenistic philosopher. The following selection presents an excerpt from a letter to a student, in which Epicurus describes what he means by pleasure, and a section from his Fragments, *in which he also focuses on individual happiness but broadens his comments to justice and injustice.*

> **Consider:** *Whether this document supports the common association of Epicureanism with indulgence in luxury or sensual pleasures; how this document reflects differences between the Classical and Hellenistic ages.*

When, therefore, we maintain that pleasure is the end, we do not mean the pleasures of profligates and those that consist in sensuality, as is supposed by some who are either ignorant or disagree with us or do not understand, but freedom from pain in the body and from trouble in the mind. For it is not continuous drinkings and revellings, not the satisfaction of lusts, nor the enjoyment of fish and other luxuries of the wealthy table, which produce a pleasant life, but sober reasoning, searching out the motives for all choice and avoidance, and banishing mere opinions, to which are due the greatest disturbance of the spirit.

Of all this the beginning and the greatest good is prudence. Wherefore prudence is a more precious thing even than philosophy: for from prudence are sprung all the other virtues, and it teaches us that it is not possible to live pleasantly without living prudently and honourably and justly (nor, again, to live a life of prudence, honour, and justice without living pleasantly). For the virtues are by nature bound up with the pleasant life, and the pleasant life is inseparable from them.

✿

II. Death is nothing to us: for that which is dissolved is without sensation; and that which lacks sensation is nothing to us.

✿

VIII. No pleasure is a bad thing in itself: but the means which produce some pleasures bring with them disturbances many times greater than the pleasures.

IX. If every pleasure could be intensified so that it lasted and influenced the whole organism or the most essential parts of our nature, pleasures would never differ from one another.

X. If the things that produce the pleasures of profligates could dispel the fears of the mind about the phenomena of the sky and death and its pains, and also teach the limits of desires (and of pains), we should never have cause to blame them: for they would be filling themselves full with pleasures from every source and never have pain of body or mind, which is the evil of life.

✿

XII. A man cannot dispel his fear about the most important matters if he does not know what is the nature of the universe but suspects the truth of some mythical story. So that without natural science it is not possible to attain our pleasures unalloyed.

✿

XXXIII. Justice never is anything in itself, but in the dealings of men with one another in any place whatever and at any time it is a kind of compact not to harm or be harmed.

XXXIV. Injustice is not an evil in itself, but only in consequence of the fear which attaches to the apprehension of being unable to escape those appointed to punish such actions.

VISUAL SOURCES

Education

Most of the few pictorial representations of Greek life that have survived are on pottery. What is portrayed on this early fifth century B.C. *cup (photo 3-1) is stylized. The intention is to show an aspect of everyday life that would be recognized by the viewers—the education of Greek boys. On the left a boy is being taught to play the harp; on the right a boy is being taught to read. The figure on the far right is probably a slave chaperon, who served as a guard and an aid in moral upbringing. On the other side of the cup (not shown) students are learning another musical instrument and writing. Since there were no state schools, instruction was limited to those who could afford a private teacher.*

Consider: *The connections between the scenes depicted on this cup and Pericles' description of Athenian society.*

Photo 3-1

Antikenmuseum, Staatliche Museen, W. Berlin/Ingrid Geske

The Women's Quarters

According to Greek social ideals, women spent most of their lives indoors at home. While the majority of Greek women were not wealthy enough to live without working, elite women might approach the ideal. The scene on this fifth-century jar used by women to fetch water from a well or communal fountain (photo 3-2) depicts the activities that form part of this ideal. Here women have gathered to share cultural activities. In the center a woman sits reading aloud from a scroll. In front of her stands another woman holding a chest of scrolls. On each side, women listen to the recitation. The perfume flask on the upper left emphasizes that this is a scene from a wealthy woman's quarters.

Photo 3-2

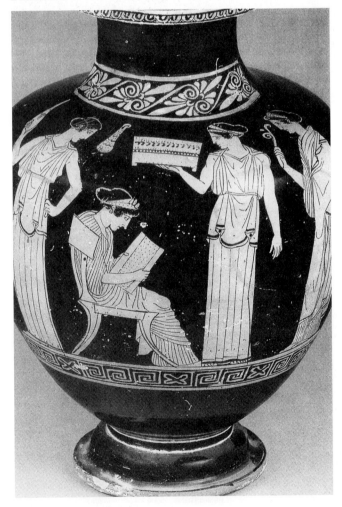

British Museum, London

The Dying Niobide:
The Classical Balance

The Dying Niobide (440?), an example of the Classical style, mixes realism and idealism (photo 3-3). The human body is depicted more or less as it appears to the human eye. Suffering shows in the mouth, perhaps fear in the eyes. Yet it is difficult to say that this is a real individual. The body is not that of a real woman but of an ideal—the artist's vision of the perfect female body. This vision fits a broader Greek cultural ideal of the human form: It reflects a balance between the private statement and the public expression, between the individual and the community, which character-ized Greeks during the Classical Age. The subject is also a lesson for the viewer. It shows the mythi-cal story of an innocent woman being killed by the gods because of her mother's excess pride. Still, the Classical balance dominates, for while there is some action, it is not overly dramatic, not shock-ing. On the whole it invites the viewer to observe and contemplate as well as to enjoy.

> **Consider:** *How* The Dying Niobide *relates to the emotional and philosophical conflicts il-lustrated by the selection from* Antigone.

Photo 3-3

Hirmer Fotoarchiv

The Old Market Woman: Hellenistic Individualism

The Old Market Woman *(second century B.C.) exemplifies the Hellenistic style (photo 3-4). Gone is the mixture of realism and idealism that characterized the Classical style. Instead, individualism and emotionalism are emphasized. A realistic individual is shown. She is far from ideal in almost every detail, from her facial lines to the basket she carries. One can empathize with the pains of old age and the situation of this individual, straining under an everyday task. No reference is made to a well-known myth or a heroic trait. This statue reflects the greater concern for the individual, the focus on the material aspects of life, and the technical brilliance of the Hellenistic Age.*

Consider: *The emotions, ideals, and experiences of the viewer being appealed to by the sculptors of this and the preceding statue.*

Photo 3-4

The Metropolitan Museum of Art, Rogers Fund, 1909

Geography and Political Configurations in Greece

Map 3-1 shows Athens and the surrounding areas during the fifth century B.C. *Like many other Greek city-states, Athens was located near the sea on a cultivated plain surrounded by mountains. The city was walled and surrounded an easily defensible high point (the acropolis). The Athenians extended the walls to protect their access to their port at Piraeus. The surrounding mountains facilitated the Athenian defense of their lands while discouraging regular communication by land with other Greek city-states. The smallness of the Athenian plain and its easy access to the sea encouraged maritime commerce, especially to obtain foods the Athenians could not grow themselves. A large number of the other Greek city-states were actually inhabited islands and port cities lacking natural geographic protection and thus were vulnerable to attack from the sea. Athens took advantage of its own protected location and its neighbors' vulnerability to become a significant naval power.*

Map 3-1   Athens in the Fifth Century B.C.

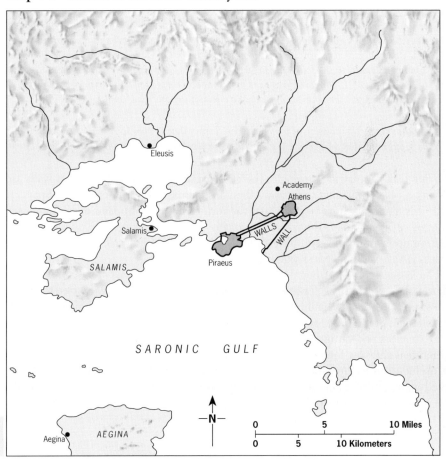

Consider: *How geography can help explain some aspects of the city-states, of the wars against Persia and between Athens and Sparta, and of the dominance over Greece achieved by Philip and Alexander.*

SECONDARY SOURCES

Goddesses, Whores, Wives, and Slaves: Women and Work in Athens

Sarah B. Pomeroy

The traditional image of Greek society is based primarily on what men did and thought. In recent decades historians have focused on the roles women played in Greek society and how those roles differed from men's roles. In the following excerpt from her well-known study of women in Greece and Rome, Sarah B. Pomeroy analyzes the economic roles played by women in Athens during the Classical Age. Here she emphasizes the effect of urban living on their lives.

Consider: *How the position of women differed from that of men in Athens; the possible effects of urbanization on women; the kind of work women engaged in and how it was valued.*

By the late fifth century B.C., owing to the need for the safety afforded by city walls, urban living replaced farming for many Athenians. Thus, when one compares Sparta to Athens, it is necessary to remember that the former never comprised more than a settlement of villages, while Athens was one of the largest Greek cities. The effect of urbanization upon women was to have their activities moved indoors, and to make their labor less visible and hence less valued.

Urban living created a strong demarcation between the activities of men of the upper and lower classes, as well as between those of men and women. Men were free to engage in politics, intellectual and military training, athletics, and the sort of business approved for gentlemen. Some tasks were regarded as banausic and demeaning, befitting slaves rather than citizens. Naturally, a male citizen who needed income was unable to maintain the ideal and was forced to labor in banausic employment. Women of the upper class, excluded from the activities of the males, supervised and—when they wished—pursued many of the same tasks deemed appropriate to slaves. Since the work was despised, so was the worker. Women's work was productive, but because it was the same as

---

Source: From *Goddesses, Whores, Wives, and Slaves* by Sarah B. Pomeroy. Copyright © 1975 by Sarah B. Pomeroy. Reprinted by permission of Schocken Books, Pantheon Books, a division of Random House, Inc.

slaves' work, it was not highly valued in the ideology of Classical Athens. The intimacy of the discussions between heroines and choruses of female slaves in tragedy and the depictions of mistress and slave on tombstones imply a bond between slave and free, for they spent much time together and their lives were not dissimilar.

✿

Women of all social classes worked mainly indoors or near the house in order to guard it. They concerned themselves with the care of young children, the nursing of sick slaves, the fabrication of clothing, and the preparation of food. The preparation of ordinary food was considered exclusively women's work.

✿

Transporting water in a pitcher balanced on the head was a female occupation. Because fetching water involved social mingling, gossip at the fountain, and possible flirtations, slave girls were usually sent on this errand.

Women did not go to market for food, and even now they do not do so in rural villages in Greece. The feeling that purchase or exchange was a financial transaction too complex for women, as well as the wish to protect women from the eyes of strangers and from intimate dealings with shopkeepers, contributed to classifying marketing as a man's occupation.

Wealthier women were distinguished by exercising a managerial role, rather than performing all the domestic work themselves.

✿

Poorer women, even citizens, went out to work, most of them pursuing occupations that were an extension of women's work in the home. Women were employed as washerwomen, as woolworkers, and in other clothing industries. They also worked as vendors, selling food or what they had spun or woven at home. Some women sold garlands they had braided. Women were also employed as nurses of children and midwives.

The Greeks: Slavery

Anthony Andrews

It has long been known that the Greeks, like other ancient peoples, practiced slavery. But focusing only on the glories of Greece sometimes leads one to forget how much slavery existed at that time and the role slavery played in supporting the Greek style of life. A historian who takes this into account is Anthony Andrews, a professor at Oxford University who has written a major text on the Greeks. In the following selection he examines Greek assumptions about slavery and the relations between slaves and masters in the Greek world.

> **Consider:** *How this analysis undermines an image of Athens as an open, democratic, and just society; what distinctions might be made between slavery in different times and societies—such as between slavery in Athens and in eighteenth-century America.*

SOURCE: Anthony Andrews, *The Greeks* (New York: Random House, 1967), pp. 133, 138–139, 142.

In the broadest terms, slavery was basic to Greek civilisation in the sense that, to abolish it and substitute free labour, if it had occurred to anyone to try this on, would have dislocated the whole society and done away with the leisure of the upper classes of Athens and Sparta. The ordinary Athenian had a very deeply ingrained feeling that it was impossible for a free man to work directly for another as his master. While it is true that free men, as well as slaves, engaged in most forms of trade and industry, the withdrawal of slaves from these tasks would have entailed a most uncomfortable reorganisation of labour and property. . . .

No easy generalisation is possible about the relations between slave and master in the Greek world, since the slave's view, as usual, is not known. In the close quarters of Greek domestic life, no distance could be preserved like that which English middle-class families used to keep between themselves and their servants—and the Greek was unlikely to refrain from talking under any circumstances. The closer relation of nurse and child, tutor and pupil, easily ripened into affection, nor need we doubt stories of the loyal slave saving his master's life on the battlefield, and the like. But at its best the relationship was bound to have unhappy elements, as that when a slave was punished it was with physical blows of the kind that a free man had the right to resent. . . .

The domestic slave who was on good terms with his master stood some chance of liberation, and the slave 'living apart' and practising his trade might hope to earn enough to buy his release. Manumission was by no means uncommon, though the practice and the formalities differed a good deal from place to place. The master often retained the right to certain services for a fixed period, or for his own lifetime. Some of those 'living apart' prospered conspicuously, giving rise to disgruntled oligarchic comment that slaves in the streets of Athens might be better dressed than free men. . . .

But the domestic slave with a bad master was in poor case, with little hope of redress, and the prospects were altogether bleaker for those who were hired out to the mines and other work—and we are not given even a distorted reflection of their feelings. But, after the Spartans had fortified their post outside Athens in 413, Thucydides tells us that over 20,000 slaves deserted to the enemy, the bulk of them 'craftsmen' (the word would cover any sort of skilled labour and need not be confined to the miners of Laurium, though no doubt many of the deserters were from there). We do not know what promises the invaders had held out to them, still less what eventually became of them, but the suggestion is clear that the life of even a skilled slave was one which he was ready to fly from on a very uncertain prospect. . . .

In the generation of Socrates, when everything was questioned, the justice of slavery was questioned also. Isolated voices were heard to say that all men were equally men, and that slavery was against nature. The defence of Aristotle, that some were naturally slaves, incapable of full human reason and needing the will of a master to complete their own, rings hollow to us, quite apart from the accident that 'naturally free' Greeks might be enslaved by the chances of war. But this was a world in which slavery, in some form or other, was universal, and no nation could remember a time when it had not been so. It is not surprising that there was no clamour for emancipation. It has been convincingly argued that the margin over bare subsistence in Greece was so small that the surplus which was needed to give leisure to the minority could only be achieved with artificially cheap labour. If that is right, there was not much alternative for Greece. For Athens, it had come, by the opening of the sixth century, to a choice between reducing citizens to slavery or extensive import of chattel slaves from abroad. Only a greatly improved technology, something like an industrial revolution, could effectively have altered these conditions.

The Ancient Greeks: Decline of the Polis

M. I. Finley

Typically, the fourth century B.C. *is seen as a period of decline, at least for the Greek polis. This decline and the reasons for it have long fascinated historians. Some point to the disillusionment following the Peloponnesian War, others to the inability of Greek city-states to control wars among themselves and ally in the face of the threat from Macedonia. In the following selection M. I. Finley, a leading historian of ancient times from Cambridge University, deals with this issue from a different point of view: The Greek polis could flourish only under unusual circumstances and only for a short period of time.*

> **Consider:** *Additional factors that could explain the "decline" of the polis; what policies or developments might have delayed the decline of the polis; whether the fate of Greek civilization was tied to that of the polis.*

All this movement, like the constant *stasis,* marked a failing of the community, and therefore of the *polis.* The more the *polis* had to hire its armed forces, the more citizens it could no longer satisfy economically, and that meant above all with land, so that they went elsewhere in order to live; the more it failed to maintain some sort of equilibrium between the few and the many, the more the cities were populated by outsiders, whether free migrants from abroad or emancipated slaves (who can be called metaphorically free migrants from within)—the less meaningful, the less real was the community. "Decline" is a tricky and dangerous word to use in this context: it has biological overtones which are inappropriate, and it evokes a continuous downhill movement in all aspects of civilization which is demonstrably false. Yet there is no escaping the evidence: the fourth century was the time when the Greek *polis* declined, unevenly, with bursts of recovery and heroic moments of struggle to save itself, to become, after Alexander, a sham *polis* in which the preservation of many external forms of *polis* life could not conceal that henceforth the Greeks lived, in Clemenceau's words, "in the sweet peace of decadence, accepting all sorts of servitudes as they came." . . .

Even fourth-century Athens was not free from signs of the general decline. Contemporary political commentators themselves made much of the fact that whereas right through the fifth century political leaders were, and were expected to be, military leaders at the same time, so that among the ten generals were regularly found the outstanding political figures (elected to the office because of their political importance, not the other way round), in the fourth century the two sides of public activity, the civil and the military, were separated. The generals were now professional soldiers, most of them quite outside politics or political influence, who often served foreign powers as mercenary commanders as well as serving their own *polis*. There are a number of reasons for the shift, among which the inadequate finances of the state rank high, but, whatever the explanation, the break was a bad thing for the *polis*, a cleavage in the responsibility of the members to their community which weakened the sense of community without producing visibly better generalship. In the navy the signs took a different form. A heavy share of the costs still fell on the richest 1200 men and the navy continued to perform well, but there was more evasion of responsibility, more need than before to compel the contributions and to pursue the defaulters at law. The crews themselves were often conscripted; voluntary enlistment could no longer provide the necessary complements. No doubt that was primarily because the treasury was too depleted to provide regular pay for long periods, just as the unwillingness of some to contribute their allotted share of the expenses resulted from an unsatisfactory system of distributing the burden, rather than from lack of patriotism. Wherever the responsibility lay, however, the result was again a partial breakdown in the *polis*.

There is no need to exaggerate: Athens nearly carried it off, and the end came because Macedon, or at least Alexander, was simply too powerful. But Macedon did exist, and so did Persia and Carthage, and later Rome. The *polis* was developed in such a world, not in a vacuum or in Cloud-Cuckoo-Land, and it grew on poor Greek soil. Was it really a viable form of political organization? Were its decline and disappearance the result of factors which could have been remedied, or of an accident—the power of Macedon—or of inherent structural weaknesses? These questions have exercised philosophers and historians ever since the late fifth century (and it is noteworthy how the problem was being posed long before the *polis* could be thought of as on its way out in any literal sense). Plato wished to rescue it by placing all authority in the hands of morally perfect philosophers. Others blame the *demos* and their misleaders, the demagogues, for every ill. Still others, especially in the past century or so, insist on the stupid failure to unite in a national state. For all their disparity, these solutions all have one thing in common: they all propose to rescue the *polis* by destroying it, by replacing it, in its root sense of a community which is at the same time a self-governing state, by something else. The *polis*, one concludes, was a brilliant conception, but one which required so rare a combination of material and institutional circumstances that it could never be realized; that it could be approximated only for a very brief period of time; that it had a past, a fleeting present, and no future. In that fleeting moment its members succeeded in capturing and recording, as man has not often done in his history, the greatness of which the human mind and spirit are capable.

Alexander the Great

Richard Stoneman

If one argues that there were great individuals who changed the course of history, Alexander (356–323 B.C.) seems to have had the right characteristics. In his short career he led the Greeks in a stunning conquest of the Persian Empire. For most historians his death in 323 marks a convenient dividing line between the Classical and Hellenistic ages. It used to be common for historians, like W. W. Tarn, to laud Alexander's greatness in deeds as well as in dreams. But as exemplified by the following selection, most historians now reject this older view. Here Richard Stoneman evaluates Alexander's personality, plans, and accomplishments.

> **Consider:** *The connections between Alexander's accomplishments and his purposes; how Alexander, often thought of as a hero, might be criticized; why Alexander's empire did not last long.*

Alexander's career was the motive force for the spread of Hellenism throughout the western Mediterranean and the Near East, and his achievement thus provided the matrix in which the Roman Empire, Christianity and other important aspects of western civilisation could take root. . . . [However] such grandiose prospects were far from Alexander's imagining and . . . his own aims and ambitions were very different. It is time to draw some of the threads together and to bring those aims and ambitions face-to-face with his actual legacy.

On the assumption, current today among most scholars, that [Alexander's "Last Plans"] . . . represent genuine plans of Alexander, we can deduce that Alexander's megalomania was increasing. He had come to believe, in some degree, his own propaganda, that made him a son of the god Ammon and possibly divine himself. Buttressed by this sublime form of self-confidence (and he had never, at any stage of his career, been short of confidence), he had become increasingly ruthless in executing his purposes. Disloyalty was instantly punished, but corruption and peculation were treated with casualness as long as the perpetrator's loyalty was not in doubt. Opportunistic and flexible, Alexander had been as quick to lose his conquests in India as he had been to gain them, abandoning them when they no longer threatened his immediate position. Babylon and Iran had become the heartland of his empire, but what kind of empire was that to be?

Administration was never to his taste, and Augustus' observation that Alexander had done surprisingly little to set in order the vast empire he had gained is a telling one. The king's state of mind seems to have been a strange one in his last months; besides his megalomania, he was perhaps already ill with the disease that killed him and suffering from a consequent *accidie*. The only activity he could conceive of that was worthy of his self-image was further conquest. Preparations were already far advanced for the invasion

---

SOURCE: Richard Stoneman, *Alexander the Great*. New York: Routledge, 1997, pp. 92–94.

of Arabia, and it is not unreasonable to believe that he had plans to conquer the west—Italy and Carthage, and perhaps beyond. Italians and Carthaginians plainly believed it.

In hindsight it may seem inevitable that an empire based purely on rapid military conquest could not be held together. It was Alexander's pleasure to have his satraps loyal to him; he was not interested in imposing a uniform style of government on his empire, and the Greek lands were virtually forgotten. It was inevitable that such an empire would collapse once his own strong personality was removed. In addition, the fact that he did nothing to appoint a successor strengthened this inevitability. . . .

But it was a world that spoke Greek. In addition, all the successor kings revered the memory of Alexander as their founder. All minted coins with his image. . . .

If we turn now from Macedon to the wider world, we can see that, although it was far from Alexander's intention to mingle cultures for any kind of altruistic or philosophical motive, it was an end result of his actions that the cultures did mix. This happened at different rates, and in different degrees, in different parts of the empire. Greece, with its strong cultural traditions, was essentially unaffected by the empire. The city-states continued their own way under Macedonian overlordship, though they had to get used to honouring 'Royal Friends'. The same is largely true of the Greek cities of Asia Minor, which were able to continue as 'independent cities' under the relatively weak rule of Antigonus and then Lysimachus. Some of the cities prospered remarkably, notably Pergamon which developed a literary and artistic culture to rival that of Alexandria itself. When the last Attalid king of Pergamon bequeathed his kingdom to Rome, the fate of the rest of Asia Minor was also sealed.

Greek Realities

Finley Hooper

Most historians stress the intellectual and scientific accomplishments of the Greeks, above all their extraordinary use of reason. In recent years historians have been pointing to the less rational and individualistic aspects of the Greeks. Finley Hooper exemplifies this trend in the following selection by focusing on the context of the supernatural and the demand to conform that typified everyday life for most Greeks.

> **Consider:** *Ways the primary documents support or refute Hooper's argument; considering this interpretation along with that of Andrews, whether it is a mistake to view the Greeks as democratic; the context Hooper is using for making his evaluation.*

For the most part, this history of the Greek people from the earliest times to the late fourth century B.C. is about a few men whose talents made all the others remembered. That would be true, in part, of any people. In ancient times, the sources of information about the average man and his life were very limited, yet one of the realities of Greek

SOURCE: Reprinted from *Greek Realities* by Finley Hooper, by permission of the Wayne State University Press. Copyright © 1967, pp. 1–3.

history is the wide disparity in outlook between the creative minority which held the spotlight and the far more numerous goatherders, beekeepers, olive growers, fishermen, seers, and sometimes charlatans, who along with other nameless folk made up the greater part of the population.

Romantic glorifications of Greece create the impression that the Greeks sought rational solutions and were imaginative and intellectually curious as a people. Actually, far from being devoted to the risks of rationality, the vast majority of the Greeks sought always the safe haven of superstition and the comfort of magic charms. Only a relatively few thinkers offered a wondrous variety of ideas in their tireless quest for truth. To study various opinions, each of which appears to have some element of truth, is not a risk everyone should take and by no means did all the ancient Greeks take it. Yet enough did, so as to enable a whole people to be associated with the beginnings of philosophy, including the objectivity of scientific inquiry.

The Greeks who belonged to the creative minority were no more like everybody else than such folk ever have been. . . .

They were restless, talkative, critical and sometimes tiresome. Yet their lives as much as their works reveal Greece, for better or for worse, in the way it really was. After Homer, lyric poets went wandering from place to place, in exile from their native cities; before the time of Aristotle, Socrates was executed. If the Greeks invented intellectualism, they were also the first to suppress it. They were, in brief, a people who showed others both how to succeed and how to fail at the things which men might try.

As has often been said, the first democratic society known to man originated in Greece. For this expression of human freedom the Greeks have deservedly received everlasting credit. Yet it is also true that democratic governments were never adopted by a majority of Greek states, and those established were bitterly contested from within and without. In Athens where democracy had its best chance, the government was always threatened by the schemes of oligarchical clubs which sought by any means possible to subvert it. Ironically, Athenian democracy actually failed because of the mistakes of those whom it benefited most, rather than through the machinations of men waiting in the wings to take over. Then, as now, beneath the surface of events there persisted the tension between the material benefits to be obtained through state intervention and the more dynamic vitality which prevails where individuals are left more free to serve and, as it happens, to exploit one another.

A historian must be careful in drawing parallels. The number of individuals in a Greek democracy whose freedom was at stake would be considerably fewer than nowadays. The history of ancient Greece came before the time when all men were created equal. Even the brilliant Aristotle accepted at face value the evidence that certain individuals were endowed with superior qualities. He saw no reason why all men should be treated alike before the law. In fact, he allowed that certain extraordinary persons might be above the law altogether. Some men seemed born to rule and others to serve. There was no common ground between them.

The egalitarian concept that every human being has been endowed by his creator with certain inalienable rights was not a part of the Greek democratic tradition. Pericles, the great Athenian statesman, said that the Athenians considered debate a necessary prelude to any wise action. At the same time, he had a narrow view as to who should do the debating. At Athens, women, foreigners and slaves were all excluded from political life. The actual citizenry was therefore a distinct minority of those living in the city.

In other Greek cities, political power continued to be vested in a small clique (an oligarchy) or in the hands of one man, and often with beneficial results. Various answers to the same political and social problems were proposed and because there were differences there were conflicts. Those who sought to reduce the conflicts also sought to curb the differences, the very same which gave Greek society its exciting vitality. Here we have one of the ironies of human history. Amid bitter often arrogant quarrelsomeness, the Greeks created a civilization which has been much admired. Yet, the price of it has been largely ignored. Hard choices are rarely popular. The Greeks provide the agonizing lesson that men do struggle with one another and in doing so are actually better off than when they live in collective submission to a single idea.

Chapter Questions

1. Evaluate the role of democracy in explaining the rise to greatness of Athens as well as the nature of Athenian society during the Classical Age.

2. Many of the documents have dealt with the nature of the city-state, emphasizing some of the tensions and changes the Greeks experienced. Basing your answers on the information and arguments presented in these sources, what do you think were the advantages and disadvantages for the Greeks of being organized into such relatively small, independent units?

3. On the one hand, the sources have focused on various admired characteristics of Greek civilization, such as their art, drama, democracy, political thought, science, and philosophy. On the other hand, the documents reveal certain criticized qualities of Greek civilization, such as the instability of the polis, the relatively common occurrence of war, the nonegalitarian attitudes of the Greeks, the negative attitude toward women, and the support of slavery. Considering this, do you think that the Greeks have been overly romanticized or appropriately admired? Why?

CHAPTER FOUR

The Rise of Rome

Roman civilization arose during the middle of the first millennium B.C. After the Romans gained independence from the ruling Etruscans in 509 B.C., they slowly established control over the Italian peninsula, the western Mediterranean, the whole Mediterranean basin, and large parts of Europe. Although Rome retained its republican form of government until the first century B.C., there was considerable political turmoil and struggle, often reflecting tensions between the lower and middle classes and the ruling elites. Eventually, the Republic was unable to support these and other tensions. After a century of "slow revolution," Augustus took command in 27 B.C., making Rome an empire in all but name. By the time the Republic was transformed into the Empire, the combination of Roman political control and Greek culture had provided considerable unity to the Mediterranean basin. This Greco-Roman civilization enjoyed full maturity following the triumph of Augustus.

The Republic's most stunning accomplishments were military, political, and administrative. Rome was in the long run consistently successful in its wars, each time extending its rule. One reason for this success was her ability to develop political, administrative, and legal policies to manage newly won territories—something at which the Greeks were much less successful. During the late Republic and particularly during the Empire, these accomplishments were facilitated and symbolized by great architectural achievements—the roads, aqueducts, public facilities, and monuments that helped hold Roman lands together. Culturally, the Romans borrowed freely from the Greeks, acknowledging Greek superiority but nevertheless adding their own style to what they borrowed.

This chapter deals with two main issues. First, what was the structure of the Roman state? This involves an examination of the Roman constitution. Second, what was the nature of Roman society during the Republic? To get at this issue, a number of documents focus on the life and education of the aristocracy, the importance of Roman religious practices, the position of women, the use of slaves, and the place of Greek culture in Roman life. The sources in this chapter should provide a background for developments during the Empire, which will be covered in the next chapter.

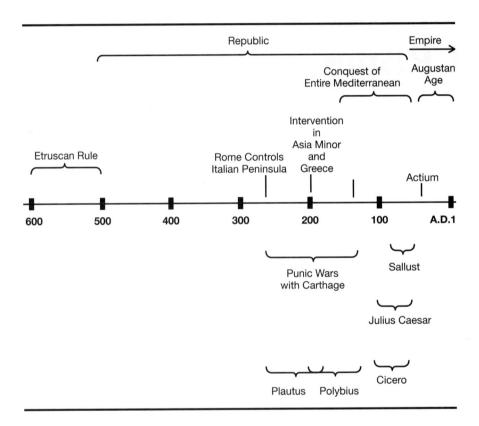

PRIMARY SOURCES

Histories: The Roman Constitution

Polybius

One of the Romans' greatest achievements was the development of political institutions that, despite problems, accommodated Rome's needs. Probably the best general description of these institutions during the Republic is provided by Polybius (205?–123 B.C.), a Greek politician and one of the greatest historians of the ancient world. He spent sixteen years in Rome, where he was in a position to observe the functioning of the Roman state and examine relevant documents. Part of his stated purpose in examining Rome's institutions was to explain why Rome had been so successful, particularly in comparison with his own Greek world. Some of his conclusions are presented in the following selection in which he describes the balanced nature of the Roman constitution.

> **Consider:** *The relative powers of the consuls, the Senate, and the people; the most important functions of the Roman government according to Polybius; the potential dangers or sources of instability in such a constitution.*

As for the Roman constitution, it had three elements, each of them possessing sovereign powers: and their respective share of power in the whole state had been regulated with such a scrupulous regard to equality and equilibrium, that no one could say for certain, not even a native, whether the constitution as a whole were an aristocracy or democracy or despotism. And no wonder: for if we confine our observation to the power of the Consuls we should be inclined to regard it as despotic; if on that of the Senate, as aristocratic; and if finally one looks at the power possessed by the people it would seem a clear case of democracy. What the exact powers of these several parts were, and still, with slight modifications, are, I will now state.

   The Consuls, before leading out the legions, remain in Rome and are supreme masters of the administration. All other magistrates, except the Tribunes, are under them and take their orders. They introduce foreign ambassadors to the Senate; bring matters requiring deliberation before it; and see to the execution of its decrees. If, again, there are any matters of state which require the authorisation of the people, it is their business to see to them, to summon the popular meetings, to bring the proposals before them, and to carry out the decrees of the majority. In the preparations for war also, and in a word in the entire administration of a campaign, they have all but absolute power. It is competent to them to impose on the allies such levies as they think good, to appoint the Military Tribunes, to make up the roll for soldiers and select those that are suitable. Besides they have absolute power of inflicting punishment on all who are under their command while on active service: and they have authority to expend as much of the public

SOURCE: Polybius, *Histories*, vol. I, trans. Evelyn S. Shuckburgh (New York: Macmillan and Co., 1889), pp. 468–471.

money as they choose, being accompanied by a quaestor[1] who is entirely at their orders. A survey of these powers would in fact justify our describing the constitution as despotic,—a clear case of royal government. Nor will it affect the truth of my description, if any of the institutions I have described are changed in our time, or in that of our posterity: and the same remarks apply to what follows.

The Senate has first of all the control of the treasury, and regulates the receipts and disbursements alike. For the Quaestors cannot issue any public money for the various departments of the state without a decree of the Senate, except for the service of the Consuls. The Senate controls also what is by far the largest and most important expenditure, that, namely, which is made by the censors[2] every *lustrum*[3] for the repair or construction of public buildings; this money cannot be obtained by the censors except by the grant of the Senate. Similarly all crimes committed in Italy requiring a public investigation, such as treason, conspiracy, poisoning, or wilful murder, are in the hands of the Senate. Besides, if any individual or state among the Italian allies requires a controversy to be settled, a penalty to be assessed, help or protection to be afforded,—all this is the province of the Senate. Or again, outside Italy, if it is necessary to send an embassy to reconcile warring communities, or to remind them of their duty, or sometimes to impose requisitions upon them, or to receive their submission, or finally to proclaim war against them,—this too is the business of the Senate. In like manner the reception to be given to foreign ambassadors in Rome, and the answers to be returned to them, are decided by the Senate. With such business the people have nothing to do. Consequently, if one were staying at Rome when the Consuls were not in town, one would imagine the constitution to be a complete aristocracy: and this has been the idea entertained by many Greeks, and by many kings as well, from the fact that nearly all the business they had with Rome was settled by the Senate.

After this one would naturally be inclined to ask what part is left for the people in the constitution, when the Senate has these various functions, especially the control of the receipts and expenditure of the exchequer; and when the Consuls, again, have absolute power over the details of military preparation, and an absolute authority in the field? There is, however, a part left the people, and it is a most important one. For the people is the sole fountain of honour and of punishment; and it is by these two things and these alone that dynasties and constitutions and, in a word, human society are held together: for where the distinction between them is not sharply drawn both in theory and practice, there no undertaking can be properly administered,—as indeed we might expect when good and bad are held in exactly the same honour. The people then are the only court to decide matters of life and death; and even in cases where the penalty is money, if the sum to be assessed is sufficiently serious, and especially when the accused have held the higher magistracies. And in regard to this arrangement there is one point deserving especial commendation and record. Men who are on trial for their lives at Rome, while sentence is in process of being voted,—if even only one of the tribes whose votes are

---

[1]Official responsible for finance and administration.

[2]Officials responsible for supervising the public census and public behavior and morals.

[3]A ceremonial purification of the Roman population after the census every five years.

needed to ratify the sentence has not voted,—have the privilege at Rome of openly departing and condemning themselves to a voluntary exile. Such men are safe at Naples or Praeneste or at Tibur, and at other towns with which this arrangement has been duly ratified on oath.

Again, it is the people who bestow offices on the deserving, which are the most honourable rewards of virtue. It has also the absolute power of passing or repealing laws; and, most important of all, it is the people who deliberate on the question of peace or war. And when provisional terms are made for alliance, suspension of hostilities, or treaties, it is the people who ratify them or the reverse.

These considerations again would lead one to say that the chief power in the state was the people's, and that the constitution was a democracy.

Such, then, is the distribution of power between the several parts of the state.

The Education of a Roman Gentleman

Cicero

Roman society during the last century of the Republic was turbulent and mobile. One way to rise in this society was through education and talent. Marcus Tullius Cicero (106–43 B.C.) rose in this way. Born into a moderately wealthy but nonaristocratic family, he became an extremely successful orator in the law courts, rose to the position of consul in 63 B.C., and became one of the most prolific, influential, and admired authors of Roman times. Cicero attributed part of his success to the excellent education he received. This is described in the following excerpt from one of his numerous letters.

> **Consider:** *The nature of this process of education; the importance of Greek culture for Cicero's education; Cicero's social and political environment.*

I daily spent the remainder of my time in reading, writing, and private declamation, I cannot say that I much relished my confinement to these preparatory exercises. The next year Quintus Varius was condemned, and banished by his own law; and I, that I might acquire a competent knowledge of the principles of jurisprudence, then attached myself to Quintus Scævola, the son of Publius, who, though he did not choose to undertake the charge of a pupil, yet, by freely giving his advice to those who consulted him, answered every purpose of instruction to such as took the trouble to apply to him. In the succeeding year, in which Sylla and Pompey were consuls, as Sulpicius, who was elected a tribune of the people, had occasion to speak in public almost every day, I had opportunity to acquaint myself thoroughly with his manner of speaking. At this time Philo, a philosopher of the first name in the Academy, with many of the principal Athenians, having deserted their native home, and fled to Rome, from the fury of Mithridates, I immediately became his scholar, and was exceedingly taken with his philosophy; and, besides the pleasure I

Source: From J. S. Watson, trans., *Cicero on Oratory and Orators* (London: Henry G. Bohn, 1855), pp. 495–499.

received from the great variety and sublimity of his matter, I was still more inclined to confine my attention to that study; because there was reason to apprehend that our laws and judicial proceedings would be wholly overturned by the continuance of the public disorders. In the same year Sulpicius lost his life; and Quintus Catulus, Marcus Antonius, and Caius Julius, three orators who were partly contemporary with each other, were most inhumanly put to death. Then also I attended the lectures of Molo the Rhodian, who was newly come to Rome, and was both an excellent pleader, and an able teacher of the art. . . .

The three following years the city was free from the tumult of arms. . . . I pursued my studies of every kind, day and night, with unremitting application. I lodged and boarded at my own house (where he lately died) Diodotus the Stoic; whom I employed as my preceptor in various other parts of learning, but particularly in logic, which may be considered as a close and contracted species of eloquence; and without which, you yourself have declared it impossible to acquire that full and perfect eloquence, which they suppose to be an open and dilated kind of logic. Yet with all my attention to Diodotus, and the various arts he was master of, I never suffered even a single day to escape me, without some exercise of the oratorical kind. I constantly declaimed in private with Marcus Piso, Quintus Pompeius, or some other of my acquaintance; pretty often in Latin, but much oftener in Greek; because the Greek furnishes a greater variety of ornaments, and an opportunity of imitating and introducing them into the Latin; and because the Greek masters, who were far the best, could not correct and improve us, unless we declaimed in that language. This time was distinguished by a violent struggle to restore the liberty of the republic; the barbarous slaughter of the three orators, Scævola, Carbo, and Antistius; the return of Cotta, Curio, Crassus, Pompey, and the Lentuli; the re-establishment of the laws and courts of judicature, and the entire restoration of the commonwealth; but we lost Pomponius, Censorinus, and Murena, from the roll of orators. I now began, for the *first* time, to undertake the management of causes, both private and public; not, as most did, with a view to learn my profession, but to make a trial of the abilities which I had taken so much pains to acquire. I had then a second opportunity of attending the instructions of Molo, who came to Rome while Sylla was dictator, to solicit the payment of what was due to his countrymen for their services in the Mithridatic war. My defence of Sextus Roscius, which was the first cause I pleaded, met with such a favourable reception, that, from that moment, I was looked upon as an advocate of the first class, and equal to the greatest and most important causes; and after this I pleaded many others, which I precomposed with all the care and accuracy I was master of. . . .

[A]fter I had been two years at the bar, and acquired some reputation in the forum, I left Rome. When I came to Athens, I spent six months with Antiochus, the principal and most judicious philosopher of the old Academy; and under this able master, I renewed those philosophical studies which I had laboriously cultivated and improved from my earliest youth. At the same time, however, I continued my *rhetorical exercises* under Demetrius the Syrian, an experienced and reputable master of the art of speaking. After leaving Athens, I traversed every part of Asia, where I was voluntarily attended by the principal orators of the country, with whom I renewed my rhetorical exercises. The chief of them was Menippus of Stratonica, the most eloquent of all the Asiatics; and if to be neither tedious nor impertinent is the characteristic of an Attic orator, he may be justly ranked in that class. Dionysius also of Magnesia, Æschylus of Cnidos, and Xenocles of

Adramyttium, who were esteemed the first rhetoricians of Asia, were continually with me. Not contented with these, I went to Rhodes, and applied myself again to Molo, whom I had heard before at Rome; and who was both an experienced pleader and a fine writer, and particularly judicious in remarking the faults of his scholars, as well as in his method of teaching and improving them. His principal trouble with me was to restrain the luxuriancy of a juvenile imagination, always ready to overflow its banks, within its due and proper channel. Thus, after an excursion of two years, I returned to Italy, not only much improved, but almost changed into a new man. The vehemence of my voice and action was considerably abated; the excessive ardour of my language was corrected; my lungs were strengthened; and my whole constitution confirmed and settled.

Menaechmi: Roman Slavery

Plautus

It should not be overlooked that the Romans, like other peoples in the ancient world, were supported by slaves. Indeed, slaves were a familiar component of everyday life for the Romans during the Republic. Some notion of the Roman treatment and perception of slaves can be gained from the following extract from Menaechmi *by Plautus (254?–184 B.C.), a Roman who wrote numerous comedies, often adapted from Greek originals. Here, Messenio, a slave, soliloquizes.*

> **Consider:** *What distinguished the "good" from the "bad" slave; the "right" way to treat a servant; the presence or absence of a sense of guilt or injustice about the institution of slavery.*

Mess. (*to himself*). This is the proof of a good servant, who takes care of his master's business, looks after it, arranges it, thinks about it, in the absence of his master diligently to attend to the affairs of his master, as much so as if he himself were present, or *even* better. It is proper that his back[1] should be of more consequence than his appetite, his legs than his stomach, whose heart is rightly placed. Let him bear in mind, those who are good for nothing, what reward is given them by their masters—lazy, worthless fellows. Stripes, fetters, the mill, weariness, hunger, sharp cold; these are the rewards of idleness. This evil do I terribly stand in awe of. Wherefore 'tis sure that to be good is better than to be bad. Much more readily do I submit to words, stripes I do detest; and I eat what is ground much more readily than supply it *ground* by myself.[2] Therefore do I obey the command of my master, carefully and diligently do I observe it; and in such manner do I pay obedience, as I think is for the interest of my back. And that *course* does profit me. Let others be just as they take it to be their interest; I shall be just as I ought to be. If I adhere to that, I shall avoid faultiness; so that I am in readiness for my master on all occasions, I shall not be much afraid. *The time* is near, when, for these deeds of mine, my master will give his reward.

SOURCE: H. T. Riley, *The Comedies of Plautus*, vol. I (London: G. Bell and Sons, Ltd., 1852), pp. 364–365.

[1]*That his back*—Ver. 970. For the purpose of keeping his back intact from the whip, and his feet from the fetters.

[2]*Ground by myself*—Ver. 979. He alludes to the custom of sending refractory slaves to the "pistrinum," where the corn was ground by a handmill, which entailed extreme labour on those grinding. He says that he would rather that others should grind the corn for him, than that he should grind it for others.

The Conspiracy of Catiline: Decline of the Republic

Sallust

The Roman Republic came to an end during the second half of the first century B.C. after a long period of conflict and civil war. Many saw this period as one of moral, social, and political decline from the more glorious and virtuous days of the Republic. Sallust (86–36 B.C.) was both a participant and an observer in this period. He became a tribune of the people in 52 B.C. and a close supporter of Julius Caesar in the following years. Later in his life he devoted himself more to historical writing. In the following selection he describes his own sense of disgust and disillusionment with the recent course of events.

> **Consider:** *The main developments that disturbed Sallust; how Sallust compared characteristics of his own times with characteristics of the early Republic; the reliability of this account.*

My earliest inclinations led me, like many other young men, to throw myself wholeheartedly into politics. There I found many things against me. Self-restraint, integrity, and virtue were disregarded; unscrupulous conduct, bribery, and profit-seeking were rife. And although, being a stranger to the vices I saw practised on every hand, I looked on them with scorn, I was led astray by ambition and, with a young man's weakness, could not tear myself away. However much I tried to dissociate myself from the prevailing corruption, my craving for advancement exposed me to the same odium and slander as all my rivals.

After suffering manifold perils and hardships, peace of mind at last returned to me, and I decided that I must bid farewell to politics for good. But I had no intention of wasting my precious leisure in idleness and sloth, or of devoting my time to agriculture or hunting—tasks fit only for slaves. I had formerly been interested in history, and some work which I began in that field had been interrupted by my misguided political ambitions. I therefore took this up again, and decided to write accounts of some episodes in Roman history that seemed particularly worthy of record—a task for which I felt myself the better qualified inasmuch as I was unprejudiced by the hopes and fears of the party man. . . .

Thus by hard work and just dealing the power of the state increased. Mighty kings were vanquished, savage tribes and huge nations were brought to their knees; and when Carthage, Rome's rival in her quest for empire, had been annihilated,[1] every land and sea lay open to her. It was then that fortune turned unkind and confounded all her enterprises. To the men who had so easily endured toil and peril, anxiety and adversity, the leisure and riches which are generally regarded as so desirable proved a burden and a curse. Growing love of money, and the lust for power which followed it, engendered every kind of evil. Avarice destroyed honour, integrity, and every other virtue, and instead taught

---

SOURCE: Sallust, *The Conspiracy of Catiline*, trans. S. A. Hanford (London: Penguin Books Ltd., 1963), pp. 174–178. Copyright © 1963. Reprinted by permission of Penguin Books Ltd.

[1] In 146 B.C.

men to be proud and cruel, to neglect religion, and to hold nothing too sacred to sell. Ambition tempted many to be false, to have one thought hidden in their hearts, another ready on their tongues, to become a man's friend or enemy not because they judged him worthy or unworthy but because they thought it would pay them, and to put on the semblance of virtues that they had not. At first these vices grew slowly and sometimes met with punishment; later on, when the disease had spread like a plague, Rome changed: her government, once so just and admirable, became harsh and unendurable. . . .

As soon as wealth came to be a mark of distinction and an easy way to renown, military commands and political power, virtue began to decline. Poverty was now looked on as a disgrace and a blameless life as a sign of ill nature. Riches made the younger generation a prey to luxury, avarice, and pride. Squandering with one hand what they grabbed with the other, they set small value on their own property while they coveted that of others. Honour and modesty, all laws divine and human, were alike disregarded in a spirit of recklessness and intemperance. To one familiar with mansions and villas reared aloft on such a scale that they look like so many towns, it is instructive to visit the temples built by our godfearing ancestors. In those days piety was the ornament of shrines; glory, of men's dwellings. When they conquered a foe, they took nothing from him save his power to harm. But their base successors stuck at no crime to rob subject peoples of all that those brave conquerors had left them, as though oppression were the only possible method of ruling an empire. I need not remind you of some enterprises that no one but an eyewitness will believe—how private citizens have often levelled mountains and paved seas for their building operations. Such men, it seems to me, have treated their wealth as a mere plaything: instead of making honourable use of it, they have shamefully misused it on the first wasteful project that occurred to them. Equally strong was their passion for fornication, guzzling, and other forms of sensuality. Men prostituted themselves like women, and women sold their chastity to every comer. To please their palates they ransacked land and sea. They went to bed before they needed sleep, and instead of waiting until they felt hungry, thirsty, cold, or tired, they forestalled their bodies' needs by self-indulgence. Such practices incited young men who had run through their property to have recourse to crime. Because their vicious natures found it hard to forgo sensual pleasures, they resorted more and more recklessly to every means of getting and spending.

VISUAL SOURCES

Evidence from Coins

Historians can generally use coins for dating and for determining changes in dynasties and regimes. For ancient times, deposits of coins are often the best evidence for the presence of a people in a particular area. They can indicate the geographic area and quantity of trade relations. By analyzing changing patterns of deposits of coins, growing trade rivalries and changes of commercial, political, or military dominance can be discovered.

The designs and representations on coins often reveal much about a society. On this Roman coin from about 137 B.C. (photo 4-1), a citizen is pictured dropping a ballot into a voting urn. This reveals something about the type of political system present in Rome at the time and indicates that Romans were particularly proud of that system. In fact, Roman citizenship and voting rights were highly valued and part of what facilitated Rome's expansion. Yet too much should not be assumed: This scene could denote a limited oligarchy as much as a democracy or anything between. The writing on the coin is evidence of some level of literacy.

Consider: *How modern American coins might reveal characteristics of American society to future historians.*

Photo 4-1

Bibliothèque Nationale, Paris

The Geographic and Cultural Environment

Map 4-1 shows some of the peoples and civilizations that occupied Italy and its immediately surrounding territory during the fifth century B.C. In the process of Rome's formation and expansion, the Romans came into direct and extended contact with these peoples. Before Rome became a dominant power, the Etruscans, Carthaginians (descendants of the Phoenicians), and Greeks had already established strong, literate, sophisticated civilizations. Understandably, then, as Rome expanded the Romans drew from and even copied many of the institutions and practices of these civilizations, particularly the closer Etruscans and Greeks. Other peoples, such as the Samnites, constituted a barrier to Roman expansion that the Romans overcame during the fifth, fourth, and third centuries B.C., usually by force of arms. Rome's geographic and cultural environment, therefore, played an important role in the development of the Roman Republic.

Map 4-1   Italy, Fifth Century B.C.

Consider: *How the experience gained during the early years of the Roman Republic laid the foundations for later Roman imperialism.*

SECONDARY SOURCES

The Ancient City: Religious Practices

Fustel de Coulanges

Ancient Rome is usually described in political, military, and cultural terms. The Romans them-selves are typically described as practical, rational, disciplined, and secular. Yet like the Greeks, they were also very religious. This is emphasized in the following selection from The Ancient City, *which has become a minor classic. Here Fustel de Coulanges, a nineteenth-century French historian, shows how central religious beliefs were to the Roman's everyday life.*

Consider: *How the Romans related to the gods; what the author means in arguing that the Roman patrician was a priest.*

We must inquire what place religion occupied in the life of a Roman. His house was for him what a temple is for us. He finds there his worship and his gods. His fire is a god; the walls, the doors, the threshold are gods; the boundary marks which surround his field are also gods. The tomb is an altar, and his ancestors are divine beings.

Each one of his daily actions is a rite; his whole day belongs to his religion. Morning and evening he invokes his fire, his Penates,[1] and his ancestors; in leaving and entering his house he addresses a prayer to them. Every meal is a religious act, which he shares with his domestic divinities. Birth, initiation, the taking of the toga, marriage, and the an-niversaries of all these events, are the solemn acts of his worship.

He leaves his house, and can hardly take a step without meeting some sacred object— either a chapel, or a place formerly struck by lightning, or a tomb; sometimes he must step back and pronounce a prayer; sometimes he must turn his eyes and cover his face, to avoid the sight of some ill-boding object.

Every day he sacrifices in his house, every month in his cury, several months a year with his gens or his tribe. Above all these gods, he must offer worship to those of the city. There are in Rome more gods than citizens.

He offers sacrifices to thank the gods; he offers them, and by far the greater number, to appease their wrath. One day he figures in a procession, dancing after a certain

---

Source: Numa Denis Fustel de Coulanges, *The Ancient City,* trans. Williard Small (Boston: Lee and Shepard, Publishers, 1874), pp. 281–283.
[1]Gods of the household.

ancient rhythm, to the sound of the sacred flute. Another day he conducts chariots, in which lie statues of the divinities. Another time it is a *lectisternium:* a table is set in a street, and loaded with provisions; upon beds lie statues of the gods, and every Roman passes bowing, with a crown upon his head, and a branch of laurel in his hand.

There is a festival for seed-time, one for the harvest, and one for the pruning of the vines. Before corn has reached the ear, the Roman has offered more than ten sacrifices, and invoked some ten divinities for the success of his harvest. He has, above all, a multitude of festivals for the dead, because he is afraid of them.

He never leaves his own house without looking to see if any bird of bad augury appears. There are words which he dares not pronounce for his life. If he experiences some desire, he inscribes his wish upon a tablet which he places at the feet of the statue of a divinity.

At every moment he consults the gods, and wishes to know their will. He finds all his resolutions in the entrails of victims, in the flight of birds, in the warning of the lightning. The announcement of a shower of blood, or of an ox that has spoken, troubles him and makes him tremble. He will be tranquil only after an expiatory ceremony shall restore him to peace with the gods.

He steps out of his house always with the right foot first. He has his hair cut only during the full moon. He carries amulets upon his person. He covers the walls of his house with magic inscriptions against fire. He knows of formulas for avoiding sickness, and of others for curing it; but he must repeat them twenty-seven times, and spit in a certain fashion at each repetition.

He does not deliberate in the senate if the victims have not given favorable signs. He leaves the assembly of the people if he hears the cry of a mouse. He renounces the best laid plans if he perceives a bad presage, or if an ill-omened word has struck his ear. He is brave in battle, but on condition that the auspices assure him the victory.

This Roman whom we present here is not the man of the people, the feeble-minded man whom misery and ignorance have made superstitious. We are speaking of the patrician, the noble, powerful, and rich man. This patrician is, by turns, warrior, magistrate, consul, farmer, merchant; but everywhere and always he is a priest, and his thoughts are fixed upon the gods. Patriotism, love of glory, and love of gold, whatever power these may have over his soul, the fear of the gods still governs everything.

Life and Leisure: The Roman Aristocrat

J. P. V. D. Balsdon

Although it is appropriate to concentrate on the major events and the important accomplishments of the Romans, at times this leads one to forget that the Romans were real people with everyday lives. The religious aspects of their lives are brought out in the selection by Fustel de Coulanges.

SOURCE: From "Life and Leisure," by J. P. V. D. Balsdon in *The Romans,* ed. by J. P. V. D. Balsdon, pp. 270–272, © 1965 by Basic Books, Inc., Publisher, New York. Reprinted with permission.

In the following selection J. P. V. D. Balsdon of Oxford focuses on the occupations, alternatives, and patterns of life open to a typical Roman aristocrat.

Consider: *The occupations most appropriate for a Roman aristocrat and the limitations he had to face; connections between this description and Cicero's life and education as revealed in the document by Cicero; any connections between this picture of Roman life and the image presented by Fustel de Coulanges.*

By upper-class standards public service was the noblest activity of man—the life of the barrister, the soldier, the administrator and the politician; for normally the senator's life embraced all those four activities. Rhetoric was a main constituent of his education and at an early age he put his learning into practice by pleading at the Bar. He climbed the ladder of a senatorial career, absent from Rome sometimes for considerable periods in which he served as an army officer or governed a province. If he committed no indiscretion, he was a life-member of the Senate—if he held the consulship, an important elder statesman from then onwards. In the Empire he might be one of the Emperor's privy counsellors.

This was not a career in which, except in the last centuries of the Republic, great fortunes were to be made. The senator therefore needed to be a wealthy man, in particular to own considerable landed property. To this he escaped when he could, particularly if he came of a good family, for the Roman aristocrat was a countryman at heart, interested in farming well, happy in the saddle, fond of hunting. He would have been shocked by the parvenu Sallust's description of farming and hunting as "occupations fit for a slave"; and other Romans no doubt were shocked too, for in the case of the farmer (and perhaps only of the farmer) the notion of work had a wide romantic fascination. Everyone liked to be reminded of Cincinnatus in the fifth century B.C., of how, when they sent for him to be dictator, they found him ploughing and how, once the business of saving Rome as dictator was accomplished, he returned happily to his farm. When Scipio Africanus found himself driven from public life, he worked on the land with his own hands.

If an aristocrat's means were not sufficient to support him in a life of public service, he might turn to business, banking, trading, tax-farming, the activities of the "Equestrian order." In this way distinguished families sometimes disappeared from politics for a generation or more and then, their wealth restored, they returned. There was nothing disgraceful about being a business man, as long as you were rich and successful enough, in which case you were likely to invest largely in land and to become one of the landowning gentry. Equestrians, whether business men or rich country residents, were fathers of senators often and sometimes sons, frequently close personal friends, Atticus of Cicero for instance.

A man who avoided or deserted "the sweat and toil" of a public career in favour of industrious seclusion—"a shady life" (*vita umbratilis*)—could excuse himself and indeed (like Cicero and Sallust when, elbowed out of an influential position in public life, they became writers) found it desirable to excuse himself. If he became a writer, then he made it clear that he wrote as an educationalist, employing his seclusion to teach valuable lessons to his readers, particularly his young readers, a purpose which nobody disparaged. But if his retirement was the retirement of self-indulgence (*desidia*), like the later life of L. Lucullus, an obsession with fantastically expensive landscape gardening and extravagant fish ponds, he was a traitor to serious and responsible standards of living (*gravitas*) and won the contempt—however envious—of all but his like-minded friends. There was no secure happiness in such a life, as serious men like Lucretius, Horace and Seneca knew.

Roman Women

Gillian Clark

Until recently most historians presented an image of Roman life that mentioned women only in passing. This void about the experience of Roman women is being filled by new scholarship, much of it written by feminist historians. In the following selection Gillian Clark analyzes the position and experience of women during the late Republic and age of Augustus, emphasizing the political, legal, and social restraints on women.

> **Consider:** *Ways in which women might influence public life despite restraints placed on them; what the characteristics of the good woman were; how one might evaluate whether Roman women were happy; how this description of Roman women compares with Balsdon's description of aristocratic Roman men.*

Women did not vote, did not serve as *iudices*,[1] were not senators or magistrates or holders of major priesthoods. They did not, as a rule, speak in the courts. . . . As a rule, women took no part in public life, except on the rare occasions when they were angry enough to demonstrate, which was startling and shocking. . . .

Women might, then, have considerable influence and interests outside their homes and families, but they were acting from within their families to affect a social system managed by men: their influence was not to be publicly acknowledged. Why were women excluded from public life? The division between arms-bearers and child-bearers was doubtless one historical cause, but the reasons publicly given were different. Women were alleged to be fragile and fickle, and therefore in need of protection; if they were not kept in their proper place they would (fragility and fickleness notwithstanding) take over. As the elder Cato . . . said . . . :

'Our ancestors decided that women should not handle anything, even a private matter, without the advice of a guardian; that they should always be in the power of fathers, brothers, husbands. . . . Call to mind all those laws on women by which your ancestors restrained their licence and made them subject to men: you can only just keep them under by using the whole range of laws. If you let them niggle away at one law after another until they have worked it out of your grasp, until at last you let them make themselves equal to men, do you suppose that you'll be able to stand them? If once they get equality, they'll be on top.' . . .

Source: Gillian Clark, "Roman Women," *Greece and Rome*, 28 (1981), 206–207, 209–210.
[1]Judges.

A social system which restricted women to domestic life, and prevailing attitudes which assumed their inferiority, must seem to us oppressive. I know of no evidence that it seemed so at the time. The legal and social constraints detailed above may have frustrated the abilities of many women and caused much ordinary human unhappiness. But there evidently were, also, many ordinarily happy families where knowledge of real live women took precedence over the theories, and women themselves enjoyed home, children, and friends. There were some women who enjoyed the political game, and who found an emotional life outside their necessary marriages. And there were certainly women who found satisfaction in living up to the standards of the time. They were, as they should be, chaste, dutiful, submissive, and domestic; they took pride in the family of their birth and the family they had produced; and probably their resolution to maintain these standards gave them the support which women in all ages have found in religious faith. But the religious feelings of Roman women, as opposed to the acts of worship in which they might take part, are something of which we know very little. . . .

The son of Murdia, in the age of Augustus, made her a public eulogy . . . [which] may make the best epitaph for the women who did not make the history books.

'What is said in praise of all good women is the same, and straightforward. There is no need of elaborate phrases to tell of natural good qualities and of trust maintained. It is enough that all alike have the same reward: a good reputation. It is hard to find new things to praise in a woman, for their lives lack incident. We must look for what they have in common, lest something be left out to spoil the example they offer us. My beloved mother, then, deserves all the more praise, for in modesty, integrity, chastity, submission, woolwork, industry, and trustworthiness she was just like other women.'

Chapter Questions

1. Describe the circumstances, options, and everyday life of a Roman aristocrat during the first century B.C. as revealed in the documents in this chapter.

2. In what ways did Greeks, Greek culture, and Greek history affect Roman civilization?

3. Describe the similarities and differences between Greek and Roman civilizations. What were some of the main strengths and weaknesses of each?

CHAPTER FIVE

The Roman Empire and the Rise of Christianity

With control in the hands of Augustus by 27 B.C., the Augustan Age began. A variety of reforms transformed the Republic into the Empire. Rome entered a period of expansion, prosperity, cultural vigor, and relative political stability that would last until the end of the second century. This was particularly so under the long rule of Augustus (27 B.C.–A.D. 14) and the five "good emperors" (A.D. 96–180).

During this same period Christianity arose. Initially, it seemed only one of many religious sects and was perceived as a version of Judaism. But through the missionary work of Paul and the internal organization of the Church, Christianity spread and became institutionalized. During the fourth century it was recognized as the state religion within the Roman Empire.

By then enormous difficulties had been experienced within the Empire. Economic, political, and military problems were so great in the third century that the Empire shrank and nearly collapsed. A revival under the strong leadership of Diocletian and Constantine during the late third and early fourth centuries proved only temporary. By the end of the fourth century, the Empire was split into a Western and an Eastern half. The West was increasingly rural, subject to invasion, and generally in decline; the East evolved into the long-lasting Byzantine Empire. By the end of the fifth century, a unified, effective Western Empire was little more than a memory.

The selections in this chapter deal with three topics. The first concerns the general nature of the Empire at its height. During this time those who predominated were the politically active Roman "gentlemen." What was their lifestyle? What were their interests? How did they relate to Classical culture? These same questions apply to some of the Roman emperors, like Marcus Aurelius, a Stoic philosopher. The documents also deal with broader questions. How was the transition from the Republic to the Empire made and what role did Augustus play in this transition? What were the connections between Roman society, culture, and religion?

The second topic is Christianity. Why was Christianity so appealing, particularly to Roman women? What explains the success of this religious movement? How did Christianity relate to Roman civilization? How did Christian theology relate to Classical philosophy?

The third topic is the decline and fall of Rome, a problem of continuing interest to historians. Some of the primary documents explore reactions to the fall. The secondary documents offer interpretations of the fall. Here the need to distinguish the Western from the Eastern Roman Empire during the decline and fall is stressed. This topic will take us up to the rise of new civilizations in lands once controlled by Rome; this will be covered in the next chapter.

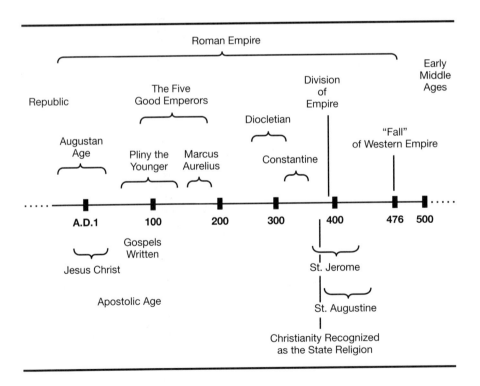

PRIMARY SOURCES

Letters: The Daily Life of a Roman Governor

Pliny the Younger

For a cultured, well-to-do Roman gentleman, the period between A.D. *96 and 180, when the Empire was at its height, was a good time to live. This is reflected in the letters of Pliny the Younger (62?–113?), a lawyer who rose to the position of governor of Bithynia in Asia Minor. In the following letter he describes a typical day while vacationing at one of his Italian villas.*

> **Consider:** *The kinds of activities most important to Pliny, at least during his stay at the villa; Pliny's view of his life and of people around him.*

TO FUSCUS

You desire to know in what manner I dispose of my day in summer-time at my Tuscan villa.

I rise just when I find myself in the humour, though generally with the sun; often indeed sooner, but seldom later. When I am up, I continue to keep the shutters of my chamber-windows closed. For under the influence of darkness and silence, I find myself wonderfully free and abstracted from those outward objects which dissipate attention, and left to my own thoughts; nor do I suffer my mind to wander with my eyes, but keep my eyes in subjection to my mind, which in the absence of external objects, see those which are present to the mental vision. If I have any composition upon my hands, this is the time I choose to consider it, not only with respect to the general plan, but even the style and expression, which I settle and correct as if I were actually writing. In this manner I compose more or less as the subject is more or less difficult, and I find myself able to retain it. Then I call my secretary, and, opening the shutters, I dictate to him what I have composed, after which I dismiss him for a little while, and then call him in again and again dismiss him.

About ten or eleven of the clock (for I do not observe one fixed hour), according as the weather recommends, I betake myself either to the terrace, or the covered portico, and there I meditate and dictate what remains upon the subject in which I am engaged. From thence I get into my chariot, where I employ myself as before, when I was walking or in my study; and find this changing of the scene preserves and enlivens my attention. At my return home I repose myself a while; then I take a walk; and after that, read aloud and with emphasis some Greek or Latin oration, not so much for the sake of strengthening my

SOURCE: Pliny, *Letters*, trans. by William Melmoth, rev. by W. M. L. Hutchinson, in vol. II of the Loeb Classical Library (Cambridge, Mass.: Harvard University Press, 1924), pp. 259–263.

elocution as my digestion; though indeed the voice at the same time finds its account in this practice. Then I walk again, am anointed, take my exercises, and go into the bath. At supper, if I have only my wife, or a few friends with me, some author is read to us; and after supper we are entertained either with music, or an interlude. When that is finished, I take my walk with my domestics, in the number of which I am not without some persons of literature. Thus we pass our evenings in various conversation; and the day, even when it is at the longest, is quickly spent.

Upon some occasions, I change the order in certain of the articles above mentioned. For instance, if I have lain longer or walked more than usual, after my second sleep and reading aloud, instead of using my chariot I get on horseback; by which means I take as much exercise and lose less time. The visits of my friends from the neighbouring towns claim some part of the day; and sometimes by a seasonable interruption, they relieve me, when I am fatigued. I now and then amuse myself with sporting, but always take my tablets into the field, that though I should catch nothing, I may at least bring home something. Part of my time, too (though not so much as they desire), is allotted to my tenants: and I find their rustic complaints give a zest to my studies and engagements of the politer kind. Farewell.

Meditations: Ideals of an Emperor and Stoic Philosopher

Marcus Aurelius

Emperor Marcus Aurelius (161–180), of great significance for what he did as well as for what he symbolized, was the last of the five "good emperors" who ruled during the relatively stable and prosperous period from the end of the first century through most of the second century. He was also an important Stoic philosopher and in his meditations captured much of the essence of the popular Hellenistic philosophy. Marcus Aurelius approached the Platonic ideal of a philosopher-king and symbolized much of what was best about Roman civilization. The following are selections from his Meditations, *written in the form of a diary toward the end of his life.*

> **Consider:** *Aurelius' standards of conduct; his attitude toward death; how he compares himself to most of those around him; the similarities between Marcus Aurelius and Pliny the Younger.*

Do not despise death, but be well content with it, since this too is one of those things which nature wills. For such as it is to be young and to grow old, and to increase and to reach maturity, and to have teeth and beard and grey hairs, and to beget, and to be pregnant and to bring forth, and all the other natural operations which the seasons of thy life bring, such also is dissolution. This, then, is consistent with the character of a reflecting man, to be neither careless nor impatient nor contemptuous with respect to death, but

SOURCE: Marcus Aurelius, "Meditations," trans. G. Long in Whitney J. Oates, ed., *The Stoic and Epicurean Philosophers* (New York: Random House, 1940), pp. 554, 584–585. Copyright © 1940. Reprinted by permission.

to wait for it as one of the operations of nature. As thou now waitest for the time when the child shall come out of thy wife's womb, so be ready for the time when thy soul shall fall out of this envelope. But if thou requirest also a vulgar kind of comfort which shall reach thy heart, thou wilt be made best reconciled to death by observing the objects from which thou art going to be removed, and the morals of those with whom thy soul will no longer be mingled. For it is no way right to be offended with men, but it is thy duty to care for them and to bear with them gently; and yet to remember that thy departure will be not from men who have the same principles as thyself. For this is the only thing, if there be any, which could draw us the contrary way and attach us to life, to be permitted to live with those who have the same principles as ourselves. But now thou seest how great is the trouble arising from the discordance of those who live together, so that thou mayest say, Come quick, O death, lest perchance I, too, should forget myself.

He who does wrong does wrong against himself. He who acts unjustly acts unjustly to himself, because he makes himself bad.

He often acts unjustly who does not do a certain thing; not only he who does a certain thing.

Thy present opinion founded on understanding, and thy present conduct directed to social good, and thy present disposition of contentment with everything which happens—that is enough.

Wipe out imagination: check desire: extinguish appetite: keep the ruling faculty in its own power. . . .

How does the ruling faculty make use of itself? For all lies in this. But everything else, whether it is in the power of thy will or not, is only lifeless ashes and smoke. . . .

Man, thou hast been a citizen in this great state (the world): what difference does it make to thee whether for five years (or three)? For that which is conformable to the laws is just for all. Where is the hardship then, if no tyrant nor yet an unjust judge sends thee away from the state, but nature who brought thee into it? The same as if a praetor who has employed an actor dismisses him from the stage.—'But I have not finished the five acts, but only three of them.'—Thou sayest well, but in life the three acts are the whole drama; for what shall be a complete drama is determined by him who was once the cause of its composition, and now of its dissolution: but thou art the cause of neither. Depart then satisfied, for he also who releases thee is satisfied.

Rome and the Early Christians

Pliny the Younger and Trajan

After the death of Christ, Christianity began to spread. Centuries would pass before it would become the major religion in the Roman world, but by the beginning of the second century it was a well-recognized sect to be contended with, particularly in the Eastern provinces. The more

SOURCE: From Dana Munro and Edith Bramhall, eds., "The Early Christian Persecutions," in Department of History of the University of Pennsylvania, ed., *Translations and Reprints from the Original Sources of European History*, vol. IV, no. 1 (Philadelphia: University of Pennsylvania Press, 1898), pp. 8–10.

Christianity spread, the more government officials were faced with the issue of how to deal with it. Generally, various religious sects and beliefs were tolerated as long as their adherents were willing to participate in official pagan rituals, which were of a combined religious and political significance. But Christian beliefs demanded exclusivity and thus prevented acceptance of official rituals; to many this constituted both religious and political subversion. This problem and a common official response to it are revealed in the following correspondence in the year 112 between Pliny the Younger, then governor of Bithynia, and the enlightened emperor Trajan.

Consider: *The circumstances under which Pliny became involved in prosecutions of Christians; what evidence this document provides about the general Roman policy toward the Christians; Roman legal practices and institutions revealed in this document; how Christians might have avoided prosecution or persecution.*

It is my custom, my Lord, to refer to you all things concerning which I am in doubt. For who can better guide my indecision or enlighten my ignorance?

I have never taken part in the trials of Christians: hence I do not know for what crime nor to what extent it is customary to punish or investigate. I have been in no little doubt as to whether any discrimination is made for age, or whether the treatment of the weakest does not differ from that of the stronger; whether pardon is granted in case of repentance, or whether he who has ever been a Christian gains nothing by having ceased to be one; whether the *name* itself without the proof of crimes, or the crimes, inseparably connected with the *name,* are punished. Meanwhile, I have followed this procedure in the case of those who have been brought before me as Christians. I asked them whether they were Christians a second and a third time and with threats of punishment; I questioned those who confessed; I ordered those who were obstinate to be executed. For I did not doubt that, whatever it was that they confessed, their stubbornness and inflexible obstinacy ought certainly to be punished. There were others of similar madness, who because they were Roman citizens, I have noted for sending to the City. Soon, the crime spreading, as is usual when attention is called to it, more cases arose. An anonymous accusation containing many names was presented. Those who denied that they were or had been Christians, ought, I thought, to be dismissed since they repeated after me a prayer to the gods and made supplication with incense and wine to your image, which I had ordered to be brought for the purpose together with the statues of the gods, and since besides they cursed Christ, not one of which things they say, those who are really Christians can be compelled to do. Others, accused by the informer, said that they were Christians and afterwards denied it; in fact they had been but had ceased to be, some many years ago, some even twenty years before. All both worshipped your image and the statues of the gods, and cursed Christ. They continued to maintain that this was the amount of their fault or error, that on a fixed day they were accustomed to come together before daylight and to sing by turns a hymn to Christ as a god, and that they bound themselves by oath, not for some crime but that they would not commit robbery, theft, or adultery, that they would not betray a trust nor deny a deposit when called upon. After this it was their custom to disperse and to come together again to partake of food, of an ordinary and harmless kind, however; even this they had ceased to do after the publication of my edict in which according to your command I had forbidden associations. Hence I believed it the more necessary to examine two female slaves, who were called deaconesses, in order to find out what was true, and to do it by torture. I found nothing but a vicious, extravagant superstition. Consequently I have postponed the examination and make haste to consult you. For it seemed to me that the subject would justify consultation, especially on account of the number of those in peril. For many of all ages, of every rank, and even of both sexes are and will be called into danger. The infection of this superstition has not only spread to the cities but even to the villages and country districts. It seems possible to stay it and bring about a reform. It is plain enough that the temples, which had been almost deserted, have begun to be frequented again, that the sacred rites, which had been neglected for a long time, have begun to be restored, and that fodder for victims, for which till now there was scarcely a purchaser, is sold. From which one may readily judge what a number of men can be reclaimed if repentance is permitted.

TRAJAN'S REPLY.

You have followed the correct procedure, my Secundus, in conducting the cases of those who were accused before you as Christians, for no general rule can be laid down as a set form. They ought not to be sought out; if they are brought before you and convicted they ought to be punished; provided that he who denies that he is a Christian, and proves this by making supplication to our gods, however much he may have been under suspicion in the past, shall secure pardon on repentance. In the case of no crime should attention be paid to anonymous charges, for they afford a bad precedent and are not worthy of our age.

The Gospel According to St. Matthew

During the first and second centuries Christianity was one of many competing sects in the Empire. But by the fourth century it had become the most influential one and was finally adopted as the official faith of the Roman Empire. From a historical point of view, a crucial problem is to explain the success of Christianity. Part of the explanation comes from an analysis of the basic teachings of Christianity. One of the most useful texts for this purpose is found in the Gospel according to St. Matthew, written toward the end of the first century, about sixty years after the recorded occurrences. The rules for conduct and the general ethical message of Christianity are revealed in the following sermon of Jesus.

> **Consider:** *To whom this message was directed; the appeal of this message to people of those times; the differences in tone and content between these selections and the selections from the Old Testament in Chapter 1.*

5: Now when he saw the crowds, he went up on a mountainside and sat down. His disciples came to him and he began to teach them, saying:

SOURCE: *The Holy Bible, New International Version* (Colorado: International Bible Society, 1983), pp. 886–889 as excerpted.

"Blessed are the poor in spirit, for theirs is the kingdom of heaven.
Blessed are those who mourn, for they will be comforted.
Blessed are the meek, for they will inherit the earth.
Blessed are those who hunger and thirst for righteousness, for they will be filled.
Blessed are the merciful, for they will be shown mercy.
Blessed are the pure in heart, for they will see God.
Blessed are the peacemakers, for they will be called sons of God.
Blessed are those who are persecuted because of righteousness, for theirs is the kingdom
of heaven.

"Blessed are you when people insult you, persecute you and falsely say all kinds of evil
against you because of me. Rejoice and be glad, because great is your reward in heaven,
for in the same way they persecuted the prophets who were before you.

✿

"You have heard that it was said, 'Do not commit adultery.' But I tell you that anyone
who looks at a woman lustfully has already committed adultery with her in his heart. If
your right eye causes you to sin, gouge it out and throw it away. It is better for you to lose
one part of your body than for your whole body to be thrown into hell. And if your right
hand causes you to sin, cut it off and throw it away. It is better for you to lose one part of
your body than for your whole body to go into hell.
"It has been said, 'Anyone who divorces his wife must give her a certificate of divorce.'
But I tell you that anyone who divorces his wife, except for marital unfaithfulness, causes
her to become an adulteress, and anyone who marries the divorced woman commits
adultery. . . .
"You have heard that it was said, 'Eye for eye, and tooth for tooth.' But I tell you, Do
not resist an evil person. If someone strikes you on the right cheek, turn to him the other
also. And if someone wants to sue you and take your tunic, let him have your cloak as
well. If someone forces you to go one mile, go with him two miles. Give to the one who
asks you, and do not turn away from the one who wants to borrow from you.
"You have heard that it was said, 'Love your neighbor and hate your enemy.' But I tell
you: Love your enemies and pray for those who persecute you, that you may be sons of
your Father in heaven. He causes his sun to rise on the evil and the good, and sends rain
on the righteous and the unrighteous. If you love those who love you, what reward will
you get? Are not even the tax collectors doing that? And if you greet only your brothers,
what are you doing more than others? Do not even pagans do that? Be perfect, therefore, as your heavenly Father is perfect.

✿

"Watch out for false prophets. They come to you in sheep's clothing, but inwardly they
are ferocious wolves. By their fruit you will recognize them. Do people pick grapes from
thornbushes, or figs from thistles? Likewise every good tree bears good fruit, but a bad
tree bears bad fruit. A good tree cannot bear bad fruit, and a bad tree cannot bear good
fruit. Every tree that does not bear good fruit is cut down and thrown into the fire. Thus,
by their fruit you will recognize them.

"Not everyone who says to me, 'Lord, Lord,' will enter the kingdom of heaven, but only he who does the will of my Father who is in heaven. Many will say to me on that day, 'Lord, Lord, did we not prophesy in your name, and in your name drive out demons and perform many miracles?' Then I will tell them plainly, 'I never knew you. Away from me, you evil-doers!'

"Therefore everyone who hears these words of mine and puts them into practice is like a wise man who built his house on the rock. The rain came down, the streams rose, and the winds blew and beat against that house; yet it did not fall, because it had its foundation on the rock. But everyone who hears these words of mine and does not put them into practice is like a foolish man who built his house on sand. The rain came down, the streams rose, and the winds blew and beat against that house, and it fell with a great crash."

When Jesus had finished saying these things, the crowds were amazed at his teaching, because he taught as one who had authority, and not as their teachers of the law.

Epistle to the Romans

St. Paul

Christianity owes its historical success not only to the content of its message but also to the organizing work of its early missionaries. St. Paul was the most important of these missionaries, traveling from the Near East to Greece and Rome with his message and organizing Christian groups during the decades after the death of Jesus. Paul's Epistle to the Romans *was written during the middle of the first century. It had a strong influence on Christian theology. The following selection focuses on the relation of Christianity to law and authority.*

> **Consider:** *The ways Paul has presented Christianity to meet the concerns of the Romans; how Christianity can be seen as compatible with Roman rule; connections between this message and the message in the Gospel according to St. Matthew.*

[21]But now, quite independently of law, God's justice has been brought to light. [22]The Law and the prophets both bear witness to it: it is God's way of righting wrong, effective through faith in Christ for all who have such faith—all, without distinction. [23]For all alike have sinned, and are deprived of the divine splendour, [24]and all are justified by God's free grace alone, through his act of liberation in the person of Christ Jesus. [25]For God designed him to be the means of expiating sin by his sacrificial death, effective through faith. God meant by this to demonstrate his justice, [26]because in his forbearance he had overlooked the sins of the past—to demonstrate his justice now in the present, showing that he is himself just and also justifies any man who puts his faith in Jesus.

SOURCE: The Epistle of Paul to the Romans (III: 21–31; XII: 6–8; XIII: 1–14), *The New English Bible.* Copyright, The Delegates of the Oxford University Press and the Syndics of the Cambridge University Press, 1961, 1970, pp. 194, 204–205. Reprinted by permission.

²⁷What room then is left for human pride? It is excluded. And on what principle? The keeping of the law would not exclude it, but faith does. ²⁸For our argument is that a man is justified by faith quite apart from success in keeping the law.

²⁹Do you suppose God is the God of the Jews alone? Is he not the God of Gentiles also? ³⁰Certainly, of Gentiles also, if it be true that God is one. And he will therefore justify both the circumcised in virtue of their faith, and the uncircumcised through their faith. ³¹Does this mean that we are using faith to undermine law? By no means: we are placing law itself on a firmer footing.

*

⁶The gifts we possess differ as they are allotted to us by God's grace, and must be exercised accordingly: the gift of inspired utterance, for example, ⁷in proportion to a man's faith; or the gift of administration, in administration. ⁸A teacher should employ his gift in teaching, and one who has the gift of stirring speech should use it to stir his hearers. If you give to charity, give with all your heart; if you are a leader, exert yourself to lead; if you are helping others in distress, do it cheerfully.

*

¹Every person must submit to the supreme authorities. There is no authority but by act of God, and the existing authorities are instituted by him; ²consequently anyone who rebels against authority is resisting a divine institution, and those who so resist have themselves to thank for the punishment they will receive. ³For government, a terror to crime, has no terrors for good behaviour. You wish to have no fear of the authorities? ⁴Then continue to do right and you will have their approval, for they are God's agents working for your good. But if you are doing wrong, then you will have cause to fear them; it is not for nothing that they hold the power of the sword, for they are God's agents of punishment, for retribution on the offender. ⁵That is why you are obliged to submit. It is an obligation imposed not merely by fear of retribution but by conscience. ⁶That is also why you pay taxes. The authorities are in God's service and to these duties they devote their energies.

⁷Discharge your obligations to all men; pay tax and toll, reverence and respect, to those to whom they are due. ⁸Leave no claim outstanding against you, except that of mutual love. He who loves his neighbour has satisfied every claim of the law. ⁹For the commandments, 'Thou shalt not commit adultery, thou shalt not kill, thou shalt not steal, thou shalt not covet', and any other commandment there may be, are all summed up in the one rule, 'Love your neighbour as yourself.' ¹⁰Love cannot wrong a neighbour; therefore the whole law is summed up in love.

¹¹In all this, remember how critical the moment is. It is time for you to wake out of sleep, for deliverance is nearer to us now than it was when first we believed. It is far on in the night; day is near. ¹²Let us therefore throw off the deeds of darkness and put on our armour as soldiers of the light. ¹³Let us behave with decency as befits the day: no revelling or drunkenness, no debauchery or vice, no quarrels or jealousies! ¹⁴Let Christ Jesus himself be the armour that you wear; give no more thought to satisfying the bodily appetites.

The City of God

St. Augustine

Christianity grew in the pagan Greco-Roman world and flourished during the ensuing Middle Ages. Christianity's ability to survive and grow amid paganism is reflected in The City of God. *Written by St. Augustine (354–430) in response to accusations that the sack of Rome by the Visigoths in 410 was caused by the pagan gods' anger at being displaced by the ascendant Christianity, this is one of the great works of Christian philosophy. St. Augustine, after studying Classical literature, becoming a professor of rhetoric, and being attracted to various philosophies and religious sects, was baptized in 387 and quickly rose to the post of Bishop of Hippo in his native Africa. He gained a reputation through his writings and became a very influential father of the Christian Church. Augustine argued that there were two cities, an eternal City of God awaiting the faithful and a worldly, sinful City of Men. The Christian Church more closely embodied the City of God and was preordained to replace Rome. The sack of Rome was thus part of God's divine plan and in no way tarnished the promise of the eternal city.*

> **Consider:** *The differences between the "heavenly" and "earthly" cities; the "proper" relationship between the two cities; ways this philosophy was conducive to the spread of Christianity within a well-ordered empire and ways this same philosophy enabled Christianity to thrive despite the decline of that empire.*

But the families which do not live by faith seek their peace in the earthly advantages of this life; while the families which live by faith look for those eternal blessings which are promised, and use as pilgrims such advantages of time and of earth as do not fascinate and divert them from God, but rather aid them to endure with greater ease, and to keep down the number of those burdens of the corruptible body which weigh upon the soul. Thus the things necessary for this mortal life are used by both kinds of men and families alike, but each has its own peculiar and widely different aim in using them. The earthly city, which does not live by faith, seeks an earthly peace, and the end it proposes, in the well-ordered concord of civic obedience and rule, is the combination of men's wills to attain the things which are helpful to this life. The heavenly city, or rather the part of it which sojourns on earth and lives by faith, makes use of this peace only because it must, until this mortal condition which necessitates it shall pass away. Consequently, so long as it lives like a captive and a stranger in the earthly city, though it has already received the promise of redemption, and the gift of the Spirit as the earnest of it, it makes no scruple to obey the laws of the earthly city, whereby the things necessary for the maintenance of this mortal life are administered; and thus, as this life is common to both cities, so there is a harmony between them in regard to what belongs to it. But, as the earthly city has had some philosophers whose doctrine is condemned by the divine teaching, and who, being deceived either by their own conjectures or by demons, supposed that many gods must be

SOURCE: Marcus Dods, ed., *The Works of Aurelius Augustine, Bishop of Hippo*, vol. II (Edinburgh, Scotland: T. and T. Clark, 1881), pp. 326–328.

invited to take an interest in human affairs, and assigned to each a separate function and a separate department,—to one the body, to another the soul; and in the body itself, to one the head, to another the neck, and each of the other members to one of the gods; and in like manner, in the soul, to one god the natural capacity was assigned, to another education, to another anger, to another lust; and so the various affairs of life were assigned,—cattle to one, corn to another, wine to another, oil to another, the woods to another, money to another, navigation to another, wars and victories to another, marriages to another, births and fecundity to another, and other things to other gods: and as the celestial city, on the other hand, knew that one God only was to be worshipped, and that to Him alone was due that service which the Greeks call λατρεία, and which can be given only to a god, it has come to pass that the two cities could not have common laws of religion, and that the heavenly city has been compelled in this matter to dissent, and to become obnoxious to those who think differently, and to stand the brunt of their anger and hatred and persecutions, except in so far as the minds of their enemies have been alarmed by the multitude of the Christians and quelled by the manifest protection of God accorded to them. This heavenly city, then, while it sojourns on earth, calls citizens out of all nations, and gathers together a society of pilgrims of all languages, not scrupling about diversities in the manners, laws, and institutions whereby earthly peace is secured and maintained, but recognising that, however various these are, they all tend to one and the same end of earthly peace. It therefore is so far from rescinding and abolishing these diversities, that it even preserves and adopts them, so long only as no hindrance to the worship of the one supreme and true God is thus introduced. Even the heavenly city, therefore, while in its state of pilgrimage, avails itself of the peace of earth, and, so far as it can without injuring faith and godliness, desires and maintains a common agreement among men regarding the acquisition of the necessaries of life, and makes this earthly peace bear upon the peace of heaven; for this alone can be truly called and esteemed the peace of the reasonable creatures, consisting as it does in the perfectly ordered and harmonious enjoyment of God and of one another in God. When we shall have reached that peace, this mortal life shall give place to one that is eternal, and our body shall be no more this animal body which by its corruption weighs down the soul, but a spiritual body feeling no want, and in all its members subjected to the will. In its pilgrim state the heavenly city possesses this peace by faith; and by this faith it lives righteously when it refers to the attainment of that peace every good action towards God and man; for the life of the city is a social life.

The Germanic Tribes

Ammianus Marcellinus

For much of Roman history, "barbarians"—most of whom were Germanic tribes—threatened the empire's borders. These pressures increased in the third and fourth centuries as Rome weakened

SOURCE: Ammianus Marcellinus, *The Later Roman Empire*, ed. and trans. by Walter Hamilton. New York: Penguin Books, 1986, pp. 412–414.

*and various nomadic and Germanic tribes, led by warrior kings, pressed against Rome's fron-
tiers. In the following selection, the Roman soldier and historian Ammianus Marcellinus
(c. 330–395) describes one of these tribes, the Alans.*

> **Consider:** *The characteristics of the Alans' nomadic life; why, according to Marcellinus,
> the Alans were such fierce fighters; how the Alans' daily life and culture differed from that
> of the Romans.*

Thus the Alans, whose various tribes there is no point in enumerating, extend over both
parts of the earth [*Europe and Asia*]. But, although they are widely separated and wander in their nomadic way over immense areas, they have in course of time come to be
known by one name and are all compendiously called Alans, because their character,
their wild way of life, and their weapons are the same everywhere. They have no huts and
make no use of the plough, but live upon meat and plenty of milk. They use wagons covered with a curved canopy of bark, and move in these over the endless desert. When they
come to a grassy place they arrange their carts in a circle and feed like wild animals; then,
having exhausted the forage available, they again settle what one might call their mobile
towns upon their vehicles, and move on. In these wagons the males couple with the
women and their children are born and reared; in fact, these wagons are their permanent
dwellings and, wherever they go, they look upon them as their ancestral home.

They drive their cattle before them and pasture them with their flocks, and they pay
particular attention to the breeding of horses. The plains there are always green and
there are occasional patches of fruit-trees, so that, wherever they go, they never lack food
and fodder. This is because the soil is damp and there are numerous rivers. Those whose
age or sex makes them unfit to fight stay by the wagons and occupy themselves in light
work, but the younger men, who are inured to riding from earliest boyhood, think it beneath their dignity to walk and are all trained in a variety of ways to be skilful warriors.
This is why the Persians too, who are of Scythian origin, are such expert fighters.

Almost all Alans are tall and handsome, with yellowish hair and frighteningly fierce
eyes. They are active and nimble in the use of arms and in every way a match for the
Huns, but less savage in their habits and way of life. Their raiding and hunting expeditions take them as far as the Sea of Azov and the Crimea, and also to Armenia and Me-
dia. They take as much delight in the dangers of war as quiet and peaceful folk in ease
and leisure. They regard it as the height of good fortune to lose one's life in battle; those
who grow old and die a natural death are bitterly reviled as degenerate cowards. Their
proudest boast is to have killed a man, no matter whom, and their most coveted trophy
is to use the flayed skins of their decapitated foes as trappings for their horses.

No temple or shrine is to be found among them, not so much as a hut thatched with
straw, but their savage custom is to stick a naked sword in the earth and worship it as the
god of war, the presiding deity of the regions over which they range. They have a wonderful way of foretelling the future. They collect straight twigs of osier, and at an appointed time sort them out uttering a magic formula, and in this way they obtain clear
knowledge of what is to come. They are all free from birth, and slavery is unknown
among them. To this day they choose as their leaders men who have proved their worth
by long experience in war. Now I must return to what remains of my main theme.

The Fall of Rome

St. Jerome

The fall of the Roman Empire, though occurring over a long period of time, was experienced as a profound shock. Even those who were not part of the Roman power structure saw the invasions and decomposition of Rome as a catastrophe. This reaction can be found in the letters of St. Jerome (340?–420), who lived through much of the decline. St. Jerome, an ascetic for part of his life and a great doctor of the Church, spent most of his life in Jerusalem and is known for his translation of the Bible into Latin.

> **Consider:** *Why Jerome was so shocked and overwhelmed by what was happening; any evidence in these letters of an incompatibility between Christianity and the Roman Empire; the methods apparently used in an effort to avoid destruction by invaders.*

Nations innumerable and most savage have invaded all Gaul. The whole region between the Alps and the Pyrenees, the ocean and the Rhine, has been devastated by the Quadi, the Vandals, the Sarmati, the Alani, the Gepidae, the hostile Heruli, the Saxons, the Burgundians, the Alemanni and the Pannonians. O wretched Empire! Mayence, formerly so noble a city, has been taken and ruined, and in the church many thousands of men have been massacred. Worms has been destroyed after a long siege. Rheims, that powerful city, Amiens, Arras, Speyer, Strasberg,—all have seen their citizens led away captive into Germany. Aquitaine and the provinces of Lyons and Narbonne, all save a few towns, have been depopulated; and these the sword threatens without, while hunger ravages within. I cannot speak without tears of Toulouse, which the merits of the holy Bishop Exuperius have prevailed so far to save from destruction. Spain, even, is in daily terror lest it perish, remembering the invasion of the Cimbri; and whatsoever the other provinces have suffered once, they continue to suffer in their fear.

I will keep silence concerning the rest, lest I seem to despair of the mercy of God. For a long time, from the Black Sea to the Julian Alps, those things which are ours have not been ours; and for thirty years, since the Danube boundary was broken, war has been waged in the very midst of the Roman Empire. Our tears are dried by old age. Except a few old men, all were born in captivity and siege, and do not desire the liberty they never knew. Who could believe this? How could the whole tale be worthily told? How Rome has fought within her own bosom not for glory, but for preservation—nay, how she has not even fought, but with gold and all her precious things has ransomed her life. . . .

Who could believe [Jerome exclaims in another passage] that Rome, built upon the conquest of the whole world, would fall to the ground? that the mother herself would become the tomb of her peoples? that all the regions of the East, of Africa and Egypt, once ruled by the queenly city, would be filled with troops of slaves and handmaidens? that to-day holy Bethlehem should shelter men and women of noble birth, who once abounded in wealth and are now beggars?

SOURCE: From James Harvey Robinson, ed., *Readings in European History*, vol. I (New York: Ginn and Co., 1904), pp. 44–45.

VISUAL SOURCES

Carved Gemstone: Augustus and the Empire Transformed

This onyx gemstone with a carved relief scene, known as the Gemma Augustrea (photo 5-1), por-
trays both a specific event and a general set of views during the early Roman Empire. Made be-
tween A.D. 10 and 20, it appears to commemorate a victory by the Romans over the Pannonians
and Germans in A.D. 12. In the lower half, moving from right to left, a man and a woman are be-
ing dragged by auxiliary soldiers (probably Macedonian allies of the Romans). On the left four
Roman soldiers raise a trophy; another barbarian couple will be tied to it. In the upper half, mov-
ing from left to right, Tiberius, who led the victorious Roman troops, descends from a chariot

Photo 5-1

Kunsthistorisches Museum, Vienna

held by Victory. The youth in armor is probably his nephew Germanicus. In the center sit the goddess Roma and Augustus, between them the sign of Capricorn (the month of his conception) and below them an eagle (the bird of the god Jupiter) and armor of the defeated. Augustus is being crowned as ruler of the civilized world by Oikoumene, while on the far right the bearded Ocean and the Earth with one of her children look on.

This scene is particularly revealing of political and religious information. It shows the transformation from the Republic to the Empire under a deified emperor in the making, for Augustus is being transformed into an equivalent of Jupiter and is clearly accepted by the rest of the gods. Moreover, his successor, Tiberius, appears to be in line for a similar fate. It also indicates the growing reach of the Roman Empire and the Romans' use of subordinate allies—the Macedonians—to exert their control. The religious figures and symbols, while Roman, also reveal affinities with Greek religious figures and symbols; artistically, the scene has a Hellenistic flavor. This is evidence for a merging of Roman and Greek cultures. Note also the balance between idealized form and realistic representation: The bodies are somewhat stylized, particularly Augustus' heroic body, but at the same time the individuals are clearly distinguished; these individuals were meant to be recognizable to the viewer.

> **Consider:** *The political implications of this scene and of the coin of some 150 years earlier shown in Chapter 4; how contemporaries might have understood the message of this scene.*

Tomb Decoration: Death and Roman Culture

The tomb decoration in photo 5-2, known as the Sarcophagus from Acilia, dates from the mid–third century. Here, a boy, perhaps the young Emperor Gordian III, is standing next to a number of other figures. To his right are perhaps his parents, and to his left important government officials (perhaps senators) as suggested by their costumes. The bundle of scrolls at the feet of the boy and the stance of the figures indicate a dedication to Classical philosophy or scholarship. Indeed, in this period, there were many tombs with scenes representing a commitment to or glorification of pagan culture—a wish by individuals to be remembered as devotees of philosophy or literature.

This commitment to pagan culture is revealed both in what this tomb decoration shows and in what it does not show. Rather than showing mythical scenes, pagan gods, or Christian beliefs, it shows secular figures glorifying literature and philosophy. It is thus evidence for the continued strength of Classical pagan culture, at least among the elite, even during a period of decline for Rome. The style also indicates a continuing Classical balance between idealized forms and realistic representation: While the robes, the bearing, and the figures are stylized, there are clear individual differences, particularly in the head of the boy and in the balding individual to his left.

> **Consider:** *How this tomb decoration compares with the Tomb of Menna (Chapter 1), the thoughts of Marcus Aurelius, and Christian beliefs.*

Photo 5-2

Museo Nazionale delle Terme

SECONDARY SOURCES

The Roman Empire: The Place of Augustus

Chester G. Starr

With the rise of power of Augustus, the Republic came to an end and the Empire began. Under the long rule of Augustus, patterns were established that would endure well beyond his death in A.D. 14. During his own time Augustus was a controversial person, and ever since scholars have tried to evaluate the man and his rule. In the following selection Chester Starr, a historian at the University of Michigan, analyzes some of the controversies over the place of Augustus in Roman history, here emphasizing his successes in the political and military fields.

> **Consider:** *The ways in which Augustus might be considered a success; how other writers and scholars might disagree with this evaluation.*

The failure of Augustus' social reforms throws into more vivid light his remarkable success in the political and military fields. Working patiently decade after decade Augustus gave the Roman world a sense of internal security based on a consciously elaborated pattern of government which embodied two principles. First came his own preeminence, and as we have seen in regard to coinage and architecture he was not bashful in stressing his own merits and achievements; no less than 150 statues and busts of the first emperor also survive. The second was his emphasis on outward cooperation with the Roman aristocracy, clothed in old constitutional forms; one may also add that on the local level Augustus, to ensure urban peace, favored the dominance of the rich and wellborn as against democracy. In sum, Augustus' reforms were essentially conservative in character. . . .

Modern historians have evaluated Augustus in many divers ways, but until recently have tended to treat him with respect, partly because of the great triumphs of literature in the "Augustan Age." Of late, however, scholars affected by the overtly arbitrary character of government in some contemporary states have approached Augustus, as the founder of a covertly arbitrary system, with little admiration. . . .

Certainly he was revered with great and genuine enthusiasm by his contemporaries both in Rome and in the provinces. In rising to the foreground as a single, unique figure Augustus had concentrated upon himself the yearnings of men for order. To this leader, more as symbol than as living creature, the subjects turned for assurance and prosperity in the material world, for a sense of security and purpose on the spiritual level. . . .

In sum Augustus steered the Empire along lines which it was to follow for centuries to come, both in its strengths and in its weaknesses; the latter often the consequence of

SOURCE: Excerpted from *The Roman Empire, 27 B.C.–A.D. 476: A Study in Survival* by Chester G. Starr. Copyright © 1982 by Oxford University Press, Inc. Reprinted by permission.

artful compromise with the Republican past. When men of later generations looked back on Augustus, they tended to have mixed emotions. His memory among common folk stood high, and the great events of his reign were long commemorated by coins, calendars, and both public and court rites and festivals. Writers of aristocratic stamp from Seneca the Elder on accepted him as inevitable and necessary to stop the Roman revolution; yet these writers rejected almost unanimously his claim that he had restored the Republic. To them the Empire was an autocratic system, and Augustus was the first autocrat. If Augustus could have heard the voices of future generations as he lay on his deathbed and begged for the applause of the bystanders, his self-satisfaction might have been diminished.

Pagan and Christian: The Appeal of Christianity

E. R. Dodds

The beginnings of Christianity coincided with the establishment of the Empire under Augustus and the early emperors who succeeded him. Numerous attempts have been made to analyze Jesus and the rise of Christianity. In the following selection E. R. Dodds views early Christianity from a historical perspective. He focuses on the appeal of Christianity and how it compares with other religions of that period.

> **Consider:** *Typical traits of mystery religions and how Christianity differed from other mystery religions; other factors that might help explain the rise of Christianity in this early period.*

In the first place, its very exclusiveness, its refusal to concede any value to alternative forms of worship, which nowadays is often felt to be a weakness, was in the circumstances of the time a source of strength. The religious tolerance which was the normal Greek and Roman practice had resulted by accumulation in a bewildering mass of alternatives. There were too many cults, too many mysteries, too many philosophies of life to choose from: you could pile one religious insurance on another, yet not feel safe. Christianity made a clean sweep. It lifted the burden of freedom from the shoulders of the individual: one choice, one irrevocable choice, and the road to salvation was clear. . . .

Secondly, Christianity was open to all. In principle, it made no social distinctions; it accepted the manual worker, the slave, the outcast, the ex-criminal; and though in the course of our period it developed a strong hierarchic structure, its hierarchy offered an open career to talent. Above all, it did not, like Neoplatonism, demand education. . . .

Thirdly, in a period when earthly life was increasingly devalued and guilt-feelings were widely prevalent, Christianity held out to the disinherited the conditional promise

---

Source: From E. R. Dodds, *Pagan and Christian in an Age of Anxiety,* pp. 133–134, 136–138, copyright 1965. Reprinted with the permission of Cambridge University Press.

of a better inheritance in another world. So did several of its pagan rivals. But Christianity wielded both a bigger stick and a juicier carrot. It was accused of being a religion of fear, and such it no doubt was in the hands of the rigorists. But it was also a religion of lively hope. . . .

But lastly, the benefits of becoming a Christian were not confined to the next world. A Christian congregation was from the first a community in a much fuller sense than any corresponding group of Isiac or Mithraist devotees. Its members were bound together not only by common rites but by a common way of life and, as Celsus shrewdly perceived, by their common danger. Their promptitude in bringing material help to brethren in captivity or other distress is attested not only by Christian writers but by Lucian, a far from sympathetic witness. Love of one's neighbour is not an exclusively Christian virtue, but in our period the Christians appear to have practised it much more effectively than any other group. The Church provided the essentials of social security: it cared for widows and orphans, the old, the unemployed, and the disabled; it provided a burial fund for the poor and a nursing service in time of plague. But even more important, I suspect, than these material benefits was the sense of belonging which the Christian community could give. Modern social studies have brought home to us the universality of the 'need to belong' and the unexpected ways in which it can influence human behaviour, particularly among the rootless inhabitants of great cities. I see no reason to think that it was otherwise in antiquity: Epictetus has described for us the dreadful loneliness that can beset a man in the midst of his fellows. Such loneliness must have been felt by millions—the urbanised tribesman, the peasant come to town in search of work, the demobilised soldier, the rentier ruined by inflation, and the manumitted slave. For people in that situation membership of a Christian community might be the only way of maintaining their self-respect and giving their life some semblance of meaning. Within the community there was human warmth: some one was interested in them, both here and hereafter. It is therefore not surprising that the earliest and the most striking advances of Christianity were made in the great cities—in Antioch, in Rome, in Alexandria. Christians were in a more than formal sense 'members one of another': I think that was a major cause, perhaps the strongest single cause, of the spread of Christianity.

Women of the Roman Empire

Jo Ann McNamara

Roman women, like Greek women, were usually in a subordinate position to men. Rome was and would remain a patriarchy. However, during the Empire and particularly as Christianity grew in importance, women's roles evolved. In the following selection Jo Ann McNamara stresses how women were able to use their family roles and religion to gain new power and choices.

SOURCE: Jo Ann McNamara, "Matres Patriae/Matres Ecclesiae: Women of the Roman Empire," in Renate Bridenthal, Claudia Koonz, and Susan Stuard, eds., *Becoming Visible: Women in European History*, 2d ed. (Boston: Houghton Mifflin, 1987), p. 108.

Consider: *Why Christianity may have been so attractive to women; how Christianity played a role in improving women's power and status.*

The Roman Republic was a patriarchy in the strictest sense of the word. Private life rested upon *patria potestas*, paternal power over the subordinate women, children, slaves, and clients who formed the Roman *familia*. The Roman matron was highly respected within limits established by a strong gender system that defined her role as the supporter of the patriarch's power. Public life was conducted in the name of the Senate and People of Rome, institutionally defined as exclusively male. In the last days of the Republic, the power of these institutions was destroyed by civil war at the same time that the army, led by its emperors (originally only a military title), carried the standards of Rome to victory over the many civilizations of the Mediterranean world and ultimately took power over the city of Rome itself.

Under the Empire, the boundaries between public and private lives became porous and women began to use their familial roles as instruments of public power. Religion, in particular, offered women a bridge across class and gender differences, from private to public life. Roman women experimented widely with a variety of pagan cults, but increasingly Christianity attracted women with a vision of a community where in Christ "There is neither Jew nor Greek, . . . neither bond nor free, . . . neither male nor female." (Galatians 3:28)

Christianity was founded at about the same time as the Roman Empire was established, and for the next three centuries the imperial government and the Christian religion developed on separate but converging tracks. As an outlawed sect, the new religion was peculiarly susceptible to the influence of wealthy and noble women. Their participation was so energetic and prominent that critics often labeled Christianity a religion of women and slaves. In the fourth and fifth centuries, when the Empire had become Christian, it consolidated new political and religious hierarchies which reinforced one another. The synthesis was basically a restructured patriarchy with Christian men firmly in control of both government and church. But Roman Law and Roman Christianity contained a wider range of choices for women regarding marriage and property which passed into the hands of Rome's European successors.

The Later Roman Empire

A. H. M. Jones

Most historians who interpret the decline and fall of the Roman Empire focus on the Western half of the Empire. In fact, the Eastern half did not fall and would not, despite some ups and downs, for another thousand years. A. H. M. Jones, a distinguished British scholar of Greece and Rome, has emphasized the significance of the Eastern Empire's different fate for analyzing the decline

---

SOURCE: A. H. M. Jones, *The Later Roman Empire*, vol. II (Oxford, England: Basil Blackwell, 1964), pp. 1026–1027, 1062–1064, 1066–1067. By permission of Basil Blackwell, Oxford.

and fall of the Western Empire. In the following selection Jones compares conditions in the two halves of the Empire, criticizing those who have theorized that the fall in the West stemmed from long-term internal weaknesses.

> **Consider:** *The primary cause for the collapse in the West according to Jones; other possible causes for the collapse in the West.*

All the historians who have discussed the decline and fall of the Roman empire have been Westerners. Their eyes have been fixed on the collapse of Roman authority in the Western parts and the evolution of the medieval Western European world. They have tended to forget, or to brush aside, one very important fact, that the Roman empire, though it may have declined, did not fall in the fifth century nor indeed for another thousand years. During the fifth century, while the Western parts were being parcelled out into a group of barbarian kingdoms, the empire of the East stood its ground. In the sixth it counter-attacked and reconquered Africa from the Vandals and Italy from the Ostrogoths, and part of Spain from the Visigoths. Before the end of the century, it is true, much of Italy and Spain had succumbed to renewed barbarian attacks, and in the seventh the onslaught of the Arabs robbed the empire of Syria, Egypt, and Africa, and the Slavs overran the Balkans. But in Asia Minor the empire lived on, and later, recovering its strength, reconquered much territory that it had lost in the dark days of the seventh century.

These facts are important, for they demonstrate that the empire did not, as some modern historians have suggested, totter into its grave from senile decay, impelled by a gentle push from the barbarians. Most of the internal weaknesses which these historians stress were common to both halves of the empire. The East was even more Christian than the West, its theological disputes far more embittered. The East, like the West, was administered by a corrupt and extortionate bureaucracy. The Eastern government strove as hard to enforce a rigid caste system, tying the *curiales* to their cities and the *coloni* to the soil. Land fell out of cultivation and was deserted in the East as well as in the West. It may be that some of these weaknesses were more accentuated in the West than in the East, but this is a question which needs investigation. It may be also that the initial strength of the Eastern empire in wealth and population was greater, and that it could afford more wastage; but this again must be demonstrated. . . .

The East then probably possessed greater economic resources, and could thus support with less strain a larger number of idle mouths. A smaller part of its resources went, it would seem, to maintain its aristocracy, and more was thus available for the army and other essential services. It also was probably more populous, and since the economic pressure on the peasantry was perhaps less severe, may have suffered less from population decline. If there is any substance in these arguments, the Eastern government should have been able to raise a larger revenue without overstraining its resources, and to levy more troops without depleting its labour force. . . .

The Western empire was poorer and less populous, and its social and economic structure more unhealthy. It was thus less able to withstand the tremendous strains imposed by its defense effort, and the internal weaknesses which it developed undoubtedly contributed to its final collapse in the fifth century. But the major cause of its fall was that it was more exposed to barbarian onslaughts which in persistence and sheer weight of numbers far exceeded anything which the empire had previously had to face. The Eastern empire, owing to its greater wealth and population and sounder economy, was better able to carry the burden of defence, but its resources were overstrained and it developed the same weaknesses as the West, if perhaps in a less acute form. Despite these weaknesses it managed in the sixth century not only to hold its own against the Persians in the East but to reconquer parts of the West, and even when, in the seventh century, it was overrun by the onslaughts of the Persians and the Arabs and the Slavs, it succeeded despite heavy territorial losses in rallying and holding its own. The internal weaknesses of the empire cannot have been a major factor in its decline.

Chapter Questions

1. What are the similarities and differences between Roman and Christian rules of conduct and ethics?

2. What traits of Classical culture and civilization do you find most admirable? Are these also traits of Christianity?

3. In what ways were conditions of Roman civilization conducive to the growth of Christianity? In what ways was Christianity nevertheless contradictory to Roman civilization?

4. How might the very success of the Roman Empire be related to its decline?

II

THE MIDDLE AGES

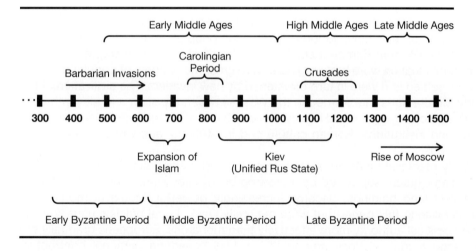

Early Middle Ages   High Middle Ages   Late Middle Ages

Carolingian Period

Barbarian Invasions

Crusades

300   400   500   600   700   800   900   1000   1100   1200   1300   1400   1500

Expansion of Islam

Kiev (Unified Rus State)

Rise of Moscow

Early Byzantine Period   Middle Byzantine Period   Late Byzantine Period

CHAPTER SIX

The Early Middle Ages

By the end of the fifth century, the Roman Empire had disintegrated in the West. In a series of invasions, various "Barbarian" peoples (mainly Germanic tribes) swept into Western Europe. Established patterns of life were disrupted and lines of communication were broken. There were great movements of population as invaders settled and were in turn threatened by new invaders. The civilization of the Early Middle Ages that formed in the West between the sixth and eleventh centuries reflected the threefold legacy of the fifth and sixth centuries: Germanic customs and institutions, Roman culture and institutions, and Christian belief and institutions.

Early medieval institutions drew from this legacy and slowly took form. The Christian Church, supported by a growing bureaucracy, numerous monasteries, and vast land holdings, became increasingly powerful. Medieval monarchies formed during this period but were generally weak. Local officials usually exercised political authority more effectively than monarchs. Europeans gradually established feudal relations among themselves based on personal contractual obligations for military service or exchange of land. An almost self-sufficient manorial economic and social system spread throughout many areas. In comparison to the preceding era, there was a broad cultural decline.

During the eighth and ninth centuries there was a temporary revival, especially under the rule of the Carolingian King Charlemagne, who conquered vast territories, centralized his own authority, and encouraged cultural activities. But not long after his death, fragmentation set in and Western Europe was again beset by invasions.

The sources in this chapter center on five broad topics. The first is the transition from Classical to medieval times: When did this transition occur, and what was its nature? Is this transition best viewed as occurring with the fall of Rome in the late fifth century or two centuries later with the rise of Islam? How was the transition experienced by observers of the time? The second topic is feudalism: How exactly should it be defined? What sort of relationships between people were characteristic of feudalism? What purposes did feudalism serve? How should feudalism be evaluated? The third topic is the reign of Charlemagne. What is the evidence for a revival of central authority and culture? What were the relations between Church and state during this period? The fourth topic concerns issues of gender characteristic of the Early Middle Ages: In what ways did the position of women change during this period? The fifth topic looks at the Early Middle Ages from a geographic perspective: How was the instability of the ninth and tenth centuries related to Western Europe's vulnerability to outside forces?

The aim in presenting these topics is to show the nature of the civilization that was developing during this time. Despite the disruptions, the apparent decline, and the relative disorganization of life between the fifth and eleventh centuries, long-lasting and distinctly European institutions were being formed.

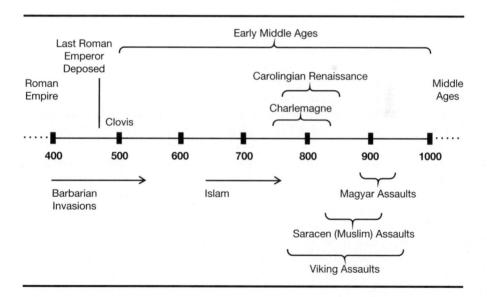

PRIMARY SOURCES

History of the Franks

Gregory of Tours

In the early years of the Middle Ages, the cultures of Rome and the invading Germanic peoples merged. One way this merger took place was through Christianity, and one of the most crucial conversions was that of Clovis (c. 466–511), king of the Franks. Under Clovis, the Franks emerged as a powerful kingdom in Gaul, and Clovis's conversion to Christianity made him more acceptable to the Romans. In the following selection from his History of the Franks, *Gregory of Tours (538–594), a Christian bishop in Gaul, describes the conversion of Clovis as well as the baptism of his army.*

> **Consider:** *The role played by queen Clotilda; what convinced Clovis to convert; why so many of his followers suddenly converted.*

The queen did not cease to urge him [Clovis] to recognize the true God and cease worshiping idols. But he could not be influenced in any way to this belief, until at last a war arose with the Alamanni, in which he was driven by necessity to confess what before he had of his free will denied. It came about that as the two armies were fighting fiercely, there was much slaughter, and Clovis's army began to be in danger of destruction. He saw it and raised his eyes to heaven, and with remorse in his heart he burst into tears and cried: "Jesus Christ, whom Clotilda asserts to be the son of the living God, who art said to give aid to those in distress, and to bestow victory on those who hope in thee, I beseech the glory of thy aid, with the vow that if thou wilt grant me victory over these enemies, and I shall know that power which she says that people dedicated in thy name have had from thee, I will believe in thee and be baptized in thy name. For I have invoked my own gods, but, as I find, they have withdrawn from aiding me; and therefore I believe that they possess no power, since they do not help those who obey them. I now call upon thee, I desire to believe thee, only let me be rescued from my adversaries." And when he said this, the Alamanni turned their backs, and began to disperse in flight. And when they saw that their king was killed, they submitted to the dominion of Clovis, saying: "Let not the people perish further, we pray; we are yours now." And he stopped the fighting, and after encouraging his men, retired in peace and told the queen how he had had merit to win the victory by calling on the name of Christ. This happened in the fifteenth year of his reign.

Then the queen asked saint Remi, bishop of Rheims, to summon Clovis secretly, urging him to introduce the king to the word of salvation. And the bishop sent for him secretly and began to urge him to believe in the true God, maker of heaven and earth, and to cease worshiping idols, which could help neither themselves nor any one else. But

SOURCE: Gregory, Bishop of Tours, *History of the Franks,* trans. Ernest Brehaut. New York: Columbia University Press, 1916, pp. 39–41.

the king said: "I gladly hear you, most holy father; but there remains one thing: the people who follow me cannot endure to abandon their gods; but I shall go and speak to them according to your words." He met with his followers, but before he could speak the power of God anticipated him, and all the people cried out together: "O pious king, we reject our mortal gods, and we are ready to follow the immortal God whom Remi preaches." This was reported to the bishop, who was greatly rejoiced, and bade them get ready the baptismal font. . . . And so the king confessed all-powerful God in the Trinity, and was baptized in the name of the Father, Son and holy Spirit, and was anointed with the holy ointment with the sign of the cross of Christ. And of his army more than 3000 were baptized.

The Origins of Feudalism

During the Middle Ages a system of feudalism developed, in part to fill the void created by the collapse of Roman authority and the weakness of centralized monarchies, and in part as a pragmatic outgrowth of various Roman institutions and German concepts of personal service and loyalty. Feudalism was essentially a series of contractual relationships between individuals, backed up by various ethical and legal doctrines. This is illustrated in the following documents dating from the seventh to the eleventh centuries.

> **Consider:** *The benefits that each party to a feudal contract expected to gain; the ideals behind the feudal relationship; the conditions for termination of the contract or relationship; the social and political conditions during these centuries suggested by these documents; the ways individuals might have attempted to secure or improve their social position in this system.*

A FRANKISH FORMULA OF COMMENDATION, SEVENTH CENTURY

Who commends himself in the power of another:

To that magnificent lord *so and so*, I, *so and so*. Since it is known familiarly to all how little I have whence to feed and clothe myself, I have therefore petitioned your piety, and your good-will has decreed to me that I should hand myself over or commend myself to your guardianship, which I have thereupon done; that is to say in this way, that you should aid and succor me as well with food as with clothing, according as I shall be able to serve you and deserve it.

And so long as I shall live I ought to provide service and honor to you, suitably to my free condition; and I shall not during the time of my life have the ability to withdraw from your power or guardianship; but must remain during the days of my life under your power or defence. Wherefore it is proper that if either of us shall wish to withdraw himself from these agreements, he shall pay *so many* shillings to the other party (*pari suo*), and this agreement shall remain unbroken. . . .

SOURCE: Edward P. Cheyney, ed., "Documents Illustrative of Feudalism," in *Translations and Reprints from the Original Sources of European History*, vol. IV, no. 3, ed. Department of History of the University of Pennsylvania (Philadelphia: University of Pennsylvania Press, 1898), pp. 3, 5, 23–24.

CAPITULARY CONCERNING FREEMEN AND VASSALS, 816

If any one shall wish to leave his lord (*seniorem*), and is able to prove against him one of these crimes, that is, in the first place, if the lord has wished to reduce him unjustly into servitude; in the second place, if he has taken counsel against his life; in the third place, if the lord has committed adultery with the wife of his vassal; in the fourth place, if he has wilfully attacked him with a drawn sword; in the fifth place, if the lord has been able to bring defence to his vassal after he has commended his hands to him, and has not done so; it is allowed to the vassal to leave him. If the lord has perpetrated anything against the vassal in these five points it is allowed the vassal to leave him. . . .

LETTER FROM BISHOP FULBERT OF CHARTRES, 1020

Asked to write something concerning the form of fealty,[1] I have noted briefly for you on the authority of the books the things which follow. He who swears fealty to his lord ought always to have these six things in memory; what is harmless, safe, honorable, useful, easy, practicable. Harmless, that is to say that he should not be injurious to his lord in his body; safe, that he should not be injurious to him in his secrets or in the defences through which he is able to be secure; honorable, that he should not be injurious to him in his justice or in other matters that pertain to his honor; useful, that he should not be injurious to him in his possessions; easy or practicable, that that good which his lord is able to do easily, he make not difficult, nor that which is practicable he make impossible to him.

However, that the faithful vassal should avoid these injuries is proper, but not for this does he deserve his holding; for it is not sufficient to abstain from evil, unless what is good is done also. It remains, therefore, that in the same six things mentioned above he should faithfully counsel and aid his lord, if he wishes to be looked upon as worthy of his benefice and to be safe concerning the fealty which he has sworn.

The lord also ought to act toward his faithful vassal reciprocally in all these things. And if he does not do this he will be justly considered guilty of bad faith, just as the former, if he should be detected in the avoidance of or the doing of or the consenting to them, would be perfidious and perjured.

Instructions to the Subjects of Charlemagne's Empire

Charlemagne

The most successful effort to reestablish central authority and revive culture during the Early Middle Ages came under the reign of Charlemagne (768–814), who was able to gain authority

SOURCE: Dana Munro, ed., "Laws of Charles the Great," in *Translations and Reprints from the Original Sources of European History*, vol. VI, no. 5, ed. Department of History of the University of Pennsylvania (Philadelphia: University of Pennsylvania Press, 1898), p. 11.

[1]The obligation of loyalty owed by a vassal to his feudal lord.

over a vast area, including most of Western and Central Europe. Charlemagne pursued policies to encourage literacy and improve the quality of religious institutions. Yet his efforts resulted in only temporary success, his empire falling apart soon after his death, with authority evolving to more local levels. The two documents that follow are instructions carried throughout Charlemagne's lands by royal agents. These documents illustrate his efforts to gain strength by mobilizing military forces and to improve culture and religion through education.

> **Consider:** *How these documents reveal the strengths and weaknesses of the central monarchy; Charlemagne's justification for his demand for better education; how these documents indicate a lack of division between religious and secular affairs.*

Concerning going to the army; the count in his county under penalty of the ban, and each man under penalty of sixty *solidi* shall go to the army, so that they come to the appointed muster at that place where it is ordered. And the count himself shall see in what manner they are prepared, that is, each one shall have a lance, shield, bow with two strings, twelve arrows. And the bishops, counts, abbots shall oversee their own men and shall come on the day of the appointed muster and there show how they are prepared. Let them have breast-plates or helmets, and let them proceed to the army, that is, in the summer.

°

Be it known, therefore, to your devotion pleasing to God, that we, together with our faithful, have considered it to be useful that the bishoprics and monasteries entrusted by the favor of Christ to our control, in addition to the order of monastic life and the intercourse of holy religion, in the culture of letters also ought to be zealous in teaching those who by the gift of God are able to learn, according to the capacity of each individual, so that just as the observance of the rule imparts order and grace to honesty of morals, so also zeal in teaching and learning may do the same for sentences, so that those who desire to please God by living rightly should not neglect to please him also by speaking correctly. For it is written: "Either from thy words thou shalt be justified or from thy words thou shalt be condemned." For although correct conduct may be better than knowledge, nevertheless knowledge precedes conduct. Therefore, each one ought to study what he desires to accomplish, so that so much the more fully the mind may know what ought to be done, as the tongue hastens in the praises of omnipotent God without the hindrances of errors. For since errors should be shunned by all men, so much the more ought they to be avoided as far as possible by those who are chosen for this very purpose alone, so that they ought to be the especial servants of truth. For when in the years just passed letters were often written to us from several monasteries in which it was stated that the brethren who dwelt there offered up in our behalf sacred and pious prayers, we have recognized in most of these letters both correct thoughts and uncouth expressions; because what pious devotion dictated faithfully to the mind, the tongue, uneducated on account of the neglect of study, was not able to express in the letter without error. Whence it happened that we began to fear lest perchance, as the skill in writing was less, so also the wisdom for understanding the Holy Scriptures might be much less than it rightly ought to be. And we all know well that, although errors of speech are dangerous, far more dangerous are errors of the understanding. Therefore, we exhort you not only not to neglect the study of letters, but also with most humble mind, pleasing to God, to study earnestly in order that you may be able more easily and more correctly to penetrate the mysteries of the divine Scriptures.

War and Conversion Under Charlemagne

Einhard

The spread of Christianity during the Early Middle Ages sometimes involved wars and forcible conversion. Charlemagne became involved in long wars against the Saxons, one of the Germanic pagan tribes on the borders of his Frankish kingdom. His efforts to subdue them permanently and bring them within his power included forcing them to convert to Christianity and dispersing them within Frankish lands. These events are described by Einhard (770–840), a scholar and member of Charlemagne's court who wrote a sympathetic biography of Charlemagne (Karl the Great).

> **Consider:** *Possible reasons for Charlemagne forcing the Saxons to convert; whether forcible conversions would have different consequences from voluntary conversions.*

Then Karl returned to the attack which he had been making upon the Saxons and which had been interrupted by the Lombard invasion. This was the longest and most severe of all his wars, for the Saxons, being barbarians and pagans like most of the tribes in Germany, were bound by the laws neither of humanity nor of religion. For a long time there had been continual disturbances along the border, since there was no natural barrier marking the boundary between the two races, except in a few places where there were heavier forests or mountains. So the Franks and the Saxons were accustomed to make almost daily raids on the territory of each other, burning, devastating, and slaying. Finally the Franks determined to put an end to this condition of affairs by conquering the Saxons. In this way that war was begun which was waged continually for thirty-three years, and which was characterized by the most violent animosity on both sides, although the Saxons suffered the greater damage. The final conquest of the Saxons would have been accomplished sooner but for their treachery. It is hard to tell how often they broke faith; surrendering to the king and accepting his terms, giving hostages and promising to accept the Christian faith and abandon their idols, and then breaking out into revolt again. This happened in almost every year of that war, but the determination of the king could not be overcome by the difficulties of the undertaking nor by the treachery of the Saxons. He never allowed a revolt to go unpunished, but immediately led or sent an army into their territory to avenge it. Finally after all the warriors had been overthrown or forced to surrender to the king, he transplanted some ten thousand men with their wives

Source: Oliver J. Thatcher and Edgar H. McNeal, eds., *A Source Book for Mediaeval History* (New York: Charles Scribner's Sons, 1905), pp. 39–40.

and children, from their home on the Elbe, to Gaul and Germany, distributing them through these provinces. Thus they were brought to accept the terms of the king, agreeing to abandon their pagan faith and accept Christianity, and to be united to the Franks; and this war which had dragged on through so many years was brought to an end.

Disorder and Destruction

The Annals of Xanten

Charlemagne brought some order to a large part of Europe, but that order was only relative and temporary. The period after his death in 814 was characterized by political disintegration, internal violence, and raids from outside forces such as the Vikings (Northmen) and Saracens (Moors). This disorder and destruction is reflected in the following selection from The Annals of Xanten, *written by ninth-century monks. These excerpts cover the years from 846 to 852.*

> **Consider:** *The impact of the Northmen and Saracens on life in Christian Europe; why Western Europeans had such difficulty defending themselves against outside forces during this period.*

(846) According to their custom the Northmen plundered Eastern and Western Frisia and burned the town of Dordrecht, with two other villages, before the eyes of Lothaire, who was then in the castle of Nimwegen, but could not punish the crime. The Northmen, with their boats filled with immense booty, including both men and goods, returned to their own country. . . .

At this same time, as no one can mention or hear without great sadness, the mother of all churches, the basilica of the apostle Peter, was taken and plundered by the Moors, or Saracens, who had already occupied the region of Beneventum. The Saracens, moreover, slaughtered all the Christians whom they found outside the walls of Rome, either within or without this church. They also carried men and women away prisoners. They tore down, among many others, the altar of the blessed Peter, and their crimes from day to day bring sorrow to Christians. Pope Sergius departed life this year.

(847) After the death of Sergius no mention of the apostolic see has come in any way to our ears. Rabanus [Maurus], master and abbot of Fulda, was solemnly chosen archbishop as the successor of Bishop Otger, who had died. Moreover the Northmen here and there plundered the Christians and engaged in a battle with the counts Sigir and Liuthar. They continued up the Rhine as far as Dordrecht, and nine miles farther to Meginhard, when they turned back, having taken their booty. . . .

(849) While King Louis was ill his army of Bavaria took its way against the Bohemians. Many of these were killed and the remainder withdrew, much humiliated, into their own country. The heathen from the North wrought havoc in Christendom as usual and grew greater in strength; but it is revolting to say more of this matter.

SOURCE: James Harvey Robinson, *Readings in European History*, vol. I (Boston: Ginn and Co., 1904), pp. 159–161.

(850) On January 1st of that season, in the octave of the Lord, towards evening, a great deal of thunder was heard and a mighty flash of lightning seen; and an overflow of water afflicted the human race during this winter. In the following summer an all too great heat of the sun burned the earth. Leo, pope of the apostolic see, an extraordinary man, built a fortification round the church of St. Peter the apostle. The Moors, however, devastated here and there the coast towns in Italy. . . . The Normans inflicted much harm in Frisia and about the Rhine. A mighty army of them collected by the river Elbe against the Saxons, and some of the Saxon towns were besieged, others burned, and most terribly did they oppress the Christians. A meeting of our kings took place on the Maas. . . .

(852) The steel of the heathen glistened; excessive heat; a famine followed. There was not fodder enough for the animals. The pasturage for the swine was more than sufficient.

The Wanderer: Life of a Medieval Warrior

Warfare and disorder marked much of the Early Middle Ages, particularly during the ninth and tenth centuries. In this society, local lords and their warrior followers often relied on each other for companionship as well as military and economic support. Opportunities and obligations might periodically take them far from home, and death always threatened them. Some of the values, joys, and difficulties of this life are reflected in the following excerpt from The Wanderer, *an epic poem probably written in the ninth or tenth century. Here the speaker, a warrior adrift because he has lost his lord and companions, looks back on his life.*

Consider: *The values of this speaker's society; the ideal relationship of the lord and his warrior follower; the advantages and disadvantages of the warrior's life.*

"Often before the day dawned I have had to speak of my cares, alone: there is now none among the living to whom I dare clearly express the thought of my heart. I know indeed that it is a fine custom for a man to lock tight his heart's coffer, keep closed the hoard-case of his mind, whatever his thoughts may be. Words of a weary heart may not withstand fate, nor those of an angry spirit bring help. Therefore men eager for fame shut sorrowful thought up fast in their breast's coffer.

"Thus I, wretched with care, removed from my homeland, far from dear kinsmen, have had to fasten with fetters the thoughts of my heart—ever since the time, many years ago, that I covered my gold-friend in the darkness of the earth; and from there I crossed the woven waves, winter-sad, downcast for want of a hall, sought a giver of treasure—a place, far or near, where I might find one in a mead-hall who should know of my people, or would comfort me friendless, receive me with gladness. He who has experienced it knows how cruel a companion sorrow is to the man who has no beloved protectors.

SOURCE: Anonymous, "The Wanderer," trans. E. Talbot Donaldson, in *The Norton Anthology of English Literature,* 4th ed., ed. by M. H. Abrams, et al. New York: W. W. Norton and Co., 1979. pp. 84–85.

Exile's path awaits him, not twisted gold—frozen thoughts in his heart-case, no joy of earth. He recalls the hall-warriors and the taking of treasure, how in youth his gold-friend made him accustomed to feasting. All delight has gone.

"He who has had long to forgo the counsel of a beloved lord knows indeed how, when sorrow and sleep together bind the poor dweller-alone, it will seem to him in his mind that he is embracing and kissing his liege lord and laying his hands and his head on his knee, as it some times was in the old days when he took part in the gift-giving. Then he wakens again, the man with no lord, sees the yellow waves before him, the sea-birds bathe, spread their feathers, frost and snow fall, mingled with hail.

"Then the wounds are deeper in his heart, sore for want of his dear one. His sorrow renews as the memory of his kinsmen moves through his mind: he greets them with glad words, eagerly looks at them, a company of warriors. Again they fade, moving off over the water; the spirit of these fleeting ones brings to him no familiar voices. Care renews in him who must again and again send his weary heart out over the woven waves.

"Therefore I cannot think why the thoughts of my heart should not grow dark when I consider all the life of men through this world—with what terrible swiftness they forgo the hall-floor, bold young retainers. So this middle-earth each day fails and falls. . . .

"Therefore the man wise in his heart considers carefully this wall-place and this dark life, remembers the multitude of deadly combats long ago, and speaks these words: 'Where has the horse gone? Where the young warrior? Where is the giver of treasure? What has become of the feasting seats? Where are the joys of the hall? Alas, the bright cup! Alas, the mailed warrior! Alas, the prince's glory! How that time has gone, vanished beneath night's cover, just as if it never had been!'"

VISUAL SOURCES

Illustration from a Gospel Book: Christianity and Early Medieval Culture

During the Early Middle Ages art became quite religious. Indeed, many of the paintings that survive from that period are miniatures from religious manuscripts, as in the case of this picture of the four evangelists from an early ninth-century Carolingian Gospel book. Each evangelist is shown writing his Gospel, and each is accompanied by his symbol: Matthew by a man, John by an eagle, Luke by a bull, and Mark by a lion.

This painting (photo 6-1) reveals a number of things about the Early Middle Ages. First, it suggests something about the position of Christianity. To this recently Christianized civilization, this scene could constitute a visual confirmation of biblical truth; the four evangelists are shown to have written, independently, similar accounts, thus testifying to the essential truth of the New Testament. Second, it exemplifies some of the uses of art in a strongly religious but relatively illiterate civilization: Here, the picture tells a story and important individuals are associated with identifying symbols. Third, the style and composition indicate that the artist was probably Byzantine or heavily influenced by Byzantine art. A Byzantine influence is also evident in a number of similar works that were part of the Carolingian revival initiated by Charlemagne. This could indicate a recognition of the superiority of Classical and Byzantine cultural productions and perhaps a sense of cultural inferiority in Western Europe.

    Consider: *What this reveals about the purposes of art during this period, and the nature of popular religion.*

Photo 6-1

Ann Münchow

Painting from an Illuminated Bible: Secular and Religious Authority

This painting (photo 6-2) shows Charles the Bald (823–877) being presented with an illuminated Bible by Count Vivian and the monks who produced it at the Monastery of St. Martin in Tours, France. It was produced around 846 and formally given to Charles in 851. The picture appears on the last page of the Bible being presented. In the upper center is Charles the Bald, a grandson of Charlemagne, seated on his throne and flanked by dignitaries. His position and authority are

Photo 6-2

Bibliothèque Nationale, Paris

denoted by his central position, crown, throne, and robes (which link him to past Roman author-
ity), as well as the hand of God above him. Below Charles stands Count Vivian, surrounded on
his right by the palace clergy and on his left by monks of St. Martin of Tours, three of whom are
holding this Bible being presented.

   The scene shows the attempted or assumed linkage between actual secular authority, which at
this time was relatively fluid, Roman authority, by then a thing of the distant past, and spiritual
authority, which remained unclear.

> **Consider:** *Reasons for the perspective, or lack of it, in this picture; similarities and differ-*
> *ences between this and the preceding painting; how this scene differs from the Gemma*
> *Augustrea (Chapter 5) and how this difference relates to differences between Roman and*
> *medieval civilizations.*

Contraction in the Early Middle Ages

The first map (map 6-1) offers evidence for the urban decline that occurred throughout Europe
during the Early Middle Ages. It shows Trier, Germany, founded by the Romans, as it was during

Map 6-1   Urban Decline, the Early Middle Ages

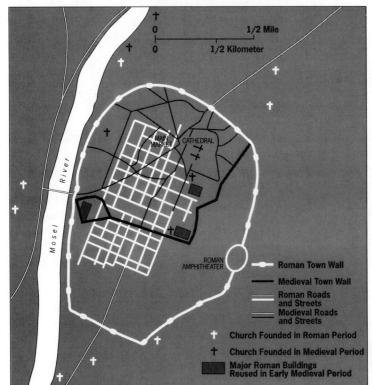

Map 6-2   Non-Christian Pressures, Ninth and Tenth Centuries

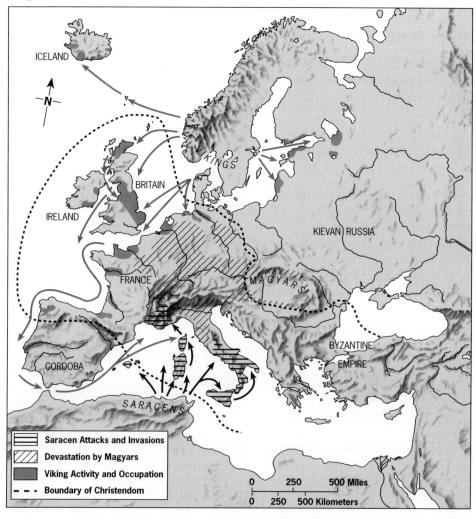

the Early Middle Ages. It became smaller, and the ordered street plan of the Romans was abandoned. Some of the Roman buildings were retained and used; some new churches were con-
structed both inside and outside the city.

Map 6-2 illustrates the relative weakness and contraction of Europe on a broader scale. Pressure was being exerted by three non-Christian groups during the ninth and tenth centuries: the
Saracens (Muslims) from the south, the Magyars from the east, and the Vikings (a general term
for groups of Scandinavians known by various names) from the north. The Saracens, adding to
the already conquered Spanish lands, took control of the western Mediterranean from Christian
hands and disrupted life with numerous raids into large areas of Southern Europe, particularly
France and Italy. The Magyars made a number of destructive raids into parts of Central, Western, and Southern Europe from their eastern homelands. The Vikings were the most mobile of all,
moving into Slavic lands to the east, England to the west, and coastal areas in Northern and
Western Europe, as well as competing with the Saracens in the Mediterranean region.

These two maps indicate some of the geopolitical problems affecting Western Christendom in the Early Middle Ages. The difficulty Christian monarchs had in resisting these invasions contributed to the political decentralization and corresponding feudalization of the period. Being unchristianized, these invaders did not respect Christian holy places or officials, which added to the disruption of organized life. Similarly, commerce suffered, as it could no longer be safely carried out. All this contributed to the increased turning inward and contraction in Europe that were indeed geographic and political realities on both a local and an international scale. Finally, with many of these invaders, particularly the Vikings, there was a merging of cultures and an influx of new strength as they eventually became Christianized and adapted to their new environments.

> **Consider:** *The ways in which the geopolitical realities of Europe in the Early Middle Ages were conducive to the growth of feudalism; the ways in which maps can support the argument that the Early Middle Ages was a period of decline in the West.*

SECONDARY SOURCES

Mohammed and Charlemagne: The Beginnings of Medieval Civilization

Henri Pirenne

Traditionally, the break between Roman civilization and the Middle Ages in the West has been dated to the Germanic invasions during the fifth century. According to this view, by the sixth century the West had experienced such change and decline in its political institutions, commerce, social life, and cities that Rome was at best a distant memory; the Early Middle Ages had begun. During the 1920s and 1930s this assumption was challenged by the Belgian historian Henri Pirenne (1862–1935). He argued that there was relative continuity during the fifth, sixth, and first half of the seventh centuries. The transition to the Middle Ages occurred between 650 to 750 as a result of the rise of Islam. Pirenne's thesis had wide acceptance for many years. Although historians have since cast doubt on important parts of this thesis, all medievalists must still deal with this interpretation. In the following excerpt Pirenne summarizes his argument.

> **Consider:** *Pirenne's explanation of why the Germanic invasions did not create the break with antiquity; Pirenne's rationale for arguing that the transition was completed by 800;*

SOURCE: Henri Pirenne, *Mohammed and Charlemagne*, trans. Bernard Miall (London: George Allen & Unwin Ltd., 1958), pp. 284–285. Reprinted by permission.

*Pirenne's view of the most important ways in which the civilization of the Middle Ages dif-
fered from that of the fifth and sixth centuries.*

From the foregoing data, it seems, we may draw two essential conclusions:

1. The Germanic invasions destroyed neither the Mediterranean unity of the ancient
world, nor what may be regarded as the truly essential features of the Roman culture
as it still existed in the 5th century, at a time when there was no longer an Emperor in
the West.

Despite the resulting turmoil and destruction, no new principles made their appearance; neither in the economic or social order, nor in the linguistic situation, nor in the existing institutions. What civilization survived was Mediterranean. It was in the regions by
the sea that culture was preserved, and it was from them that the innovations of the age
proceeded: monasticism, the conversion of the Anglo-Saxons, the *ars Barbarica,* etc.

The Orient was the fertilizing factor: Constantinople, the centre of the world. In 600
the physiognomy of the world was not different in quality from that which it had revealed
in 400.

2. The cause of the break with the tradition of antiquity was the rapid and unexpected
advance of Islam. The result of this advance was the final separation of East from West,
and the end of the Mediterranean unity. Countries like Africa and Spain, which had always been parts of the Western community, gravitated henceforth in the orbit of Baghdad. In these countries another religion made its appearance, and an entirely different
culture. The Western Mediterranean, having become a Musulman lake, was no longer
the thoroughfare of commerce and of thought which it had always been.

The West was blockaded and forced to live upon its own resources. For the first time
in history the axis of life was shifted northwards from the Mediterranean. The decadence
into which the Merovingian monarchy lapsed as a result of this change gave birth to a
new dynasty, the Carolingian, whose original home was in the Germanic North.

With this new dynasty the Pope allied himself, breaking with the Emperor, who, en-
grossed in his struggle against the Musulmans, could no longer protect him. And so the
Church allied itself with the new order of things. In Rome, and in the Empire which it
founded, it had no rival. And its power was all the greater inasmuch as the State, being
incapable of maintaining its administration, allowed itself to be absorbed by the feudality, the inevitable sequel of the economic regression. All the consequences of this change
became glaringly apparent after Charlemagne. Europe, dominated by the Church and
the feudality, assumed a new physiognomy, differing slightly in different regions. The
Middle Ages—to retain the traditional term—were beginning. The transitional phase
was protracted. One may say that it lasted a whole century—from 650 to 750. It was during this period of anarchy that the tradition of antiquity disappeared, while the new elements came to the surface.

This development was completed in 800 by the constitution of the new Empire,
which consecrated the break between the West and the East, inasmuch as it gave to the
West a new Roman Empire—the manifest proof that it had broken with the old Empire,
which continued to exist in Constantinople.

The Carolingian West:
The Genesis of Feudal
Relationships

David Nicholas

Scholars have long differed over the precise meaning of feudalism. In the following selection David Nicholas surveys this scholarly debate, pointing out some of the problems with the different approaches. He then argues that the term "feudal relations," emphasizing vassalage and the fief as the key components of the feudal bond, is more useful than the term "feudalism."

> **Consider:** *The ways scholars have disagreed over feudalism; why feudal relations might be a better term; the ways this interpretation might be supported by the primary sources in this chapter.*

The Frankish age witnessed the birth of feudal relations, in the stage that the American medievalist Joseph Strayer called the feudalism of the armed retainer, as distinguished from the later feudalism of the counts and other great lords. The term 'feudalism' has occasioned considerable dispute among scholars. It is applied by Marxists and some capitalist politicians for any economic or political regime that they consider aristocratic or oppressive. Others have identified it with decentralisation of governmental function, but this ignores the fact that those areas where feudal bonds were most completely developed, France and England, became centralised states, while non-feudal Germany and Italy split into numerous principalities. Forces other than extent of feudalisation were involved in these cases, but lords of feudal vassals had a measure of control over their fiefs that princes did not have over allodial (public, non-feudal) land.

Some have defined feudalism very broadly, including the non-honourable bonds of serf to landlord as an economic feudalism. Others prefer to avoid the term entirely, since 'feudalism' is a modern word that was not used during the Middle Ages. Much of the confusion comes from the 'all or nothing' approach of some historians. Although some lords compiled lists of their fiefholders, there was never a feudal 'system'. 'Feudal relations' seems preferable, for even feudal'ism' suggests more rigidity than was ever present. Feudal relations developed gradually. We learn much about them in the late Merovingian and Carolingian periods, but the sources then say little more until the eleventh century and particularly the twelfth. When the records recommence, they show that feudal bonds had been evolving in many but not all parts of Europe in the intervening period.

For while the word 'feudalism' did not exist, Latin and the vernacular languages had words for vassal and fief, the necessary component parts of the feudal bond. Vassalage was a personal tie of man to lord that developed characteristics that set it apart from

---

SOURCE: From David Nicholas, *The Evolution of the Medieval World, 312–1500.* Reprinted by permission of Longman Group UK.

other such bonds. The vassal, the subordinate party, owed honourable obligations, notably military service, that did not compromise his social rank. In the language of contemporary texts, he was a 'free man in a relationship of dependence'. Not all vassals held fiefs. Princes throughout the Middle Ages continued to maintain warriors in their households. It is inexact to speak of these people as being in a feudal bond with their lords, for they lived in proximity to their lords and did not hold fiefs. The fief was the proprietary nexus between vassal and lord and was held on conditions of tenure that were sharply different from non-feudal property. Vassals who held fiefs were expected to use the income of those properties to pay the costs of performing their own vassalic obligations. They were not maintained directly in the lords' households. Pope Gregory VII (1073–85), whose vassals included Robert Guiscard, the ruler of much of southern Italy, and who claimed the right to give Hungary and England in fief to their kings, would have been astonished at some scholars' notion that he was fighting for a figment of his imagination. Although there was no feudal system, to deny the existence of vassalage and fiefholding is to deny fact.

An Evaluation of Feudalism

Daniel D. McGarry

Feudalism developed gradually during the Early Middle Ages, becoming a prevailing system in many areas between the ninth and thirteenth centuries. By the Late Middle Ages, the feudal system was in decline, though elements of it would remain well into the early modern period. Since the Renaissance, scholars have often evaluated medieval feudalism negatively, emphasizing its weakness and localism. In recent decades, scholars have looked at feudalism more positively, emphasizing its adaptiveness to certain historical circumstances. In the following selection Daniel McGarry evaluates the shortcomings and the positive features of feudalism.

> **Consider:** *Whether you agree with McGarry's evaluation of what feudalism's "shortcomings" were and what its "positive" characteristics were; whether the strengths of feudalism outweigh its weaknesses.*

While feudalism had serious shortcomings, it also rendered valuable services. On the negative side, it resulted in numerous small, semi-independent local governments, incapable of providing many needed public services. Usually roads and bridges were inadequately maintained, while excessive tolls and duties were collected, and brigands and pirates flourished. Excessive emphasis was placed upon personal relationships, to the neglect of concepts of the community and public welfare. The components of the body politic were too loosely bound together by oaths and customs, with a minimum of firm enforceable obligations. The central government was too dependent upon voluntary cooperation and moral responsibility. Obligations were often so indeterminate as to admit

SOURCE: Reprinted with permission of Macmillan Publishing Company from *Medieval History and Civilization* by Daniel D. McGarry. Copyright © 1976 by Macmillan Publishing Company, Inc.

of easy evasion. Confusion frequently prevailed, private wars were common, and commerce was severely handicapped.

On the positive side, feudalism was a realistic adaptation to existing circumstances: a flexible workable compromise between Germanic and Roman elements. In a time of great insecurity, it provided local defense and government, without entirely sacrificing unity. It was just flexible enough, on the one hand, and just conservative enough on the other, to surmount contemporary challenges yet allow for future reunification. Those states, such as France and England, where feudalism prevailed in the early Middle Ages emerged strong and united at the close of the Middle Ages, whereas those such as Germany and Italy where mixed political patterns were maintained, emerged weak and divided. Feudalism helped to give Western Europe a military proficiency which eventually enabled it to spread its colonies and civilization over the world. It encouraged the contract theory of government, according to which government is the result of a free agreement among the governed; and it contained the principle that all government is limited. Many favorable features of feudalism, first applied only to the upper classes, were progressively extended downward to benefit all the people. Feudal great councils eventually evolved into general representative assemblies, known as Parliaments, Cortes, Estates, Diets, etc. The principle of "No taxation without representation" or "No new taxes without popular consent" is traceable back to the feudal requirement of the imposition of other than customary aids upon the aristocracy. The modern "code of the gentleman," and many of our ideals of courtesy, good manners, and fair play also derive from feudalism.

Sanctity and Power: The Dual Pursuit of Medieval Women

Jo Ann McNamara and Suzanne F. Wemple

Too often it has been assumed that the position of women changed little throughout the Early Middle Ages. In the following selection two medieval historians, Jo Ann McNamara of Hunter College and Suzanne Wemple of Barnard College, argue that by the ninth century the situation for many women had vastly improved.

Consider: *How marriage customs changed to the benefit of women; the social effects of changes in women's inheritance rights.*

By the ninth century a complex series of social advances had produced a vastly improved situation for the individual woman vis-à-vis the family interest to which she had previously been subordinated. Women were able to ensure their independence within the limits of whatever social sphere they occupied by their control of some property of their own. The Germanic custom of bride purchase practically disappeared. Instead of giving a purchase price to the bride's family, the groom endowed her directly with the bride gift, usually a piece of landed property over which she had full rights. To this, he frequently added the morning gift following the consummation of the marriage. In addition to the economic independence derived through marriage, the women of the ninth century enjoyed an increased capacity to share in the inheritance of property. Women had always been eligible to receive certain movable goods from either their own relatives or from their husbands but now law and practice allowed women to inherit immovables. A reason for this trend may be discerned from a deed from the eighth century in which a doting father left equal shares of his property to his sons and daughters. He justified his act by explaining that discrimination between the sexes was an "impious custom" that ran contrary to God's law and to the love he felt for all of his children.

Women's ability to inherit property had far-reaching social effects, which modern demographers are still investigating. Although a young woman still could not marry a man against her family's will, her independence after marriage was greatly enhanced if she possessed her own property. After their father's death, Charlemagne's daughters were able to withdraw from the court of their brother and lead independent lives because Charlemagne had endowed them with substantial property. As widows, too, women acquired increased status if they were allowed to control their sons' and their deceased husbands' property. The most dramatic example of this permanently affected the political future of England. The daughter of Alfred the Great, Ethelflaeda, widow of the king of Mercia, devoted her long reign to cooperation with her brother in the pursuit of their father's policy of containing the Norse invaders. Together they established a strong, centralized kingdom centered on Wessex. After a life of campaigning against Danish, Irish, and Norwegian enemies, she succeeded in willing the kingdom away from her own daughter, the rightful heiress, and leaving it to her brother. This act destroyed the independence of Mercia with its rival claims to Anglo-Saxon supremacy and assured that the English kingdom would be dominated by Wessex and the line of Alfred. Ironically, Ethelflaeda's indisputable contribution to the future of England deprived another woman of her right to rule.

Chapter Questions

1. In what ways was feudalism an effective answer to problems facing Europeans during the Early Middle Ages? In what ways did feudalism create new problems? Do you think the advantages of feudalism outweighed its disadvantages?

2. How would you justify calling this era a period of decline? What are some of the problems in so interpreting the Early Middle Ages? How might it be described as something other than a decline?

3. In what ways did the West differ politically, militarily, and culturally in the Early Middle Ages from the preceding Roman Empire?

CHAPTER SEVEN

The Medieval East

As Europe entered the Early Middle Ages, events took a different course in other areas of the West. In the Eastern Roman Empire, relative stability was maintained. The Empire, now centered at Constantinople, evolved into the Byzantine Empire and would survive until the fifteenth century. The part of the Mediterranean world farther south and east was unified during the seventh and eighth centuries under the rapidly expanding Islamic Empire, which eventually gained control over most of the Mediterranean region and extended into Spain and southern France. Finally, to the north and east of Byzantium, the East Slavs founded a civilization centered around the Principality of Kiev.

Compared to Western Europe during most of the Early Middle Ages, the Byzantine and Islamic civilizations were quite sophisticated, organized, and powerful. Islam was the largest, the most dynamic, and to Western Europeans, the most threatening of these.

This chapter concentrates primarily on Islam. Islam is often examined from the narrow Western perspective of how it affected Europe. It is emphasized as a preserver and transmitter of Classical civilization, as a civilization that developed certain inventions, techniques, and products that Europeans found useful, and as a foreign threat to Christendom in the West. While some documents address questions related to this important perspective, most focus on Islamic civilization in its own right. A first set of questions has to do with religion in the Islamic world. What was the nature of the Islamic faith and how is it reflected in the Koran? What were the connections between the Islamic faith and Christianity? What were some of the similarities and differences between the two? A second set of questions deals with aspects of Islamic culture. What intellectual traditions were valued in the Islamic world? What opportunities were available to scholars in this world? How was an education obtained? What were the connections between the Islamic faith and pictorial art? A third set of questions explores aspects of Islamic society. Of what significance was the Arabic background to the growth of Islam? In what ways was Islamic society physically recognizable? How did Islamic customs differ from customs in other societies?

Several documents deal with the civilizations Islam came into contact with as well as with Islam itself. Was Islam oriented primarily toward the West or toward the East? What roles did the central government and the emperor play in the Byzantine state? What was the role of law in the Byzantine Empire, and how does this role reflect connections between Byzantine civilization and Roman civilization? Finally, how did the Rus (from the Principality of Kiev) appear to Islamic observers of the time?

Together these documents should provide a balanced picture of Islam and an introduction to Byzantium and Kiev during the Early Middle Ages. At the end of this period Europe starts to recover and to gain a new dynamism; this topic will be the subject of the next chapter.

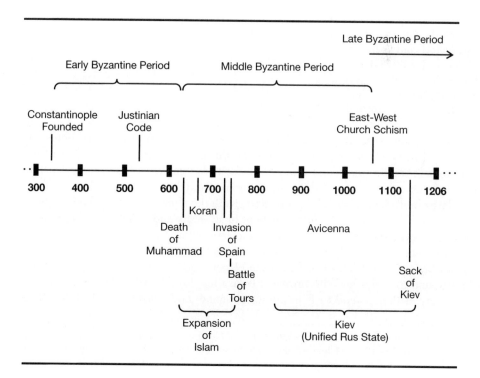

PRIMARY SOURCES

The Koran

The Koran is to the Islamic faith what the Bible is to Christianity. For believers it contains the word of Allah, God, as revealed to his prophet Muhammad and recorded by Muhammad's followers twenty years after Muhammad's death in 632. Over the next hundred years Arab Muslims spread Islam and their own control from the Arabian peninsula north and east through the Persian Empire and parts of Asia Minor and west through North Africa as far as Spain. Islam did not reject all of Christianity or Judaism. According to the faithful, Muhammad was the last and most important of the prophets, among whom were also included Moses and Jesus. The following selections from the Koran reveal some of the main beliefs and attitudes of the Islamic faith.

Consider: *Attitudes toward struggle and dissent; how these selections compare with those from the Old and New Testaments in Chapters 1 and 5; Islamic views of women.*

SAY: HE IS ONE GOD;
God the Eternal.
He begetteth not, nor is begotten;
Nor is there one like unto Him.

❖

MAGNIFY the name of thy LORD, THE MOST HIGH,
Who created, and fashioned,
And decreed, and guided,
Who bringeth forth the pasturage,
Then turneth it dry and brown.

❖

It is not righteousness that ye turn your face towards the east or the west, but righteousness is [in] him who believeth in God and the Last day, and the Angels, and the Scripture, and the Prophets, and who giveth wealth for the love of God to his kinsfolk and to orphans and the needy and the son of the road and them that ask and for the freeing of slaves, and who is instant in prayer, and giveth the alms; and those who fulfil their covenant when they covenant, and the patient in adversity and affliction and in time of violence, these are they who are true, and these are they who fear God.

SAY: We believe in God, and what hath been sent down to thee, and what was sent down to Abraham, and Ishmael, and Isaac, and Jacob, and the tribes, and what was given to Moses, and to Jesus, and the prophets from their Lord,—we make no distinction between any of them,—and to Him are we resigned: and whoso desireth other than

SOURCE: Stanley Lane-Poole, *The Speech and Table-Talk of the Prophet Mohammed* (London: Macmillan, 1882), pp. 15, 32, 83, 133–137. J. M. Rodwell, trans., *The Koran* (London: J. M. Dent, 1871), pp. 411, 415.

Resignation [Islām] for a religion, it shall certainly not be accepted from him, and in the life to come he shall be among the losers.

✿

Fight in the path of God with those who fight with you;—but exceed not; verily God loveth not those who exceed.—And kill them wheresoever ye find them, and thrust them out from whence they thrust you out; for dissent is worse than slaughter; but fight them not at the Sacred Mosque, unless they fight you there: but if they fight you, then kill them: such is the reward of the infidels! But if they desist, then verily God is forgiving and merciful.—But fight them till there be no dissent, and the worship be only to God;—but, if they desist, then let there be no hostility save against the transgressors.

✿

Men are superior to women on account of the qualities with which God hath gifted the one above the other, and on account of the outlay they make from their substance for them. Virtuous women are obedient, careful, during *the husband's* absence, because God hath of them been careful. . . . *other* women who seem good in your eyes, marry *but* two, or three, or four; and if ye *still* fear that ye shall not act equitably, then one only; or the slaves whom ye have acquired: this will make justice on your part easier.

Autobiography of a Muslim Scholar

Avicenna

Avicenna (980–1037) was an outstanding example of the many Muslim individuals who produced great achievements in creative and intellectual endeavors. Known primarily as a philosopher, Avicenna was also a mathematician, physician, theologian, astronomer, and philologist. He wrote extensively, and some of his works were later translated and circulated in Europe. The following is a selection from his autobiography, indicating the breadth of his learning as well as aspects of social and cultural life in the Islamic world.

> **Consider:** *The attitude of Avicenna's family toward learning and knowledge; the most respected kinds of learning and intellectual authorities; ways an intellectual could survive or move up in the Islamic world.*

My father was a man of Balkh, and he moved from there to Bukhara during the days of Nuh ibn Mansūr; in his reign he was employed in the administration, being governor of a village-centre in the outlying district of Bukhara called Kharmaithan. Near by is a village named Afshana, and there my father married my mother and took up his residence;

SOURCE: From A. J. Arberry, *Aspects of Islamic Civilization* (London: George Allen & Unwin Ltd., 1967), pp. 136–139. Reprinted by permission of George Allen & Unwin Ltd. and The University of Michigan Press.

I was also born there, and after me my brother. Later we moved to Bukhara, where I was put under teachers of the Koran and of letters. By the time I was ten I had mastered the Koran and a great deal of literature, so that I was marvelled at for my aptitude.

Now my father was one of those who has responded to the Egyptian propagandist (who was an Ismaili); he, and my brother too, had listened to what they had to say about the Spirit and the Intellect, after the fashion in which they preach and understand the matter. They would therefore discuss these things together, whilst I listened and comprehended all that they said; but my spirit would not assent to their argument. Presently they began to invite me to join the movement, rolling on their tongues talk about philosophy, geometry, Indian arithmetic; and my father sent me to a certain vegetable-seller who used the Indian arithmetic, so that I might learn it from him. Then there came to Bukhara a man called Abū 'Abd Allāh al-Nātilī who claimed to be a philosopher; my father invited him to stay in our house, hoping that I would learn from him also. Before his advent I had already occupied myself with Muslim jurisprudence, attending Ismā'īl the Ascetic; so I was an excellent enquirer, having become familiar with the methods of postulation and the techniques of rebuttal according to the usages of the canon lawyers. I now commenced reading the *Isagoge* with al-Nātilī. When he mentioned to me the definition of *genus* as a term applied to a number of things of different species in answer to the question 'What is it?' I set about verifying this definition in a manner such as he had never heard. He marvelled at me exceedingly, and warned my father that I should not engage in any other occupation but learning. Whatever problem he stated to me, I showed a better mental conception of it than he. So I continued until I had read all the straightforward parts of Logic with him; as for the subtler points, he had no acquaintance with them.

From then onwards I took to reading texts by myself; I studied the commentaries, until I had completely mastered the science of Logic. Similarly with Euclid I read the first five or six figures with him, and thereafter undertook on my own account to solve the entire remainder of the book. Next I moved on to the *Almagest;* when I had finished the prolegomena and reached the geometrical figures, al-Nātilī told me to go on reading and to solve the problems by myself; I should merely revise what I read with him, so that he might indicate to me what was right and what was wrong. The truth is that he did not really teach this book; I began to solve the work, and many were the complicated figures of which he had no knowledge until I presented them to him, and made him understand them. Then al-Nātilī took leave of me, setting out for Gurganj.

I now occupied myself with mastering the various texts and commentaries on natural science and metaphysics, until all the gates of knowledge were open to me. Next I desired to study medicine, and proceeded to read all the books that have been written on this subject. Medicine is not a difficult science, and naturally I excelled in it in a very short time, so that qualified physicians began to read medicine with me. I also undertook to treat the sick, and methods of treatment derived from practical experience revealed themselves to me such as baffle description. At the same time I continued between whiles to study and dispute on law, being now sixteen years of age.

The next eighteen months I devoted entirely to reading; I studied Logic once again, and all the parts of philosophy. During all this time I did not sleep one night through, nor devoted my attention to any other matter by day. I prepared a set of files; with each proof I examined, I set down the syllogistic premises and put them in order in the files, then I examined what deductions might be drawn from them. I observed methodically the conditions of the premises, and proceeded until the truth of each particular problem was confirmed for me. Whenever I found myself perplexed by a problem, or could not find the middle term in any syllogism, I would repair to the mosque and pray, adoring the All-Creator, until my puzzle was resolved and my difficulty made easy. At night I would return home, set the lamp before me, and busy myself with reading and writing; whenever sleep overcame me or I was conscious of some weakness, I turned aside to drink a glass of wine until my strength returned to me; then I went back to my reading. If ever the least slumber overtook me, I would dream of the precise problem which I was considering as I fell asleep; in that way many problems revealed themselves to me whilst sleeping. So I continued until I had made myself master of all the sciences; I now comprehended them to the limits of human possibility. All that I learned during that time is exactly as I know it now; I have added nothing more to my knowledge to this day.

I was now a master of Logic, natural sciences and mathematics. I therefore returned to metaphysics; I read Aristotle's *Metaphysica,* but did not understand its contents and was baffled by the author's intention; I read it over forty times until I had the text by heart. Even then I did not understand it or what the author meant, and I despaired within myself, saying, 'This is a book which there is no way of understanding.' But one day at noon I chanced to be in the booksellers' quarter, and a broker was there with a volume in his hand which he was calling for sale. He offered it to me, but I returned it to him impatiently, believing that there was no use in this particular science. However, he said to me: 'Buy this book from me; it is cheap, and I will sell it to you for four dirhams. The owner is in need of the money.' So I bought it, and found that it was a book by Abū Nasr al-Fārābī *On the Objects of the Metaphysica.* I returned home and hastened to read it; and at once the objects of that book became clear to me, for I had it all by heart. I rejoiced at this, and upon the next day distributed much in alms to the poor in gratitude to Almighty God.

Now the Sultan of Bukhara at that time was Nūh ibn Mansūr, and it happened that he fell sick of a malady which baffled all the physicians. My name was famous among them because of the breadth of my reading; they therefore mentioned me in his presence, and begged him to summon me. I attended the sick-room, and collaborated with them in treating the royal patient. So I came to be enrolled in his service. One day I asked his leave to enter their library, to examine the contents and read the books on medicine; he granted my request, and I entered a mansion with many chambers, each chamber having chests of books piled one upon another. In one apartment were books on language and poetry, in another law, and so on; each apartment was set aside for books on a single science. I glanced through the catalogue of the works of the ancient Greeks, and asked for those which I required; and I saw books whose very names are as yet unknown to many—works which I had never seen before and have not seen since. I read these books, taking notes of their contents; I came to realize the place each man occupied in his particular science.

So by the time I reached my eighteenth year I had exhausted all these sciences. My memory for learning was at that period of my life better than it is now, but today I am more mature; apart from this my knowledge is exactly the same, nothing further having been added to my store since then.

The Institutes of Justinian: Byzantium and the Legacy of Roman Law

A principal way that continuity was maintained between the Byzantine Empire and its predecessor, the Roman Empire, was through the use of the Justinian Code. Initiated in 528 during the reign of Emperor Justinian (527–565), this code contained a compilation of Roman laws, a growing collection of new laws, and a manual for students (the Institutes*). The following are selections from the Preamble and Book One of the* Institutes.

Consider: *How the Germanic invasions of the fifth and sixth centuries were met in Byzantium; the purposes of the* Institutes; *the role of law in the Byzantine Empire.*

PREAMBLE

In the Name Of Our Lord Jesus Christ.

THE EMPEROR CÆSAR FLAVIUS JUSTINIANUS, VANQUISHER OF THE ALAMANI, GOTHS, FRANCS, GERMANS, ANTES, ALANI, VANDALS, AFRICANS, PIOUS, HAPPY, GLORIOUS, TRIUMPHANT CONQUEROR, EVER AUGUST, TO THE YOUTH DESIROUS OF STUDYING THE LAW, GREETING.

The imperial majesty should be not only made glorious by arms, but also strengthened by laws, that, alike in time of peace and in time of war, the state may be well governed, and that the emperor may not only be victorious in the field of battle, but also may by every legal means repel the iniquities of men who abuse the laws, and may at once religiously uphold justice and triumph over his conquered enemies.

1. By our incessant labours and great care, with the blessing of God, we have attained this double end. The barbarian nations reduced under our yoke know our efforts in war; to which also Africa and very many other provinces bear witness, which, after so long an interval, have been restored to the dominion of Rome and our empire, by our victories gained through the favour of heaven. All nations moreover are governed by laws which we have either promulgated or arranged.

2. When we had arranged and brought into perfect harmony the hitherto confused mass of imperial constitutions, we then extended our care to the endless volumes of ancient law; and sailing as it were across the mid ocean, have now completed, through the favour of heaven, a work we once despaired of.

3. When by the blessing of God this task was accomplished, we summoned the most eminent Tribonian, master and ex-quæstor of our palace, together with the illustrious Theophilus and Dorotheus, professors of law, all of whom have on many occasions proved to us their ability, legal knowledge, and obedience to our orders; and we specially charged them to compose, under our authority and advice, Institutes, so that you may no more learn the first elements of law from old and erroneous sources, but apprehend them by the clear light of imperial wisdom; and that your minds and ears may receive nothing that

SOURCE: *The Institutes of Justinian,* trans. Thomas C. Sandars (London: Longmans, Green, 1874), pp. 1–7.

is useless or misplaced, but only what obtains in actual practice. So that, whereas, formerly, the foremost among you could scarcely, after four years' study, read the imperial constitutions, you may now commence your studies by reading them, you who have been thought worthy of an honour and a happiness so great as that the first and last lessons in the knowledge of the law should issue for you from the mouth of the emperor.

4. When therefore, by the assistance of the same eminent person Tribonian and that of other illustrious and learned men, we had compiled the fifty books, called Digests or Pandects, in which is collected the whole ancient law, we directed that these Institutes should be divided into four books, which might serve as the first elements of the whole science of law.

5. In these books a brief exposition is given of the ancient laws, and of those also, which, overshadowed by disuse, have been again brought to light by our imperial authority.

6. These four books of Institutes thus compiled, from all the Institutes left us by the ancients, and chiefly from the commentaries of our Gaius, both from his Institutes and his Journal, and also from many other commentaries, were presented to us by the three learned men we have above named. We read and examined them, and have accorded to them all the force of our constitutions.

7. Receive, therefore, with eagerness, and study with cheerful diligence, these our laws, and show yourselves persons of such learning that you may conceive the flattering hope of yourselves being able, when your course of legal study is completed, to govern our empire in the different portions that may be entrusted to your care.

Given at Constantinople on the eleventh day of the calends of December, in the third consulate of the Emperor Justinian, ever August.

BOOK ONE

Justice is the constant and perpetual wish to render every one his due.

1. Jurisprudence is the knowledge of things divine and human; the science of the just and the unjust.

2. Having explained these general terms, we think we shall commence our exposition of the law of the Roman people most advantageously, if we pursue at first a plain and easy path, and then proceed to explain particular details with the utmost care and exactness. For, if at the outset we overload the mind of the student, while yet new to the subject and unable to bear much, with a multitude and variety of topics, one of two things will happen—we shall either cause him wholly to abandon his studies, or, after great toil, and often after great distrust of himself (the most frequent stumbling-block in the way of youth), we shall at last conduct him to the point, to which, if he had been led by an easier road, he might, without great labour, and without any distrust of his own powers, have been sooner conducted.

3. The maxims of law are these: to live honestly, to hurt no one, to give every one his due.

4. The study of law is divided into two branches; that of public and that of private law. Public law regards the government of the Roman Empire; private law, the interest of individuals. We are now to treat of the latter, which is composed of three elements, and consists of precepts belonging to natural law, to the law of nations, and to the civil law.

The Rus: Cross-Cultural Contact

Ibn Fadlan

Throughout the Early Middle Ages the civilizations that succeeded Rome came into contact with one another through conquest, trade, diplomacy, and migration. These contacts were particularly frequent in border areas where some assimilation between cultures occurred. This is illustrated in the following document written by Ibn Fadlan, a diplomat sent in 921 from Baghdad to a town on the Volga in modern Russia. He comments on the Swedish Rus of the Volga, who by this time had started to merge with Slavic peoples in the nearby Principality of Kiev.

> **Consider:** *How social and economic distinctions among the Rus were manifested; what this document reveals about the customs of Ibn Fadlan; the purposes and means that enabled these representatives from different cultures to meet.*

I saw the Rus when they arrived on their trading mission and anchored at the River Atul [Volga]. Never had I seen people of more perfect physique; they are tall as date-palms, and reddish in colour. They wear neither coat nor mantle, but each man carries a cape which covers one half of his body, leaving one hand free. Their swords are Frankish in pattern, broad, flat, and fluted. Each man has [tattooed upon him] trees, figures, and the like from the finger-nails to the neck. Each woman carries on her bosom a container made of iron, silver, copper, or gold—its size and substance depending on her man's wealth. Attached to the container is a ring carrying her knife which is also tied to her bosom. Round her neck she wears gold or silver rings; when a man amasses 10,000 *dirhems* he makes his wife one gold ring; when he has 20,000 he makes two; and so the woman gets a new ring for every 10,000 *dirhems* her husband acquires, and often a woman has many of these rings. Their finest ornaments are green beads made from clay. They will go to any length to get hold of these; for one *dirhem* they procure one such bead and they string these into necklaces for their women.

They are the filthiest of god's creatures. They do not wash after discharging their natural functions, neither do they wash their hands after meals. They are as stray donkeys. They arrive from their distant lands and lay their ships alongside the banks of the Atul, which is a great river, and there they build big wooden houses on its shores. Ten or twenty of them may live together in one house, and each of them has a couch of his own where he sits and diverts himself with the pretty slave-girls whom he has brought along to offer for sale. He will make love with one of them in the presence of his comrades, sometimes this develops into a communal orgy, and, if a customer should turn up to buy a girl, the Rus will not let her go till he has finished with her.

Every day they wash their faces and heads, all using the same water which is as filthy as can be imagined. This is how it is done. Every morning a girl brings her master a large bowl of water in which he washes his face and hands and hair, combing it also over the

---

SOURCE: Johannes Brøndsted, *The Vikings*, trans. Kalle Skov (Baltimore, Md.: Penguin Books, 1965), pp. 264–266. Copyright © 1965. Reprinted by permission of Penguin Books Ltd.

bowl, then blows his nose and spits into the water. No dirt is left on him which doesn't go into the water. When he has finished the girl takes the same bowl to his neighbour—who repeats the performance—until the bowl has gone round to the entire household. All have blown their noses, spat, and washed their faces and hair in the water.

On anchoring their vessels, each man goes ashore carrying bread, meat, onions, milk, and *nabid* [beer?], and these he takes to a large wooden stake with a face like that of a human being, surrounded by smaller figures, and behind them tall poles in the ground. Each man prostrates himself before the large post and recites: 'O Lord, I have come from distant parts with so many girls, so many sable furs (and whatever other commodities he is carrying). I now bring you this offering.' He then presents his gift and continues 'Please send me a merchant who has many *dinars* and *dirhems,* and who will trade favourably with me without too much bartering.' Then he retires. If, after this, business does not pick up quickly and go well, he returns to the statue to present further gifts. If results continue slow, he then presents gifts to the minor figures and begs their intercession, saying, 'These are our Lord's wives, daughters, and sons.' Then he pleads before each figure in turn, begging them to intercede for him and humbling himself before them. Often trade picks up, and he says 'My Lord has requited my needs, and now it is my duty to repay him.' Whereupon he sacrifices goats or cattle, some of which he distributes as alms. The rest he lays before the statues, large and small, and the heads of the beasts he plants upon the poles. After dark, of course, the dogs come and devour the lot—and the successful trader says, 'My Lord is pleased with me, and has eaten my offerings.'

If one of the Rus falls sick they put him in a tent by himself and leave bread and water for him. They do not visit him, however, or speak to him, especially if he is a serf. Should he recover he rejoins the others; if he dies they burn him. If he happens to be a serf, however, they leave him for the dogs and vultures to devour. If they catch a robber they hang him in a tree until he is torn to shreds by wind and weather.

VISUAL SOURCES

Manuscript Illuminations: Scenes from the Life of Muhammad

These three manuscript illuminations show scenes from the life of Muhammad. In the first (photo 7-1), the boy Muhammad is being recognized as a prophet by the Christian monk Bahira, on the right with two accompanying sages. Muhammad has already been recognized by followers on the left and is apparently even recognized by the bowing camels on the right. The recognition is confirmed by the anointing angel Gabriel above. In the second (photo 7-2), Muhammad rides into a city backed up by armed followers and is apparently accepted by the city's inhabitants. Again,

Photo 7-1

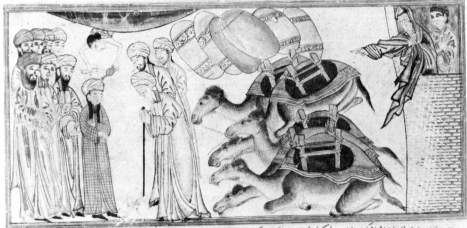

مَعَهُ احَوالهُ وكَانَتْ تَجمِع مَلِك الاحَوَال مَوَافَضَةً ومُنَاسِبَة لمَا قَرَاهُ تَحْبِراً انَهُ الكُتُب وَرَايَ خَاتَم النَّبُوَةِ بَيْنَ كَتِفَيهِ ثُمَّ سَأَلَ ابَا طَالِب عَنهُ وَقَالَ لَمَن هَذَا الصَّبَى

قَالَ هَذَا وَابَى فَقَالَ الرَّاهِبُ لَيْنَبَغَى انَّ لَا يَكُونُ لِهَذَا ابُ بَلْ يَكُونُ والِدَهُ قَدمَاتَ وَدِيَكُونُ فِيهَا فَقَالَ هَذَا ابْنُ اخِى فَقَالَ مَاذَا فَعَلَ والِدُهُ ثُمَّ قَالَ الرَّاهِبُ وَدِكَانَتْ امُهُ حَامِلَة بِهِ وَقَالَ لَهُ حَمَى اصَّت

Edinburgh University Library, Or.Ms. 20, fol. 43v.

Photo 7-2

وَقَطَعَ جَمِيعُ عَلَّمَ قَالُوا انَّا الخُرُج فَقَالَ النَّبِى علَيهِ السَلَم انَّ لَا ابُدَّنَ لَكُم الآنَ مَطِلُوكُم وَظَلَمَكُم لَكَنَّ ارَحَرَجُم حَرَجوب
اولَادَكُم وتَرَكُوا امْوَالُكُم وسَلَبِكُم وصَوَابِذَلِكَ وكَانُوا الحَرَبِيُون يَسُومُ بِاعَدِهِم وِالَى المُومِينُ وكَان عَلَيْهِمُ مَحَا نَهُمُ ثُمَّ
عَبْ سُومَا فَانَقُذِهِمْ عَن حَوَالِ المَدِينَة وكَان مُسْتَوْلَى الخَرَاجِ محَمَد بنِ سَلَمَة مَضَوْا اولَادَهُم وَنِسَاءَهُم وسِتَمَائَة جَمَل قَمَا الخَبَارَدَهَ كَانَ ارُب

Edinburgh University Library, Or.Ms. 161, fol. 6v.

Photo 7-3

Edinburgh University Library

Muhammad's authority is shown by the presence of the angel Gabriel, who anoints him. In the third (photo 7-3), Muhammad is preaching to his disciples during his final visit to Mecca. Both Muhammad and the disciples are displayed with halos.

These pictures disclose similarities and differences between the Islamic and Christian religions. These pictures come not from an illustrated Koran but from an early-fourteenth-century Islamic history book and are quite rare, for plastic or pictorial art was not sanctioned by Islamic theology; thus there developed no tradition of religious painting corresponding to the ecclesiastical art supported by the Christian Church. The content of the pictures reveals connections to Christianity: the recognition by Christian monks of Muhammad's authority, the importance of the biblical angel Gabriel, and even the use of halos to identify Muhammad and the disciples. The rapid spread of Islam by the legitimate use of arms is suggested in the second picture. The style of the pictures indicates the vast geographic extent of Islam by the fourteenth century, for it derives from Far Eastern, perhaps Mongolian, influence.

      Consider: *The characteristics of Islam revealed by these scenes.*

The Byzantine Empire and the Expansion of Islam

The first map (map 7-1) shows the Byzantine Empire at the beginning of the seventh century. It indicates that despite the fall of the Roman Empire in the West, most of the Mediterranean still remained in Byzantine hands. Moreover, as the successors to Rome in the West became Christian, almost the whole Mediterranean basin remained Christian. Map 7-2 shows the same area in 750. It reveals not only the rapid rise of Islam, but also the dramatic decline of territory controlled by the Byzantine Empire. The Mediterranean basin is now divided between Christians and Muslims.

Map 7-1   The Byzantine Empire, c. 600

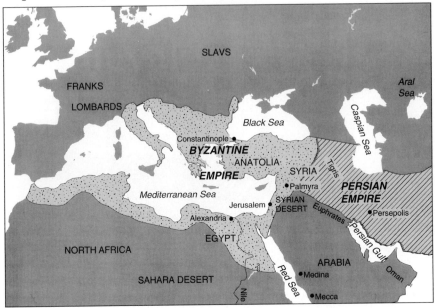

Map 7-2   The Byzantine Empire and Islam in the West, 750

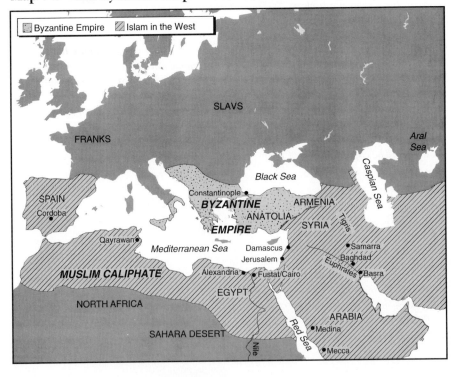

Map 7-3   Islam in the West, 750–1500

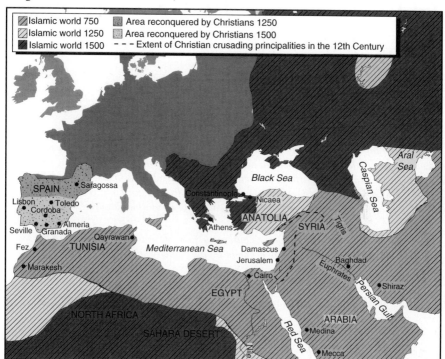

The third map (map 7-3) shows the same region in the period between 750 and 1500. In most areas, Islam had continued to expand, though it had lost lands it once controlled in the Iberian peninsula. By 1500, the Byzantine Empire had fallen to Islamic forces. The Mediterranean basin remained divided between Christians and Muslims. Together these maps reveal the changing fortunes of the successors to Rome between 500 and 1500.

> **Consider:** What these maps reveal about divisions within the once unified Mediterranean basin; how these divisions might have affected relations between Europeans and cultures to the South and East.

SECONDARY SOURCES

Byzantium: The Empire of New Rome

Cyril Mango

One of the outstanding characteristics of the Byzantine Empire was the authority of its central government, headed by the emperor. Indeed, historians often attribute the ability of the Byzantine Empire to survive so long in part to the strength of this central government. In the following selection Cyril Mango, a recognized authority on Byzantium from Oxford and Harvard, analyzes the position of the emperor and the central government in the Byzantine Empire.

> **Consider:** *The sources of the emperor's authority; possible limits on the power of the emperor; the distinction between government by the emperor and government by the imperial palace.*

A sixth-century abbot is reported to have addressed these words to a novice:

> If the earthly emperor intended to appoint you a patrician or a chamberlain, to give you a dignity in his palace (that palace which will vanish like a shadow or a dream), would you not scorn all your possessions and rush to him with all haste? Would you not be willing to undergo every kind of pain and toil, even to risk death for the sake of witnessing that day when the emperor, in the presence of his senate, will receive you and take you into his service?

Few Byzantines, we may imagine, would have behaved differently, since the most obvious characteristic of the Byzantine polity was the overwhelming power of the central government. Short of rebellion, there was no effective counterweight to this power except in delay, inefficiency, corruption or simply distance. This remained true until the gradual disintegration of central governance which we may place approximately in the eleventh century.

In theory the emperor's authority knew no limits save those imposed by divine laws. . . . in practice the emperor was a man who dwelt in the imperial palace of Constantinople, far removed from the public gaze, surrounded by his court. More often than not, he owed his position to an unformulated, but generally respected, principle of heredity; alternatively, he may have been co-opted by his predecessor, chosen by an influential group or he may have owed his throne to a successful rebellion. Strangely enough, the Byzantine State never evolved a theory of imperial succession. A man became emperor by the will of God, his election was signalled by acclamation on the part of the army and the senate, and confirmed, from the fifth century onwards, by a religious coronation performed by the patriarch of Constantinople. To outside observers this system looked

SOURCE: From Cyril Mango, *Byzantium: The Empire of New Rome*, pp. 32–33, copyright 1980 Weidenfeld and Nicholson. Reprinted by permission of the publisher.

curiously unstable and ill-defined: some Arab authors believed that the Roman emperor owed his position to victory and was dismissed if he was unsuccessful. But whatever the circumstances of the emperor's accession, he could not govern single-handed. His principal ministers were chosen at his pleasure and the effective power they wielded was not expressed by their titles. Some emperors—the more forceful ones—assumed a preponderant role in the conduct of affairs, while others were content to leave it to a relative or to one or more officials. While it was generally believed that the emperor had a duty to lead his armies in the field, many emperors did not do so, either through incapacity or because they feared a rebellion during their absence from the capital. There was so much variation in practice that it may be more accurate to speak of government by the imperial palace rather than by the emperor.

The Arabs in History

Bernard Lewis

Islam started as an Arabic religion, and its early conquests were made by Arabs. One of the questions that has concerned historians is the relative importance of Islam as a religion and the Arabs as a people in explaining the conquests and spread of Islam during the seventh and eighth centuries. In the following selection Bernard Lewis, a historian of the Middle East, deals with this question and focuses particularly on the Arabic language as the key legacy of the early conquests.

> **Consider:** *Lewis' argument that the expansion was not of Islam, but of the Arab nation; what, according to Lewis, the role of religion was in the conquests; the significance of the Arabic language within the Islamic (or Arab) Empire.*

Initially the great conquests were an expansion not of Islam but of the Arab nation, driven by the pressure of over-population in its native peninsula to seek an outlet in the neighbouring countries. It is one of the series of migrations which carried the Semites time and again into the Fertile Crescent and beyond. The expansion of the Arabs is not as sudden as might at first appear. In periods when the dam holding the Arabs in their peninsula was too strong to allow a direct break-through, the pressure of over-population found partial relief in a steady infiltration of Arab elements into the border lands. There is much evidence of important Arab infiltration during the sixth and seventh centuries, in particular into the Euphrates basin, Palestine and south-east Syria. The Byzantine towns of Bosra and Gaza, to name but two, had important Arab populations even before the conquests, and there can be little doubt that the conquerors found many of their kinsmen already settled in the nearest of the countries they conquered.

The role of religion in the conquests is over-estimated by earlier writers and has perhaps been under-estimated by some modern scholars. Its importance lies in the temporary psychological change which it wrought in a people who were naturally excitable and temperamental, unaccustomed to any sort of discipline, willing to be persuaded, but

SOURCE: Bernard Lewis, *The Arabs in History,* 3d ed. (London: Hutchinson University Library, 1964), pp. 55–56, 132.

never to be commanded. It made them for a time more self-confident and more amenable to control. In the Wars of Conquest it was the symbol of Arab unity and victory. That the driving force of the conquests was worldly rather than religious is shown by their outstanding figures—men of the type of Khālid and 'Amr, men whose interest in religion was perfunctory and utilitarian. With few exceptions the truly converted and the pietists played little part in the creation of the Arab Empire.

°

The conquests made Arabic an imperial language, soon also the language of a great and diverse culture. Arabic expanded to meet these two needs, partly by borrowing new words and expressions, but mainly by development from within, forming new words from old roots, giving new meanings to old words. As an example of the process we may choose the Arabic word for "absolute", a notion quite unnecessary to the pre-Islamic Arabs. It is *mujurrad,* the passive participle of *jarrada,* to strip bare or denude, a term normally used of locusts and connected with the words *jarāda,* locust, and *jarīda,* leaf. The language created in this way possessed a vivid, concrete and pictorial vocabulary, with each term having deep roots in a purely Arab past and tradition. It allowed of the direct and uncushioned impact of ideas on the mind through concrete and familiar words and of unrestricted penetration to and from the deeper layers of consciousness.

The Arabic language, thus enriched, remained the sole instrument of culture for long after the fall of the purely Arab kingdom. With the language of the Arabs came their poetry as its classical model and the world of ideas embedded therein—concrete, not abstract, though often subtle and allusive; rhetorical and declamatory, not intimate and personal; recitative and spasmodic, not epic and sustained; a literature where the impact of words and form counted for more than the transmission of ideas.

It was the Arabisation of the conquered provinces rather than their military conquest that is the true wonder of the Arab expansion. By the eleventh century Arabic had become not only the chief idiom of everyday use from Persia to the Pyrenees, but also the chief instrument of culture, superseding old culture languages like Coptic, Aramaic, Greek and Latin. As the Arabic language spread, the distinction between Arab conqueror and Arabised conquered faded into relative insignificance, and while all who spoke Arabic and professed Islam were felt to belong to a single community the term Arab was restricted once again to the nomads who had originally borne it or was used as a title of aristocratic descent with no great economic or social significance.

The Islamic World

Albert Hourani

Islam expanded rapidly during the seventh and eighth centuries. Wherever Islamic peoples went they carried their customs and institutions, over time creating what would be recognized as an

SOURCE: Reprinted by permission of the publishers from *A History of the Arab People* by Albert Hourani, Cambridge, Mass.: The Belknap Press of Harvard University Press. Copyright © 1991 by Albert Hourani.

Islamic world. In the following selection Albert Hourani, a prominent historian, analyzes the ways that a sense of identity was being established in the Islamic world, focusing particularly on the buildings and objects that allowed people to see and feel that they were within an Islamic land.

> **Consider:** *How buildings, artifacts, and art might help create a sense of Islamic identity; in what other ways a sense of unity within Islam was created.*

By the third and fourth Islamic centuries (the ninth or tenth century A.D.) something which was recognizably an 'Islamic world' had emerged. A traveller around the world would have been able to tell, by what he saw and heard, whether a land was ruled and peopled by Muslims. These external forms had been carried by movements of peoples: by dynasties and their armies, merchants moving through the worlds of the Indian Ocean and the Mediterranean Sea, and craftsmen attracted from one city to another by the patronage of rulers or the rich. They were carried also by imported and exported objects expressing a certain style: books, metalwork, ceramics and particularly perhaps textiles, the staple of long-distance trade.

The great buildings above all were the external symbols of this 'world of Islam'. At a later period regional styles of mosque building would appear, but in the early centuries there were some common features to be found from Cordoba to Iraq and beyond. In addition to the great mosques were smaller ones for bazaars, quarters or villages, where prayer was offered but the Friday sermon was not preached; these were likely to be built of local materials and reflect local tastes and traditions. . . .

A second type of building was that which expressed the power of the ruler. Among them were great works of public utility, caravanserais on the trade-routes, and aqueducts or other waterworks; in the parched countries of the Middle East and the Maghrib, to bring water to the inhabitants of the cities was an act of sound policy, and irrigation of the land was a practice which spread with the expansion of the Arabs in the Mediterranean. It was the palaces, however, which best expressed imperial greatness: pleasure pavilions set amidst gardens and running water, emblems of a secluded paradise, and official palaces, centres of government and justice as well as of princely life. . . .

The houses built in this period by the Muslim population of the cities have disappeared, but enough has remained of the artefacts used in them to show that some of them contained works of art similar to those in the palaces. Books were transcribed and illustrated for merchants and scholars; glass, metalwork and pottery were made for them; textiles were especially important—floors were covered with carpets, low settee-frames had textile coverings, walls were hung with carpets or cloths. All these show, on the whole, the same kind of decoration as that of religious buildings, formalized plants and flowers, geometrical designs and Arabic words. . . .

By the tenth century, then, men and women in the Near East and the Maghrib lived in a universe which was defined in terms of Islam. The world was divided into the Abode of Islam and the Abode of War, and places holy to Muslims or connected with their early history gave the Abode of Islam its distinctive feature. Time was marked by the five daily prayers, the weekly sermon in the mosque, the annual fast in the month of Ramadan and the pilgrimage to Mecca, and the Muslim calendar.

Islam also gave men an identity by which to define themselves in regard to others. Like all men, Muslims lived at different levels. They did not think of Judgement and Heaven all the time. Beyond their individual existence, they defined themselves for most daily purposes in terms of the family or broader kinship group, the herding unit or tribe, the village or rural district, the quarter or city. Beyond these, however, they were aware of belonging to something broader: the community of believers (the *umma*). The ritual acts which they performed in common, the acceptance of a shared view of man's destiny in this world and the next, linked them with each other and separated them from those of other faiths, whether living among them in the Abode of Islam or beyond its frontiers.

Within this 'world of Islam', at an intermediate level between it and the small cohesive units of everyday life, there were identities of a kind which did not, on the whole, create such strong and lasting loyalties. Service or obedience to a dynasty, particularly if it was long-lasting, could create such a loyalty. Sharing a language too must have created a sense of ease in communication, and a kind of pride.

The Eastern Orientation of Islam

Peter Brown

Westerners often assume that Islamic civilization centered around the Mediterranean and that if not for the resistance put up by Europeans and the Byzantine Empire, Islam would have extended its control to the lands north of the Mediterranean. In the following selection Peter Brown of Oxford and the University of California disputes this view, arguing that Persia acquired great economic importance as the Mediterranean cities declined. In turn, the Islamic Empire became centered in Persia and was oriented toward the East rather than the West.

> **Consider:** *How Persia pulled the Islamic Empire eastward; why, according to Brown, the foundation of Baghdad was more important than military defeats in halting the Arab advance on Europe.*

Mesopotamia regained a central position that it had lost since the days of Alexander the Great. Baghdad, with its circular city wall, owed nothing to the great cities of the Roman empire: it was an avatar of the round cities of Assyria and central Asia. The Mediterranean cities declined as the great caravans by-passed them, bringing trade by camel along the oceans of sand that stretched from the Sahara to the Gobi Desert. In North Africa and Syria, the villages that had sent their oil and grain across the sea to Rome and Constantinople disappeared into the sand. The Mediterranean coast, from being the heart of the civilized world, imperceptibly diminished in significance, as the numbed extremity of a great Eurasian empire.

SOURCE: From Peter Brown, *The World of Late Antiquity*, pp. 202–203, copyright 1971 Thames and Hudson, Ltd.

For the new commercial opportunities were in Persian hands. And, in Persian hands, the eternal lure of Further Asia reasserted itself, as in the early Sassanian period. The mosque and the fire temple could be seen beside the market-places of Lohang and Canton. Chinese prisoners of war from central Asia brought the art of papermaking to Baghdad in 751. Sinbad the Sailor would not have considered the Mediterranean worth his trouble: for the wealth and interests of the Abbasid empire poured eastwards, down the Tigris and Euphrates, to the sea route that linked Basra directly with Canton.

The eastward pull of the vast mass of Persia in the Islamic empire was the salvation of Europe. It was not the Greek fire of the Byzantine navy outside Constantinople in 717, nor the Frankish cavalry of Charles Martel at Tours in 732, that brought the Arab war-machine to a halt. It was the foundation of Baghdad. With the establishment of the Abbasid califate, the slow-moving ideals of an organized and expensive imperial administration replaced the fearful mobility of the Beduin armies. In the new civilian world, the soldier was as much out of place as he had been among the otiose aristocrats of the fourth-century West. The bloodsucking relationships of the Holy War, by which the early Arabs had first impinged on the outside world, gave way to a meticulous diplomacy modelled on the protocol of the Persian *ancien régime*. At the court of the califs, the world appeared to revolve like clockwork round Baghdad, as in the dreamlike ceremonial of the king of kings. Just before he was crowned Roman emperor of the West in 800, Charlemagne received from Harun al-Rashid a great cloak and a pet elephant called Abul Abaz. Little did the Frankish monarch know it, but in this gift the calif had merely repeated the time-honoured gesture of Khusro I Anoshirwan when, at the great Spring festival, the king of kings had lavished gifts of animals and cast-off clothing on his humble servants.

In the western imagination, the Islamic empire stands as the quintessence of an oriental power. Islam owed this crucial orientation neither to Muhammad nor to the adaptable conquerors of the seventh century, but to the massive resurgence of eastern, Persian traditions in the eighth and ninth centuries.

Chapter Questions

1. In what ways does Islamic civilization reflect a common Greco-Roman background with medieval Europe and Byzantium and yet constitute a civilization strikingly different from either?

2. How can the sources in this chapter be used to support the argument that between the seventh and tenth centuries the "center of civilization" was among non-European peoples?

3. What characteristics of Byzantine civilization help explain its strength and long life?

CHAPTER EIGHT

The High Middle Ages: The Eleventh and Twelfth Centuries

During the eleventh and twelfth centuries Western Europe gained new dynamism. The population increased and would continue to do so into the thirteenth century. This was accompanied by an internal expansion, involving increased clearing and farming of land, and an external expansion, with Europeans settling in new lands to the east and venturing on crusades to the Holy Land. Commerce revived, including long-range trade facilitated by newly won control over parts of the Mediterranean formerly dominated by Islam and Byzantium. Towns and cities grew, accompanied by corresponding social and political changes, as urban groups gained power and prestige. Within the Catholic Church, reforms were instituted, such as those initiated by the Cluniac monasteries. The papacy became more assertive, claiming greater powers and challenging monarchs for authority. In a variety of ways there was a broad cultural revival, perhaps most clearly exemplified by the establishment of new institutions of learning that would develop into universities by the early thirteenth century. Through these and other developments, a more stable civilization was being formed that we can recognize as European.

The sources in this chapter concentrate on three main aspects of the eleventh and twelfth centuries. The first is what many historians feel was the most central issue of the time: What would the relationship between Church and state be? This issue was manifested in the Investiture Controversy, especially in the struggle between Pope Gregory VII and Emperor Henry IV, but more broadly a controversy that generally marked the High Middle Ages. The second is a broad and deeply significant development, the growth of commerce and industry. The documents show urban revival, growing trade within Europe, and new long-distance commerce. The documents also cast light on the type of individuals most involved— the growing class of merchants. The third is the social and psychological nature of life during this period, a topic that has recently been of particular interest to historians. How was serfdom experienced and viewed? How did people of different classes relate to each other? How were women viewed? In what ways was the psychic life of individuals related to the physical and social environment of the Middle Ages?

A sense of the dynamism characteristic of the High Middle Ages during these two centuries should emerge from these materials. In the next chapter the crusades, which reflect this same expansive dynamism, will be examined.

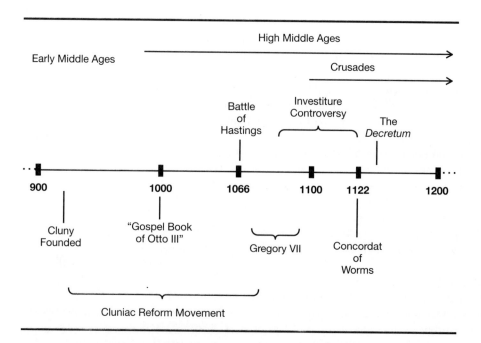

PRIMARY SOURCES

Letters: Secular and Ecclesiastical Authority
Pope Gregory VII

Throughout the Middle Ages the line between secular and ecclesiastical authority was often unclear. During the eleventh century the papacy was growing in stature and power, particularly under Gregory VII's pontificate (1073—1085). Gregory VII, who brought the reforming spirit to his office, soon came into conflict with Emperor Henry IV of the Holy Roman Empire over who had the right to appoint people to high offices in the Church and who had control over properties and revenues connected with ecclesiastical offices. This controversy was not solved until well into the twelfth century, and similar struggles between Church and state continued to arise in succeeding centuries. The following set of papal propositions, found among the letters of Gregory VII (ca. 1075), indicates some of the powers the papacy was claiming for itself during this period.

Consider: *In what matters the papacy asserted its powers and over whom; the ways in which these powers might have threatened the powers of secular rulers.*

The Roman church was founded by God alone.

The Roman bishop alone is properly called universal.

He alone may depose bishops and reinstate them.

His legate, though of inferior grade, takes precedence, in a council, of all bishops and may render a decision of deposition against them.

He alone may use the insignia of empire.

The pope is the only person whose feet are kissed by all princes.

His title is unique in the world.

He may depose emperors.

No council may be regarded as a general one without his consent.

No book or chapter may be regarded as canonical without his authority.

A decree of his may be annulled by no one; he alone may annul the decrees of all.

He may be judged by no one.

No one shall dare to condemn one who appeals to the papal see.

The Roman church has never erred, nor ever, by the witness of Scripture, shall err to all eternity.

He may not be considered Catholic who does not agree with the Roman church.

The pope may absolve the subjects of the unjust from their allegiance.

SOURCE: From James Harvey Robinson, ed., *Readings in European History*, vol. I (Boston: Ginn, 1904), p. 274.

The Life of Saint Godric: A Merchant Adventurer

Reginald of Durham

Trade and the number of people involved in commerce grew during the eleventh and twelfth centuries, not only in the Mediterranean area but in Northern Europe as well. In some cases individuals were able to start with little and over the years amass considerable wealth. This is illustrated in the following selection from The Life of Saint Godric. *Godric lived during the twelfth century, closing out his career as a merchant by going on a pilgrimage to Jerusalem and giving his wealth to the Church. His biography was written by a friend and disciple, the monk Reginald of Durham.*

Consider: *How this document might be used to show that the main elements of capitalism were present as far back as the twelfth century; what this document shows about the potential for social mobility during the Middle Ages.*

He chose not to follow the life of a husbandman, but rather to study, learn and exercise the rudiments of more subtle conceptions. For this reason, aspiring to the merchant's trade, he began to follow the chapman's way of life, first learning how to gain in small bargains and things of insignificant price; and thence, while yet a youth, his mind advanced little by little to buy and sell and gain from things of greater expense. For, in his beginnings, he was wont to wander with small wares around the villages and farmsteads of his own neighbourhood; but, in process of time, he gradually associated himself by compact with city merchants. Hence, within a brief space of time, the youth who had trudged for many weary hours from village to village, from farm to farm, did so profit by his increase of age and wisdom as to travel with associates of his own age through towns and boroughs, fortresses and cities, to fairs and to all the various booths of the marketplace, in pursuit of his public chaffer. . . . At first, he lived as a chapman for four years in Lincolnshire, going on foot and carrying the smallest wares; then he travelled abroad, first to St. Andrews in Scotland and then for the first time to Rome. On his return, having formed a familiar friendship with certain other young men who were eager for merchandise, he began to launch upon bolder courses, and to coast frequently by sea to the foreign lands that lay around him. Thus, sailing often to and fro between Scotland and Britain, he traded in many divers wares and, amid these occupations, learned much worldly wisdom. . . . For he laboured not only as a merchant but also as a shipman . . . to Denmark and Flanders and Scotland; in all which lands he found certain rare, and therefore more precious, wares, which he carried to other parts wherein he knew them to be least familiar, and coveted by the inhabitants beyond the price of gold itself; wherefore he exchanged these wares for others coveted by men of other lands; and thus he

SOURCE: G. G. Coulton, *Social Life in Britain from the Conquest to the Reformation* (Cambridge, England: Cambridge University Press, 1918), pp. 415–419.

chaffered most freely and assiduously. Hence he made great profit in all his bargains, and gathered much wealth in the sweat of his brow; for he sold dear in one place the wares which he had bought elsewhere at a small price.

Then he purchased the half of a merchant-ship with certain of his partners in the trade; and again by his prudence he bought the fourth part of another ship. At length, by his skill in navigation, wherein he excelled all his fellows, he earned promotion to the post of steersman. . . .

And now he had lived sixteen years as a merchant, and began to think of spending on charity, to God's honour and service, the goods which he had so laboriously acquired. He therefore took the cross as a pilgrim to Jerusalem, and, having visited the Holy Sepulchre, came back to England by way of St. James [of Compostella].

The Art of Courtly Love

Andreas Capellanus

The historian is always faced with a serious problem in writing about social life during the High Middle Ages, for literacy was not widespread and few documents on social life remain. This is the case with sexual practices and the social attitudes of the elite toward the peasants. The historian is forced to rely on documents that deal only indirectly with such topics, such as the following selection from The Art of Courtly Love *(ca. 1185), by Andreas Capellanus. It is perhaps a surprise to learn that the author was a chaplain at the court of Marie de France at Troyes. He wrote from and for an aristocratic point of view. Here, Andreas Capellanus comments on the love of peasants.*

> **Consider:** *Evidence in this document for the attitudes of the aristocracy toward peasants; the information provided here about the sexual attitudes and practices of medieval people; what this document indicates about the functions of the medieval clergy.*

CHAPTER XI. THE LOVE OF PEASANTS

But lest you should consider that what we have already said about the love of the middle class applies also to farmers, we will add a little about their love. We say that it rarely happens that we find farmers serving in Love's court, but naturally, like a horse or a mule, they give themselves up to the work of Venus, as nature's urging teaches them to do. For a farmer hard labor and the uninterrupted solaces of plough and mattock are sufficient. And even if it should happen at times, though rarely, that contrary to their nature they are stirred up by Cupid's arrows, it is not expedient that they should be instructed in the theory of love, lest while they are devoting themselves to conduct which is not natural to

Source: Andreas Capellanus, *The Art of Courtly Love,* trans. John Jay Parry (New York: Columbia University Press, 1941), pp. 149–150.

them the kindly farms which are usually made fruitful by their efforts may through lack of cultivation prove useless to us. And if you should, by some chance, fall in love with some of their women, be careful to puff them up with lots of praise and then, when you find a convenient place, do not hesitate to take what you seek and to embrace them by force. For you can hardly soften their outward inflexibility so far that they will grant you their embraces quietly or permit you to have the solaces you desire unless first you use a little compulsion as a convenient cure for their shyness. We do not say these things, however, because we want to persuade you to love such women, but only so that, if through lack of caution you should be driven to love them, you may know, in brief compass, what to do.

The Decretum: Medieval Women—Not in God's Image

Gratian

In the eyes of the medieval Church, the position of women was a problem. On one hand, women were, in theory, spiritual equals to men: their souls were as worthy as men's. On the other hand, women were acknowledged as legally and socially subordinate to men: for example, the priesthood was limited to men. In attitudes and in practice, the latter view of women as subject to men predominated. A particularly strong statement of this view can be found in the following selection from the Decretum, *a systematization of Church law written around 1140 by Gratian, a jurist from northern Italy.*

> **Consider:** *The image of women revealed in this document; how Gratian justifies this view of the position of women; some of the possible consequences of this attitude.*

Women should be subject to their men. The natural order for mankind is that women should serve men and children their parents, for it is just that the lesser serve the greater.

The image of God is in man and it is one. Women were drawn from man, who has God's jurisdiction as if he were God's vicar, because he has the image of the one God. Therefore woman is not made in God's image.

Woman's authority is nil; let her in all things be subject to the rule of man. . . . And neither can she teach, nor be a witness, nor give a guarantee, nor sit in judgment.

Adam was beguiled by Eve, not she by him. It is right that he whom woman led into wrongdoing should have her under his direction, so that he may not fail a second time through female levity. [*Corpus Iuris Canonici*]

SOURCE: Excerpts from *Not in God's Image* by Julia O'Faolain and Lauro Martines. Copyright © 1973 by Julia O'Faolain and Lauro Martines. Reprinted by permission of Harper & Row, Publishers, Inc.

VISUAL SOURCES

The Gospel Book of Otto III: Church and State

In photo 8-1, this page from an illuminated manuscript, the Gospel Book of Otto III (c. 1000), commemorates Emperor Otto III of the Holy Roman Empire receiving homage from the four parts of the Empire: Sclavinia, Germania, Gallia, and Roma. On Otto's left are two barons, and on his right two members of the clergy. The crowned Otto sits on a throne under a canopy, holding a cross-inscribed orb in his left hand and the scepter in his right, both symbolizing his universal authority. He is clothed in gowns that hark back to Roman imperial costumes. In style and ceremonial arrangement, this picture resembles Byzantine models.

Photo 8-1

Bayerische Staatsbibliothek

This picture exemplifies the efforts of the Holy Roman emperors to unify the authority of Church and state in their own being and office. Otto is pictured as superior to separate parts of the empire, feudal lords, and ecclesiastical authorities, himself the legitimate heir to Roman authority and a divinely ordained king. A letter from Berbert of Aurillac supports this: "Ours, ours is the Roman Empire, Italy, fertile in fruits, Lorraine and Germany, fertile in men offer their resources and even the strong kingdoms of the Slavs are not lacking to us. Our august emperor of the Romans art thou, Caesar, who, sprung from the noblest blood of the Greeks [Otto's mother was a Byzantine princess], surpass the Greeks in empire and govern the Romans by hereditary right, but both you surpass in genius and eloquence."

Consider: *Ways suggested by this illuminated manuscript that secular rulers struggled with the Church for authority.*

Medieval Expansion

The first of these maps (map 8-1) is of a local area in northeastern France. It shows the unplanned growth of settlements during and after the twelfth century. In general, settlements prior

Map 8-1   Unplanned Settlement (France)

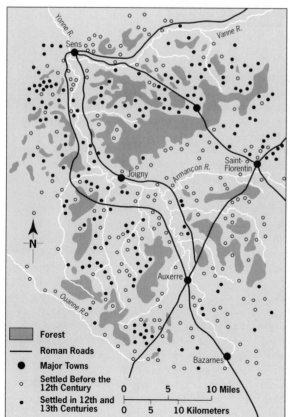

Map 8-2   Planned Settlement (Germany)

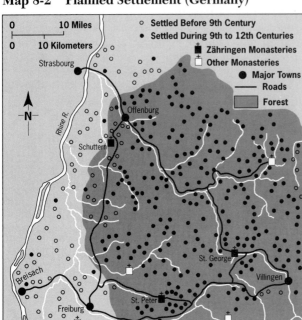

to the twelfth century were along old Roman roads or waterways; the newer settlements tended to be in the less desirable areas requiring greater clearing and cultivation. Map 8-2 shows the growth of settlements in the Black Forest in Germany between the ninth and twelfth centuries; in fact, most of the growth took place during the eleventh and twelfth centuries. In this case, however, much of the settlement was planned and carried out by the dukes of Zähringen and some of the monasteries under their control, particularly St. Peter and St. George. By the end of the first half of the twelfth century, the Zähringens had founded the strategically located towns of Freiburg, Villingen, and Offenburg, which enabled them to gain control over the whole area. The third map (map 8-3) shows a related pattern. Here, a series of towns along the road between Paris and Orléans was founded in the twelfth century by French kings anxious to effect their control over the area. Map 8-4 places the information provided by the first three maps in the context of twelfth-century Europe. Together, all four maps reveal the internal expansion of Europe during the eleventh and twelfth centuries, how that expansion was connected to geographic and commercial factors, and how political motivations played a role in the pattern of this expansion.

The last map (map 8-5) shows the external expansion of Europe and Christendom during this same period. This was carried out by the newly expanding Byzantine Empire, by the now Christianized Vikings (Normans), by military efforts with directly religious overtones both national (the reconquest in Spain) and international (the crusades to the Holy Land), and by a combination of political and commercial expansion by Italian and north German cities and states.

The external and internal expansions complement each other and provide evidence of the general dynamism of the High Middle Ages and of some of the connections between demographic growth, commercial activity, political consolidation, and military assertiveness.

Map 8-3   Strategic Settlement (Paris-Orléans Road)

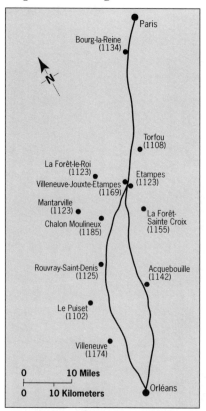

Map 8-4   Twelfth-Century Europe

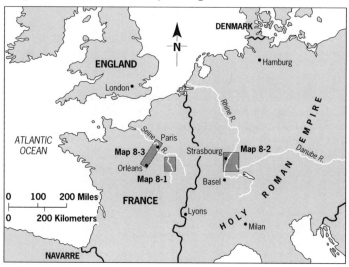

Map 8-5   External Expansion

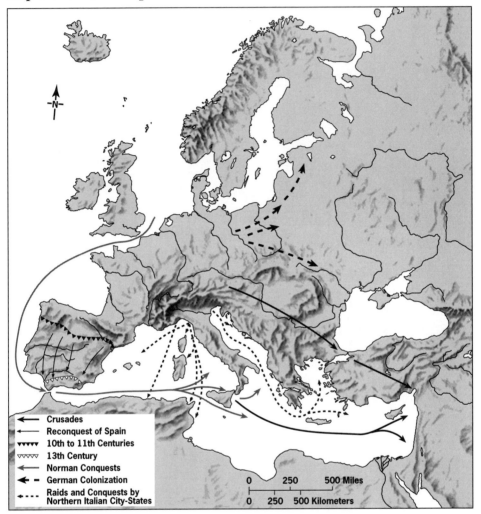

Consider: *The ways in which maps can reveal both the expansion of a civilization and how the expansion took place; how differences between the Early and High Middle Ages are revealed when these maps are compared with those in Chapter 6.*

SECONDARY SOURCES

Medieval Values

Jacques Le Goff

The medieval world was permeated by certain values that colored how people tended to think about the world and to behave in society. Here generalizations are difficult, and in analyzing values scholars often have difficulty leaving their own values aside. In the following selection Jacques Le Goff, a well-known French medievalist, analyzes the fundamental values with which men of the Middle Ages thought, acted, and lived. Here he focuses on their social and political concerns, above all hierarchy, authority, rebellion, and liberty.

> **Consider:** *What exactly these medieval values were and how they fit together; what "justice" might mean to medieval men; how one's social station might relate to these values.*

. . . [M]en of the Middle Ages thought, acted, and lived with several fundamental values. . . .

Hierarchy: The duty of medieval man was to remain where God had placed him. Rising in society was a sign of pride; demotion was a shameful sin. The organization of society that God had ordained was to be respected, and it was based on the principle of hierarchy. Earthly society, modeled on celestial society, was to reproduce the hierarchy of the angels and the archangels. . . .

Authority and Authorities: On the social and political levels, medieval man had to obey his superiors, who were prelates if he was a cleric, the king, the lord, the city fathers, or community leaders if he was a layman. On the intellectual and mental level he had to show loyalty to the authorities, the first of which was the Bible, followed by authorities imposed by historical Christianity: the Fathers of the church in late antiquity, the university *magistri* in the age of the universities in and after the thirteenth century. The abstract and superior value of *auctoritas*, of authority, inherited from classical antiquity, was imposed upon him, embodied in a great number of different "authorities." The greatest intellectual and social virtue required of medieval man was obedience, justified by religion.

The Rebel: Nevertheless (increasingly after the year 1000, and again after the thirteenth century), a growing number of medieval men refused to accept unchallenged the domination of hierarchical superiors and authorities. For a long time, the principal form of

SOURCE: From Le Goff & Cochrane, *Medieval Callings*, pp. 33–35, ed. by Jacques Le Goff, trans. by Lydia Cochrane. © 1990 University of Chicago Press. Reprinted by permission of the publisher.

contestation and rebellion was religious: it was heresy. Within the framework of feudalism, it then took the form of the revolt of the vassal against the lord when the latter abused his power or neglected his duties. In the university context contestation was intellectual. Social revolt finally arrived to both city and countryside in the forms of strikes, riots, and workers' and peasants' revolts. The great century for revolt was the fourteenth, from England and Flanders to Tuscany and Rome. When necessary, medieval man had learned how to become a rebel.

Liberty and Liberties: Liberty was one of medieval man's time-honored values. It motivated his principal revolts. The church, paradoxically, gave the signal, as it was under the banner of *Libertas Ecclesiae*—the freedom of the church—that the church, the pope at its head, demanded its independence from a lay world that had subjugated it through feudalization. From the mid-eleventh century, liberty was the password of the great movement for reform begun under Gregory the Great.

Later, aware of their strength and eager to sweep away obstacles to the great surge that had begun with the year 1000, peasants and new city-dwellers demanded and obtained freedom, or, more often, freedoms. The enfranchisement of the serfs corresponded to the concession of charters or liberties to the burghers of the towns and cities. These were above all freedoms (in the plural)—liberties that were actually privileges.

The Mold for Medieval Women: Social Status

Margaret Wade Labarge

Gender alone greatly affected the life of medieval women, but there were several other factors that interacted with gender to influence the sort of life a medieval woman might lead. Perhaps the most important other factor was social status. In the following selection from A Small Sound of the Trumpet: Women in Medieval Life, *Margaret Wade Labarge analyzes the importance of social status for medieval women.*

> **Consider:** *The differences between upper- and lower-class women; how status interacts with gender differences; how the primary sources in this chapter might support Labarge's analysis.*

. . . [S]ocial status was even more important for a medieval woman than her physical inheritance, for it defined how she would be regarded by others, whom she could marry or what form of religious life she might undertake. Status was determined by birth, for medieval thinkers firmly believed that royal and noble blood was indeed different from the substance which pulsed in the veins of the bourgeois and the peasants, and that it should

---

SOURCE: From *A Small Sound of the Trumpet* by Margaret Wade Labarge. Copyright © 1986 by Margaret Wade Labarge. Reprinted by permission of Beacon Press.

not be intermingled with that of a lower rank. It was this solid conviction which accounted for the fury of widows and wards whose lords sold their marriages and thus their fiefs to men below their own station and explains their willingness to pay large sums to avoid such disparagement. Women shared the status of their family and their husband all the way up and down the social scale, though a married woman was always a step below her husband for he was her lord and master. Nevertheless, such subordination was restricted only to her husband; all other men, if of lower rank, must display respect for her higher status, for actual behaviour was based primarily on the subservience exacted by rank. . . .

The consciousness of their privileged position protected the women of the upper classes, but worked to the disadvantage of those lower down the scale. Courtesy was a noble virtue; it was not considered necessary towards poor townswomen or, even more noticeably, towards peasant women, because their low rank excluded them from consideration. Most men felt that violence, even rape, practised on such base creatures quite literally did not count and should be overlooked. Such an attitude was encouraged by the fact that high tempers and violence were general in the Middle Ages in both sexes. In addition, the law recognized the right of men of all classes to beat their wives, so long as they did not kill them or do excessive damage. It appears to have been a frequently exercised right, for many of the cautionary tales warn women of the wisdom of being humble and not arousing their husband's wrath, lest a beating and permanent disfigurement or worse should follow. The women themselves seem to have been quick with words and occasionally with blows.

The Merchant

Aron Ja. Gurevich

The eleventh and twelfth centuries saw the growth of towns and cities, which marked a new dynamism in Western civilization. One reason for this growth was the revival of commerce. Here the medieval merchant played a central role, but the merchant was important to medieval society in several ways. In the following selection Aron Ja. Gurevich analyzes the roles played by the medieval merchant and the type of person the great merchant was.

> **Consider:** *The ways the merchant supported medieval society; the social and psychological differences between the merchant and others; whether this interpretation is supported by the document on St. Godric.*

The position of men of affairs in medieval society was extremely contradictory. By lending money to the nobles and the monarchs (whose insolvency or refusal to pay often caused the failure of great banks), and by acquiring landed property, concluding marriages with knightly families, and pursuing noble titles and crests, the mercantile patriciate became

SOURCE: From Aron Ja. Gurevich, "The Merchant," in *Medieval Callings*, pp. 281–282, ed. by Jacques Le Goff, trans. by Lydia Cochrane. © 1990 University of Chicago Press. Reprinted by permission of the publisher.

deeply entrenched in feudal society, to the point of being an inevitable and fundamental element of it. Crafts, commerce, the city, and finance were all organic parts of fully developed feudalism. At the same time, however, money was sapping the traditional bases of aristocratic domination—land and warfare—and pauperizing the artisan class and the peasants, since the great enterprises launched by merchants employed wage-workers. When in the late Middle Ages money became a powerful social force, large-scale international commerce and the spirit of gain that moved the merchants became the heralds of a new economic and social order: capitalism.

In spite of all his efforts to "root himself" in the structure of feudalism and adapt himself to it, the great merchant was a totally different psychological and social type from the feudal lord. He was a knight of profit who risked his life not on the battlefield but in his office or his shop, on board a merchant ship, or in his bank. To the warlike virtues and the impulsive emotivity of the nobles he opposed careful calculation and cause-and-effect thinking; to irrationality, he opposed rationality. In the milieu of men of affairs a new type of religious sentiment came to be elaborated in a paradoxical combination of faith in God and fear of castigation in the otherworld, on the one hand, and, on the other, a mercantile approach to "good works" that expected indemnification and compensation, which were to be expressed as material prosperity.

The Making of the Middle Ages: Serfdom

R. W. Southern

For large masses of people serfdom was the overriding condition of life during the Middle Ages. At times observers have tended to romanticize the Middle Ages and the bucolic life of the peasantry. But in the following selection R. W. Southern of Oxford University, author of the highly acclaimed The Making of the Middle Ages, *reflects most historians' views in arguing that serfdom was a condition characterized by servitude; the serf's lack of liberty was recognized by contemporaries as harmful and degrading. This selection illustrates the advantages of looking at the Middle Ages from the inside, from the point of view of the people of that time.*

Consider: *The evidence Southern provides to support his argument; how this interpretation fits with the selection from* The Art of Courtly Love *that discusses love and the peasants; conditions that might have mitigated the negative aspects of serfdom.*

To nearly all men serfdom was, without qualification, a degrading thing, and they found trenchant phrases to describe the indignity of the condition. The serf's family was always referred to by lawyers as his brood, his *sequela,* and the poets delighted to exercise their ingenuity in describing the physical deformity of the ideal serf. Hard words break no bones, but they are hard to bear for all that, and they became harder as time went on.

Source: R. W. Southern, *The Making of the Middle Ages* (New Haven, Conn.: Yale University Press, 1953), pp. 106–107.

Men well knew, however theologians might seem to turn common notions inside out, the difference between the yoke of servitude and the honour of liberty—or, to use the expressive phrase of Giraldus Cambrensis, the *hilaritas libertatis:* "There is nothing," he wrote, "which so stirs the hearts of men and incites them to honourable action like the lightheartedness of liberty; and nothing which so deters and depresses them like the oppression of servitude." If we consider only the practical effects of serfdom and notice how little the lines of economic prosperity follow those of personal status; if we reflect on the many impediments to free action, to which even the mightiest were subjected in such delicate matters as marriage and the bequeathing of property, it may seem surprising that the pride of liberty was so strong, and the contempt for serfdom so general: yet such was the case. However much the hierarchical principle of society forced men into relationships at all levels of society in which rights and restraints were inextricably mixed up, the primitive line which divided liberty from servitude was never forgotten.

Feudal Society: The Psychic World of Medieval People

Marc Bloch

A full picture of the Middle Ages requires a concrete, empathetic sense of how people experienced everyday life at that time. But perhaps the hardest task for the historian is to understand and convey feelings and attitudes of people in the distant past. Few historians have attempted to do this in any "scientific" or rigorous way, although in recent years there has been a growing interest in this kind of scholarship. A pioneering effort in this direction was made by the French medievalist Marc Bloch. In the following selection Bloch relates the physical and social environment of the Middle Ages to the psychic world of the inhabitants of that time.

> **Consider:** *The evidence that supports Bloch's claim that emotional instability was characteristic of the feudal era; how this approach compares with the approaches of Southern and Pirenne.*

The men of the two feudal ages were close to nature—much closer than we are; and nature as they knew it was much less tamed and softened than we see it today. The rural landscape, of which the waste formed so large a part, bore fewer traces of human influence. The wild animals that now only haunt our nursery tales—bears and, above all, wolves—prowled in every wilderness, and even amongst the cultivated fields. So much was this the case that the sport of hunting was indispensable for ordinary security, and almost equally so as a method of supplementing the food supply. People continued to pick wild fruit and to gather honey as in the first ages of mankind. In the construction of implements and tools, wood played a predominant part. The nights, owing to the wretched lighting, were darker; the cold, even in the living quarters of the castles, was more

SOURCE: Reprinted from *Feudal Society* by Marc Bloch, trans. L. A. Manyon, University of Chicago Press, 1961, pp. 72–73. Reprinted by permission of The University of Chicago Press. Copyright © 1961.

intense. In short, behind all social life there was a background of the primitive, of submission to uncontrollable forces, of unrelieved physical contrasts. There is no means of
measuring the influence which such an environment was capable of exerting on the
minds of men, but it could hardly have failed to contribute to their uncouthness. . . .

Infant mortality was undoubtedly very high in feudal Europe and tended to make
people somewhat callous toward bereavements that were almost a normal occurrence.
As to the life of adults, even apart from the hazards of war it was usually short. . . .

Among so many premature deaths, a large number were due to the great epidemics
which descended frequently upon a humanity ill-equipped to combat them; among the
poor another cause was famine. Added to the constant acts of violence these disasters
gave life a quality of perpetual insecurity. This was probably one of the principal reasons
for the emotional instability so characteristic of the feudal era, especially during its first
age. A low standard of hygiene doubtless also contributed to this nervous sensibility. . . .

. . . Finally, we must not leave out of account the effects of an astonishing sensibility
to what were believed to be supernatural manifestations. It made people's minds constantly and almost morbidly attentive to all manner of signs, dreams, or hallucinations.
This characteristic was especially marked in monastic circles where the influence of mor-
tifications of the flesh and the repression of natural instincts were joined to that of a
mental attitude vocationally centered on the problems of the unseen. No psychoanalyst
has ever examined dreams more earnestly than the monks of the tenth or the eleventh
century. Yet the laity also shared the emotionalism of a civilization in which moral or social convention did not yet require well-bred people to repress their tears and their rap-
tures. The despairs, the rages, the impulsive acts, the sudden revulsions of feeling
present great difficulties to historians, who are instinctively disposed to reconstruct the
past in terms of the rational. But the irrational is an important element in all history and
only a sort of false shame could allow its effects on the course of political events in feudal Europe to be passed over in silence.

Chapter Questions

1. For a long time it was believed that the Middle Ages, the years 500 to 1500, consti-
    tuted an era of little change, offering little in comparison to the Greco-Roman civi-
    lization that preceded it and the Renaissance that succeeded it. In what ways do the
    sources in this chapter *not* support this interpretation?

2. In what ways were developments during the eleventh and twelfth centuries prob-
    lematic or advantageous to the Church? To the monarchies?

3. What options were available to people in different classes or stations of life—
    peasants, merchants, Church officials, and kings—to make changes in their lives?

CHAPTER NINE

The High Middle Ages: The Crusades and the East

Part of the dynamism of the High Middle Ages was manifested in the crusades. These crusades were officially initiated by the Church in an effort to spread Christianity, principally at the expense of Islam. The earliest crusades, which were the most successful, contributed to the long-term reconquest of Spain by Christian forces and the establishment of Christian control in the Holy Land for much of the twelfth century. The crusades increased contact between Western Europeans and the other two inheritors of the Roman world, Islam and Byzantium. At this time Byzantium was beginning a long period of decline that would culminate with the fall of Constantinople in 1453. Islam was no longer the expansive power it had once been, but it remained a formidable opponent with considerable resources.

The documents in this chapter emphasize three themes: the crusades, the interaction between these three civilizations occasioned by the crusades, and the importance of Byzantium. First, how did the papacy justify the crusades? How does this justification compare with other factors motivating Europeans to join these crusades? What do the crusades reveal about medieval society and institutions during these centuries? Second, what were the reactions of the Byzantines to the crusades and to the Europeans? How did Muslims view Western Europeans and their customs? How did Europeans relate to Byzantines and Muslims? Of what significance to the balance of power among these three civilizations were the crusades? Finally, what were some of Byzantium's main accomplishments? What was the significance of the final fall of Constantinople?

An examination of these materials will broaden our picture of the High Middle Ages. Some of the developments emphasized here and in the preceding chapter will come to greater fruition in the thirteenth century, as will be seen in the next chapter.

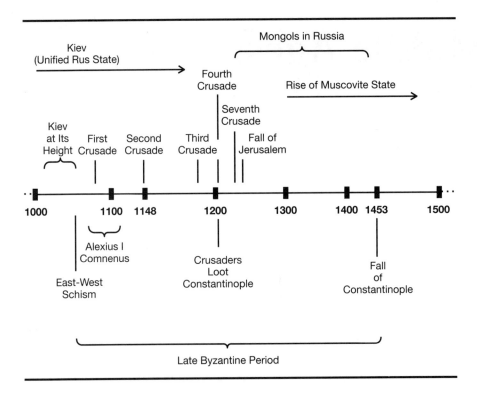

PRIMARY SOURCES

The Opening of the Crusades
Pope Urban II

The series of crusades initiated in the eleventh century brought the West into greater contact with Byzantium and Islam. These crusades demonstrated the expansiveness of the West during the High Middle Ages as well as the increasing power and activism of the papacy. The first of these crusades was called for in 1095 by Pope Urban II in response to a request for help from the Byzantine Emperor Alexius Comnenus. At the Council of Clermont, Urban made the following plea, recorded by Robert the Monk.

> **Consider:** *How Urban justified his call for a crusade; what Urban might have hoped to gain from this crusade; to whom this plea was addressed.*

"From the confines of Jerusalem and from the city of Constantinople a grievous report has gone forth and has repeatedly been brought to our ears; namely, that a race from the kingdom of the Persians, an accursed race, a race wholly alienated from God, 'a generation that set not their heart aright, and whose spirit was not steadfast with God,' has violently invaded the lands of those Christians and has depopulated them by pillage and fire. They have led away a part of the captives into their own country, and a part they have killed by cruel tortures. They have either destroyed the churches of God or appropriated them for the rites of their own religion. They destroy the altars, after having defiled them with their uncleanness. . . . The kingdom of the Greeks is now dismembered by them and has been deprived of territory so vast in extent that it could not be traversed in two months' time.

"On whom, therefore, is the labor of avenging these wrongs and of recovering this territory incumbent, if not upon you,—you, upon whom, above all other nations, God has conferred remarkable glory in arms, great courage, bodily activity, and strength to humble the heads of those who resist you? Let the deeds of your ancestors encourage you and incite your minds to manly achievements:—the glory and greatness of King Charlemagne, and of his son Louis, and of your other monarchs, who have destroyed the kingdoms of the Turks and have extended the sway of the holy Church over lands previously pagan. Let the holy sepulcher of our Lord and Saviour, which is possessed by the unclean nations, especially arouse you, and the holy places which are now treated with ignominy and irreverently polluted with the filth of the unclean. Oh, most valiant soldiers and descendants of invincible ancestors, do not degenerate, but recall the valor of your progenitors.

SOURCE: From James Harvey Robinson, ed., *Readings in European History,* vol. I (Boston: Ginn, 1904), pp. 314–317.

"But if you are hindered by love of children, parents, or wife, remember what the Lord says in the Gospel, 'He that loveth father or mother more than me is not worthy of me.' 'Every one that hath forsaken houses, or brethren, or sisters, or father, or mother, or wife, or children, or lands, for my name's sake, shall receive an hundredfold, and shall inherit everlasting life.' Let none of your possessions retain you, nor solicitude for your family affairs. For this land which you inhabit, shut in on all sides by the seas and surrounded by the mountain peaks, is too narrow for your large population; nor does it abound in wealth; and it furnishes scarcely food enough for its cultivators. Hence it is that you murder and devour one another, that you wage war, and that very many among you perish in intestine strife.

"Let hatred therefore depart from among you, let your quarrels end, let wars cease, and let all dissensions and controversies slumber. Enter upon the road to the Holy Sepulcher; wrest that land from the wicked race, and subject it to yourselves. That land which, as the Scripture says, 'floweth with milk and honey' was given by God into the power of the children of Israel. Jerusalem is the center of the earth; the land is fruitful above all others, like another paradise of delights. This spot the Redeemer of mankind has made illustrious by his advent, has beautified by his sojourn, has consecrated by his passion, has redeemed by his death, has glorified by his burial.

"This royal city, however, situated at the center of the earth, is now held captive by the enemies of Christ and is subjected, by those who do not know God, to the worship of the heathen. She seeks, therefore, and desires to be liberated and ceases not to implore you to come to her aid. From you especially she asks succor, because, as we have already said, God has conferred upon you above all other nations great glory in arms. Accordingly, undertake this journey eagerly for the remission of your sins, with the assurance of the reward of imperishable glory in the kingdom of heaven."

Crusaders' Motives

Ekkehard of Aurach

Different sources evidence a variety of motivations for the groups of people joining the crusades. The following is an account of Ekkehard of Aurach, a contemporary of the first crusade and a well-known German historian.

Consider: *How this account compares with that of Urban II; how this account adds to the significance of the first crusade.*

The West Franks were easily induced to leave their fields, since France had, during several years, been terribly visited now by civil war, now by famine, and again by sickness. . . . Among the other nations, the common people, as well as those of higher rank, related

SOURCE: From James Harvey Robinson, ed., *Readings in European History*, vol. I (Boston: Ginn, 1904), p. 318.

that, aside from the apostolic summons, they had in some instances been called to the land of promise by certain prophets who had appeared among them, or through heavenly signs and revelations. Others confessed that they had been induced to pledge themselves by some misfortune. A great part of them started forth with wife and child and laden with their entire household equipment.

Inducements for the Crusades
Pope Eugenius III

In succeeding crusades popes used various means to induce people to participate. The following document indicates the privileges granted to crusaders by Pope Eugenius III in 1146. Such privileges were also offered by other popes for other crusades.

> **Consider:** *The inducements envisioned by Eugenius to be effective; evidence for the power of the papacy during the twelfth century.*

Moreover, in virtue of the authority vested by God in us, we, who with paternal care provide for your safety and the needs of the Church, have promised and granted to those who from a spirit of devotion have resolved to enter upon and accomplish this holy and necessary undertaking, that full remission of sins which our predecessor, Pope Urban, granted. We have also commanded that their wives and children, their property and possessions, shall be under the protection of the holy Church, of ourselves, of the archbishops, bishops, and other prelates of the Church of God. Moreover we ordain, by our apostolic authority, that until their return or death is fully proven, no lawsuit shall be instituted hereafter in regard to any property of which they were in peaceful possession when they took the cross.

Those who with pure hearts enter upon this sacred journey, and who are in debt, shall pay no interest. And if they, or others for them, are bound by oath or promise to pay interest, we free them by our apostolic authority. And after they have sought aid of their relatives, or of the lords of whom they hold their fiefs, if the latter are unable or unwilling to advance them money, we allow them freely to mortgage their lands and other possessions to churches, ecclesiastics, or other Christians, and their lords shall have no redress.

Following the example of our predecessor, and through the authority of omnipotent God and of St. Peter, prince of the apostles, which is vested in us by God, we grant absolution and remission of sins, so that those who devoutly undertake and accomplish this holy journey, or who die by the way, shall obtain absolution for all their sins which they confess with humble and contrite heart, and shall receive from him who grants to each his due reward the prize of eternal life.

SOURCE: From James Harvey Robinson, ed., *Readings in European History,* vol. I (Boston: Ginn, 1904), pp. 337–338.

The Alexiad: A Byzantine View of the Crusades

Princess Anna Comnena

Alexius I Comnenus, the Byzantine emperor from 1081 to 1118, expected a relatively small number of mercenary soldiers when he sent his request to Pope Urban II in 1095. Instead, he was faced with a massive army of crusaders, many of whom were not truly soldiers. His reaction to the approach of the crusaders reflects some of the distrust and hostility between the Byzantines and the Europeans. The following is an account by Anna Comnena, the daughter of Alexius I and the author of The Alexiad, *written forty years after the events occurred.*

> **Consider:** *Why Alexius feared the coming of the crusaders, who supposedly were responding to his call for help; the motives of the crusaders in the eyes of the Byzantines.*

Before he had enjoyed even a short rest, he heard a report of the approach of innumerable Frankish armies. Now he dreaded their arrival for he knew their irresistible manner of attack, their unstable and mobile character and all the peculiar natural and concomitant characteristics which the Frank retains throughout; and he also knew that they were always agape for money, and seemed to disregard their truces readily for any reason that cropped up. For he had always heard this reported of them, and found it very true. However, he did not lose heart, but prepared himself in every way so that, when the occasion called, he would be ready for battle. And indeed the actual facts were far greater and more terrible than rumour made them. For the whole of the West and all the barbarian tribes which dwell between the further side of the Adriatic and the pillars of Heracles, had all migrated in a body and were marching into Asia through the intervening Europe, and were making the journey with all their household. The reason of this upheaval was more or less the following. A certain Frank, Peter by name, nicknamed Cucupeter, had gone to worship at the Holy Sepulchre and after suffering many things at the hands of the Turks and Saracens who were ravaging Asia, he got back to his own country with difficulty. But he was angry at having failed in his object, and wanted to undertake the same journey again. However, he saw that he ought not to make the journey to the Holy Sepulchre alone again, lest worse things befall him, so he worked out a cunning plan. This was to preach in all the Latin countries that 'the voice of God bids me announce to all the Counts in France that they should all leave their homes and set out to worship at the Holy Sepulchre, and to endeavour whole-heartedly with hand and mind to deliver Jerusalem from the hand of the Hagarenes.' And he really succeeded. For after inspiring the souls of all with this quasi-divine command he contrived to assemble the Franks from all sides, one after the other, with arms, horses and all the other paraphernalia of war. And they were all so zealous and eager that every highroad was full of them. And those Frankish soldiers were accompanied by an unarmed host more numerous than the sand or the

---

SOURCE: Anna Comnena, *The Alexiad of the Princess Anna Comnena,* trans. Elizabeth A. S. Dawes (London: Kegan Paul, Trench, Trubner, 1928), p. 248. Reprinted by permission of Routledge & Kegan Paul Ltd.

stars, carrying palms and crosses on their shoulders; women and children, too, came away from their countries. And the sight of them was like many rivers streaming from all sides, and they were advancing towards us through Dacia generally with all their hosts.

And such an upheaval of both men and women took place then as had never occurred within human memory, the simpler-minded were urged on by the real desire of worshipping at our Lord's Sepulchre, and visiting the sacred places; but the more astute, especially men like Bohemund and those of like mind, had another secret reason, namely, the hope that while on their travels they might by some means be able to seize the capital itself, looking upon this as a kind of corollary.

Memoirs: European and Muslim Interactions

Usāmah Ibn-Munqidh

There was considerable interaction between Europeans and Muslims, particularly in the Holy Lands, where Europeans temporarily established feudal kingdoms. Such interactions provide us with useful insights into the nature of both peoples, as indicated in the following excerpt from an eleventh-century memoir written by a Syrian. Here he comments on the characteristics of the Franks.

> **Consider:** *The Muslim customs and values revealed in this document; how this perception of Europeans compares with that of Alexius I; the ways in which this observer felt that Muslims were superior to Franks.*

Their lack of sense.—Mysterious are the works of the Creator, the author of all things! When one comes to recount cases regarding the Franks, he cannot but glorify Allah (exalted is he!) and sanctify him, for he sees them as animals possessing the virtues of courage and fighting, but nothing else; just as animals have only the virtues of strength and carrying loads. I shall now give some instances of their doings and their curious mentality.

In the army of King Fulk, son of Fulk, was a Frankish reverend knight who had just arrived from their land in order to make the holy pilgrimage and then return home. He was of my intimate fellowship and kept such constant company with me that he began to call me "my brother." Between us were mutual bonds of amity and friendship. When he resolved to return by sea to his homeland, he said to me:

> My brother, I am leaving for my country and I want thee to send with me thy son (my son, who was then fourteen years old, was at that time in my company) to our country, where he can see the knights and learn wisdom and chivalry. When he returns, he will be like a wise man.

SOURCE: Philip K. Hitti, ed. and trans., *An Arab-Syrian Gentleman and Warrior in the Period of the Crusades: Memoirs of Usāmah Ibn-Munqidh (Kitāb al-I'Tibār)* (New York: Columbia University Press, 1929), pp. 161, 164. Copyright © 1977 by Philip K. Hitti.

Thus there fell upon my ears words which would never come out of the head of a sensible man; for even if my son were to be taken captive, his captivity could not bring him a worse misfortune than carrying him into the lands of the Franks. However, I said to the man:

> By thy life, this has exactly been my idea. But the only thing that prevented me from carrying it out was the fact that his grandmother, my mother, is so fond of him and did not this time let him come out with me until she exacted an oath from me to the effect that I would return him to her.

Thereupon he asked, "Is thy mother still alive?" "Yes," I replied. "Well," said he, "disobey her not."

Another wants to show to a Moslem God as a child.—I saw one of the Franks come to al-Amīr Muʿīn-al-Dīn (may Allah's mercy rest upon his soul!) when he was in the Dome of the Rock and say to him, "Dost thou want to see God as a child?" Muʿīn-al-Dīn said, "Yes." The Frank walked ahead of us until he showed us the picture of Mary with Christ (may peace be upon him!) as an infant in her lap. He then said, "This is God as a child." But Allah is exalted far above what the infidels say about him!

Franks lack jealousy in sex affairs.—The Franks are void of all zeal and jealousy. One of them may be walking along with his wife. He meets another man who takes the wife by the hand and steps aside to converse with her while the husband is standing on one side waiting for his wife to conclude the conversation. If she lingers too long for him, he leaves her alone with the conversant and goes away.

VISUAL SOURCES

Conflict and Cultural Exchange

The crusades were but one type of contact between Islam and Western Christendom. In some areas of Europe, such as the Iberian Peninsula and Sicily, there was extensive interaction on a daily basis between Christians and Muslims in the centuries before, during, and after the Great Crusades to the Near East. This interaction is revealed in an illustration from a manuscript of rules for games compiled for King Alfonso X of Castile during the second half of the thirteenth century (photo 9-1). It shows a Christian on the left playing a game of chess with a Muslim on the right. This picture suggests the twin aspects of contact between Islam and Western Christendom—military conflict, since chess is a game of war and the two opponents here are Muslim and Christian, and peaceful contact, since a game is being transmitted to the West as were the system of Arabic numerals, the works of Greek philosophers, and agricultural techniques.

> **Consider:** *The ways in which peaceful cultural interactions might have taken place; other kinds of evidence for cultural interactions between Islam and Western Christendom.*

Photo 9-1

MAS, Barcelona; courtesy Patrimonio Nacional, Madrid

SECONDARY SOURCES

The Great Significance of the Crusades

Henri Pirenne

In terms of rescuing Jerusalem from Islamic hands, the crusades were at best only temporarily successful. But as part of a European expansion reflecting a new strength in comparison to competing civilizations, the first crusade had great significance. More than most historians, Henri Pirenne has focused on the broad connections between Islam and medieval Europe. In the following selection he stresses the importance of the first crusade and related events of the eleventh century.

Consider: *The significance of the first crusade for the balance of power between Christianity and Islam.*

SOURCE: Excerpts from Henri Pirenne, *Medieval Cities: Their Origins and the Revival of Trade*, trans. Frank D. Halsey (copyright 1925, © 1952 by Princeton University Press; Princeton Paperback, 1969), pp. 90–91. Reprinted by permission of Princeton University Press.

Before the counter-attack of Christianity, Islam thus gave way little by little. The launching of the First Crusade (1096) marked its definite recoil. In 1097 a Genoese fleet sailed towards Antioch, bringing to the Crusaders reinforcements and supplies. Two years later Pisa sent out vessels "under the orders of the Pope" to deliver Jerusalem. From that time on the whole Mediterranean was opened, or rather reopened, to western shipping. As in the Roman era, communications were reestablished from one end to the other of that essentially European sea.

The Empire of Islam, in so far as the sea was concerned, came to an end. To be sure, the political and religious results of the Crusade were ephemeral. The kingdom of Jerusalem and the principalities of Edessa and Antioch were reconquered by the Muslims in the twelfth century. But the sea remained in the hands of the Christians. They were the ones who held undisputed economic mastery over it. All the shipping in the ports of the Levant came gradually under their control. Their commercial establishments multiplied with surprising rapidity in the ports of Syria, Egypt and the isles of the Ionian Sea. The conquest of Corsica (1091), of Sardinia (1022) and of Sicily (1058-1090) took away from the Saracens the bases of operations which, since the ninth century, had enabled them to keep the west in a state of blockade. The ships of Genoa and Pisa kept the sea routes open. They patronized the markets of the east, whither came the products of Asia, both by caravan and by the ships of the Red Sea and the Persian Gulf, and frequented in their turn the great port of Byzantium. The capture of Amalfi by the Normans (1073), in putting an end to the commerce of that city, freed them from her rivalry.

The Meaning of the Middle Ages: The Crusades Minimized

Norman F. Cantor

Not all historians agree that the crusades were of great significance. In recent years historians have tended to deemphasize their importance. This is exemplified in the following selection by Norman Cantor.

Consider: *What, according to Cantor, was most important about the crusades; how this interpretation differs from Pirenne's.*

Historians used to believe that the Crusades reopened the Mediterranean to east-west trade after centuries of isolation and thus made a critical contribution to the economic and intellectual development of Europe. It is true that the Crusades were inspired in part by commercial motives: from the middle of the tenth century, Venetian and Genoese merchants had aspired to take over certain commercial ventures from the Arabs and Byzantines and to acquire new ports in the eastern Mediterranean. The Crusades helped the Italian merchants in both ambitions, but that does not imply that they

SOURCE: From Norman F. Cantor, *The Meaning of the Middle Ages: A Sociological and Cultural History.* Copyright © 1973 by Allyn and Bacon, Inc., Boston. Reprinted with permission.

opened up the Mediterranean—east-west trade had never completely disappeared, and in the ninth and tenth centuries, long before the Crusades, it was growing fast spurred on by the growth of the Italian cities.

It is true that the Christian world absorbed a great deal of Muslim philosophy, medicine, science, and literature in the late eleventh and twelfth centuries, but the Crusades did not contribute to this phenomenon—indeed, they probably inhibited it by stirring up religious fanaticism and hatred of Muslims. The intellectual exchange between Christians and Muslims did not take place among soldiers on a battlefield but in the cosmopolitan centers of southern Europe (especially those in Spain and Sicily) where Christians and Muslims lived side by side.

The tangible, institutional impact of the Crusades on the development of Europe was very slight: the institution of monarchy was affected almost not at all, and even the Church (apart from a slight rise in papal prestige) was not much affected by the Crusades in the twelfth century. Eventually two different kinds of crusading movements developed: external Crusades, directed mainly against Arabs, and internal Crusades against enemies within Christendom. The latter—the crusading ideal turned inward—had enormous impact upon the development of European civilization, but this was not fully realized until the thirteenth century.

The most important legacy of the crusading movement was the sanctification of violence in pursuit of ideological ends. This was not a new concept, but it took on new force when the pope and the flower of Christian chivalry acted it out in holy wars. The underlying concept outlived its religious origin, and eventually it was absorbed in the institution of monarchy. When the European kings grew more powerful, in the twelfth and thirteenth centuries, they secularized the concept of justifiable violence and extended it into the political sphere. The defense of the realm and its head became a moral duty, and the state gradually replaced the Church as a holy cause.

The Byzantine Empire: Defeat, Decline, and Resilience

Robert Browning

In 1453 Constantinople fell, providing historians with a convenient date for the end of the long-lasting Byzantine Empire. However, by that date the Byzantine Empire was only a shadow of what it had been three centuries earlier. In the following selection Robert Browning argues that we must look back to 1204 to explain why the Byzantine Empire collapsed. He goes on to analyze the importance of its long though weakened existence after that date for the Western world in general.

Consider: *Why the Latin invasion of 1204 was so important; why the long existence of the Byzantine Empire might have been so important to the Western world.*

Source: From Robert Browning, *The Byzantine Empire*, rev. ed., pp. 255, 291. Washington, D.C.: The Catholic University of America Press, 1992. Reprinted by permission.

If the historian is asked why the Byzantine Empire, after more than a thousand years of vigorous life, collapsed so ignominiously, he will doubtless reply that there was no single reason. Factors of many kinds were at work, from improvements in seagoing ships to climatic changes in central Asia, from the growing independence of landed proprietors to debasement of the coinage in order to increase the money supply. If there was a single fatal blow, it was struck in 1204 when the territory of the empire still stretched from the Adriatic to the gates of Syria, and not in 1453, when Constantinople fell to the rulers of a vast, enveloping empire as an over-ripe fruit falls from a tree. It was the power vacuum created by the Latin invasion which enabled the orthodox Slav states of the Balkans to strike out on a course of their own, freed from the field of force of Byzantium, and in the end condemned them to fall one by one to the Ottoman conqueror. Rivalry and intrigue replaced the firm and traditional political leadership which might have enabled the Balkan world, with its immense manpower and its largely common culture, to offer effective resistance. . . .

The capture of Constantinople by the crusaders in 1204 and the establishment of Latin rule over the ruins of the Byzantine Empire brought with them the destruction of those institutions within which Byzantine art, letters, and thought flourished. There was no longer an emperor and a court to provide patronage. The Church still survived, but much of its wealth was now in western hands and its hierarchy scattered and impoverished. Many monasteries, however, continued to provide, albeit on a reduced scale, the conditions for the execution of works of art and the copying of manuscripts. The cultivated metropolitan milieu by which and for which so much of the literature and art of the twelfth century had been produced existed no longer. Its members had fled as refugees to one or another of the regions still outside Latin control, or had sunk into obscurity. . . .

There was no longer any career in the bureaucracy of Church or state awaiting those with a classical literary education. The imperial factories had vanished in the general débâcle, and their silk weavers, mosaicists, goldsmiths, and other craftsmen were scattered to the four winds, unable to pass on their centuries-old skills to a following generation.

Fortunately, Byzantine society and Byzantine culture remained in being until the western world was mature enough to want to learn from them. What they learned was not a dead body of doctrine or an artistic iconography, but rather the living and developing tradition of a society which carried a great cultural heritage without being overburdened or paralyzed by it.

Chapter Questions

1. What role did the crusades play in struggles for power between secular and religious authorities both within Europe and between Europe and competing civilizations?
2. How might the crusades have been perceived by the following twelfth-century figures: a pope, a Frankish aristocrat, a Muslim scholar, and a Byzantine prince?
3. In what ways might one argue that the crusades were of great historical significance? In what ways might one argue that the crusades were of little historical significance?

CHAPTER TEN

The High Middle Ages: The Thirteenth Century

The pinnacle of the High Middle Ages, the thirteenth century was a period in which the dynamic trends already under way during the two preceding centuries came to fruition. Within the Church new reforming orders like the Franciscans and Dominicans were founded and the papacy made even more unprecedented claims to power. With these claims the papacy continued to come into conflict with monarchs who had themselves gained in stature and power in certain areas, particularly England and France. Commerce continued to thrive, but by this time merchants, artisans, and even cities were organizing their own institutions, like guilds and leagues, reflecting their growing power and permanency. The culture of the Middle Ages flourished during this century. Magnificent Gothic cathedrals, some started in the twelfth century, rose throughout Europe. Universities expanded, becoming important centers of learning as well as recruiting grounds for members of the growing state and ecclesiastical bureaucracies. Medieval scholasticism dominated the period intellectually and received its finest statement in the work of St. Thomas Aquinas.

In this chapter some of the connections between religious, political, social, and cultural trends of thirteenth-century Europe are examined. Some documents concentrate primarily on theoretical and practical relations between the Church, the state, and society. How did the papacy justify its claims over secular authority? How did the Church react to the challenges presented by the growing urban centers? How did the Church control its clergy, who had such concrete contact with all classes in traditional society? How was the Church affected by the growing body of and new respect for Classical law and thought?

The documents also shed light on the relations between monarchs, nobles, and towns—the three lay competitors for power. How did the strength of central authority vary in different parts of Europe? How did monarchs, nobles, and towns compete with one another for power and authority? How did the balance between the monarchs, nobles, and towns shift in the Holy Roman Empire under Frederick II? How did the newly assertive cities deal with the development of commerce and urban growth, as seen in the formation of leagues and various urban institutions such as guilds?

Finally, the sources show how some of these relations were reflected in the culture and society of the period. What constituted social injustice? What problems did urban areas have with crime and violence? How was the position of the aristocracy reflected in pictorial art? How was the new respect for Classical law

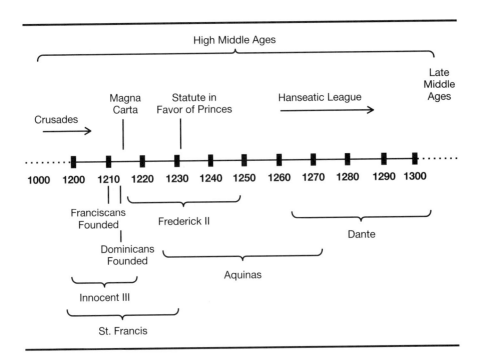

connected to medieval constitutionalism? How did Christian intellectuals relate Classical pagan thought and medieval Christian doctrines in this thirteenth-century environment?

What emerges from these materials is a picture of a flourishing civilization—medieval Europe at its height. During the following century Europe entered a period of disruption and transformation—the Late Middle Ages. This will be examined in the next chapter.

PRIMARY SOURCES

Papal Proclamation of Supremacy

Pope Innocent III

The struggles between Church and state, so apparent during the Investiture Controversy, abated in the twelfth century but did not disappear. Popes continued to claim vast powers for themselves and managed to make some of those claims stick. The pinnacle of papal authority occurred during Innocent III's pontificate (1198–1216). Pope Innocent came into conflict with the rulers of the Empire, England, France, and others over political and religious issues. In the following papal proclamation Innocent III presents a theory for the proper jurisdictions of pontifical authority and royal power.

> **Consider:** *Innocent III's justification for the supremacy of papal authority; how a king might respond to this argument.*

Just as the founder of the universe established two great lights in the firmament of heaven, a greater one to preside over the day and a lesser to preside over the night, so too in the firmament of the universal church, which is signified by the word heaven, he instituted two great dignities, a greater one to preside over souls as if over day and a lesser one to preside over bodies as if over night. These are the pontifical authority and the royal power. Now just as the moon derives its light from the sun and is indeed lower than it in quantity and quality, in position and in power, so too the royal power derives the splendor of its dignity from the pontifical authority. . . .

SOURCE: From Brian Tierney, *The Crisis of Church and State, 1050–1300* (Englewood Cliffs, N.J.: Prentice-Hall Inc., 1964), p. 132. Copyright © 1964. Reprinted by permission.

A Church Register:
Clerical Administration
Archbishop Eudes of Rouen

Much of the administration of the medieval Church was carried out by bishops, the more consci-
entious of whom made periodic visits to the local clergy and Church establishments in their
areas. The following is an excerpt from the register of the Archbishop Eudes of Rouen, who held
that office from 1242 to 1267. To judge from his extensive records, he took his responsibilities
seriously and rather meticulously attempted to improve the practices of his clergy.

> **Consider:** *The kinds of problems that bothered Eudes; Eudes' view of the proper*
> *behavior for the clergy.*

OCTOBER 24. We visited the abbey of St-Etienne-de-Caen, where there are sixty-three
monks. All but three are priests. In one of the priories there are rabbit dogs; we forbade
the monks who are staying there to become hunters. There are some who do not confess
every month; we enjoined them to correct this. It used to be their practice that all those
ministering [to the celebrants] at all Masses, save those [Masses] for the dead, received
Communion, but this practice, through negligence, has gradually been abandoned; we
enjoined the abbot and prior to have this custom more fully observed by all. The cloister
is badly kept; we enjoined them to correct this. Traveling monks do not observe the fasts
of the Rule; we enjoined them to correct this. In the priories they do not observe the
fasts of the Rule and they eat meat freely; we enjoined them to correct this. They owe fifteen hundred pounds, but about as much is owed to them; they have an income of four
thousand pounds. Total for procuration: seven pounds, ten shillings, ten pence.

JUNE 30. We visited the deanery of Meulan at Chars. We found that the priest at
Courdimanche has occasionally celebrated Mass though he is under suspension and that
he kept a concubine; he rides horseback dressed in a short mantle, and he runs about too
much. Item, the priest at Courcelles does not keep residence well nor is he in the habit
of wearing his gown. Item, the priest at Hérouville only rarely wears a gown. Item, the
priest at Valmondois sells his services; he is noted for having money, is contentious, and
is given to drinking. Item, the priest at Vaux is a trader and had, and still has, a certain
vineyard which he holds as security from a certain wastrel to whom he had loaned his too
precious coins; he does not say his Hours well and sometimes he comes to Mass straight
from his bed. Item, the priest at Chars is ill famed of a certain widow; he runs about too
much. . . . Item, the priest at Longuesse is ill famed of Eugénie, his parishioner, and has
had children by her; he promised us that if he should be ill famed of these matters again
he would regard his church as resigned.

JULY 3. We visited the priory of Notre-Dame-de-Chaumont. Only two monks are
there, and there should be three. They do not confess every month as the Statutes of

---

SOURCE: From Jeremiah F. O'Sullivan, ed., *The Register of Eudes of Rouen*, trans. Sydney M. Brown (New
York: Columbia University Press, 1964), pp. 43–45, 293.

Pope Gregory require. They have no written copy of their Rule, nor a copy of the Statutes. They do not hold chapter, nor do they receive the minor penances. They do not keep the fasts of the Rule; they eat meat when it is not necessary. They use feather beds, though we had warned them about this before. Instead this time, and in the presence of their own abbot of St-Germer, we enjoined them with firmness to correct their deficiencies. They have an income of one hundred pounds; they owe about thirty pounds.

The Rule of St. Francis

St. Francis of Assisi

There were periodic Christian reform movements during the High Middle Ages. The most important movement during the thirteenth century was initiated by the Franciscans, a group of pious laymen who gathered around Francis of Assisi (1181?–1226). Francis, who had been born into a merchant family and was headed for a secular career, had experienced a deeply emotional conversion, given up his worldly goods, and pursued a life of asceticism, preaching, and poverty. He and his followers did not withdraw to a cloistered life, but traveled extensively and were particularly active in urban areas. While still not formally approved by the Church, this organization constituted a potential threat. But by 1223, when the following version of St. Francis' rule was adopted, the papacy had officially recognized the Franciscans as an orthodox order.

Consider: *Reasons such an order might be so successful; the functions such an order might perform for society or for the Church; how the record of behavior described in the previous document compares with the standard set up under the Rule of St. Francis.*

This is the rule and life of the Minor Brothers, namely, to observe the holy gospel of our Lord Jesus Christ by living in obedience, in poverty, and in chastity. Brother Francis promises obedience and reverence to Pope Honorius and to his successors who shall be canonically elected, and to the Roman Church. The other brothers are bound to obey brother Francis, and his successors. . . .

I counsel, warn, and exhort my brothers in the Lord Jesus Christ that when they go out into the world they shall not be quarrelsome or contentious, nor judge others. But they shall be gentle, peaceable, and kind, mild and humble, and virtuous in speech, as is becoming to all. They shall not ride on horseback unless compelled by manifest necessity or infirmity to do so. When they enter a house they shall say, "Peace be to this house." According to the holy gospel, they may eat of whatever food is set before them.

I strictly forbid all the brothers to accept money or property either in person or through another. Nevertheless, for the needs of the sick, and for clothing the other brothers, the ministers and guardians may, as they see that necessity requires, provide through spiritual friends, according to the locality, season, and the degree of cold which may be expected in the region where they live. But, as has been said, they shall never receive money or property.

SOURCE: Oliver J. Thatcher and Edgar H. McNeal, eds. and trans., *A Source Book for Medieval History* (New York: Scribner's, 1905), pp. 499–507.

Those brothers to whom the Lord has given the ability to work shall work faithfully and devotedly, so that idleness, which is the enemy of the soul, may be excluded and not extinguish the spirit of prayer and devotion to which all temporal things should be subservient. As the price of their labors they may receive things that are necessary for themselves and the brothers, but not money or property. And they shall humbly receive what is given them, as is becoming to the servants of God and to those who practise the most holy poverty.

The brothers shall have nothing of their own, neither house, nor land, nor anything, but as pilgrims and strangers in this world, serving the Lord in poverty and humility, let them confidently go asking alms. Nor let them be ashamed of this, for the Lord made himself poor for us in this world. This is that highest pitch of poverty which has made you, my dearest brothers, heirs and kings of the kingdom of heaven, which has made you poor in goods, and exalted you in virtues. . . .

I strictly forbid all the brothers to have any association or conversation with women that may cause suspicion. And let them not enter nunneries, except those which the pope has given them special permission to enter. Let them not be intimate friends of men or women, lest on this account scandal arise among the brothers or about brothers.

Summa Theologica

St. Thomas Aquinas

By the thirteenth century much of the intellectual and cultural heritage of Classical times, particularly Aristotelian thought, was being reacquired in Europe. This posed a problem for the Church, for it was not clear whether pagan ideas and the reasoning of Greeks such as Aristotle contradicted the Christian view of the universe as it had developed during the Middle Ages. One of the main tasks of a line of thirteenth-century scholars, among them Albertus Magnus (1193?–1280), St. Thomas Aquinas (1225–1274), St. Bonaventure (1221–1274), and Duns Scotus (1265?–1308?), was to make compatible this pagan thought and Church orthodoxy based on faith. In doing this, these scholastics tended to be encyclopedic, covering almost all the concerns of medieval people. The most encyclopedic and important of these was Aquinas, an Italian Dominican who taught at the University of Paris and elsewhere. In the following selection from his Summa Theologica, *Aquinas addresses the question of whether the existence of God can be proved.*

Consider: *The reasoning used here; the audience being addressed by Aquinas.*

The existence of God can be proved in five ways.

The first and more manifest way is the argument from motion. It is certain, and evidence to our senses, that in the world some things are in motion. Now whatever is in motion is put in motion by another, for nothing can be in motion except it is in potentiality

---

SOURCE: St. Thomas Aquinas, *The Summa Theologica of St. Thomas Aquinas*, Part I, XXI–XXVI, 2d rev. ed., trans. Fathers of the English Dominican Province (New York: Benziger Brothers, 1920), pp. 24–27.

to that towards which it is in motion; whereas a thing moves inasmuch as it is in act. For motion is nothing else than the reduction of something from potentiality to actuality. But nothing can be reduced from potentiality to actuality, except by something in a state of actuality. Thus that which is actually hot, as fire, makes wood, which is potentially hot, to be actually hot, and thereby moves and changes it. Now it is not possible that the same thing should be at once in actuality and potentiality in the same respect, but only in different respects. For what is actually hot cannot simultaneously be potentially hot; but it is simultaneously potentially cold. It is therefore impossible that in the same respect and in the same way a thing should be both mover and moved, *i.e.,* that it should move itself. Therefore, whatever is in motion must be put in motion by another. If that by which it is put in motion be itself put in motion, then this also must needs be put in motion by another, and that by another again. But this cannot go on to infinity, because then there would be no first mover, and, consequently, no other mover; seeing that subsequent movers move only inasmuch as they are put in motion by the first mover; as the staff moves only because it is put in motion by the hand. Therefore it is necessary to arrive at a first mover, put in motion by no other; and this everyone understands to be God.

The second way is from the nature of the efficient cause. In the world of sense we find there is an order of efficient causes. There is no case known (neither is it, indeed, possible) in which a thing is found to be the efficient cause of itself; for so it would be prior to itself, which is impossible. Now in efficient causes it is not possible to go on to infinity, because in all efficient causes following in order, the first is the cause of the intermediate cause, and the intermediate is the cause of the ultimate cause, whether the intermediate cause be several, or one only. Now to take away the cause is to take away the effect. Therefore, if there be no first cause among efficient causes, there will be no ultimate, nor any intermediate cause. But if in efficient causes it is possible to go to infinity, there will be no first efficient cause, neither will there be an ultimate effect, nor any intermediate efficient causes; all of which is plainly false. Therefore it is necessary to admit a first efficient cause, to which everyone gives the name of God.

The third way is taken from possibility and necessity, and runs thus. We find in nature things that are possible to be and not to be, since they are found to be generated, and to corrupt, and consequently, they are possible to be and not to be. But it is impossible for these always to exist, for that which is possible not to be at some time is not. Therefore, if everything is possible not to be, then at one time there could have been nothing in existence. Now if this were true, even now there would be nothing in existence, because that which does not exist only begins to exist by something already existing. Therefore, if at one time nothing was in existence, it would have been impossible for anything to have begun to exist; and thus even now nothing would be in existence—which is absurd. Therefore, not all beings are merely possible, but there must exist something the existence of which is necessary. But every necessary thing either has its necessity caused by another, or not. Now it is impossible to go on to infinity in necessary things which have their necessity caused by another, as has been already proved in regard to efficient causes. Therefore we cannot but postulate the existence of some being having of itself its own necessity, and not receiving it from another, but rather causing in others their necessity. This all men speak of as God.

The fourth way is taken from the gradation to be found in things. Among beings there are some more and some less good, true, noble, and the like. But 'more' and 'less' are predicated of different things, according as they resemble in their different ways something which is the maximum, as a thing is said to be hotter according as it more nearly resembles that which is hottest; so that there is something which is truest, something best, something noblest, and consequently, something which is uttermost being; for those things that are greatest in truth are greatest in being, as it is written in *Metaph.* ii. Now the maximum in any genus is the cause of all in that genus; as fire, which is the maximum of heat, is the cause of all hot things. Therefore there must also be something which is to all beings the cause of their being, goodness, and every other perfection; and this we call God.

The fifth way is taken from the governance of the world. We see that things which lack intelligence, such as natural bodies, act for an end, and this is evident from their acting always, or nearly always, in the same way, so as to obtain the best result. Hence it is plain that not fortuitously, but designedly, do they achieve their end. Now whatever lacks intelligence cannot move towards an end, unless it be directed by some being endowed with knowledge and intelligence; as the arrow is shot to its mark by the archer. Therefore some intelligent being exists by whom all natural things are directed to their end; and this being we call God.

Political Authority: The Emperor, the Princes, and the Towns

Frederick II

The papacy was not the only force competing with royal authority for power during the thirteenth century. Within their realms, kings faced relatively powerful and independent princes and cities. This was particularly true in the German lands of the Holy Roman Empire. A development that significantly shifted the balance in favor of independent princes occurred during Frederick II's reign (1212–1250). Frederick was a dynamic emperor who was concerned with acquiring control over his lands in Italy. To enable him to concentrate his efforts there, Frederick made the following grant of privileges to his German princes in 1231.

> **Consider:** *The ways in which this grant strengthened the position of the princes against the emperor; how this grant strengthened the position of the princes against the independent towns; methods that could have been used to strengthen royal authority.*

1. No new castles or cities shall be erected by us or by anyone else to the prejudice of the princes.

SOURCE: From Oliver J. Thatcher and Edgar H. McNeal, eds. and trans., *A Source Book for Medieval History* (New York: Scribner's, 1905), pp. 238–240.

2.   New markets shall not be allowed to interfere with the interests of former ones.
3.   No one shall be compelled to attend any market against his will.
4.   Travellers shall not be compelled to leave the old highways, unless they desire to do so.
5.   We will not exercise jurisdiction within the ban-mile of our cities.
6.   Each prince shall possess and exercise in peace according to the customs of the land the liberties, jurisdiction, and authority over counties and hundreds which are in his own possession or are held as fiefs from him.
7.   Centgrafs shall receive their office from the prince or from the person who holds the land as a fief.
8.   The location of the hundred court shall not be changed without the consent of the lord.
9.   No nobleman shall be amenable to the hundred court.
10. The citizens who are known as *phalburgii* [*i.e.,* persons or corporations existing outside the city, but possessing political rights within it] shall be expelled from the cities.
11. Payments of wine, money, grain, and other rents, which free peasants have formerly agreed to pay [to the emperor], are hereby remitted, and shall not be collected henceforth.
12. The serfs of princes, nobles, ministerials, and churches shall not be admitted to our cities.
13. Lands and fiefs of princes, nobles, ministerials, and churches, which have been seized by our cities, shall be restored and shall never again be taken.
14. The right of the princes to furnish safe-conduct within the lands which they hold as fiefs from us shall not be infringed by us or by anyone else.
15. Inhabitants of our cities shall not be compelled by our judges to restore any possessions which they may have received from others before they moved there.
16. Notorious, condemned, and proscribed persons shall not be admitted to our cities; if they have been, they shall be driven out.
17. We will never cause any money to be coined in the land of any of the princes which shall be injurious to his coinage.
18. The jurisdiction of our cities shall not extend beyond their boundaries, unless we possess special jurisdiction in the region.
19. In our cities the plaintiff shall bring suit in the court of the accused.
20. Lands or property which are held as fiefs shall not be pawned without the consent of the lord from whom they are held.
21. No one shall be compelled to aid in the fortifying of cities unless he is legally bound to render that service.
22. Inhabitants of our cities who hold lands outside shall pay to their lords or advocates the regular dues and services, and they shall not be burdened with unjust exactions.
23. If serfs, freemen subject to advocates, or vassals of any lord, shall dwell within any of our cities, they shall not be prevented by our officials from going to their lords.

Decrees of the Hanseatic League

Increased trade and the corresponding growth of cities dependent on that trade created common problems and interests, encouraging some cities to make cooperative agreements or form leagues. This cooperation occurred mostly in commercial areas where central royal authority was relatively weak, as in northern Italy, where the Lombard League was formed, and in northern Germany, where the Hanseatic League was established during the thirteenth century. The prominence of the Hanseatic League rose further in the fourteenth and fifteenth centuries. The following are decrees issued by the Hanseatic League between 1260 and 1264.

Consider: *The primary concerns of league members on which they felt they could cooperate; who was perceived as the principal threat to the independence of the towns.*

We wish to inform you of the action taken in support of all merchants who are governed by the law of Lübeck.

(1) Each city shall, to the best of her ability, keep the sea clear of pirates, so that merchants may freely carry on their business by sea. (2) Whoever is expelled from one city because of a crime shall not be received in another. (3) If a citizen is seized [by pirates, robbers, or bandits] he shall not be ransomed, but his sword-belt and knife shall be sent to him [as a threat to his captors]. (4) Any merchant ransoming him shall lose all his possessions in all the cities which have the law of Lübeck. (5) Whoever is proscribed in one city for robbery or theft shall be proscribed in all. (6) If a lord besieges a city, no one shall aid him in any way to the detriment of the besieged city, unless the besieger is his lord. (7) If there is a war in the country, no city shall on that account injure a citizen from the other cities, either in his person or goods, but shall give him protection. (8) If any man marries a woman in one city, and another woman from some other city comes and proves that he is her lawful husband, he shall be beheaded. (9) If a citizen gives his daughter or niece in marriage to a man [from another city], and another man comes and says that she is his lawful wife, but cannot prove it, he shall be beheaded.

This law shall be binding for a year, and after that the cities shall inform each other by letter of what decisions they make.

Ordinances of the Guild Merchants of Southampton

One way medieval merchants responded to the growth of commerce and industry in urban areas was to form guilds. While the specific origin of guilds is unclear—they may at first have been

---

SOURCE: From Oliver J. Thatcher and Edgar H. McNeal, eds. and trans., *A Source Book for Medieval History* (New York: Scribner's, 1905), pp. 611–612.

SOURCE: Edward P. Cheyney, ed., "English Towns and Gilds," in *Translations and Reprints from the Original Sources of European History,* vol. II, no. 1, ed. Department of History of the University of Pennsylvania (Philadelphia: University of Pennsylvania Press, 1898), pp. 12–15.

only fraternal-religious groups—by the thirteenth and fourteenth centuries they could be found in most cities. They tended to develop into independent organizations that monopolized commerce and played an important social role in the community. The following selections are taken from ordinances dating back to the thirteenth century of the Guild Merchants of Southampton, England.

> **Consider:** *The ways in which this guild attempted to control commerce and industry; what services the guild performed for its members; how the principles and practices of guilds fit with the argument that capitalism was widespread in medieval times; similarities and differences between the concerns of this guild and those of the Hanseatic League.*

§7. And when a gildsman dies, all those who are of the Gild and are in the city shall attend the service for the dead, and gildsmen shall bear the body and bring it to the place of burial. And whoever will not do this shall pay according to his oath, two pence, to be given to the poor. And those of the ward where the dead man shall be ought to find a man to watch over the body the night that the dead shall lie in his house. And so long as the service of the dead shall last, that is to say, the vigil and the mass, there ought to burn four candles of the Gild, each candle of two pounds weight or more, until the body is buried. And these four candles shall remain in the keeping of the steward of the Gild.

✿

§9. And when a gildsman dies, his eldest son or his next heir shall have the seat of his father, or of his uncle, if his father was not a gildsman, and of no other one; and he shall give nothing for his seat. . . .

✿

§11. And if a gildsman shall be imprisoned in England in time of peace, the alderman, with the steward, and with one of the skevins shall go, at the cost of the Gild, to procure the deliverance of the one who is in prison.

§12. And if any gildsman strikes another with his fist; and, is convicted thereof, he shall lose the Gild until he shall have bought it back for ten shillings, and taken the oath of the Gild again like a new member. And if a gildsman strikes another with a stick, or a knife, or any other weapon, whatever it may be, he shall lose the Gild and the franchise, and shall be held as a stranger until he shall have been reconciled to the good men of the Gild and has made recompense to the one whom he has injured; and has paid a fine to the Gild of twenty shillings, and this shall not be remitted.

✿

§15. And if a gildsman reviles or slanders another gildsman, and a complaint of it comes to the alderman, and, if he is reasonably convicted thereof, he shall pay two shillings fine to the Gild, and if he is not able to pay he shall lose the Gild.

§16. And if anyone, who is of the franchise, speaks evil of a gildsman, and is convicted of this before the alderman, he shall pay five shillings for a fine, or lose the franchise.

✿

§19. And no one in the city of Southampton shall buy anything to sell again in the same city, unless he is of the Gild Merchant or of the franchise. . . .

§20. And no one shall buy honey, fat, salt herrings, or any kind of oil, or millstones, or fresh hides, or any kind of fresh skins, unless he is a gildsman; nor keep a tavern for wine, nor sell cloth at retail, except in market or fair days; nor keep grain in his granary beyond five quarters, to sell at retail, if he is not a gildsman; and whoever shall do this and be convicted, shall forfeit all to the king.

§22. If any gildsman falls into poverty and has not the wherewithal to live, and is not able to work or to provide for himself, he shall have one mark from the Gild to relieve his condition when the Gild shall sit. . . .

§23. And no private man or stranger shall bargain for or buy any kind of merchandise coming into the city before a burgess of the Gild Merchant, so long as the gildsman is present and wishes to bargain for and buy this merchandise; and if any one does so and is convicted, that which he buys shall be forfeited to the king.

§24. And anyone who is of the Gild Merchant shall share in all merchandise which another gildsman shall buy or any other person, whoever he is, if he comes and demands part and is there where the merchandise is bought, and also if he gives satisfaction to the seller and gives security for his part. But no one who is not a gildsman is able or ought to share with a gildsman, without the will of the gildsman.

Chambermaids

Bartholomaeus Anglicus

Most women were neither wealthy nor of high position. Few options were available to them. Many had to become servants, serving as chambermaids. The life they faced is described in the following excerpt from a book of writings gathered by a thirteenth-century English Franciscan, Bartholomaeus Anglicus. The book was translated and widely circulated in the fourteenth century.

> **Consider:** *What limitations a chambermaid faced; what penalties could be imposed upon her; ways in which her position might differ from that of a male servant.*

A chambermaid is a servant employed by the master or mistress of the house to do the heaviest and foulest jobs. She is fed coarse food, clad in the meanest cloth, and bears the burden of servitude. If she has children, they are the master's serfs. If she is a serf herself, she may not marry whom she chooses, and anyone who does marry her, falling into servitude, can be sold like an animal by the master. If freed, the serving maid can be recalled to serfdom for ingratitude. Chambermaids are frequently beaten, abused, and tormented, and scarcely given a chance to console themselves by laughter or distractions. . . .

SOURCE: Excerpts from *Not in God's Image* by Julia O'Faolain and Lauro Martines. Copyright © 1973 by Julia O'Faolain and Lauro Martines. Reprinted by permission of Harper & Row, Publishers, Inc.

Rabanus says that chambermaids have this characteristic: they rebel against their masters and mistresses and get out of hand if they are not kept down. . . . Serfs and that sort are kept in place only through fear.

VISUAL SOURCES

Medieval Life

While there was considerable change throughout the High and Late Middle Ages, many fundamental aspects of life remained much the same. In photo 10-1, a late-medieval illustration by Pol de Limbourg from the Très Riches Heures du Duc de Berry, *a book of prayers for each day of the year, shows a typical October day. A peasant sows seeds in a small, recently plowed field. Just behind, a scarecrow in the form of an archer guards another field. In the background flows the Seine with some aristocrats on its bank under the walls of the Louvre, the Gothic castle of the French kings in Paris. The basic reliance on agriculture, the importance of the seasons, the sharp contrast between the social classes, and the increasingly large castles symbolizing military prowess and status remained typical of medieval life.*

Consider: *The nature of the peasant's life as portrayed by this artist; how an aristocratic viewer of this illustration might react.*

Secularization and the Medieval Knight

This illustration from a book produced shortly after 1300 (photo 10-2) shows two knights jousting in a tournament. The knights are distinguished by their costumes. The knight on the left falls in defeat with a pierced helmet; the winner suffers only a broken lance. Meanwhile, aristocratic women view the scene in apparent admiration.

This sort of pageantry was growing in a period when the traditional function of knighthood was becoming obsolete. Earlier in the Middle Ages knights were owners of horses and armor who served in the cavalry and upheld certain chivalric values. According to a twelfth-century source the knight was "to protect the Church, to fight against treachery, to respect the priesthood, to fend off injustice from the poor, to make peace in [his] own province, to shed blood for [his] brethren, and if needs must, to lay down [his] life." By the thirteenth and fourteenth centuries new military tactics diminished the importance of knights, centralizing monarchies weakened their independence, and spreading wealth enabled even the middle class to purchase knighthood. As shown in this picture, however, knighthood still survived and even helped define masculinity and femininity.

The book itself, the Codex Manesse, *indicates a growing secularization in society during the thirteenth century. It is a collection of popular poems and songs of chivalry and love written in the vernacular rather than in Latin.*

Consider: *The images of masculinity and femininity conveyed by this illustration; any connections between these images and medieval values; the distinctions between the image and reality of medieval knighthood.*

Photo 10-1

Chantilly, Musée Condé. Photographie Giraudon

Photo 10-2

Universitätsbibliothek, Heidelberg

SECONDARY SOURCES

The Outlaws of Medieval Legend: Social Rank and Injustice

Maurice Keen

Today, the social system of the Middle Ages seems unjust, particularly for the poor, who suffered the most. Yet one must be careful in applying modern standards to an earlier era. In the following selection Maurice Keen of Oxford argues that the poor did not have such a critical view of the social system and the laws that supported such a hierarchical structure. Rather, criticism was directed toward corruption within the system. In his interpretation Keen makes creative use of evidence from medieval ballads and legends.

Consider: *The common view or ideal that justified the social system to the medieval mind; what sort of behavior created a sense of injustice in the minds of medieval people.*

The middle ages were profoundly respectful to hereditary rank and they did not question its title to homage. They did on the other hand question the right of those whose actions belied any nobility of mind to the enjoyment of the privileges of noble status. They were not indignant against an unjust social system, but they were indignant against unjust social superiors. The ballad makers accepted this contemporary attitude and echoed it in their poems.

This explains why the ballads have nothing to say of the economic exploitation of the poor, of the tyranny of lords of manors whose bondmen were tied to the soil and bound by immemorial custom to till their land for him. For we might expect, from what we know of the social system of the countryside in the middle ages, to find Robin, as the champion of the poor, freeing serfs from bondage, harbouring runaway villeins in his band, and punishing the stewards of estates whose conduct was every whit as harsh and unjust as that of the offices of the law. But the middle ages did not view social injustice, as we do, in terms of the exploitation of one class by another; they admired the class system as the co-operation for the common well-being of the different estates of men. They recognized three different classes in their society; the knights and lords, whose business it was to protect Christendom in arms, the clerks who had charge of its spiritual well-being and whose duty was prayer, and the common men whose business it was to till the soil. Each rank had its obligation to discharge its proper duties without complaint, and,

SOURCE: Maurice Keen, *The Outlaws of Medieval Legend* (London: Routledge and Kegan Paul, 1961), pp. 154–155. Reprinted by permission.

in the case particularly of the first two classes, not to abuse the privileges which its function gave it. That they were made to 'swink and toil' gave the peasants no ground for complaint; their occupation, as one preacher quaintly put it, lay in 'grobbynge about the erthe, as erynge and dungynge and sowynge and harwying' and 'this schuld be do justlie and for a good ende, withoute feyntise or falshede or gruechynge of hire estaat'. But those who failed to discharge their duties and abused their position had no right to a place in the system, nor to the profits of association. 'They neither labour with the rustics . . . nor fight with the knights, nor pray and chant with the clergy; therefore,' says the great Dominican, Bromyard, of such men 'they shall go with their own abbot, of whose Order they are, namely the Devil, where no Order exists but horror eternal'.

The law's object is ultimately to uphold social justice, and to the middle ages social justice meant a hierarchical social system. The trouble came when those who belonged to a high class used the wealth, which was given them to uphold their proper rank, to corrupt the law and abuse it for their own profit. Their ultimate sin was the use of their originally rightful riches to purchase more than was their due. For this reason, those who were shocked by flagrant injustice into attacking the accepted system criticized not the economic oppression which is almost automatically implied, but the corruption of evil men whose personal greed destroyed the social harmony of what they regarded as the ideal system. The method which these men employed was to buy the law, and to control by their position its application. It is for this reason that the outlaw ballads, whose heroes are the champions of the poor, are silent about the multitudinous economic miseries of the medieval peasant, and are concerned only or at least chiefly with an endless feud against the corrupt representatives of the law. Contemporary opinion diagnosed the disease which was gnawing at society as the personal corruption of those in high rank; that such disease was the inevitable accompaniment of their hierarchic system they simply could not see. This is why the animus in the outlaw ballads is against oppression by those who own the law, not against exploitation by those who own the land.

Life in Cities:
Violence and Fear

Jacques Rossiaud

The growth of cities after the eleventh century created what we now recognize as typical urban problems. One such problem was keeping the peace. Cities in Western Europe were often places of violence and fear. As part of a trend toward studying social life, historians have increasingly studied crime and violence in medieval cities. In the following selection Jacques Rossiaud analyzes violent acts in the cities of Western Europe, emphasizing how urban violence fostered anxiety.

SOURCE: From Jacques Rossiaud, "The City-Dweller and Life in Cities and Towns," in *Medieval Callings*, pp. 152–154, ed. by Jacques Le Goff, trans. by Lydia Cochrane. © 1990 University of Chicago Press. Reprinted by permission of the publisher.

Consider: *Who tended to commit most of the violent acts; possible explanations for urban violence; what the effects of this violence might be.*

The history of the cities of Western Europe is shot through with episodes of violence, fear, and revolution, episodes in which family honor, participation in the municipal council, or working conditions were at stake. Such conflicts opposed "magnate" and "popular" factions. In Italy they opposed actual political parties dominated by clans, and in the bigger cities of Flanders they turned into true class wars punctuated by massacres, exilings, and destruction. Such conflicts were frequent between 1250 and 1330, and they resulted everywhere in a defeat of the old rich land and an enlargement of oligarchies. A second wave of unrest of a more clearly social character (the *ciompi* in Florence and Siena, the *maillotins* in Paris, and so forth) battered the urban world in the late fourteenth century. The defeat of the lower orders did not put an end to the tensions, which were transformed into an occasional brief terror, here and there, but were more usually expressed in continual but muted, "atomized" conflicts difficult to distinguish from common delinquency in the documentation. Stones thrown at night through a master's windows, a creditor brutalized, a brawl between two rival groups of workers were easily ascribed to ordinary violence by the judges.

In other words, many city-dwellers, even if they lived through long and difficult periods of tension, escaped the horrors of riots and repression, but they all had to face an atmosphere of violence on an almost daily basis. There is little need to accumulate examples: in Florence, Venice, Paris, Lille, Dijon, Avignon, Tours, or Foix, the judicial archives reveal an impressive series of cold-blooded vendettas, of *chaudes mêlées* between individuals or groups settled with knives or iron-tipped sticks, and of rapes, often collective, that marked for life poor girls beaten and dragged from their rooms at night.

These violent acts were for the most part committed by youths or adult men, often of modest social condition, but who were indistinguishable from law-abiding citizens. . . .

Wine—drunkenness was often an excuse—does not explain everything, nor do the arms that everyone carried in spite of municipal ordinances. The example came from on high: even in Reims at the beginning of the fourteenth century, the judges were incapable of keeping clans from resolving their quarrels by means of arms. However, civic violence (executions, torture, forcing a criminal to run through the city streets as the crowd jeered and struck him) was offered as a spectacle, and the domestic moral code allowed blows. Justice, what is more, did not inspire belief; it was more dreaded than appreciated, and it was inefficient and costly. When he was scoffed at, the individual turned to immediate vengeance. He did so to safeguard his honor: it was in the name of honor that young men punished girls who, to their minds, transgressed its canons. Like violence, honor was a value widespread in urban societies: prominent citizens were called "honorable." There was no reputation without honor and no honor without authority. The rich man's wealth and friends lent support to his honor; the working man without wealth held his reputation to be an essential capital. . . .

Violence fostered anxiety. On occasion the notables denounced it, but they did not really seek to extirpate it (either in Venice or Dijon). For humble folk this fear added to other obsessions—of being abandoned amid general indifference, as with Dame Poverty, whom Jean de Meun described as covered with an old sack, "a bit apart from the others . . . crouched down and hunched over like a poor dog," sad, shamed, and unloved.

Solitude

Georges Duby

Whether in urban or rural areas, people of the High Middle Ages spent much of their everyday lives in the company of others. What we in our times think of as privacy was not quite the same in medieval society. Not only were living spaces more communal, but people were expected to work, play, and travel in groups. In the following selection A History of Private Life, *Georges Duby describes this crowded, communal society and the difficulties facing anyone seeking solitude.*

Consider: *How groups formed in various occupations and activities; how Duby analyzes private space; the problems facing an individual longing for solitude.*

People crowded together cheek by jowl, living in promiscuity, sometimes in the midst of a mob. In feudal residences there was no room for individual solitude, except perhaps in the moment of death. When people ventured outside the domestic enclosure, they did so in groups. No journey could be made by fewer than two people, and if it happened that they were not related, they bound themselves by rites of brotherhood, creating an artificial family that lasted as long as the journey required. By age seven, at which time young aristocratic males were considered persons of sex, they left the woman's world and embarked upon a life of adventure. Yet throughout their lives they remained surrounded, in the strong sense of the word—whether they were dedicated to the service of God and sent to study with a schoolmaster or joined a group of other young men in aping the gestures of a leader, their new father, whom they followed whenever he left his house to defend his rights by force of arms or force of words or to hunt in his forests. Their apprenticeship over, new knights received their arms as a group, a mob organized as a family. (Generally the lord's son was dubbed along with the sons of the vassals.) From that time forth the young knights were always together, linked in glory and in shame, vouching for and standing as hostage for one another. As a group, accompanied by servants and often by priests, they raced from tourney to tourney, court to court, skirmish to skirmish, displaying their loyalties by showing the colors or shouting the same rallying cry. The devotion of these young comrades enveloped their leader in an indispensable mantle of domestic familiarity, an itinerant household.

Thus, in feudal society, private space was divided, composed of two distinct areas: one fixed, enclosed, attached to the hearth; the other mobile, free to move through public

SOURCE: George Duby, "Solitude: Eleventh to Thirteenth Century," in *A History of Private Life,* vol. III, Philippe Aries and Georges Duby, eds. Cambridge, Mass.: Belknap Press of Harvard University Press, 1987, pp. 509–510.

space, yet embodying the same hierarchies and held together by the same controls. Within this mobile cell peace and order were maintained by a power whose mission was to organize a defense against the intrusion of the public authorities, for which purpose an invisible wall, as solid as the enclosure that surrounded the house, was erected against the outside world. This power enveloped and restrained the individuals of the household, subjecting them to a common discipline. Power meant constraint. And if private life meant secrecy, it was a secrecy shared by all members of the household, hence fragile and easily violated. If private life meant independence, it was independence of a collective sort. In the eleventh and twelfth centuries collective privacy did exist. But can we detect any signs of personal privacy within the collective privacy?

Feudal society was so granular in structure, composed of such compact curds, that any individual who attempted to remove himself from the close and omnipresent conviviality, to be alone, to construct his own private enclosure, to cultivate his garden, immediately became an object of either suspicion or admiration, regarded as either a rebel or a hero and in either case considered "foreign"—the antithesis of "private." The person who stood apart, even if his intention was not deliberately to commit evil, was inevitably destined to do so, for his very isolation made him more vulnerable to the Enemy's attacks. No one would run such a risk who was not deviant or possessed or mad; it was commonly believed that solitary wandering was a symptom of insanity. Men and women who traveled the roads without escort were believed to offer themselves up as prey, so it was legitimate to take everything they had. In any case, it was a pious work to place them back in some community, regardless of what they might say, to restore them by force to that clearly ordered and well-managed world where God intended them to be, a world composed of private enclosures and of the public spaces between them, through which people moved only in cortege.

Ecological Conditions and Demographic Change

David Herlihy

Most historians feel that the medieval expansion ended between 1300 and 1350 and that changes occurred that marked the following century as one of contraction, disruption, and decline. Traditionally, these changes have been analyzed from political, military, and religious perspectives. In the following selection David Herlihy of Harvard focuses on the economic aspects of this change, particularly the economic limitations that prevented the medieval expansion from continuing much beyond the thirteenth century.

> **Consider:** *Obstacles hindering economic expansion by 1300; the social and political effects that might have stemmed from these economic changes; other factors that might account for the end of the medieval expansion.*

Source: David Herlihy, "Ecological Conditions and Demographic Change," in *One Thousand Years: Western Europe in the Middle Ages*, ed. Richard L. DeMolen (Boston: Houghton Mifflin, 1974), p. 32.

Medieval expansion, however, never achieved a true breakthrough, never reached what some economists today term the stage of "takeoff," in which a built-in capacity for continuing growth is developed. By around 1300, certain obstacles were beginning to hinder economic expansion. One was the relative stagnation of technology. In spite of important technological discoveries that introduced the Middle Ages, peasants in 1300 were working the land much as their ancestors had several centuries before. However, technological stagnation alone does not seem to have imposed a rigid ceiling on growth. Paradoxically, many peasants in the late thirteenth century were not working the soil according to the best known and available methods. Their chief handicap was not lack of knowledge but lack of capital, for the best methods were based upon the effective use of cattle to supply both labor and manure. Insofar as we can judge, many small cultivators of the thirteenth century could not afford cattle and had to work their plots with their own unaided and inefficient efforts.

A second limitation upon expansion was the failure to develop institutions and values that would maintain appropriate levels of investment, especially in agriculture. In spite of the growth of cities, a large part of Europe's lands was controlled by military and clerical aristocracies, which were not likely to reinvest their profits received in rent. The great landlords were rather prone to spend their rents on conspicuous but economically barren forms of consumption such as manor houses, castles, churches, wars, the maintenance of a lavish style of living. They were also likely to demand from the towns money in loans for such unproductive expenditures.

A third limiting factor seems to have been the growing scarcity of resources, especially good land. As the best soils were taken under cultivation, the still growing population had to rely increasingly upon poorer, marginal lands, which required more effort and capital to assure a good return. The European economy was burdened by a growing saturation in the use of its readily available resources, and it had neither the technology nor the capital to improve its returns from what it possessed. In the opinion of many historians today, this saturation in the use of resources not only ended the economic advance of the central Middle Ages but precipitated a profound demographic and economic crisis in the fourteenth century.

Chapter Questions

1. Some historians have described the thirteenth century as the period in which medieval civilization attained a remarkable balance. In what ways was this period so balanced?

2. In what ways were the main characteristics of the thirteenth century simply a further extension of trends already evident during the eleventh and twelfth centuries? What new developments appeared during the thirteenth century?

3. What evidence does the chapter provide of the struggle for authority that persisted through this period?

CHAPTER ELEVEN

The Late Middle Ages

The fourteenth century and the first half of the fifteenth saw decline, disruption, and disintegration. This period, usually referred to as the Late Middle Ages, has been described in terms such as "the decline of the Middle Ages" and "the waning of the Middle Ages." Certain developments support these descriptions. Demographically, the population increase of the High Middle Ages was over by the end of the thirteenth century. During the following century population decreased significantly, due in great part to poor harvests, disease, and war. Geographically, European expansion temporarily ended. Religiously, the Church faced a series of problems: The papacy suffered from increasing conflict with powerful European monarchs; heretical movements spread; the Church itself became divided during the Great Schism; and the papacy was threatened by a revolt of its own high clergy in the Conciliar Movement. Economically, wages and prices varied greatly, as did the availability of labor and goods; this disrupted relations among various social groups. Politically, almost unending conflict led to an unusually intense period of wars, the most serious of which was the Hundred Years' War between England and France.

To illustrate the disruptive developments of the Late Middle Ages, the selections in this chapter concentrate on two specific topics: problems facing the Church and the mid-fourteenth-century plague. What was the nature of the Conciliar Movement, which threatened the pope's authority? How was the Church threatened by heresy? How did it deal with heresy? What were the social and psychological consequences of the plague? How was the plague related to religious views of Europeans? How did institutions react to the consequences of the plague?

Although this chapter views the Late Middle Ages largely as a period of disruption and decline, it was also a period of continuity. Many aspects of medieval civilization would continue for centuries, evolving only very slowly. To show both the continuity and the decline characteristic of this era, the nature of society in the Late Middle Ages and the psychological characteristics of the period are analyzed. How was this society organized? What were typical members of this society like? What were the attitudes toward women and marriage? How were psychological trends reflected by conceptions of death? What sorts of rebellions occurred?

In sum, the materials paint a picture in marked contrast to our image of the High Middle Ages. But while the decline during the Late Middle Ages was real, the same period witnessed an extraordinary social and cultural revival in Italy, which will be the concern of the next chapter.

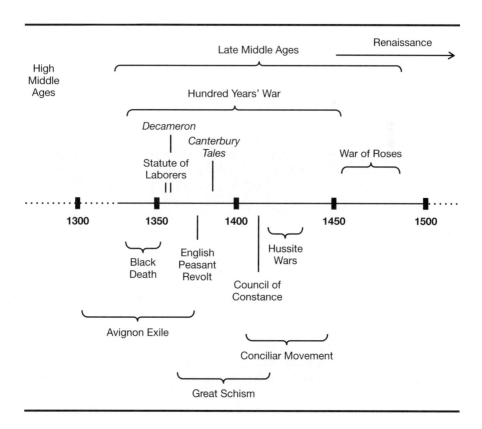

PRIMARY SOURCES

Attack on the Papacy: The Conciliar Movement

From 1378 to 1417 the Catholic Church was divided, with competing popes reigning simultane-
ously, each claiming authority. In an effort to end this schism, Church councils met at Pisa (1409)
and then at Constance (1414–1417). These councils constituted the high point of a developing
Conciliar Movement—an effort to place ultimate authority in the hands of a general Church
council and diminish the powers of the pope. The council at Pisa worsened the situation by in-
stalling a third pope, but at Constance the schism was ended with the election of a single pope,
Martin V. He and his successors repudiated the Conciliar Movement over the next few decades.
Yet the Conciliar Movement represented a strong current of opinion within the Church and re-
vealed the depth of the problems facing the Church. The following two documents are decrees
passed during the Council of Constance at the height of this movement.

Consider: *The intent of the Decree Sacrosancta; why the council felt it necessary also to*
pass the Decree Frequens; how the council justified its authority.

DECREE SACROSANCTA

In the name of the Holy and indivisible Trinity; of the Father, Son, and Holy Ghost.
Amen.

This holy synod of Constance, forming a general council for the extirpation of the present schism and the union and reformation, in head and members, of the church of God,
legitimately assembled in the Holy Ghost, to the praise of Omnipotent God, in order that
it may the more easily, safely, effectively and freely bring about the union and reformation
of the church of God, hereby determines, decrees, ordains and declares what follows:—

It first declares that this same council, legitimately assembled in the Holy Ghost,
forming a general council and representing the Catholic Church militant, has its power
immediately from Christ, and everyone, whatever his state or position, even if it be the
Papal dignity itself, is bound to obey it in all those things which pertain to the faith and
the healing of the said schism, and to the general reformation of the Church of God, in
head and members.

It further declares that anyone, whatever his condition, station or rank, even if it be the
Papal, who shall contumaciously refuse to obey the mandates, decrees, ordinances or instructions which have been, or shall be issued by this holy council, or by any other general council, legitimately summoned, which concern, or in any way relate to the above

SOURCE: From James Harvey Robinson, ed., "The Pre-Reformation Period," in *Translations and Reprints from*
the Original Sources of European History, vol. III, no. 6, ed. Department of History of the University of Pennsylvania (Philadelphia: University of Pennsylvania Press, 1898), pp. 30–31.

mentioned objects, shall, unless he repudiate his conduct, be subjected to condign penance and be suitably punished, having recourse, if necessary, to the other resources of the law.

°

DECREE FREQUENS

A frequent celebration of general councils is an especial means for cultivating the field of the Lord and effecting the destruction of briars, thorns, and thistles, to-wit, heresies, errors and schism, and of bringing forth a most abundant harvest. The neglect to summon these, fosters and develops all these evils, as may be plainly seen from a recollection of the past and a consideration of existing conditions. Therefore, by a perpetual edict, we sanction, decree, establish and ordain that general councils shall be celebrated in the following manner, so that the next one shall follow the close of this present council at the end of five years. The second shall follow the close of that, at the end of seven years and councils shall thereafter be celebrated every ten years in such places as the Pope shall be required to designate and assign, with the consent and approbation of the council, one month before the close of the council in question, or which, in his absence, the council itself shall designate. Thus, with a certain continuity, a council will always be either in session, or be expected at the expiration of a definite time.

Manual of the Inquisitor

Bernard Gui

Heresy, always a concern for the Church, had by the fourteenth century become such a serious problem that the Church turned to formal institutions such as the Inquisition to deal with it. One of the best-known and longest-lasting heretical movements was that of the Waldensians in southern France and northern Italy. Originally, they were followers of Peter Waldo, who pursued a life of piety and religious belief. The Waldensians were officially condemned in the thirteenth century but survived to be persecuted in the fourteenth century. The following is a selection from the Manual of the Inquisitor, *compiled by Bernard Gui, a Dominican monk and bishop who became a zealous inquisitor in southern France from 1307 to 1324.*

> **Consider:** *The main crimes of the Waldensians according to Gui; the nature of the threat posed by these crimes; the similarities and differences between the threats posed by this heresy and those of the Conciliar Movement.*

Disdain for ecclesiastical authority was and still is the prime heresy of the Waldenses. Excommunicated for this reason and delivered over to Satan, they have fallen into innumerable errors, and have blended the errors of earlier heretics with their own concoctions.

SOURCE: Bernard Gui, *Manual of the Inquisitor,* in *Introduction to Contemporary Civilization in the West,* vol. I, 3d ed., ed. Contemporary Civilization Staff of Columbia College, Columbia University (New York: Columbia University Press, 1960), pp. 198–202, 204. Reprinted by permission.

The misled believers and sacrilegious masters of this sect hold and teach that they are in no way subject to the lord Pope or Roman Pontiff, or to the other prelates of the Roman Church, and that the latter persecute and condemn them unjustly and improperly. Moreover, they declare that they cannot be excommunicated by this Roman Pontiff and these prelates, and that obedience is owed to none of them when they order and summon the followers and masters of the said sect to abandon or abjure this sect, although this sect be condemned as heretical by the Roman Church. . . .

Moreover, the sect does not accept canonical authority, or the decretals or constitutions of the Sovereign Pontiff, any more than the regulations concerning fasts and the observance of the feasts or the decrees of the Fathers. Straying from the straight road, they recognize no authority therein, scorn them, reject and condemn them.

Moreover, the followers of the sect are even more perniciously mistaken concerning the sacrament of penance and the power of the keys. They declare they have received—this is their doctrine and their teaching—from God and none other, like the apostles who held it of Christ, the power of hearing the confessions of men and women who desire to confess to them, of granting them absolution and of prescribing penance. Thus they hear confessions, grant absolution and prescribe penance, although they have not been ordained as priests or clerics by a bishop of the Roman Church and although they are just laymen. They in no way claim to hold this power from the Roman Church, on the contrary, they deny it; and in fact, they hold it neither from God nor from His Church, since they have been cast out from the Church by this very Church, outside which there is neither true penance nor salvation.

Moreover, this same sect hold up to ridicule the indulgences established and granted by the prelates of the Church, saying they are worthless.

Moreover, they are in error with respect to the sacrament of the Eucharist. They claim, not publicly but secretly, that in the sacrament of the altar the bread and wine do not become body and blood of Christ when the priest who celebrates or consecrates is a sinner; and by sinner they mean any man who does not belong to their sect. Moreover, they claim, on the contrary, that any upright man, even a layman, without having received priestly ordination from the hands of a Catholic bishop, may consecrate the body and blood of Christ, provided he be of their sect. They believe that women too can do this, subject to the same condition. Thus they hold that any holy man is a priest.

The Rebellions of 1381

Sir John Froissart

The Late Middle Ages were marked by several rebellions by the lower classes. One of the most important of these was the 1381 rebellion of peasants and artisans in England. Led by John Ball, Wat Tyler, and Jack Straw, the rebellion threatened the upper classes before it was crushed and

SOURCE: Sir John Froissart, *Chronicles of England, France, Spain*, vol. I, trans. Thomas Johnes (New York: The Colonial Press, 1904), pp. 211–215.

its leaders were executed. Events of the rebellion are described in the following selection by Sir John Froissart (1333?–1400?), a French chronicler of the Hundred Years' War between England and France.

> **Consider:** *Ways John Ball appealed to the poor; how the rebels gained strength; the discontents of the poor; how rebellion might spread throughout England and elsewhere.*

While these conferences were going forward there happened great commotions among the lower orders in England, by which that country was nearly ruined. In order that this disastrous rebellion may serve as an example to mankind, I will speak of all that was done from the information I had at the time. It is customary in England, as well as in several other countries, for the nobility to have great privileges over the commonalty; that is to say, the lower orders are bound by law to plough the lands of the gentry, to harvest their grain, to carry it home to the barn, to thrash and winnow it; they are also bound to harvest and carry home the hay. All these services the prelates and gentlemen exact of their inferiors; and in the counties of Kent, Essex, Sussex, and Bedford, these services are more oppressive than in other parts of the kingdom. In consequence of this the evil disposed in these districts began to murmur, saying, that in the beginning of the world there were no slaves, and that no one ought to be treated as such, unless he had committed treason against his lord, as Lucifer did against God; but they had done no such thing, for they were neither angels nor spirits, but men formed after the same likeness as these lords who treated them as beasts. This they would bear no longer; they were determined to be free, and if they labored or did any work, they would be paid for it. A crazy priest in the country of Kent, called John Ball, who for his absurd preaching had thrice been confined in prison by the Archbishop of Canterbury, was greatly instrumental in exciting these rebellious ideas. Every Sunday after mass, as the people were coming out of church, this John Ball was accustomed to assemble a crowd around him in the marketplace and preach to them. On such occasions he would say, "My good friends, matters cannot go on well in England until all things shall be in common; when there shall be neither vassals nor lords; when the lords shall be no more masters than ourselves. How ill they behave to us! For what reason do they thus hold us in bondage? Are we not all descended from the same parents, Adam and Eve? And what can they show, or what reason can they give, why they should be more masters than ourselves? They are clothed in velvet and rich stuffs, ornamented with ermine and other furs, while we are forced to wear poor clothing. They have wines, spices, and fine bread, while we have only rye and the refuse of the straw; and when we drink it must be water. They have handsome seats and manors, while we must brave the wind and rain in our labors in the field: and it is by our labor they have wherewith to support their pomp. We are called slaves, and if we do not perform our service we are beaten, and we have no sovereign to whom we can complain or who would be willing to hear us. Let us go to the King and remonstrate with him; he is young, and from him we may obtain a favorable answer, and if not we must ourselves seek to amend our condition."

With such language as this did John Ball harangue the people of his village every Sunday after mass. The archbishop, on being informed of it, had him arrested and imprisoned for two or three months by way of punishment; but the moment he was out of prison, he returned to his former course. Many in the city of London, envious of the rich and noble, having heard of John Ball's preaching, said among themselves that the country was badly governed, and that the nobility had seized upon all the gold and silver. These wicked Londoners, therefore, began to assemble in parties, and to show signs of rebellion; they also invited all those who held like opinions in the adjoining counties to come to London, telling them that they would find the town open to them and the commonalty of the same way of thinking as themselves, and that they would so press the King that there should no longer be a slave in England.

By this means the men of Kent, Essex, Sussex, Bedford, and the adjoining counties, in number about 60,000, were brought to London, under command of Wat Tyler, Jack Straw, and John Ball. . . . At Canterbury the rebels entered the Church of St. Thomas, where they did much damage; they also pillaged the apartments of the archbishop, saying as they were carrying off the different articles, "The Chancellor of England has had this piece of furniture very cheap; he must now give us an account of his revenues, and of the large sums which he has levied since the coronation of the King." After this they plundered the abbey of St. Vincent, and then, leaving Canterbury, took the road toward Rochester. As they passed they collected people from the villages right and left, and on they went like a tempest, destroying all the houses belonging to attorneys, King's proctors, and the archbishop, which came in their way. At Rochester they met with the same welcome as at Canterbury, for all the people were anxious to join them. . . .

In other countries of England the rebels acted in a similar manner, and several great lords and knights, such as the Lord Manley, Sir Stephen Hales, and Sir Thomas Cossington, were compelled to march with them. Now observe how fortunately matters turned out, for had these scoundrels succeeded in their intentions, all the nobility of England would have been destroyed; and after such success as this the people of other nations would have rebelled also, taking example from those of Ghent and Flanders, who at the time were in actual rebellion against their lord; the Parisians, indeed, the same year acted in a somewhat similar manner; upward of 20,000 of them armed themselves with leaden maces and caused a rebellion. . . .

The Decameron:
The Plague in Florence

Giovanni Boccaccio

In the middle of the fourteenth century, a devastating plague swept across Europe. In some cities almost half of the population was lost, and for those who were left alive the effects were long-lasting. One survivor was Giovanni Boccaccio (1313–1375), a well-known humanist of the

SOURCE: Giovanni Boccaccio, *The Decameron*, in *Stories of Boccaccio*, trans. John Payne (London: Bibliophilist Library, 1903), pp. 1–6.

Italian Renaissance. His best-known work is The Decameron, *written between 1348 and 1353 when the plague struck Florence. Boccaccio initiated the work with a description of the plague, an excerpt of which follows.*

> **Consider:** *How people reacted to the plague; the general understanding of the cause of the plague and how it spread.*

In the year then of our Lord 1348, there happened at Florence, the finest city in all Italy, a most terrible plague; which, whether owing to the influence of the planets, or that it was sent from God as a just punishment for our sins, had broken out some years before in the Levant, and after passing from place to place, and making incredible havoc all the way, had now reached the west. There, spite of all the means that art and human foresight could suggest, such as keeping the city clear from filth, the exclusion of all suspected persons, and the publication of copious instructions for the preservation of health; and notwithstanding manifold humble supplications offered to God in processions and otherwise; it began to show itself in the spring of the aforesaid year, in a sad and wonderful manner. Unlike what had been seen in the east, where bleeding from the nose is the fatal prognostic, here there appeared certain tumours in the groin or under the armpits, some as big as a small apple, others as an egg; and afterwards purple spots in most parts of the body; in some cases large and but few in number, in others smaller and more numerous—both sorts the usual messengers of death. To the cure of this malady, neither medical knowledge nor the power of drugs was of any effect; whether because the disease was in its own nature mortal, or that the physicians (the number of whom, taking quacks and women pretenders into the account, was grown very great) could form no just idea of the cause, nor consequently devise a true method of cure; whichever was the reason, few escaped; but nearly all died the third day from the first appearance of the symptoms, some sooner, some later, without any fever or accessory symptoms. What gave the more virulence to this plague, was that, by being communicated from the sick to the hale, it spread daily, like fire when it comes in contact with large masses of combustibles. Nor was it caught only by conversing with, or coming near the sick, but even by touching their clothes, or anything that they had before touched. . . .

These facts, and others of the like sort, occasioned various fears and devices amongst those who survived, all tending to the same uncharitable and cruel end; which was, to avoid the sick, and every thing that had been near them, expecting by that means to save themselves. And some holding it best to live temperately, and to avoid excesses of all kinds, made parties, and shut themselves up from the rest of the world; eating and drinking moderately of the best, and diverting themselves with music, and such other entertainments as they might have within doors; never listening to anything from without, to make them uneasy. Others maintained free living to be a better preservative, and would baulk no passion or appetite they wished to gratify, drinking and revelling incessantly from tavern to tavern, or in private houses (which were frequently found deserted by the owners, and therefore common to every one), yet strenuously avoiding, with all this brutal indulgence, to come near the infected. And such, at that time, was the public distress, that the laws, human and divine, were no more regarded; for the officers, to put them in force, being either dead, sick, or in want of persons to assist them, every one did just as he pleased. A third sort of people chose a method between these two: not confining themselves to rules of diet like the former, and yet avoiding the intemperance of the latter; but eating and drinking what their appetites required, they walked everywhere with odours and nosegays to smell to; as holding it best to corroborate the brain: for the whole atmosphere seemed to them tainted with the stench of dead bodies, arising partly from the distemper itself, and partly from the fermenting of the medicines within them. Others with less humanity, but perchance, as they supposed, with more security from danger, decided that the only remedy for the pestilence was to avoid it: persuaded, therefore, of this, and taking care for themselves only, men and women in great numbers left the city, their houses, relations, and effects, and fled into the country; as if the wrath of God had been restrained to visit those only within the walls of the city; or else concluding, that more ought to stay in a place thus doomed to destruction.

Thus divided as they were in their views, neither did all die, nor all escape; but falling sick indifferently, as well those of one as of another opinion; they who first set the example by forsaking others, now languished themselves without pity. I pass over the little regard that citizens and relations showed to each other; for their terror was such, that a brother even fled from his brother, a wife from her husband, and, what is more uncommon, a parent from his own child. Hence numbers that fell sick could have no help but what the charity of friends, who were very few, or the avarice of servants supplied; and even these were scarce and at extravagant wages, and so little used to the business that they were fit only to reach what was called for, and observe when their employer died; and this desire of getting money often cost them their lives. . . .

Not to dwell upon every particular of our misery, I shall observe, that it fared no better with the adjacent country; for, to omit the different boroughs about us, which presented the same view in miniature with the city, you might see the poor distressed labourers, with their families, without either the aid of physicians, or help of servants, languishing on the highways, in the fields, and in their own houses, and dying rather like cattle than human creatures. The consequence was that, growing dissolute in their manners like the citizens, and careless of everything, as supposing every day to be their last, their thoughts were not so much employed how to improve, as how to use their substance for their present support. The oxen, asses, sheep, goats, swine, and the dogs themselves, ever faithful to their masters, being driven from their own homes, were left to roam at will about the fields, and among the standing corn, which no one cared to gather, or even to reap; and many times, after they had filled themselves in the day, the animals would return of their own accord like rational creatures at night.

What can I say more, if I return to the city? unless that such was the cruelty of Heaven, and perhaps of men, that between March and July following, according to authentic reckonings, upwards of a hundred thousand souls perished in the city only; whereas, before that calamity, it was not supposed to have contained so many inhabitants. What magnificent dwellings, what noble palaces were then depopulated to the last inhabitant! what families became extinct! what riches and vast possessions were left, and no known heir to inherit them! what numbers of both sexes, in the prime and vigour of youth, whom in the morning neither Galen, Hippocrates, nor Aesculapius himself, would have denied to be in perfect health, breakfasted in the morning with their living friends, and supped at night with their departed friends in the other world!

Statute of Laborers

King Edward III

The Black Death that struck Florence between 1347 and 1350 came to England, causing a loss of lives so severe that there was an almost immediate shortage of laborers. Under these conditions surviving laborers could demand higher wages and apparently did. This hurt the powerful commercial and landed classes, who turned for help to government authorities. One response was the Statute of Laborers (1351), issued by King Edward III and directed against changes in prices and wages. An excerpt of this statute follows.

> **Consider:** *The economic and social consequences of the plague in England; the king's response to this economic problem; the standards used to evaluate proper wages.*

The King to the sheriff of Kent, greeting: Because a great part of the people, and especially of workmen and servants, have lately died in the pestilence, many seeing the necessity of masters and great scarcity of servants, will not serve unless they may receive excessive wages, and others preferring to beg in idleness rather than by labor to get their living; we, considering the grievous incommodities which of the lack especially of ploughmen and such laborers may hereafter come, have upon deliberation and treaty with the prelates and the nobles and learned men assisting us, with their unanimous counsel ordained:

That every man and woman of our realm of England, of what condition he be, free or bond, able in body, and within the age of sixty years, not living in merchandize, nor exercising any craft, nor having of his own whereof he may live, nor land of his own about whose tillage he may occupy himself, and not serving any other; if he be required to serve in suitable service, his estate considered, he shall be bound to serve him which shall so require him; and take only the wages, livery, meed, or salary which were accustomed to be given in the places where he oweth to serve, the twentieth year of our reign of England, or five or six other common years next before.

If any reaper, mower, or other workman or servant, of what estate or condition that he be, retained in any man's service, do depart from the said service without reasonable cause or license, before the term agreed, he shall have pain of imprisonment; and no one, under the same penalty, shall presume to receive or retain such a one in his service.

No one, moreover, shall pay or promise to pay to any one more wages, liveries, meed, or salary than was accustomed, as is before said. . . .

SOURCE: Edward P. Cheyney, ed., "England in the Time of Wycliffe," in *Translations and Reprints from the Original Sources of European History*, vol. II, no. 5, ed. Department of History of the University of Pennsylvania (Philadelphia: University of Pennsylvania Press, 1898), pp. 3–4.

The Canterbury Tales

Geoffrey Chaucer

One of the best literary descriptions of representative individuals during the Late Middle Ages comes from Geoffrey Chaucer's Canterbury Tales. *Written during the last quarter of the four-teenth century by this English poet, soldier, politician, and diplomat, it recounts the tales told by a group of imaginary English pilgrims. In the prologue, excerpted here, Chaucer presents a somewhat stereotypical and subtly sarcastic image of people representative of a medieval world already on the wane.*

> **Consider:** *The various roles these people were supposed to play in medieval society according to this document; the extent to which this is both an accurate and a distorted source of medieval history.*

The KNIGHT was a very distinguished man. From the beginning of his career he had loved chivalry, loyalty, honourable dealing, generosity, and good breeding. He had fought bravely in the king's service, beside which he had travelled further than most men in hea-then as well as in Christian lands. Wherever he went he was honoured for his valour. . . .

He was always outstandingly successful; yet though distinguished he was prudent, and his bearing as modest as a maid's. In his whole life he never spoke discourteously to any kind of man. He was a true and perfect noble knight. But, speaking of his equipment, his horses were good, yet he was not gaily dressed. He wore a tunic of thick cotton cloth, rust-marked from his coat of mail; for he had just come back from his travels and was making his pilgrimage to render thanks. . . .

There was also a NUN, a Prioress, who smiled in an unaffected and quiet way; . . . At table she showed her good breeding at every point: she never let a crumb fall from her mouth or wetted her fingers by dipping them too deeply into the sauce; and when she lifted the food to her lips she took care not to spill a single drop upon her breast. Eti-quette was her passion. So scrupulously did she wipe her upper lip that no spot of grease was to be seen in her cup after she had drunk from it; and when she ate she reached daintily for her food. Indeed she was most gay, pleasant and friendly. She took pains to imitate courtly behaviour and cultivate a dignified bearing so as to be thought a person deserving of respect. Speaking of her sensibility, she was so tender-hearted and compas-sionate that she would weep whenever she saw a mouse caught in a trap, especially if it were bleeding or dead. . . .

With her she had another NUN, her chaplain and three PRIESTS.

There was a remarkable fine-looking MONK, who acted as estate-steward to his monastery and loved hunting: a manly man, well fitted to be an abbot. He kept plenty of fine horses in his stable, and when he went out riding people could hear the bells on his bridle jingling in the whistling wind as clear and loud as the chapel bell of the small convent of which he was the head. Because the Rule of St Maur or of St Benedict was

---

SOURCE: Geoffrey Chaucer, *The Canterbury Tales,* trans. David Wright (New York: Random House, 1964), pp. 3–8, 11–12. Copyright © 1964 by David Wright. Reprinted by permission of Literistic, Ltd.

old-fashioned and somewhat strict, this Monk neglected the old precepts and followed the modern custom. He did not give two pins for the text which says hunters cannot be holy men, or that a monk who is heedless of his Rule—that is to say a monk out of his cloister—is like a fish out of water. In his view this saying was not worth a bean; and I told him his opinion was sound. Why should he study and addle his wits with everlasting poring over a book in cloisters, or work with his hands, or toil as St Augustine commanded? How is the world to be served? Let St Augustine keep his hard labour for himself! Therefore the Monk, whose whole pleasure lay in riding and the hunting of the hare (over which he spared no expense) remained a hard rider and kept greyhounds swift as birds. . . .

Next there was a MERCHANT with a forked beard who rode seated on a high saddle, wearing a many-coloured dress, boots fastened with neat handsome clasps, and upon his head a Flanders beaver hat. He gave out his opinions with great pomposity and never stopped talking about the increase of his profits. In his view the high seas between Harwich and Holland should be cleared of pirates at all costs. He was an expert at the exchange of currency. This worthy citizen used his head to the best advantage, conducting his money-lending and other financial transactions in a dignified manner; none guessed he was in debt. He was really a most estimable man; but to tell the truth his name escapes me. . . .

With us there was a good religious man, a poor PARSON, but rich in holy thoughts and acts. He was also a learned man, a scholar, who truly preached Christ's Gospel and taught his parishioners devoutly. Benign, hardworking, and patient in adversity—as had often been put to the test—he was loath to excommunicate those who failed to pay their tithes. To tell the truth he would rather give to the poor of his parish what had been offered him by the rich, or from his own pocket; for he managed to live on very little. Wide as was his parish, with houses few and far between, neither rain nor thunder nor sickness nor misfortune stopped him from going on foot, staff in hand, to visit his most distant parishioners, high or low. To his flock he set this noble example: first he practised, then he preached. . . . He never looked for ceremony and deference, nor was his conscience of the over-scrupulous and specious sort. He taught the Gospel of Christ and His twelve apostles: but first he followed it himself.

The Goodman of Paris: Instructions on Being a Good Wife

Sources on the history of women during the Late Middle Ages are not abundant, and only recently have historians engaged in a fuller search for them. An exception is the relatively well known Goodman of Paris. *Written in the form of a letter by a Parisian merchant to his wife, it was an idealized manual of the duties of a wealthy wife from the point of view of an anonymous*

SOURCE: Eileen Power, trans., *The Goodman of Paris* (London: Routledge & Kegan Paul, 1928), pp. 43–46. Reprinted by permission.

merchant. In the following excerpt from this late-fourteenth-century work, the author introduces and outlines what he will be discussing.

> **Consider:** *The position and role of women at this time according to this document; the purposes of marriage according to this author.*

THE FIRST SECTION

The first section of the three is necessary to gain the love of God and the salvation of your soul, and also to win the love of your husband and to give you in this world that peace which should be in marriage. And because these two things, namely the salvation of your soul and the comfort of your husband, be the two things most chiefly necessary, therefore are they here placed first. And this first section contains nine articles.

The first article speaketh of worshipping and thanking our Saviour and his Blessed Mother at your waking and your rising, and of apparelling yourself seemingly.

The second article is of fit companions, and of going to Church, and of choosing your place, of wise behaviour, of hearing mass and of making confession.

The third article is that you should love God and his Blessed Mother and serve them continually and set and keep yourself in their grace.

The fourth article is that you should dwell in continence and chastity, after the ensample of Susanna, of Lucrece, and others.

The fifth article is that you should love your husband (whether myself or another) after the ensample of Sarah, Rebecca and Rachel.

The sixth article is that you should be humble and obedient to him after the ensample of Griselda, of the woman who would not rescue her husband from drowning, and of the Mother of God who answered "fiat" etc., of Lucifer, of the *puys*, of the bailly of Tournay, of the monks and the husbands, of madame d'Andresel, of Chaumont and of the Roman woman.

The seventh that you be careful and heedful of his person.

The eighth that you be silent in hiding his secrets, after the ensample of Papirius, of the woman who laid eight eggs, of the Venetian woman, of the woman who returned from St James (of Compestollo), and of the advocate.

The ninth and last article showeth that if your husband try to act foolishly or so acteth, you must wisely and humbly withdraw him therefrom, like unto Melibeus and dame Jehanne la Quentine.

THE SECOND SECTION

The second section is necessary to increase the profit of the household, gain friends and save one's possessions; to succour and aid oneself against the ill fortunes of age to come, and it contains six [*sic*] articles.

The first article is that you have care of your household, with diligence and perseverence and regard for work; take pains to find pleasure therein and I will do likewise on my part, and so shall we reach the castle whereof it is spoken.

The second article is that at the least you take pleasure and have some little skill in the care and cultivation of a garden, grafting in due season and keeping roses in winter.

The third article is that you know how to choose varlets, doorkeepers, handymen or other strong folk to perform the heavy work that from hour to hour must be done, and likewise labourers etc. And also tailers, shoemakers, bakers, pastry-makers, etc. And in particular how to set the household varlets and chambermaids to work, to sift and winnow grain, clean dresses, air and dry, and how to order your folk to take thought for the sheep and horses and to keep and amend wines.

The fourth article is that you, as sovereign mistress of your house, know how to order dinners, suppers, dishes and courses, and be wise in that which concerns the butcher and the poulterer, and have knowledge of spices.

The fifth article is that you know how to order, ordain, devise and have made all manner of pottages, civeys, sauces and all other meats, and the same for sick folk.

THE THIRD SECTION

The third section tells of games and amusements that be pleasant enough to keep you in countenance and give you something to talk about in company, and contains three articles.

The first article is all concerned with amusing questions, which be shown forth and answered in strange fashion by the hazard of dice and by rooks and kings.

The second article is to know how to feed and fly the falcon.

The third article tells of certain other riddles concerning counting and numbering, which be subtle to find out and guess.

VISUAL SOURCES

The Church Besieged

Some of the problems facing the Church and its sense of being besieged by evil forces are illustrated in this fifteenth-century manuscript illumination (photo 11-1). In the center stands the pope, flanked by Church officials trying to defend the Church, symbolized as a medieval fortress. The attackers in the foreground are heretics, as indicated by blindness that represents their inability to see the truth. They are flanked by attacking women who represent various cardinal sins.

> **Consider:** *The problems facing the Church and the appropriate cures according to this illumination; any connections between this illumination and the documents on the Conciliar Movement and heresy; how this illumination reveals attitudes toward women.*

Photo 11-1

Bibliothèque Nationale, Paris

The Triumph of Death

With war, famine, and especially plague striking fourteenth- and fifteenth-century Europe, death became a common theme of art. Typically, the plague was viewed as God's punishment for human sins, and thus only the Church might do something about the plague. Yet religion and everything else seemed impotent against death. This is shown in the numerous illustrations focusing on the theme of death. The engraving shown in photo 11-2 of The Triumph of Death, *from Petrarch's* Trionfi, *was made by a Venetian artist between 1470 and 1480. Here king, clergy, and commoners all fall helplessly under Death's cart. The souls of the dead are taken either by angels, on the upper left, or devils, on the upper right.*

> **Consider:** *Attitudes toward death reflected by such popular scenes; any ways these scenes reflect attitudes similar to those revealed by Boccaccio.*

Photo 11-2

British Museum, London

Unrest in the
Late Middle Ages

This map (map 11-1) gives some idea of the geographic extent of the social and religious unrest in fourteenth-century Europe. England was affected by a combination of urban and rural revolts as well as religious heresy. Their geographic locations suggest that the revolts and the heresy may

Map 11-1   Social and Religious Unrest in Fourteenth-Century Europe

have been connected. What is not shown on this map would also add to the picture of turmoil and unrest: the numerous political and military disturbances, the religious divisions of the Great Schism (1378–1417), the spread of the plague, and the actual disappearance of settlements founded in the three preceding centuries.

> **Consider:** *Connections among political disturbances, religious divisions, plagues, and population loss that could be revealed by maps.*

Food and Crime

Chart 11-1 provides another indication of the disruptions affecting Europe in the fourteenth century. Here the rise and fall in the price of wheat and the number of crimes between 1300 and 1350 in Norfolk, England, are compared. Fluctuations in food supplies are thus revealed, as well as clear connections between the price of wheat and the number of crimes committed.

> **Consider:** *How the information in this chart might relate to social, political, or even religious unrest.*

Chart 11-1   Crime and the Price of Wheat in Fourteenth-Century Norfolk, England

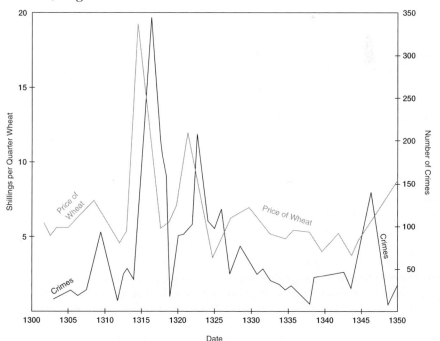

SECONDARY SOURCES

The Crisis of the Late Middle Ages

Francis Oakley

Most historians agree that during the fourteenth and fifteenth centuries, medieval civilization suffered a crisis. What are less clear are the exact nature of that crisis and its causes. In the following selection Francis Oakley focuses on problems within the Church, wars, and economic difficulties as being the core of the crisis of the Late Middle Ages.

Consider: *Whether the problems within the Church should be considered causes or symptoms of the general crisis; the social consequences of wars and economic depression.*

One of the most persistent features of ecclesiastical life from the early fourteenth century onward had been the extension once more of royal or princely control over the local churches. In ways subtle and not so subtle the work of the Gregorian reformers was being undone, and rulers were moved increasingly to assert their sovereign jurisdiction over all groups and institutions—clergy and churches included—within the territorial boundaries of their states. By the early fifteenth century the kings of France and England, in particular, had become adept at the art of marshaling national antipapal feeling in order to bring pressure on the papacy to concede them a handsome share of the taxes levied on their national churches and of the benefices or ecclesiastical positions belonging thereto. Given the difficulties that the Avignonese popes and the popes of the schism had had to face, they had had little choice but to yield to such diplomatic blackmail, even though by so doing they had committed the church piecemeal to a revolution that would ultimately leave to their successors nothing more than a theoretically supreme authority, the substance of power having passed in fact into the hands of kings, princes, and rulers of city-states like Venice. . . .

Historians have frequently chosen to take this transformation of the church and the accompanying decline of papal fortunes as symptomatic of a more profound crisis in the very soul of medieval civilization itself. It is easy enough to understand why they should have been tempted to do so. The outbreak in 1296 of the war between France and England, which had led so rapidly to the disastrous confrontation with Boniface VIII, had marked the end of a comparatively peaceful era and the beginning of the prolonged struggle between the two major European powers, which, punctuated with intermittent truces and periods of peace, was to drag on well into the fifteenth century. While it lasted it caused a great deal of devastation in France and sponsored in that country a recrudescence of the aristocratic feuds and rival private armies characteristic of the an-archic early phase of feudalism. A similar growth of what has been called "bastard feudalism" occurred in England during the dynastic conflicts between the Yorkist and Lancastrian claimants to the throne which broke out in 1450 after the end of the war with France and which have gone down in history as the "Wars of the Roses." The four-teenth and fifteenth centuries marked, then, at best a pause in the development of the English and French states and at worst a positive setback. Certainly, they witnessed the breakdown of public order and the growth of violence to a degree that would have been unimaginable in the late thirteenth century.

To the social dislocations caused by invasion and civil war must also be added the tribulations consequent to the ending in the early fourteenth century of the great eco-nomic boom that had gathered force in the tenth century, accelerated in the eleventh and twelfth centuries, and reached its peak in the thirteenth. Even before the advent of the Black Death (1348–50), population expansion had ceased, serious and widespread famines had reappeared, and the European economy had begun to slide into a financial crisis and a depression that was to last until the latter part of the fifteenth century and even, in some sectors, into the sixteenth.

The Black Death: A Socioeconomic Perspective

Millard Meiss

Historians have argued that the Black Death, along with other mid-fourteenth-century develop-ments, led to important economic and social changes that characterized the Late Middle Ages. Most concretely, historians point to increasing wages and greater opportunities for social mobil-ity as directly stimulated by the demographic ravages of the plague. In the following selection Millard Meiss makes this interpretation in examining the consequences of the plague in Florence and Siena.

> **Consider:** *The economic and social consequences of the Black Death in northern Italy; the groups that benefited most after the Black Death, and why; the ways in which this inter-pretation is supported by Boccaccio's account.*

In the immediate wake of the Black Death we hear of an unparalleled abundance of food and goods, and of a wild, irresponsible life of pleasure. Agnolo di Tura writes that in Siena "everyone tended to enjoy eating and drinking, hunting, hawking, and gaming," and Matteo Villani laments similar behavior in Florence. . . .

This extraordinary condition of plenty did not, of course, last very long. For most peo-ple the frenzied search for immediate gratification, characteristic of the survivors of

SOURCE: From Meiss, Millard, *Painting in Florence and Sienna After the Black Death*, pp. 67–69. Copyright © 1978 by Princeton University Press. Reprinted by permission of Princeton University Press.

calamities, was likewise short-lived. Throughout the subsequent decades, however, we continue to hear of an exceptional difference to accepted patterns of behavior and to institutional regulations, especially among the mendicant friars. It seems, as we shall see, that the plague tended to promote an unconventional, irresponsible, or self-indulgent life, on the one hand, and a more intense piety or religious excitement, on the other. Villani tells us, in his very next sentences, of the more lasting consequences of the epidemic:

"Men thought that, through the death of so many people, there would be abundance of all produce of the land; yet, on the contrary, by reason of men's ingratitude, everything came to unwonted scarcity and remained long thus; . . . most commodities were more costly, by twice or more, than before the plague. And the price of labor, and the products of every trade and craft, rose in disorderly fashion beyond the double. Lawsuits and disputes and quarrels and riots arose everywhere among citizens in every land, by reason of legacies and successions; . . . Wars and divers scandals arose throughout the world, contrary to men's expectation."

Conditions were similar in Siena. Prices rose to unprecedented levels. The economy of both Florence and Siena was further disrupted during these years by the defection of almost all the dependent towns within the little empire of each city. These towns seized as an opportunity for revolt the fall of the powerful Florentine oligarchy in 1343, and the Sienese in 1355. The two cities, greatly weakened, and governed by groups that pursued a less aggressive foreign policy, made little attempt to win them back.

The small towns and the countryside around the two cities were not decimated so severely by the epidemic, but the people in these regions felt the consequences of it in another way. Several armies of mercenaries of the sort that all the large states had come to employ in the fourteenth century took advantage of the weakness of the cities. . . .

The ravages of the mercenary companies accelerated a great wave of immigration from the smaller towns and farms into the cities that had been initiated by the Black Death. Most of the newcomers were recruits for the woolen industry, who were attracted by relatively high wages. But the mortality offered exceptional opportunities also for notaries, jurists, physicians, and craftsmen. In both Florence and Siena the laws controlling immigration were relaxed, and special privileges, a rapid grant of citizenship, or exemption from taxes were offered to badly needed artisans or professional men, such as physicians. . . .

In addition to bringing into the city great numbers of people from the surrounding towns and country, the Black Death affected the character of Florentine society in still another way. Through irregular inheritance and other exceptional circumstances, a class of *nouveaux riches* arose in the town and also in decimated Siena. Their wealth was accentuated by the impoverishment of many of the older families, such as the Bardi and the Peruzzi, who had lost their fortunes in the financial collapse. In both cities, too, many tradesmen and artisans were enriched to a degree unusual for the *popolo minuto*. Scaramella sees as one of the major conflicts of the time the struggle between the old families and this *gente nuova*. Outcries against both foreigners and the newly rich, never lacking in the two cities, increased in volume and violence. Antagonism to "the aliens and the ignorant" coalesced with antagonism to the new municipal regime; the government, it was said, had been captured by them.

A Psychological Perspective
of the Black Death

William L. Langer

Most historians have long been reluctant to view historical developments from a psychological perspective. In recent decades historians have been challenged to apply psychological insights to history. In 1957 William L. Langer, then president of the American Historical Association, issued such a challenge to historians in his presidential address to the annual convention. In the following selection from that address, Langer suggests how modern psychology might be used to interpret the Black Death and related developments.

> **Consider:** *How a psychologist might explain various behaviors related to the Black Death; how* The Triumph of Death *fits with this interpretation.*

The Black Death was worse than anything experienced prior to that time and was, in all probability, the greatest single disaster that has ever befallen European mankind. In most localities a third or even a half of the population was lost within the space of a few months, and it is important to remember that the great visitation of 1348–1349 was only the beginning of a period of pandemic disease with a continuing frightful drain of population. . . .

At news of the approach of the disease a haunting terror seizes the population, in the Middle Ages leading on the one hand to great upsurges of repentance in the form of flagellant processions and on the other to a mad search for scapegoats, eventuating in large-scale pogroms of the Jews. The most striking feature of such visitations has always been the precipitate flight from the cities, in which not only the wealthier classes but also town officials, professors and teachers, clergy, and even physicians took part. The majority of the population, taking the disaster as an expression of God's wrath, devoted itself to penitential exercises, to merciful occupations, and to such good works as the repair of churches and the founding of religious houses. On the other hand, the horror and confusion in many places brought general demoralization and social breakdown. Criminal elements were quick to take over, looting the deserted houses and even murdering the sick in order to rob them of their jewels. Many, despairing of the goodness and mercy of God, gave themselves over to riotous living, resolved, as Thucydides says, "to get out of life the pleasures which could be had speedily and which would satisfy their lusts, regarding their bodies and their wealth alike as transitory." Drunkenness and sexual immorality were the order of the day. "In one house," reported an observer of the London plague of 1665, "you might hear them roaring under the pangs of death, in the next tippling, whoring and belching out blasphemies against God." . . .

The age was marked, as all admit, by a mood of misery, depression, and anxiety, and by a general sense of impending doom. Numerous writers in widely varying fields have

SOURCE: William L. Langer, "The Next Assignment," *The American Historical Review*, vol. LXIII, no. 2 (January 1958), pp. 292–293, 295–298. Reprinted by permission.

commented on the morbid preoccupation with death, the macabre interest in tombs, the gruesome predilection for the human corpse. Among painters the favorite themes were Christ's passion, the terrors of the Last Judgment, and the tortures of Hell, all depicted with ruthless realism and with an almost loving devotion to each repulsive detail. Altogether characteristic was the immense popularity of the Dance of Death woodcuts and murals, with appropriate verses, which appeared soon after the Black Death and which, it is agreed, expressed the sense of the immediacy of death and the dread of dying unshriven. Throughout the fifteenth and sixteenth centuries these pitilessly naturalistic pictures ensured man's constant realization of his imminent fate.

The origins of the Dance of Death theme have been generally traced to the Black Death and subsequent epidemics, culminating in the terror brought on by the outbreak of syphilis at the end of the fifteenth century. Is it unreasonable, then, to suppose that many of the other phenomena I have mentioned might be explained, at least in part, in the same way? We all recognize the late Middle Ages as a period of popular religious excitement or overexcitement, of pilgrimages and penitential processions, of mass preaching, of veneration of relics and adoration of saints, of lay piety and popular mysticism. It was apparently also a period of unusual immorality and shockingly loose living, which we must take as the continuation of the "devil-may-care" attitude of one part of the population. This the psychologists explain as the repression of unbearable feelings by accentuating the value of a diametrically opposed set of feelings and then behaving as though the latter were the real feelings. But the most striking feature of the age was an exceptionally strong sense of guilt and a truly dreadful fear of retribution, seeking expression in a passionate longing for effective intercession and in a craving for direct, personal experience of the Deity, as well as in a corresponding dissatisfaction with the Church and with the mechanization of the means of salvation as reflected, for example, in the traffic in indulgences.

These attitudes, along with the great interest in astrology, the increased resort to magic, and the startling spread of witchcraft and Satanism in the fifteenth century were, according to the precepts of modern psychology, normal reactions to the sufferings to which mankind in that period was subjected.

Chapter Questions

1. If you wanted to interpret the Late Middle Ages as a period of decline, what arguments and evidence would you emphasize? If you wanted to interpret this period primarily as one of transition, what arguments and evidence would you emphasize?

2. In what ways was the general character of the Late Middle Ages exemplified by the plague and reactions to it?

III

RENAISSANCE, REFORMATION, AND EXPANSION

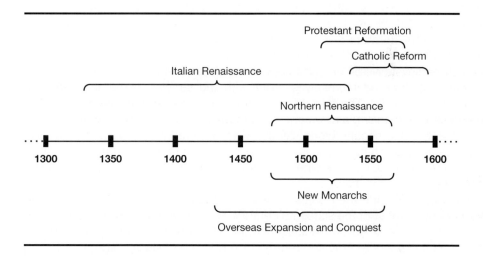

CHAPTER TWELVE

The Renaissance

Although in many ways a period of decline and disintegration, the Late Middle Ages also witnessed an extraordinary outburst of cultural and intellectual creativity known as the Renaissance. The Renaissance started in the fourteenth century in the cities of northern Italy, where scholars and a social elite became more interested in the literature and ideas of ancient Greece and Rome. As interest in Classical civilization grew, so did a tendency to reject many of the ideas and practices of medieval civilization. While remaining deeply religious, people of the Renaissance concerned themselves more with the secular, physical world than medieval people did. The term that best encompasses the meaning of the Renaissance is *humanism:* a new concern with people as powerful, creative individuals in a dynamic secular world. All this was reflected in the literature, art, and societies of northern Italian cities from the fourteenth century through the beginning of the sixteenth century, when invasions and other problems led to a decline of the Renaissance in Italy.

In Northern Europe the Renaissance started during the fifteenth century and lasted through most of the sixteenth century. This Renaissance was heavily influenced by the earlier Italian Renaissance; indeed, it was common for people to travel south across the Alps and return north with the ideas and styles they were exposed to in northern Italy. Nevertheless, the Northern Renaissance had some roots and characteristics that distinguished it from the Italian Renaissance. Above all, it was more integrated with Christian concerns. For example, more emphasis was placed on learning Classical languages to improve translations of the Bible, studying Classical literature for its relation to Christian ideals and life, and producing artistic creations with predominantly religious themes.

This chapter concentrates on one broad issue: the Renaissance. Examined here are traits historians define as typical of the Renaissance, such as literary humanism, humanistic education, and humanism in general. What was literary humanism? How was the development of humanism reflected in educational changes such as the new emphasis on the liberal arts? What problems were faced by those involved in humanism? Artistic and political trends that reflect this humanism are also explored. In what ways did Renaissance art differ from medieval art? How are some of the main elements of the Renaissance reflected in the art of the period? How did political theory mirror characteristics of the Renaissance? What was the nature of the Renaissance in the North? How were some of the connections between medieval concerns and Renaissance style reflected in the art of the Northern Renaissance? Above all, the materials concern efforts by people of that time as well as modern scholars to distinguish the Renaissance as a whole from the preceding Middle Ages. How did important figures of the Italian Renaissance view the Middle Ages? How sharp was the break, if any, with the Middle Ages? How should the Renaissance be interpreted as a whole? Efforts to answer questions such as these have caused considerable scholarly disagreement, most notably over the interpretation by Jacob Burckhardt, which emphasizes the modernity and distinctness of the Italian Renaissance. Secondary sources exemplify this tradition of controversy over the meaning of the Renaissance.

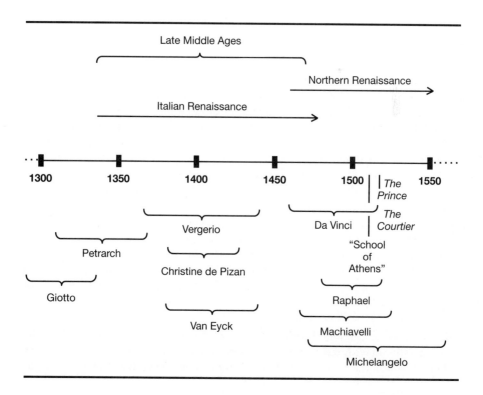

PRIMARY SOURCES

A Letter to Boccaccio: Literary Humanism

Francesco Petrarch

Literary humanism, a movement to revive Classical literature and the values expressed in Classical writings, was central to the early Renaissance. This trend, which originated in northern Italy during the fourteenth century, represented a broadening in focus from otherworldly concerns and people as religious beings, which was typical of the Middle Ages, to include the problems of people and nature in this world. The individual most commonly associated with it and perhaps most responsible for its spread was the Florentine Francesco Petrarch (1304–1374). Best known for his love sonnets to Laura, he also collected and translated many Classical works and wrote numerous letters—often extolling the Classical authors and even writing in their style. In the following selection from a 1362 letter to his friend Boccaccio, Petrarch offered reassurance and responded to charges typically made against humanistic learning.

Consider: *The nature of the charges Petrarch is refuting; how Petrarch related humanism to religion; Petrarch's perception of the benefits of literary humanism.*

Neither exhortations to virtue nor the argument of approaching death should divert us from literature; for in a good mind it excites the love of virtue, and dissipates, or at least diminishes, the fear of death. To desert our studies shows want of self-confidence rather than wisdom, for letters do not hinder but aid the properly constituted mind which possesses them; they facilitate our life, they do not retard it. Just as many kinds of food which lie heavy on an enfeebled and nauseated stomach furnish excellent nourishment for one who is well but famishing, so in our studies many things which are deadly to the weak mind may prove most salutary to an acute and healthy intellect, especially if in our use of both food and learning we exercise proper discretion. If it were otherwise, surely the zeal of certain persons who persevered to the end could not have roused such admiration. Cato, I never forget, acquainted himself with Latin literature as he was growing old, and Greek when he had really become an old man. Varro, who reached his hundredth year still reading and writing, parted from life sooner than from his love of study. Livius Drusus, although weakened by age and afflicted with blindness, did not give up his interpretation of the civil law, which he carried on to the great advantage of the state. . . .

Besides these and innumerable others like them, have not all those of our own religion whom we should wish most to imitate devoted their whole lives to literature, and grown old and died in the same pursuit? Some, indeed, were overtaken by death while

SOURCE: James Harvey Robinson and Henry Winchester Rolfe, *Petrarch: The First Modern Scholar and Man of Letters* (New York: Haskell House, 1898), pp. 391–395.

still at work reading or writing. To none of them, so far as I know, did it prove a disadvantage to be noted for secular learning. . . .

While I know that many have become famous for piety without learning, at the same time I know of no one who has been prevented by literature from following the path of holiness. The apostle Paul was, to be sure, accused of having his head turned by study, but the world has long ago passed its verdict upon this accusation. If I may be allowed to speak for myself, it seems to me that, although the path to virtue by the way of ignorance may be plain, it fosters sloth. The goal of all good people is the same, but the ways of reaching it are many and various. Some advance slowly, others with more spirit; some obscurely, others again conspicuously. One takes a lower, another a higher path. Although all alike are on the road to happiness, certainly the more elevated path is the more glorious. Hence ignorance, however devout, is by no means to be put on a plane with the enlightened devoutness of one familiar with literature. Nor can you pick me out from the whole array of unlettered saints, an example so holy that I cannot match it with a still holier one from the other group.

On the Liberal Arts

Peter Paul Vergerio

Closely associated with the rise of literary humanism was a new emphasis on the more broadly defined "liberal arts." This emphasis was manifested in a new concern with education; a change in educational curriculum constituted an institutional development that was enduring and that had wide-ranging effects. The first to express this emphasis systematically in an educational program was Peter Paul Vergerio (1370–1444). He taught in several Italian universities, and in his main treatise, On the Liberal Arts, *he rejected much of the content and methods of medieval education. Vergerio presents his views on the growing importance of the liberal arts in the following selection from a letter written to Ubertinus of Carrara.*

> **Consider:** *What is particularly humanistic rather than scholastic or medieval about this view; how Vergerio justifies his choice of the three subjects in this proposed curriculum; what Petrarch might think of this letter.*

Your grandfather, Francesco I, a man distinguished for his capacity in affairs and for his sound judgment, was in the habit of saying that a parent owes three duties to his children. The first of these is to bestow upon them names of which they need not feel ashamed. For not seldom, out of caprice, or even indifference, or perhaps from a wish to perpetuate a family name, a father in naming his child inflicts upon him a misfortune which clings to him for life. The second obligation is this: to provide that his child be brought up in a city of distinction, for this not only concerns his future self-respect, but is closely connected with the third and most important care which is due from father to

SOURCE: From William Harrison Woodward, *Vittorino da Feltre and Other Humanist Educators* (Cambridge, England: Cambridge University Press; New York: Bureau of Publications, Teachers College, Columbia University, 1963), pp. 96–97, 106–107. Reprinted by permission.

son. This is the duty of seeing that he be trained in sound learning. For no wealth, no possible security against the future, can be compared with the gift of an education in grave and liberal studies. By them a man may win distinction for the most modest name, and bring honour to the city of his birth however obscure it may be. But we must remember that whilst a man may escape from the burden of an unlucky name, or from the contempt attaching to a city of no repute, by changing the one or quitting the other, he can never remedy the neglect of early education. The foundation, therefore, of this last must be laid in the first years of life, the disposition moulded whilst it is susceptible and the mind trained whilst it is retentive.

This duty, common indeed to all parents, is specially incumbent upon such as hold high station. For the lives of men of position are passed, as it were, in public view; and are fairly expected to serve as witness to personal merit and capacity on the part of those who occupy such exceptional place amongst their fellow men. . . .

We come now to the consideration of the various subjects which may rightly be included under the name of 'Liberal Studies.' Amongst these I accord the first place to History, on grounds both of its attractiveness and of its utility, qualities which appeal equally to the scholar and to the statesman. Next in importance ranks Moral Philosophy, which indeed is, in a peculiar sense, a 'Liberal Art,' in that its purpose is to teach men the secret of true freedom. History, then, gives us the concrete examples of the precepts inculcated by philosophy. The one shews what men should do, the other what men have said and done in the past, and what practical lessons we may draw therefrom for the present day. I would indicate as the third main branch of study, Eloquence, which indeed holds a place of distinction amongst the refined Arts. By philosophy we learn the essential truth of things, which by eloquence we so exhibit in orderly adornment as to bring conviction to differing minds. And history provides the light of experience—cumulative wisdom fit to supplement the force of reason and the persuasion of eloquence. For we allow that soundness of judgment, wisdom of speech, integrity of conduct are the marks of a truly liberal temper.

The City of Ladies

Christine de Pizan

Most of the great cultural figures of the Renaissance were men. Nevertheless, some women were able to produce works, achieve recognition, and defend women against male detractors. The most famous of these was Christine de Pizan (1363?–1431?). Born in Venice, she moved with her family to Paris, where her father became a physician and astrologer at the French royal court. Unusually well educated, she wrote several poems and books, the most widely read of which was The City of Ladies *(1405). In the following excerpt Christine de Pizan questions an allegorical figure representing Lady Reason about women's political and educational abilities and about men's low opinions of women.*

SOURCE: Excerpts from *The Book of the City of Ladies* by Christine de Pizan, translated by Earl Jeffrey Richards. Copyright © 1982 by Persea Books, Inc. Reprinted by permission of Persea Books, Inc.

Consider: *What the common assumptions and arguments about women are; how Christine de Pizan attacks those assumptions and arguments; ways in which her writing embodies traits of the Renaissance.*

11. CHRISTINE ASKS REASON WHY WOMEN ARE NOT IN THE SEATS OF LEGAL COUNSEL; AND REASON'S RESPONSE.

. . . though God has given women great understanding—and there are many such women—because of the integrity to which women are inclined, it would not be at all appropriate for them to go and appear so brazenly in the court like men, for there are enough men who do so. What would be accomplished by sending three men to lift a burden which two can carry easily? But if anyone maintained that women do not possess enough understanding to learn the laws, the opposite is obvious from the proof afforded by experience, which is manifest and has been manifested in many women—just as I will soon tell—who have been very great philosophers and have mastered fields far more complicated, subtle, and lofty than written laws and man-made institutions. Moreover, in case anyone says that women do not have a natural sense for politics and government, I will give you examples of several great women rulers who have lived in past times. And so that you will better know my truth, I will remind you of some women of your own time who remained widows and whose skill governing—both past and present—in all their affairs following the deaths of their husbands provides obvious demonstration that a woman with a mind is fit for all tasks.

36. AGAINST THOSE MEN WHO CLAIM IT IS NOT GOOD FOR WOMEN TO BE EDUCATED.

Following these remarks, I, Christine, spoke, "My lady, I realize that women have accomplished many good things and that even if evil women have done evil, it seems to me, nevertheless, that the benefits accrued and still accruing because of good women—particularly the wise and literary ones and those educated in the natural sciences whom I mentioned above—outweigh the evil. Therefore, I am amazed by the opinion of some men who claim that they do not want their daughters, wives, or kins-women to be educated because their mores would be ruined as a result."

She responded, "Here you can clearly see that not all opinions of men are based on reason and that these men are wrong. For it must not be presumed that mores necessarily grow worse from knowing the moral sciences, which teach the virtues, indeed, there is not the slightest doubt that moral education amends and ennobles them. How could anyone think or believe that whoever follows good teaching or doctrine is the worse for it? Such an opinion cannot be expressed or maintained. I do not mean that it would be good for a man or a woman to study the art of divination or those fields of learning which are forbidden—for the holy Church did not remove them from common use without good reason—but it should not be believed that women are the worse for knowing what is good. . . .

"Thus, not all men (and especially the wisest) share the opinion that it is bad for women to be educated. But it is very true that many foolish men have claimed this because it displeased them that women knew more than they did. . . .

If it were customary to send little girls to school and to teach them the same subjects as are taught to boys, they would learn just as fully and would understand the subtleties of all arts and sciences. Indeed maybe they would understand them better . . . for just as women's bodies are more soft than men's, so too their understanding is more sharp. . . . If they understand less it is because they do not go out and see so many different places and things but stay home and mind their own work. For there is nothing which teaches a reasonable creature so much as the experience of many different things.

The Prince
Niccolò Machiavelli

The Italian Renaissance developed in an environment in which politics took on an increasingly competitive, secular tone. Within each Italian state, parties fought for power while at the same time the states fought each other for dominance or advantage. After 1492, Italy was invaded numerous times by Spain, France, and the Holy Roman Empire. These developments are reflected in the life and work of the great Renaissance political theorist Niccolò Machiavelli (1469–1527).

Born in Florence when it was under the rule of the Medicis, Machiavelli initiated his career in the Florentine civil service in 1498 during the period when the Medicis were out of power, replaced by a republican government. He rose to important diplomatic posts within the government, but was forced into retirement when the Medici family came back to power in 1512. He never gave up hope of returning to favor, and he wrote his most famous work, The Prince *(1513), in part as an application to the Medici rulers for a job in the Florentine government. The book has since become a classic treatise in political theory, above all for the way that it divorces politics from theology and metaphysics. The following selections from* The Prince *illustrate its style and some of its main themes.*

Consider: *The ways in which this work reflects values or practices typical of the Renaissance; how these same principles might be applied to twentieth-century politics.*

It now remains to be seen what are the methods and rules for a prince as regards to his subjects and friends. And as I know that many have written of this, I fear that my writing about it may be deemed presumptuous, differing as I do, especially in this matter, from the opinions of others. But my intention being to write something of use to those who understand, it appears to me more proper to go to the real truth of the matter than to its imagination; and many have imagined republics and principalities which have never been seen or known to exist in reality; for how we live is so far removed from how we ought to live, that he who abandons what is done for what ought to be done, will rather learn to bring about his own ruin than his preservation. A man who wishes to make a profession of goodness in everything must necessarily come to grief among so many who are not good. Therefore it is necessary for a prince, who wishes to maintain himself, to learn

SOURCE: From *The Prince and the Discourses* by Niccolò Machiavelli, translated by Luigi Ricci and revised by E. R. P. Vincent (1935), pp. 56, 65–66, by permission of Oxford University Press.

how not to be good, and to use this knowledge and not use it, according to the necessity of the case. . . .

It is not, therefore, necessary for a prince to have all the above-named qualities, but it is very necessary to seem to have them. I would even be bold to say that to possess them and always to observe them is dangerous, but to appear to possess them is useful. Thus it is well to seem merciful, faithful, humane, sincere, religious, and also to be so; but you must have the mind so disposed that when it is needful to be otherwise you may be able to change to the opposite qualities. And it must be understood that a prince, and especially a new prince, cannot observe all those things which are considered good in men, being often obliged, in order to maintain the state, to act against faith, against charity, against humanity, and against religion. And, therefore, he must have a mind disposed to adapt itself according to the wind, and as the variations of fortune dictate, and, as I said before, not deviate from what is good, if possible, but be able to do evil if constrained.

A prince must take great care that nothing goes out of his mouth which is not full of the above-named five qualities, and, to see and hear him, he should seem to be all mercy, faith, integrity, humanity, and religion. And nothing is more necessary than to seem to have this last quality, for men in general judge more by the eyes than by the hands, for every one can see, but very few have to feel. Everybody sees what you appear to be, few feel what you are, and those few will not dare to oppose themselves to the many, who have the majesty of the state to defend them; and in the actions of men, and especially of princes, from which there is no appeal, the end justifies the means. Let a prince therefore aim at conquering and maintaining the state, and the means will always be judged honourable and praised by every one, for the vulgar is always taken by appearances and the issue of the event; and the world consists only of the vulgar, and the few who are not vulgar are isolated when the many have a rallying point in the prince.

The Book of the Courtier

Baldesar Castiglione

In the Italian states, the most prestigious life took place in the courts of rulers. While Machiavelli wrote about methods and rules for the successful prince, others described the qualities necessary for men or women hoping to rise or maintain their position in court life. The most famous of these writers was the Italian diplomat Baldesar Castiglione (1478–1529), who wrote The Book of the Courtier *while a member of the Duke of Urbino's court. In the following excerpt, Castiglione describes first, the best qualities of the courtier—the ideal "Renaissance man"—and second, the virtues and actions best suited to women of the court.*

> **Consider:** *Why Castiglione considers noble birth important; what talents Castiglione thinks are most important for the courtier's success; how a woman's path to success at court differs from a man's.*

Source: Baldesar Castiglione, *The Book of the Courtier,* trans. by Charles S. Singleton. New York: Doubleday, 1959, pp. 28–30, 32–34, 70, 206.

"Thus, I would have our Courtier born of a noble and genteel family; because it is far less becoming for one of low birth to fail to do virtuous things than for one of noble birth, who, should he stray from the path of his forebears, stains the family name, and not only fails to achieve anything but loses what has been achieved already. For noble birth is like a bright lamp that makes manifest and visible deeds both good and bad, kindling and spurring on to virtue as much for fear of dishonor as for hope of praise. . . .

Besides his noble birth, I would wish the Courtier favored in this other respect, and endowed by nature not only with talent and with beauty of countenance and person, but with that certain grace which we call an 'air,' which shall make him at first sight pleasing and lovable to all who see him; and let this be an adornment informing and attending all his actions, giving the promise outwardly that such a one is worthy of the company and the favor of every great lord." . . .

"But to come to some particulars: I hold that the principal and true profession of the Courtier must be that of arms . . . which I wish him to exercise with vigor; and let him be known among the others as bold, energetic, and faithful to whomever he serves. . . . The more our Courtier excels in this art, the more will he merit praise; although I do not deem it necessary that he have the perfect knowledge of things and other qualities that befit a commander, for since this would launch us on too great a sea, we shall be satisfied, as we have said, if he have complete loyalty and an undaunted spirit, and be always seen to have them. . . .

Therefore, let the man we are seeking be exceedingly fierce, harsh, and always among the first, wherever the enemy is; and in every other place, humane, modest, reserved, avoiding ostentation above all things as well as that impudent praise of himself by which a man always arouses hatred and disgust in all who hear him."

"I would have him more than passably learned in letters, at least in those studies which we call the humanities. Let him be conversant not only with the Latin language, but with Greek as well, because of the abundance and variety of things that are so divinely written therein. Let him be versed in the poets, as well as in the orators and historians, and let him be practiced also in writing verse and prose, especially in our own vernacular; for, besides the personal satisfaction he will take in this, in this way he will never want for pleasant entertainment with the ladies, who are usually fond of such things. . . . These studies, moreover, will make him fluent, and (as Aristippus said to the tyrant) bold and self-confident in speaking with everyone. However, I would have our Courtier keep one precept firmly in mind, namely, in this as in everything else, to be cautious and reserved rather than forward, and take care not to get the mistaken notion that he knows something he does not know."

❋ ❋ ❋

I think that in her ways, manners, words, gestures, and bearing, a woman ought to be very unlike a man; for just as he must show a certain solid and sturdy manliness, so it is seemly for a woman to have a soft and delicate tenderness, with an air of womanly sweetness in her every movement, which, in her going and staying, and in whatever she says, shall always make her appear the woman without any resemblance to a man.

"Now, if this precept be added to the rules which these gentlemen have taught the Courtier, then I think she ought to be able to follow many such and adorn herself with the best accomplishments, as signor Gasparo says. For I hold that many virtues of the mind are as necessary to a woman as to a man; also, gentle birth; to avoid affectation, to be naturally graceful in all her actions, to be mannerly, clever, prudent, not arrogant, not envious, not slanderous, not vain, not contentious, not inept, to know how to gain and hold the favor of her mistress and of all others, to perform well and gracefully the exercises that are suitable for women. And I do think that beauty is more necessary to her than to the Courtier, for truly that woman lacks much who lacks beauty. Also she must be more circumspect, and more careful not to give occasion for evil being said of her, and conduct herself so that she may not only escape being sullied by guilt but even by the suspicion of it, for a woman has not so many ways of defending herself against false calumnies as a man has."

VISUAL SOURCES

The School of Athens: Art and Classical Culture

Raphael

Raphael's famous fresco in the Vatican, The School of Athens, *painted between 1508 and 1511, is one of the most revealing masterpieces of Renaissance art (photo 12-1). It shows the major Greek philosophers arranged in different positions and groups according to their philosophical inclinations. In the center stands Plato, pointing upward to confirm his commitment to his theory of ideas and holding a copy of his* Timaeus *in his left hand, and Aristotle, pointing downward to indicate his empirical orientation. Correspondingly, the left side of the painting is filled with metaphysical philosophers with a statue of Apollo (patron of poetry) overhead, while the right side shows physical scientists under a statue of Athena (goddess of reason). Socrates is on the left, counting out points on his fingers to a group of younger men. Sprawled on the steps in the center is Diogenes. At the lower left Phythagoras demonstrates his mathematics on a tablet. The figures of Classical authors and gods are actually portraits of Raphael's contemporaries as well. The figure of Plato is probably Leonardo da Vinci. Writing in the center foreground is the brooding, pessimistic philosopher Heraclitus, a portrait of Michelangelo. On the right bending over a geometric diagram is Euclid, a portrait of the architect Bramante. Behind him Ptolemy holds a globe, while on the far right the artist, Raphael, looks out of the picture.*

In content, then, this painting is a tribute to Greek philosophy, which played such an important role in the Italian Renaissance. However, it goes further. Raphael belonged to a group of thinkers and artists who met to discuss philosophy, much as in this picture, but as implied in the picture, both the Platonic and Aristotelian points of view were respected in the Renaissance. Moreover, the artists, architects, sculptors, philosophers, and writers who served as models for the figures in this painting knew and communicated with each other; thus this fresco displays the many interconnections of the cultural elite in northern Italy, particularly in Florence. Even this fresco's specific location in the Vatican is revealing. On the opposing wall is another fresco, Raphael's Disputa, *which depicts the great Christian theologians of various eras. The placement*

Photo 12-1

The Vatican Museum

of these two frescos symbolizes values characteristic of the Renaissance: glorification of pagan culture without rejecting Christianity. Finally, the use of perspective and the newness of the architectural design exemplify the Renaissance traits of realism and bold innovation.

> **Consider:** *The way in which this reflects a society and attitudes different from those of the Middle Ages.*

Giovanni Arnolfini and His Bride: Symbolism and the Northern Renaissance

Jan van Eyck

It should not be concluded even in art that the Renaissance constituted a sudden and complete break with the past. Even when in style and subject matter paintings reflect the realism, humanism, and individualism of the Renaissance, they also reflect medieval assumptions and concerns that remained.

This can be seen in a Northern Renaissance masterpiece, Giovanni Arnolfini and His Bride, painted in 1434 by the Flemish artist Jan van Eyck (photo 12-2). The scene appears to be quite

Photo 12-2

The National Gallery, London

secular: Giovanni Arnolfini, an Italian businessman residing in Bruges, is standing with his bride in a private bridal chamber taking marriage vows (at this time two people could contract a legitimate marriage outside the Church). Around them various objects that might typically be found in such a room are quite realistically depicted. To the medieval eye these objects have well-known symbolic meaning that give this scene considerable religious and cultural significance. The single lighted candle was the traditional nuptial candle, symbolizing Christ and implying divine light. The convex mirror reflected the chamber, testifying to the presence of two witnesses (one of whom was the artist, van Eyck, who tells us just above the mirror that "Jan van Eyck was here"), and represented the all-seeing eye of God. The shoes (to the left), so appropriate for the muddy streets of Bruges, are off, indicating that this couple is standing on holy ground. The dog in the foreground symbolizes fidelity. The ripening peaches to the left on the chest and windowsill represent fertility and perhaps paradise lost. On the post of a chair near the bed is a carved Margaret, patron saint of childbirth. The pose of the couple suggests relationships between husband and wife: He is dominating by his frontal pose; she is deferentially turned toward him.

Thus this painting is both a realistic depiction of two individuals with distinct personalities (as revealed particularly in their faces) in a natural setting and a symbolic representation of the meanings of marriage in the fifteenth century, with all its religious implications. And that this is a portrait of an Italian merchant and his bride in a room furnished with items coming from all areas of Europe, in Bruges, a northern center of banking and commerce, reflects the growing importance and wealth of the middle class and international trade during this period.

Consider: *The ways this reflects a society and attitudes similar to those of the Middle Ages.*

SECONDARY SOURCES

The Civilization of the Renaissance in Italy

Jacob Burckhardt

Modern interpretations of the Renaissance almost uniformly start with the Swiss historian Jacob Burckhardt's The Civilization of the Renaissance in Italy, *first published in 1860. Burckhardt rejected a chronological approach and pictured the Italian Renaissance of the fourteenth and fifteenth centuries as a whole, strikingly distinct from the preceding Middle Ages and clearly a superior civilization. Until the 1920s, historians almost unanimously accepted his interpretation. After that time various aspects of his thesis were attacked, particularly by medievalists. In recent decades, however, Burckhardt's work has gained new respectability, at least as an idealized*

SOURCE: Jacob Burckhardt, *The Civilization of the Renaissance in Italy*, trans. S. G. C. Middlemore (London: George Allen and Unwin, Ltd.; New York: The Macmillan Co., 1890), p. 129.

cultural history of the Italian Renaissance. In any case, all historians who approach this topic must deal with Burckhardt's argument, some of the central points of which appear in the following excerpt.

> **Consider:** *What most distinguishes the Italian Renaissance from the preceding Middle Ages according to Burckhardt; any support the primary documents might provide for this argument; how a proud medievalist might respond to this argument.*

In the Middle Ages both sides of human consciousness—that which was turned within as that which was turned without—lay dreaming or half awake beneath a common veil. The veil was woven of faith, illusion, and childish prepossession, through which the world and history were seen clad in strange hues. Man was conscious of himself only as a member of a race, people, party, family, or corporation—only through some general category. In Italy this veil first melted into air; an *objective* treatment and consideration of the state and of all the things of this world became possible. The *subjective* side at the same time asserted itself with corresponding emphasis; man became a spiritual *individual,* and recognised himself as such. In the same way the Greek had once distinguished himself from the barbarian, and the Arabian had felt himself an individual at a time when other Asiatics knew themselves only as members of a race. . . .

In far earlier times we can here and there detect a development of free personality which in Northern Europe either did not occur at all, or could not display itself in the same manner. . . . But at the close of the thirteenth century Italy began to swarm with individuality; the charm laid upon human personality was dissolved; and a thousand figures meet us each in its own special shape and dress. Dante's great poem would have been impossible in any other country of Europe, if only for the reason that they all still lay under the spell of race. For Italy the august poet, through the wealth of individuality which he set forth, was the most national herald of his time. But this unfolding of the treasures of human nature in literature and art—this many-sided representation and criticism— will be discussed in separate chapters; here we have to deal only with the psychological fact itself. This fact appears in the most decisive and unmistakable form. The Italians of the fourteenth century knew little of false modesty or of hypocrisy in any shape; not one of them was afraid of singularity, of being and seeming unlike his neighbours.

The Myth of
the Renaissance

Peter Burke

Many historians attacked Burckhardt's interpretation and the legacy built up around it. These historians argued that Burckhardt overemphasized how modern the Renaissance was. They

---

Source: From Peter Burke, *The Renaissance*, pp. 1, 3–5. Reprinted with permission by Humanities Press International, Inc., Atlantic Highlands, NJ, 07716; and The Macmillan Press, Ltd.

stressed how much the Renaissance, even in Italy, was still part of the medieval world. Other historians have responded that criticisms of Burckhardt go too far. In the following selection Peter Burke criticizes Burckhardt's idea of the Renaissance as a myth and describes the main objections to it.

> **Consider:** *Why, according to Burke, Burckhardt's idea of the Renaissance is a myth; how a supporter of Burckhardt might respond; whether the sources give greater support to Burckhardt's or Burke's interpretation.*

Jacob Burckhardt defined the period in terms of two concepts, 'individualism' and 'modernity'. 'In the Middle Ages', according to Burckhardt, 'human consciousness . . . lay dreaming or half awake beneath a common veil. . . . Man was conscious of himself only as a member of a race, people, party, family, or corporation—only through some general category.' In Renaissance Italy, however, 'this veil first melted into air . . . man became a spiritual *individual*, and recognised himself as such'. Renaissance meant modernity. The Italian was, Burckhardt wrote, 'the first-born among the sons of modern Europe'. The fourteenth-century poet Petrarch was 'one of the first truly modern men'. The great re-newal of art and ideas began in Italy, and at a later stage the new attitudes and the new artistic forms spread to the rest of Europe.

This idea of the Renaissance is a myth. . . .

Burckhardt's mistake was to accept the scholars and artists of the period at their own valuation, to take this story of rebirth at its face value and to elaborate it into a book. To the old formulae of the restoration of the arts and the revival of classical antiquity, he added new ones such as individualism, realism, and modernity. . . .

This nineteenth-century myth of the Renaissance is still taken seriously by many peo-ple. Television companies and organisers of package tours still make money out of it. However, professional historians have become dissatisfied with this version of the Re-naissance, even if they continue to find the period and the movement attractive. The point is that the grand edifice erected by Burckhardt and his contemporaries has not stood the test of time. More exactly, it has been undermined by the researches of the medievalists in particular. Their arguments depend on innumerable points of detail, but they are of two main kinds.

In the first place, there are arguments to the effect that so-called 'Renaissance men' were really rather medieval. They were more traditional in their behaviour, assumptions and ideals than we tend to think—and also more traditional than they saw themselves. Hindsight suggests that even Petrarch, 'one of the first truly modern men', according to Burckhardt, had many attitudes in common with the centuries he described as 'dark'. . . .

In the second place, the medievalists have accumulated arguments to the effect that the Renaissance was not such a singular event as Burckhardt and his contemporaries once thought and that the term should really be used in the plural. There were various 'renascences' in the Middle Ages, notably in the twelfth century and in the age of Charle-magne. In both cases there was a combination of literary and artistic achievements with a revival of interest in classical learning, and in both cases contemporaries described their age as one of restoration, rebirth or 'renovation'.

Machiavelli and the Renaissance

Federico Chabod

Reactions to and appreciations of Machiavelli's thought in The Prince *form an apparently contra-dictory history in themselves. On the one hand, few thinkers in the history of political theory rank more highly than Machiavelli; he is recognized as being the first modern political theorist. On the other hand, there is a more popular tradition of rejecting his ideas as immoral; the term* Machiavellian *is pejorative, referring to political opportunism and ruthlessness. In the following selection Federico Chabod, an Italian historian who has written extensively on Machiavelli, ana-lyzes Machiavelli and the significance of his ideas.*

Consider: *Why Machiavelli's ideas are so appropriate to the historical realities of his time; how the selections from* The Prince *support this interpretation of Machiavelli.*

The *leitmotiv* of Machiavelli's posthumous life was his great assertion as a thinker, repre-senting his true and essential contribution to the history of human thought, namely, the clear recognition of the autonomy and the necessity of politics, 'which lies outside the realm of what is morally good or evil.' Machiavelli thereby rejected the medieval concept of 'unity' and became one of the pioneers of modern spirit. . . .

For Machiavelli accepted the political challenge in its entirety; he swept aside every criterion of action not suggested by the concept of *raison d'état,* i.e., by the exact evalu-ation of the historical moment and the constructive forces which *The Prince* must em-ploy in order to achieve his aim; and he held that the activities of rulers were limited only by their capacity and energy. Hence, he paved the way for absolute governments, which theoretically were completely untrammelled, both in their home and in their foreign policies.

If this was made possible by the Florentine Secretary's recognition of the autonomy of politics, it depended, conversely, on his own peculiar conception of the State, which he identified with the government, or rather with its personal Head. Accordingly, in *The Prince* all his attention was riveted on the human figure of the man who held the reins of government and so epitomized in his person the whole of public life. Such a conception, determined directly by the historical experience which Machiavelli possessed in such outstanding measure and presupposing a sustained effort on the part of the central gov-ernment, was essential to the success and pre-eminence of his doctrine.

This was a turning-point in the history of the Christian world. The minds of political theorists were no longer trammelled by Catholic dogma. The structure of the State was not yet threatened in other directions by any revolt of the individual conscience. An en-tire moral world, if it was not eclipsed, had at any rate receded into the shadows, nor was

---

SOURCE: Federico Chabod, *Machiavelli and the Renaissance,* trans. David Moore (Cambridge, Mass.: Harvard University Press, 1960), pp. 116–118. Copyright © 1958 by Federico Chabod. Reprinted by permission.

any other at once forthcoming to take its place and to inspire a new fervour of religious belief; hence, political thought could express itself without being confused by considerations of a different character. It was an era in which unitarian States were being created amid the ruins of the social and political order of the Middle Ages, an era in which it was necessary to place all the weapons of resistance in the hands of those who had still to combat the forces of feudalism and particularism. It was, in short, an era in which it was essential that the freedom and grandeur of political action and the strength and authority of central government should be clearly affirmed. Only thus was it possible to obliterate once and for all the traces of the past and to offer to the society of the future, in the guise of a precept, the weapons which would preserve the life of the united nation in the face of disruptive elements old and new.

This was the great achievement of Niccolò Machiavelli, who accordingly became the legitimate representative of politics and government, the man who was at once admired and hated, followed and opposed, throughout two centuries of European history; and it was on him that the eyes of men were to be fixed, because only he, a poor, weary citizen of a city divided against itself, had proclaimed with an eloquence that was now muted the nature of the arms which the sovereign authority must employ in order to achieve victory.

Northern Sources of the Renaissance

Charles G. Nauert

Most modern scholars argue that there were some differences between the Italian and Northern European Renaissances. Perhaps most obviously, the Northern Renaissance came later. More importantly, while heavily influenced by Italian humanism, humanism in Northern Europe was more tied to Christian culture and concerns. In the following selection Charles Nauert explains differences between the Italian and Northern Renaissance and argues that the North accepted Renaissance culture only when that culture came to suit the particular historical needs of the North.

> **Consider:** *The ways the Northern Renaissance differed from the Italian Renaissance; how Nauert explains these differences.*

The North itself would never have accepted Renaissance culture if that culture had not suited its needs. The reorganized, powerful monarchies of the late fifteenth and early sixteenth centuries needed a new ideal for their servants and courtiers, and the emphasis on public service, on personal merit, and on learning provided an attractive substitute for the traditional manners of the unlettered, unruly, and discredited feudal classes. The new ideal contained enough emphasis on social class and military prowess to make it

SOURCE: From Charles G. Nauert, *The Age of Renaissance and Reformation*, pp. 116–117. Reprinted by permission of Charles G. Nauert, Jr. © 1981.

credible to a society where the hereditary nobility still counted for much. For the kings, it offered the added advantage of servants who were refined and cultivated, and who would wield the pen as well as the sword for their master.

In addition to the monarchs and their courts, other important groups in the North also found humanistic culture attractive. The powerful, self-confident merchant oligarchies that governed the important towns, especially the prospering towns of the Rhine Valley and of south Germany, found in humanism a cultural ideal far more suited to the needs and prejudices of urban magnates than were the chivalric and scholastic traditions of the Middle Ages. The large group of would-be Church reformers found the characteristic Renaissance repudiation of the recent past and the desire to return to the original sources quite attractive, for the Roman past included the apostolic and early patristic age, when the Church was still pure and uncorrupted. . . .

The humanism that grew up in the North was not a mere copy of the Italian culture, but a grafting of Italian elements into a cultural tradition that varied from country to country. Obviously, for example, Germans or even Frenchmen could not revere the ancient Romans as their ancestors in quite the same sense that Italians could.

What did develop everywhere was a revulsion against the heritage of the immediate past (often more open and violent than in Italy because scholastic traditions and a clerical spirit had much greater strength in the North), and the conscious adoption of an idealized Greek and Roman Antiquity as the model for reforming literature, education, and the whole ideal of the educated man. Even more than in Italy, Northern humanists enthusiastically looked to the apostolic and patristic age of the Church as a valuable part of the ancient heritage they sought to restore. This emphasis on ancient Christianity, combined with the widespread movements of lay piety that flourished in the lower Rhine Valley and other parts of Northern Europe, explains why humanism north of the Alps directed much of its reformist activity toward reform of the Church and deepening of personal religious experience.

Chapter Questions

1. In what ways was the Renaissance a new development, strikingly different from the preceding Middle Ages? How might the "newness" of these developments be minimized or reinterpreted as an evolutionary continuation of the Middle Ages?

2. According to the sources in this chapter, what was particularly humanistic about the cultural productions and the attitudes of the Renaissance?

CHAPTER THIRTEEN

The Reformation

The Roman Catholic Church managed to hold together throughout the Middle Ages despite internal discord, heretical movements, and conflicts with secular authorities. In the sixteenth century the Protestant Reformation split it apart. The Reformation was initiated in 1517 by Martin Luther's challenges to official Church doctrine and papal authority. The movement spread in Germany, Northern Europe, and other parts of Europe. By mid-century a related but different form of Protestantism initiated in Geneva by John Calvin had become more dynamic, dominating the struggle against Catholicism in Central Europe and parts of France, Scotland, and England. Meanwhile, Catholic forces fought back politically and militarily under the leadership of the Holy Roman Emperor and Spain, and religiously through the Council of Trent and the Jesuits.

The importance of religious beliefs, the passion involved in the Reformation, and the historical significance of this division in the Western Christian Church have made the Reformation the object of intensive study. Moreover, a relatively large number of Reformation documents have been preserved.

Although representing a broad sampling of Reformation themes, the selections in this chapter center on three related topics. The first involves the much debated question of causes. Clearly, there was a combination of social, religious, political, and economic causes, but which predominated? What were some of the connections among these causes? The second also deals with causes of the Reformation, but from a somewhat different perspective. What moved Luther to reject Catholicism and develop new doctrines? What was the appeal of Lutheranism and Calvinism? In what ways were Catholic organizations such as the Jesuits and Carmelites able to attract members and play such an important role in Catholic reform? The third takes a more comparative perspective, concentrating on the differences and similarities among the faiths. How closely related were Calvinism and Lutheranism? Why did Lutheranism lose some of its dynamic force while Calvinism spread? How were both Lutheranism and Calvinism related to Catholicism on the one hand and to other Protestant sects on the other? How did the Reformation affect women? What was the nature of Catholic reform during the sixteenth century? Finally, the sources should shed light on the overall significance of the Reformation, one of the most profound revolutions in European history.

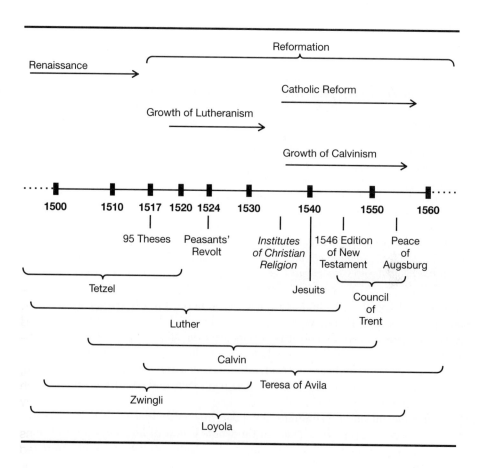

PRIMARY SOURCES

The Spark for the Reformation: Indulgences

Johann Tetzel

Although there were many causes of the Reformation, the immediate issue that sparked Luther into the position of a reformer was the sale of indulgences. Indulgences were remissions or exemptions for penance in purgatory due to an individual for the sins he had committed in life. They could be granted by the papacy because of the doctrine that it could draw on the treasury of merit or pool of spiritual wealth left by Christ and extraordinarily good Christians over time. As with some other practices of the Church, what was once used primarily for spiritual purposes, such as rewarding acts of penitence, was by the early sixteenth century being "abused" for secular purposes, such as providing money for Church officers. This was apparently the case with the sale of indulgences by Johann Tetzel (1465?–1519), a persuasive, popular Dominican friar who was appointed by Archbishop Albert of Mainz in 1517 to sell indulgences in Germany. Proceeds of the sale were to be split between Albert and the papacy. The following is an excerpt from a sermon on indulgences by Tetzel.

> **Consider:** *The most convincing "selling points" made by Tetzel; the requirements for obtaining effective indulgences; how Tetzel might have defended himself against attacks on this sale of indulgences as an abuse.*

You may obtain letters of safe conduct from the vicar of our Lord Jesus Christ, by means of which you are able to liberate your soul from the hands of the enemy, and convey it by means of contrition and confession, safe and secure from all pains of Purgatory, into the happy kingdom. For know, that in these letters are stamped and engraven all the merits of Christ's passion there laid bare. Consider, that for each and every mortal sin it is necessary to undergo seven years of penitence after confession and contrition, either in this life or in Purgatory.

How many mortal sins are committed in a day, how many in a week, how many in a month, how many in a year, how many in the whole extent of life! They are well-nigh numberless, and those that commit them must needs suffer endless punishment in the burning pains of Purgatory.

But with these confessional letters you will be able at any time in life to obtain full indulgence for all penalties imposed upon you, in all cases except the four reserved to the Apostolic See. Thence throughout your whole life, whenever you wish to make confession,

SOURCE: From James Harvey Robinson and Merrick Whitcomb, eds., "Period of the Early Reformation in Germany," in *Translations and Reprints from the Original Sources of European History*, vol. II, no. 6, ed. Department of History of the University of Pennsylvania (Philadelphia: University of Pennsylvania Press, 1898), pp. 4–5.

you may receive the same remission, except in cases reserved to the Pope, and afterwards, at the hour of death, a full indulgence as to all penalties and sins, and your share of all spiritual blessings that exist in the church militant and all its members.

Do you not know that when it is necessary for anyone to go to Rome, or undertake any other dangerous journey, he takes his money to a broker and gives a certain per cent— five or six or ten—in order that at Rome or elsewhere he may receive again his funds intact, by means of the letters of this same broker? Are you not willing, then, for the fourth part of a florin, to obtain these letters, by virtue of which you may bring, not your money, but your divine and immortal soul, safe and sound into the land of Paradise?

Justification by Faith
Martin Luther

The early leader of the Reformation was Martin Luther (1483–1546). Born in Germany to a wealthy peasant family, Luther became an Augustinian monk and a professor of theology at the University of Wittenberg. While at this post in 1517, he became involved in the indulgence problem with Tetzel and issued rather academic challenges in his ninety-five theses. News of this act quickly spread, and a major controversy developed. Although originally intending to stimulate only modest reforms within the Catholic Church, Luther soon found himself espousing doctrines markedly differing from those authorized by the Church and taking actions that eventually resulted in his expulsion from the Church.

Luther himself attributed his spiritual evolution to certain crucial experiences. The most important of these was his first formulation of the doctrine of "justification by faith," which constituted the core of his beliefs and much of the basis for Protestantism. In the following excerpts from his autobiographical writings, Luther describes this experience.

Consider: *What Luther meant by "justification by faith"; why this doctrine might have been so appealing to many Catholics; why this doctrine might have been threatening to the Catholic Church.*

I greatly longed to understand Paul's Epistle to the Romans and nothing stood in the way but that one expression, "the justice of God," because I took it to mean that justice whereby God is just and deals justly in punishing the unjust. My situation was that, although an impeccable monk, I stood before God as a sinner troubled in conscience, and I had no confidence that my merit would assuage him. Therefore I did not love a just and angry God, but rather hated and murmured against Him. Yet I clung to the dear Paul and had a great yearning to know what he meant.

Night and day I pondered until I saw the connection between the justice of God and the statement that "the just shall live by his faith." Then I grasped that the justice of God is that righteousness by which through grace and sheer mercy God justifies us through faith. Thereupon I felt myself to be reborn and to have gone through open doors into

SOURCE: From Roland H. Bainton, *The Age of Reformation* (New York: D. Van Nostrand Co., Inc., 1956), pp. 97–98. Reprinted by permission.

paradise. The whole of Scripture took on a new meaning, and whereas before the "justice of God" had filled me with hate, now it became to be inexpressibly sweet in greater love. This passage of Paul became to me a gate to heaven. . . .

If you have a true faith that Christ is your Saviour, then at once you have a gracious God, for faith leads you in and opens up God's heart and will, that you should see pure grace and overflowing love. This it is to behold God in faith that you should look upon His fatherly, friendly heart, in which there is no anger nor ungraciousness. He who sees God as angry does not see Him rightly but looks only on a curtain, as if a dark cloud had been drawn across his face.

On the Bondage of the Will

Martin Luther

A central distinction between Luther's views and those of Catholicism concerned the power of free will and good works to effect salvation. According to Catholicism, people had the ability to contribute to their own salvation by choosing to engage in good deeds, pious acts, approved behavior, and so forth. Luther rejected this, arguing that people were powerless to effect their own salvation, that salvation was granted only by God out of his mercy. The following is an excerpt from Luther's On the Bondage of the Will, *written in 1520 in response to a defense of free will and good works by the famous Christian humanist Erasmus.*

> **Consider:** *How Luther's arguments here follow from his ideas about justification by faith; the characteristics of God in Luther's eyes.*

I frankly confess that, for myself, even if it could be, I should not want 'free-will' to be given me, nor anything to be left in my own hands to enable me to endeavour after salvation; not merely because in face of so many dangers, and adversities, and assaults of devils, I could not stand my ground and hold fast my 'free-will' (for one devil is stronger than all men, and on these terms no man could be saved); but because, even were there no dangers, adversities, or devils, I should still be forced to labour with no guarantee of success, and to beat my fists at the air. If I lived and worked to all eternity, my conscience would never reach comfortable certainty as to how much it must do to satisfy God. Whatever work I had done, there would still be a nagging doubt as to whether it pleased God, or whether He required something more. The experience of all who seek righteousness by works proves that; and I learned it well enough myself over a period of many years, to my own great hurt. But now that God has taken my salvation out of the control of my own will, and put it under the control of His, and promised to save me, not according to my working or running, but according to His own grace and mercy, I have the comfortable certainty that He is faithful and will not lie to me, and that He is also great and powerful, so that no devils or opposition can break Him or pluck me from Him. 'No one,' He

SOURCE: Martin Luther, *On the Bondage of the Will*, trans. J. I. Packer and O. R. Johnston (London: James Clarke & Co., 1957), pp. 313–314. Reprinted by permission.

says, 'shall pluck them out of my hand, because my Father which gave them me is greater than all' (John 10.28–29). Thus it is that, if not all, yet some, indeed many, are saved; whereas, by the power of 'free-will' none at all could be saved, but every one of us would perish.

Furthermore, I have the comfortable certainty that I please God, not by reason of the merit of my works, but my reason of His merciful favour promised to me; so that, if I work too little, or badly, He does not impute it to me, but with fatherly compassion pardons me and makes me better. This is the glorying of all the saints in their God.

Condemnation of Peasant Revolt

Martin Luther

In 1524 a major peasant revolt broke out in Germany. Long-standing economic and social conflicts came to a head as peasants rose against their lords, the German princes. The peasants expected to be supported by Luther, who had so recently turned on the Church in the name of Christian liberty. Luther's concerns, however, were primarily spiritual; he did not intend his challenge to papal authority to be extended to social and political authority in general. Hesitant at first, Luther clearly sided with the princes as the peasant revolt spread and became more serious. Luther lost much popular support, particularly among peasants, who turned instead to more radical groups like the Anabaptists. But Luther gained important political allies among the princes, who savagely put down the revolt. Lutheranism became cast as a movement that supported strong secular authority. The following is an excerpt from Luther's condemnation of the peasant revolt.

> **Consider:** *Any inconsistency between this document and Luther's previous actions or what Luther says in the other documents; how this helps explain the successes and failures of Lutheranism.*

In my preceding pamphlet [on the "Twelve Articles"] I had no occasion to condemn the peasants, because they promised to yield to law and better instruction, as Christ also demands (Matt. vii. I). But before I can turn around, they go out and appeal to force, in spite of their promises, and rob and pillage and act like mad dogs. From this it is quite apparent what they had in their false minds, and that what they put forth under the name of the gospel in the "Twelve Articles" was all vain pretense. In short, they practice mere devil's work, and it is the arch-devil himself who reigns at Mühlhausen, indulging in nothing but robbery, murder, and bloodshed; as Christ says of the devil in John viii. 44, "he was a murderer from the beginning." Since, therefore, those peasants and miserable wretches allow themselves to be led astray and act differently from what they declared, I likewise must write differently concerning them; and first bring their sins before their

SOURCE: From James Harvey Robinson, ed., *Readings in European History*, vol. II (Boston: Ginn, 1904), pp. 106–108.

eyes, as God commands (Isa. lviii. I; Ezek. ii. 7), whether perchance some of them may come to their senses; and, further, I would instruct those in authority how to conduct themselves in this matter.

With threefold horrible sins against God and men have these peasants loaded themselves, for which they have deserved a manifold death of body and soul.

First, they have sworn to their true and gracious rulers to be submissive and obedient, in accord with God's command (Matt. xxii. 21), "Render therefore unto Caesar the things which are Caesar's," and (Rom. xiii. I), "Let every soul be subject unto the higher powers." But since they have deliberately and sacrilegiously abandoned their obedience, and in addition have dared to oppose their lords, they have thereby forfeited body and soul, as perfidious, perjured, lying, disobedient wretches and scoundrels are wont to do. Wherefore St. Paul judges them, saying (Rom. xiii. 2), "And they that resist shall receive to themselves damnation." The peasants will incur this sentence, sooner or later; for God wills that fidelity and allegiance shall be sacredly kept.

Second, they cause uproar and sacrilegiously rob and pillage monasteries and castles that do not belong to them, for which, like public highwaymen and murderers, they deserve the twofold death of body and soul. It is right and lawful to slay at the first opportunity a rebellious person, who is known as such, for he is already under God's and the emperor's ban. Every man is at once judge and executioner of a public rebel; just as, when a fire starts, he who can extinguish it first is the best fellow. Rebellion is not simply vile murder, but is like a great fire that kindles and devastates a country; it fills the land with murder and bloodshed, makes widows and orphans, and destroys everything, like the greatest calamity. Therefore, whosoever can, should smite, strangle, and stab, secretly or publicly, and should remember that there is nothing more poisonous, pernicious, and devilish than a rebellious man. Just as one must slay a mad dog, so, if you do not fight the rebels, they will fight you, and the whole country with you.

Third, they cloak their frightful and revolting sins with the gospel, call themselves Christian brethren, swear allegiance, and compel people to join them in such abominations. Thereby they become the greatest blasphemers and violators of God's holy name, and serve and honor the devil under the semblance of the gospel, so that they have ten times deserved death of body and soul, for never have I heard of uglier sins. And I believe also that the devil foresees the judgment day, that he undertakes such an unheard-of measure; as if he said, "It is the last and therefore it shall be the worst; I'll stir up the dregs and knock the very bottom out." May the Lord restrain him! Lo, how mighty a prince is the devil, how he holds the world in his hands and can put it to confusion: who else could so soon capture so many thousands of peasants, lead them astray, blind and deceive them, stir them to revolt, and make them the willing executioners of his malice. . . .

And should the peasants prevail (which God forbid!),—for all things are possible to God, and we know not but that he is preparing for the judgment day, which cannot be far distant, and may purpose to destroy, by means of the devil, all order and authority and throw the world into wild chaos,—yet surely they who are found, sword in hand, shall perish in the wreck with clear consciences, leaving to the devil the kingdom of this world and receiving instead the eternal kingdom. For we are come upon such strange times that a prince may more easily win heaven by the shedding of blood than others by prayers.

Institutes of the Christian Religion: Predestination

John Calvin

Lutheranism was the dominant movement of the first decades of the Reformation. But by mid-century it had lost much of its dynamism and remained confined primarily to major portions of Germany and Scandinavia. Leadership of the expanding Protestant movement in other parts of Europe fell to John Calvin (1509–1564). Born in France and trained as a lawyer and Classical scholar in French universities, Calvin had an important religious experience and adopted many of Luther's doctrines. Because of his views, he fled France for Geneva in the 1530s, eventually establishing a theocratic government there in the 1540s. While agreeing with most of the doctrines of Lutheranism, Calvin stressed the notion of predestination. This is illustrated in the following excerpt from the Institutes of the Christian Religion *(1536), Calvin's rigorously logical masterpiece, which systematically establishes and explains the Calvinist Christian theology. Here, he stresses the importance of justification by faith and calling—striving to live a good life doing that which one has been called upon by God to do—as evidence that one has already been elected by God for salvation.*

> **Consider:** *How Calvinism avoids the danger of passivity and resignation that might be implied in this conception of predestination; how these views compare with Luther's views on free will and good works; why this doctrine would be threatening to Catholicism.*

The covenant of life is not preached equally to all, and among those to whom it is preached, does not always meet with the same reception. This diversity displays the unsearchable depth of the divine judgment, and is without doubt subordinate to God's purpose of eternal election. But if it is plainly owing to the mere pleasure of God that salvation is spontaneously offered to some, while others have no access to it, great and difficult questions immediately arise, questions which are inexplicable, when just views are not entertained concerning election and predestination. . . .

By predestination we mean the eternal decree of God, by which he determined with himself whatever he wished to happen with regard to every man. All are not created on equal terms, but some are preordained to eternal life, others to eternal damnation; and, accordingly, as each has been created for one or other of these ends, we say that he has been predestinated to life or to death. . . .

We say, then, that Scripture clearly proves this much, that God by his eternal and immutable counsel determined once for all those whom it was his pleasure one day to admit to salvation, and those whom, on the other hand, it was his pleasure to doom to destruction. We maintain that this counsel, as regards the elect, is founded on his free mercy, without any respect to human worth, while those whom he dooms to destruction are excluded from access to life by a just and blameless, but at the same time incomprehensible judgment. In regard to the elect, we regard calling as the evidence of election,

SOURCE: John Calvin, *Institutes of the Christian Religion*, vol. II, trans. Henry Beveridge (Edinburgh, Great Britain: Calvin Translation Society, 1845), pp. 529, 534, 540.

and justification as another symbol of its manifestation, until it is fully accomplished by the attainment of glory. But as the Lord seals his elect by calling and justification, so by excluding the reprobate either from the knowledge of his name or the sanctification of his Spirit, he by these marks in a manner discloses the judgment which awaits them. I will here omit many of the fictions which foolish men have devised to overthrow predestination. There is no need of refuting objections which the moment they are produced abundantly betray their hollowness. I will dwell only on those points which either form the subject of dispute among the learned, or may occasion any difficulty to the simple, or may be employed by impiety as specious pretexts for assailing the justice of God.

Constitution of the Society of Jesus

The Catholic Church was not passive in the face of the challenges from Protestant reformers. In a variety of ways the Church reformed itself from within and took the offensive against Protestants in doctrine and deed. Probably the most effective weapon of Catholic reform was the Society of Jesus (the Jesuits) founded by Ignatius Loyola (1491–1556). Loyola, a soldier who had turned to the religious life while recovering from wounds, attracted a group of highly disciplined followers who offered their services to the pope. In 1540, the pope formally accepted their offer. The Jesuits became an arm of the Church in combating Protestantism, spreading Catholicism to foreign lands and gaining influence within Catholic areas of Europe. The following is an excerpt from the Constitution of the Society of Jesus, approved by Pope Paul III in 1540.

> **Consider:** *The characteristics of this organization that help explain its success; how, in tone and content, this document differs from Lutheran and Calvinist documents.*

He who desires to fight for God under the banner of the cross in our society,—which we wish to distinguish by the name of Jesus,—and to serve God alone and the Roman pontiff, his vicar on earth, after a solemn vow of perpetual chastity, shall set this thought before his mind, that he is a part of a society founded for the especial purpose of providing for the advancement of souls in Christian life and doctrine and for the propagation of faith through public preaching and the ministry of the word of God, spiritual exercises and deeds of charity, and in particular through the training of the young and ignorant in Christianity and through the spiritual consolation of the faithful of Christ in hearing confessions; and he shall take care to keep first God and next the purpose of this organization always before his eyes. . . .

All the members shall realize, and shall recall daily, as long as they live, that this society as a whole and in every part is fighting for God under faithful obedience to one most holy lord, the pope, and to the other Roman pontiffs who succeed him. And although we are taught in the gospel and through the orthodox faith to recognize and steadfastly profess that all the faithful of Christ are subject to the Roman pontiff as their head and as

SOURCE: James Harvey Robinson, ed., *Readings in European History*, vol. II (Boston: Ginn, 1904), pp. 162–163.

the vicar of Jesus Christ, yet we have adjudged that, for the special promotion of greater humility in our society and the perfect mortification of every individual and the sacrifice of our own wills, we should each be bound by a peculiar vow, in addition to the general obligation, that whatever the present Roman pontiff, or any future one, may from time to time decree regarding the welfare of souls and the propagation of the faith, we are pledged to obey without evasion or excuse, instantly, so far as in us lies, whether he send us to the Turks or any other infidels, even to those who inhabit the regions men call the Indies; whether to heretics or schismatics, or, on the other hand, to certain of the faithful.

The Way of Perfection

Teresa of Avila

While the Society of Jesus was the best-known Catholic religious order founded during the Reformation, other orders were founded or reformed and played roles in reasserting the strength of Catholicism. Many of these were women's orders that emphasized meditation, prayer, and mystical religious experiences. The most famous leader of these women's orders was Saint Teresa of Avila (1515–1582), a Spanish saint and founder of the reformed order of Carmelites. The following excerpt is from her book The Way of Perfection.

> **Consider:** *How she reacted to the Lutheran Reformation; ways this religious order and Catholicism might be appealing to women.*

When this convent was originally founded, for the reasons set down in the book which, as I say, I have already written, and also because of certain wonderful revelations by which the Lord showed me how well He would be served in this house, it was not my intention that there should be so much austerity in external matters, nor that it should have no regular income: on the contrary, I should have liked there to be no possibility of want. I acted, in short, like the weak and wretched woman that I am, although I did so with good intentions and not out of consideration for my own comfort.

At about this time there came to my notice the harm and havoc that were being wrought in France by these Lutherans and the way in which their unhappy sect was increasing. This troubled me very much, and, as though I could do anything, or be of any help in the matter, I wept before the Lord and entreated Him to remedy this great evil. I felt that I would have laid down a thousand lives to save a single one of all the souls that were being lost there. And, seeing that I was a woman, and a sinner, and incapable of doing all I should like in the Lord's service, and as my whole yearning was, and still is, that, as He has so many enemies and so few friends, these last should be trusty ones, I determined to do the little that was in me—namely, to follow the evangelical counsels as perfectly as I could, and to see that these few nuns who are here should do the same,

SOURCE: E. Allison Peers, ed. and trans., *The Complete Works of Saint Teresa of Jesus*, vol. II (London and New York: Sheed and Ward, 1950), pp. 3, 13.

confiding in the great goodness of God, Who never fails to help those who resolve to forsake everything for His sake. . . .

It seems over-bold of me to think that I can do anything towards obtaining this. But I have confidence, my Lord, in these servants of Thine who are here, knowing that they neither desire nor strive after anything but to please Thee. For Thy sake they have left the little they possessed, wishing they had more so that they might serve Thee with it. Since Thou, my Creator, art not ungrateful, I do not think Thou wilt fail to do what they beseech of Thee, for when Thou wert in the world, Lord, Thou didst not despise women, but didst always help them and show them great compassion. *Thou didst find more faith and no less love in them than in men, and one of them was Thy most sacred Mother, from whose merits we derive merit, and whose habit we wear, though our sins make us unworthy to do so. We can do nothing in public that is of any use to Thee, nor dare we speak of some of the truths over which we weep in secret, lest Thou shouldst not hear this our just petition. Yet, Lord, I cannot believe this of Thy goodness and righteousness, for Thou art a righteous Judge, not like judges in the world, who, being, after all, men and sons of Adam, refuse to consider any woman's virtue as above suspicion. Yes, my King, but the day will come when all will be known. I am not speaking on my own account, for the whole world is already aware of my wickedness, and I am glad that it should become known; but, when I see what the times are like, I feel it is not right to repel spirits which are virtuous and brave, even though they be the spirits of women.*

VISUAL SOURCES

Luther and the New Testament

The frontispiece of Luther's 1546 edition of the New Testament (photo 13-1) reveals much about the Protestant Reformation. First, most words are written in German, not Latin, thus reflecting the Protestant view that the Bible should be read by everyone. The place is Wittenberg, where Luther initiated the Reformation by posting his ninety-five theses in 1517. The year, 1546, was that of Luther's death. In the picture Christ on the cross is flanked by the praying Luther on the right and his patron, the elector of Saxony, on the left. This symbolizes the two unified in the central Protestant belief of justification by faith, the actual political-religious alliance of the two that was so important for the spread of Lutheranism in Germany, and the compatibility of Church and state according to Lutheranism. The general simplicity and lack of ornamentation of this work reflect Lutheranism and part of what it rejected about Catholicism. The book itself, produced mechanically, indicates the importance of the recently invented printing press for the Reformation.

Consider: *How this frontispiece might explain or symbolize the causes of the Reformation.*

Photo 13-1

ORAVIT, DOCVIT, CHRISTVS, FIT VICTIMA, VICTOR

Das newe Testament,
auffs new zugericht.

Doct: Mart: Luth:

Witeberg.
Gedruckt durch Hans Lufft,
1 5 4 6.

Staatliche Lutherhalle, Wittenberg

Luther and the Catholic Clergy Debate

Sebald Beham

Both Catholics and Protestants often used art to propogate their views in the Reformation debate. Nuremberg artist Sebald Beham's 1525 woodcut (photo 13-2) appeared in a broadsheet with a text by Hans Sachs entitled Luther and the Artisans. *On the left are the "godless"—members of trades, including a painter holding a stick and brush, a bell caster, and a fisherman with his net—all relying on religious commissions from the Catholic church. They complain that Luther has unjustly attacked the clergy for practices such as the sale of indulgences and rental of church lands. They are led by a nun and a priest, who points an accusing finger at Luther. On the right is a group of humble peasants—representing the "common man"—led by Martin Luther, who uses the Bible to answer charges against him and instruct his accusers to seek the kingdom of God. Christ, above in a circle of clouds and holding orb and scepter as Lord of the world, casts his judgment against the clergy by including his scepter to Luther's side.*

Consider: *What this painting reveals about the Reformation; how this painting compares to the previous illustration.*

Photo 13-2

Staatlichen Museen zu Berlin/Bildarchiv Preussischer Kulturbesitz

Loyola and Catholic Reform

Peter Paul Rubens

*In this painting by Peter Paul Rubens (photo 13–3), commissioned by the Jesuits in 1619,
Ignatius Loyola is shown preaching and casting out demons from the Church. In the center*

Photo 13-3

Kunsthistorisches Museum, Vienna

Loyola, with a halo and backed on his right by the clergy, preaches. He is supported above by angels. To the upper left the demons flee from their victims below, who are both overwhelmed and newly hopeful from the experience.

A comparison with (photo 13-1), the frontispiece of the 1546 edition of Luther's German translation of the New Testament, reveals part of the nature of Catholic reform. Here, the emphasis is on the Church's intervening between God and man, on the importance of the sacraments, and on the need for an ordained priesthood. The Catholic Church was willing to utilize the wealth and splendor available to it in its cause, as demonstrated not only by Loyola's robes and the grandeur of this Church interior, but in the commissioning of a leading artist like Rubens to paint in the new, elaborate, rich baroque style.

> **Consider:** *If you view this picture and the previous two as propaganda pieces, in what ways might they be appealing, and to whom?*

SECONDARY SOURCES

What Was the Reformation?

Euan Cameron

Historians usually agree that the Reformation comprised the general religious transformations in Europe during the sixteenth century. However, they often disagree on what exactly was at the core of the Reformation. In the following selection Euan Cameron argues that the essence of the Reformation was a combination of religious reformers' protests and laymen's political ambitions.

> **Consider:** *How the protests by churchmen and scholars combined with the ambitions of politically active laymen to become the essence of the Reformation; what this interpretation implies about the causes for the Reformation.*

The Reformation, the movement which divided European Christianity into catholic and protestant traditions, is unique. No other movement of religious protest or reform since antiquity has been so widespread or lasting in its effects, so deep and searching in its criticism of received wisdom, so destructive in what it abolished or so fertile in what it created. . . .

The European Reformation was not a simple revolution, a protest movement with a single leader, a defined set of objectives, or a coherent organization. Yet neither was it a floppy or fragmented mess of anarchic or contradictory ambitions. It was a series of

SOURCE: From Euan Cameron, *The European Reformation*, pp. 1–2, © 1991. Reprinted by permission of Oxford University Press.

parallel movements; within *each* of which various sorts of people with differing perspectives for a crucial period in history combined forces to pursue objectives which they only partly understood.

First of all, the Reformation was a protest by churchmen and scholars, privileged classes in medieval society, against their own superiors. Those superiors, the Roman papacy and its agents, had attacked the teachings of a few sincere, respected academic churchmen which had seemed to threaten the prestige and privilege of clergy and papacy. Martin Luther, the first of those protesting clerics, had attacked 'the Pope's crown and the monks' bellies', and they had fought back, to defend their status. The protesting churchmen—the 'reformers'—responded to the Roman counter-attack not by silence or furtive opposition, but by publicly denouncing their accusers in print. Not only that: they developed their teachings to make their protest more coherent, and to justify their disobedience.

Then the most surprising thing of all, in the context of medieval lay people's usual response to religious dissent, took place. Politically active laymen, not (at first) political rulers with axes to grind, but rather ordinary, moderately prosperous householders, took up the reformers' protests, identified them (perhaps mistakenly) as their own, and pressed them upon their governors. This blending and coalition—of reformers' protests and laymen's political ambitions—is the essence of the Reformation. It turned the reformers' movement into a new form of religious dissent: it became not a 'schism', in which a section of the catholic Church rose in political revolt against authority, without altering beliefs or practices; nor yet a 'heresy', whereby a few people deviated from official belief or worship, but without respect, power, or authority. Rather it promoted a new pattern of worship and belief, publicly preached and acknowledged, which *also* formed the basis of new religious *institutions* for all of society, within the whole community, region, or nation concerned.

A Political Interpretation of the Reformation

G. R. Elton

In more recent times the religious interpretation of the Reformation has been challenged by political historians. This view is illustrated by the following selection from the highly authoritative New Cambridge Modern History. *Here, G. R. Elton of Cambridge argues that while spiritual and other factors are relevant, primary importance for explaining why the Reformation did or did not take hold rests with political history.*

Consider: *How Elton supports his argument; the ways in which Cameron might refute this interpretation.*

Source: From G. R. Elton, ed., *The New Cambridge Modern History,* vol. II, *The Reformation* (Cambridge, England: Cambridge University Press, 1958), p. 5. Reprinted by permission.

The desire for spiritual nourishment was great in many parts of Europe, and movements of thought which gave intellectual content to what in so many ways was an inchoate search for God have their own dignity. Neither of these, however, comes first in explaining why the Reformation took root here and vanished there—why, in fact, this complex of antipapal 'heresies' led to a permanent division within the Church that had looked to Rome. This particular place is occupied by politics and the play of secular ambitions. In short, the Reformation maintained itself wherever the lay power (prince or magistrates) favoured it; it could not survive where the authorities decided to suppress it. Scandinavia, the German principalities, Geneva, in its own peculiar way also England, demonstrate the first; Spain, Italy, the Habsburg lands in the east, and also (though not as yet conclusively) France, the second. The famous phrase behind the settlement of 1555—*cuius regio eius religio*—was a practical commonplace long before anyone put it into words. For this was the age of uniformity, an age which held at all times and everywhere that one political unit could not comprehend within itself two forms of belief or worship.

The tenet rested on simple fact: as long as membership of a secular polity involved membership of an ecclesiastical organisation, religious dissent stood equal to political disaffection and even treason. Hence governments enforced uniformity, and hence the religion of the ruler was that of his country. England provided the extreme example of this doctrine in action, with its rapid official switches from Henrician Catholicism without the pope, through Edwardian Protestantism on the Swiss model and Marian papalism, to Elizabethan Protestantism of a more specifically English brand. But other countries fared similarly. Nor need this cause distress or annoyed disbelief. Princes and governments, no more than the governed, do not act from unmixed motives, and to ignore the spiritual factor in the conversion of at least some princes is as false as to see nothing but purity in the desires of the populace. The Reformation was successful beyond the dreams of earlier, potentially similar, movements not so much because (as the phrase goes) the time was ripe for it, but rather because it found favour with the secular arm. Desire for Church lands, resistance to imperial and papal claims, the ambition to create self-contained and independent states, all played their part in this, but so quite often did a genuine attachment to the teachings of the reformers.

The Catholic Reformation

John C. Olin

The history of the Catholic Church during the sixteenth century is almost as controversial as the history of the Protestant Reformation. Indeed, variations on the terminology used, from "Catholic reform," "Catholic Reformation," and "Catholic revival" to "Counter Reformation" reflect important differences in historians' interpretations of that history. The hub of the controversy is the extent to which reform and revival in the Catholic Church was a reaction to the Protestant

SOURCE: John C. Olin, "The Catholic Reformation," in *The Meaning of the Renaissance and Reformation*, ed. Richard L. DeMolen (Boston: Houghton Mifflin Co., 1974), pp. 268, 289–290.

Reformation or a product of forces independent of the Protestant Reformation. In the following selection John C. Olin, a historian specializing in Reformation studies, addresses this issue and analyzes the nature of Catholic reform during the sixteenth century.

> **Consider:** *For Olin, the problems in labeling Catholic reform the Counter Reformation; what the inner unity and coherence of the Catholic reform movement was.*

Catholic reform in all its manifestations, potential and actual, was profoundly influenced by the crisis and subsequent schism that developed after 1517. It did not suddenly arise then, but it was given new urgency, as well as a new setting and a new dimension, by the problems that Protestantism posed. What had been, and probably would have remained, a matter of renewal and reform within the confines of religious and ecclesiastical tradition became also a defense of that tradition and a struggle to maintain and restore it. A very complex pattern of Catholic activity unfolded under the shock of religious revolt and disruption. It cannot satisfactorily be labeled the Counter Reformation, for the term is too narrow and misleading. There was indeed a reaction to Protestantism, but this factor, as important as it is, neither subsumes every facet of Catholic life in the sixteenth century nor adequately explains the source and character of the Catholic revival.

Our initial task, then, is to break through the conventional stereotype of Protestant Reformation and Catholic Counter Reformation to view Catholic reform in a more comprehensive and objective way. This will entail consideration of the reaction to schism and the advance of Protestantism, but this subject can neither serve as a point of departure nor be allowed to usurp the stage. The survival of Catholicism and its continued growth suggest another perspective, as do the lives and devotion of so many of the most important Catholic figures of this time. Indeed, if the real significance of the Catholic Reformation must be found in its saints, as has recently been remarked, then emphasis on schism, controversy, and the more secular reflexes of ecclesiastical man may be slightly misplaced.

❖

Certain basic lineaments stand out in the Catholic reform movement, from the days of Savonarola and Ximenes to the close of the Council of Trent. The first and the most obvious was the widespread awareness of the need for reform and the serious efforts made to achieve it. This movement was in the beginning scattered and disparate, a matter of individual initiative and endeavor rather than a coordinated program affecting the church as a whole. Ximenes is the major example of an ecclesiastical or institutional reformer prior to 1517. Erasmus and the Christian humanists, however widespread and deep their influence, worked in a private capacity, so to speak, and sought essentially personal reorientation and renewal, though they did envision a broader reform of Christian life and society. With the pontificate of Paul III, Catholic reform became more concerted and official, and reached out to encompass the entire church. The arrival of Contarini in Rome in 1535 ushered in the new era. New blood was infused into the papal administration, the early Jesuits were organized and began their extensive activities, and the General Council was finally convened at Trent. Despite its diversity, the movement had an inner unity and coherence and followed an identifiable and continuous course.

Of what did this inner unity and coherence consist? It was manifested in the first place in the desire for religious reform. . . . [W]hat features distinguish the Catholic reformers and link them in a common endeavor[?] As we see it, two characteristics run like a double rhythm through the Catholic Reformation: the preoccupation of the Catholic reformers with individual or personal reformation, and their concern for the restoration and renewal of the Church's pastoral mission. In short, Catholic reform had a marked personal and pastoral orientation.

The Catholic reformers focused on the individual Christian and his spiritual and moral life. They sought essentially a *reformatio in membris* rather than dogmatic or structural change. The members of Christ's church must lead better Christian lives and be instructed and guided along that path. This is the burden of Savonarola's prophetic preaching, the goal of Erasmus and the Christian humanists, the objective of Ignatius Loyola and his *Spiritual Exercises.* The Theatines, Capuchins, and Jesuits emphasized this in terms of the greater commitment and sanctification of their members. The reforms of Ximenes in Spain, Giberti in Verona, and the Council of Trent for the universal church had this as an underlying purpose in their concern for the instruction and spiritual advancement of the faithful. . . .

Such a focus presupposes concern for the reform of the institutional church as well, for if men are to be changed by religion, then religion itself must be correctly represented and faithfully imparted. Thus the church's pastoral mission—the work of teaching, guiding, and sanctifying its members—must be given primacy and rendered effective. Hence the stress on training priests, selecting good men as bishops and insisting that they reside in their dioceses, instructing the young and preaching the gospel, restoring discipline in the church, and rooting out venality and unworthiness in the service of Christ and the salvation of souls. The Bark of Peter was not to be scuttled or rebuilt, but to be steered back to its original course with its crew at their posts and responsive to their tasks. The state of the clergy loomed large in Catholic reform. If their ignorance, corruption, or neglect had been responsible for the troubles that befell the church, as nearly everyone affirmed, then their reform required urgent attention and was the foundation and root of all renewal. This involved personal reform, that of the priests and bishops who are the instruments of the church's mission, and its purpose and consequence were a matter of the personal reform of the faithful entrusted to their care. The immediate objective, however, was institutional and pastoral. The church itself was to be restored so that its true apostolate might be realized.

The Legacy of the Reformation

Steven E. Ozment

Various historians have identified widespread changes stemming from the Reformation. The most obvious of these were the changes in religious affiliation and the conflicts between Protestants

---

SOURCE: From Steven E. Ozment, *The Age of Reformation*, pp. 435–436. Copyright 1980. Reprinted by permission of the Yale University Press.

and Catholics that developed. However, there were other cultural and social changes stemming from the Reformation that directly affected daily life. In the following selection Steven Ozment analyzes the legacy of the Reformation, emphasizing how it displaced many of the beliefs, practices, and institutions of daily life.

> **Consider:** *How the changes emphasized by Ozment might have affected daily life; what connections there might be between the Reformation and witchcraft according to Ozment.*

Viewed in these terms, the Reformation was an unprecedented revolution in religion at a time when religion penetrated almost the whole of life. The Reformation constituted for the great majority of people, whose social status and economic condition did not change dramatically over a lifetime, an upheaval in the world as they knew it, regardless of whether they were pious Christians or joined the movement. In the first half of the sixteenth century cities and territories passed laws and ordinances that progressively ended or severely limited a host of traditional beliefs, practices, and institutions that touched directly the daily life of large numbers of people: mandatory fasting; auricular confession; the veneration of saints, relics, and images; the buying and selling of indulgences; pilgrimages and shrines; wakes and processions for the dead and dying; endowed masses in memory of the dead; the doctrine of purgatory; Latin Mass and liturgy; traditional ceremonies, festivals, and holidays; monasteries, nunneries, and mendicant orders; the sacramental status of marriage; extreme unction, confirmation, holy orders, and penance; clerical celibacy; clerical immunity from civil taxation and criminal jurisdiction; nonresident benefices; papal excommunication and interdict; canon law; papal and episcopal territorial government; and the traditional scholastic education of clergy. Modern scholars may argue over the degree to which such changes in the official framework of religion connoted actual changes in personal beliefs and habits. Few, however, can doubt that the likelihood of personal change increased with the incorporation of Protestant reforms in the laws and institutions of the sixteenth century. As historians write the social history of the Reformation, I suspect they will discover that such transformations in the religious landscape had a profound, if often indirect, cultural impact.

While the Reformation influenced the balance of political power both locally and internationally, it was not a political revolution in the accepted sense of the term; a major reordering of traditional social and political groups did not result, although traditional enemies often ended up in different religious camps and the higher clergy was displaced as a political elite. The larger social impact of the Reformation lay rather in its effectively displacing so many of the beliefs, practices, and institutions that had organized daily life and given it security and meaning for the greater part of a millennium. Here the reformers continued late medieval efforts to simplify religious, and enhance secular, life. If scholars of popular religion in Reformation England are correct, Protestant success against medieval religion actually brought new and more terrible superstitions to the surface. By destroying the traditional ritual framework for dealing with daily misfortune and worry, the Reformation left those who could not find solace in its message—and there were many—more anxious than before, and especially after its leaders sought by coercion what they discovered could not be gained by persuasion alone. Protestant "disenchantment" of the world in this way encouraged new interest in witchcraft and the occult, as the religious heart and mind, denied an outlet in traditional sacramental magic and pilgrimage piety, compensated for new Protestant sobriety and simplicity by embracing superstitions even more socially disruptive than the religious practices set aside by the Reformation.

Women in the Reformation

Marilyn J. Boxer and Jean H. Quataert

The great figures of the Reformation were men, and traditionally focus has been on their struggles and their doctrines. In recent years scholars have questioned what role women played in the Reformation and whether the Reformation benefited women socially or in any aspect of public life. These questions are addressed by Marilyn J. Boxer and Jean H. Quataert, both specializing in women's studies, in the following excerpt from their book Connecting Spheres.

> **Consider:** *Ways women helped spread the Reformation; why the Reformation did not greatly change women's place in society.*

Defying stereotypes, women in good measure also were instrumental in spreading the ideas of the religious Reformation to the communities, towns, and provinces of Europe after 1517. In their roles as spouses and mothers they were often the ones to bring the early reform ideas to the families of Europe's aristocracy and to those of the common people in urban centers as well. The British theologian Richard Hooker (1553?–1600) typically explained the prominence of women in reform movements by reference to their "nature," to the "eagerness of their affection," not to their intelligence or ability to make conscious choices. Similarly, Catholic polemicists used notions about women's immature and frail "nature" to discredit Protestantism.

The important role played by women in the sixteenth-century Reformation should not surprise us, for they had been equally significant in supporting earlier heresies that challenged the established order and at times the gender hierarchy, too. Many medieval anticlerical movements that extolled the virtues of lay men praised lay women as well. . . .

Since the message of the Reformation, like that of the earlier religious movements, meant a loosening of hierarchies, it had a particular appeal to women. By stressing the individual's personal relationship with God and his or her own responsibility for behavior, it affirmed the ability of each to find truth by reading the original Scriptures. Thus, it offered a greater role for lay participation by women, as well as men, than was possible in Roman Catholicism. . . .

[Nevertheless,] the Reformation did not markedly transform women's place in society, and the reformers had never intended to do so. To be sure, they called on men and women to read the Bible and participate in religious ceremonies together. But Bible-reading reinforced the Pauline view of woman as weak-minded and sinful. When such

---

SOURCE: Excerpted from *Connecting Spheres: Women in the Western World, 1500 to the Present,* edited by Marilyn J. Boxer and Jean H. Quataert. Copyright © 1987 by Oxford University Press, Inc.

practice took a more radical turn in the direction of lay prophesy, as occurred in some Reform churches southwest of Paris, or in the coming together of women to discuss "unchristian pieces" as was recorded in Zwickau, reformers—Lutheran and Calvin alike—pulled back in horror. The radical or Anabaptist brand of reform generally offered women a more active role in religious life than did Lutheranism, even allowing them to preach. "Admonished to Christian righteousness" by more conservative Protestants, Anabaptists were charged with holding that "marriage and whoredom are one and the same thing." The women were even accused of having "dared to deny their husbands' marital rights." During an interrogation one woman explained that "she was wed to Christ and must therefore be chaste, for which she cited the saying, that no one can serve two masters."

The response of the magisterial Reformers was unequivocal. The equality of the Gospel was not to overturn the inequalities of social rank or the hierarchies of the sexual order. As the Frenchman Pierre Viret explained it in 1560, appealing to the old polarities again, the Protestant elect were equal as Christians and believers—as man and woman, master and servant, free and serf. Further, while the Reformation thus failed to elevate women's status, it deprived them of the emotionally sustaining presence of female imagery, of saints and protectors who long had played a significant role at crucial points in their life cycles. The Reformers rejected the special powers of the saints and downplayed, for example, Saints Margaret and Ann, who had been faithful and succoring companions for women in childbirth and in widowhood. With the rejection of Mary as well as the saints, nuns, and abbesses, God the Father was more firmly in place.

Chapter Questions

1. What were the most important differences between Catholicism and Protestantism in the sixteenth century? In what ways do these differences explain the appeal of each faith and the causes of the Reformation?

2. Considering the information in the preceding chapter, how might the Reformation be related to some of the intellectual and cultural developments of the Renaissance?

3. In what ways would it be accurate to describe Luther and his doctrines—and indeed the Reformation in general—as more medieval and conservative than humanistic and modern?

CHAPTER FOURTEEN

Overseas Expansion and New Politics

Between the mid-fifteenth and mid-sixteenth centuries much of Europe gained a new political and economic strength, which had been missing during the Late Middle Ages. This was manifested in a number of ways. First, central governments acquired new authority and power under a series of talented monarchs, often referred to by historians as the "new monarchs." This was particularly so in England, France, and Spain, but even in the Holy Roman Empire, where the emperor was often relatively weak, Emperor Charles V rose in stature and power. Second, European states supported a new wave of expansion into the rest of the world. Led by Portugal and then Spain, these states sent explorers, missionaries, merchants, colonists, and armed forces throughout the world, quickly establishing vast empires. Third, modern diplomacy was developed, enabling states to have recognized representatives with authority and expertise in foreign countries. This reflected and facilitated the new political strength and competitiveness of European states.

Sources in this chapter deal with each of these aspects of the new political and economic strength of fifteenth- and sixteenth-century Europe. In particular, questions related to exploration and expansion are addressed. What were the motives for expansion? Why did the expansion occur at this time? What connections were there between expansion and nationalism? What were the consequences of expansion? Some documents concern political developments of the period, particularly the reign of Charles V, the most renowned ruler of the time. What were his role and position? How were they affected by expansion? What were some of the connections between his position and the new commercial and financial prosperity?

In short, the sources in this chapter reveal a new political and economic strength that relates to the religious, cultural, and intellectual developments covered in the two preceding chapters. While this Renaissance civilization did not represent a complete break with the civilization of the Middle Ages, the selections emphasize what is different and more recognizably "modern" about this period. Historical patterns were being established that would characterize Europe for several succeeding generations, as will be seen in the following chapters.

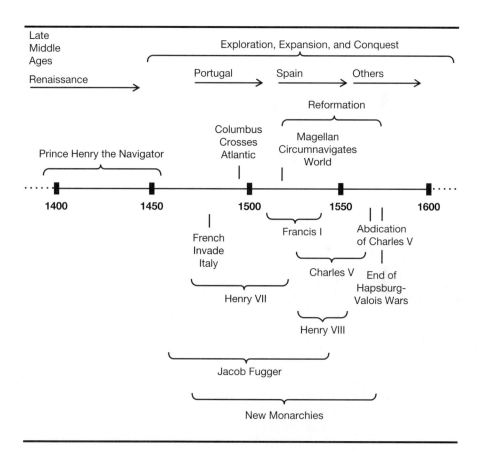

PRIMARY SOURCES

The Chronicle of the Discovery and Conquest of Guinea

Gomes Eannes de Azurara

The great geographic expansion and conquests of the fifteenth and sixteenth centuries were initiated by Prince Henry (the Navigator) of Portugal (1394–1460). Although he did not person-ally participate in the explorations, he established a naval school and base of operations on the southwestern tip of Portugal from which he sent expeditions down the west coast of Africa. One of the clearest explanations of the motives for this effort has been provided by Gomes Eannes de Azurara, a friend of Prince Henry (referred to as "the Lord Infant"), who chronicled the voyages of 1452–1453 at the request of King Alfonso V.

> **Consider:** *The explanations that sound more like rationalizations than reasons for explorations; whether economic, military, and religious motives are complementary or contradictory; ways this document reflects the history of a country engaged with Islam.*

We imagine that we know a matter when we are acquainted with the doer of it and the end for which he did it. And since in former chapters we have set forth the Lord Infant as the chief actor in these things, giving as clear an understanding of him as we could, it is meet that in this present chapter we should know his purpose in doing them. And you should note well that the noble spirit of this Prince, by a sort of natural constraint, was ever urging him both to begin and to carry out very great deeds. For which reason, after the taking of Ceuta he always kept ships well armed against the Infidel, both for war, and because he had also a wish to know the land that lay beyond the isles of Canary and that Cape called Bojador, for that up to his time, neither by writings, nor by the memory of man, was known with any certainty the nature of the land beyond that Cape. Some said indeed that Saint Brandan had passed that way; and there was another tale of two galleys rounding the Cape, which never returned. But this doth not appear at all likely to be true, for it is not to be presumed that if the said galleys went there, some other ships would not have endeavoured to learn what voyage they had made. And because the said Lord Infant wished to know the truth of this,—since it seemed to him that if he or some other lord did not endeavour to gain that knowledge, no mariners or merchants would ever dare to attempt it—(for it is clear that none of them ever trouble themselves to sail to a place where there is not a sure and certain hope of profit)—and seeing also that no other prince took any pains in this matter, he sent out his own ships against those parts, to have manifest certainty of them all. And to this he was stirred up by his zeal for the

SOURCE: Gomes Eannes de Azurara, *The Chronicle of the Discovery and Conquest of Guinea*, vol. I, trans. Charles Raymond Beazley and Adgar Prestage (London: The Hakluyt Society, 1896), pp. 27–29.

service of God and of the King Edward his Lord and brother, who then reigned. And this was the first reason of his action.

The second reason was that if there chanced to be in those lands some population of Christians, or some havens, into which it would be possible to sail without peril, many kinds of merchandise might be brought to this realm, which would find a ready market, and reasonably so, because no other people of these parts traded with them, nor yet people of any other that were known; and also the products of this realm might be taken there, which traffic would bring great profit to our countrymen.

The third reason was that, as it was said that the power of the Moors in that land of Africa was very much greater than was commonly supposed, and that there were no Christians among them, nor any other race of men; and because every wise man is obliged by natural prudence to wish for a knowledge of the power of his enemy; therefore the said Lord Infant exerted himself to cause this to be fully discovered, and to make it known determinately how far the power of those infidels extended.

The fourth reason was because during the one and thirty years that he had warred against the Moors, he had never found a Christian king, nor a lord outside this land, who for the love of our Lord Jesus Christ would aid him in the said war. Therefore he sought to know if there were in those parts any Christian princes, in whom the charity and the love of Christ was so ingrained that they would aid him against those enemies of the faith.

The fifth reason was his great desire to make increase in the faith of our Lord Jesus Christ and to bring to him all the souls that should be saved,—understanding that all the mystery of the Incarnation, Death, and Passion of our Lord Jesus Christ was for this sole end—namely the salvation of lost souls—whom the said Lord Infant by his travail and spending would fain bring into the true path. For he perceived that no better offering could be made unto the Lord than this; for if God promised to return one hundred goods for one, we may justly believe that for such great benefits, that is to say for so many souls as were saved by the efforts of this Lord, he will have so many hundreds of guerdons in the kingdom of God, by which his spirit may be glorified after this life in the celestial realm. For I that wrote this history saw so many men and women of those parts turned to the holy faith, that even if the Infant had been a heathen, their prayers would have been enough to have obtained his salvation. And not only did I see the first captives, but their children and grandchildren as true Christians as if the Divine grace breathed in them and imparted to them a clear knowledge of itself.

Letter to Lord Sanchez, 1493

Christopher Columbus

The voyages of Christopher Columbus (1451–1506) opened the New World to Europe and marked the entry of Spain into the process of exploration, expansion, and conquest initiated by Portugal. Columbus was a Genoese explorer who, after great difficulties, convinced the Spanish

SOURCE: *Select Letters of Christopher Columbus*, trans. and ed. R. H. Hajor (London: The Hakluyt Society, 1847), pp. 6–10.

monarchs, Queen Isabella and King Ferdinand, to support his voyages across the Atlantic. He expected to discover a western route to Asia and its riches. Instead, he landed on several islands of the Caribbean, which he assumed were part of Asia. The following letter to Lord Raphael Sanchez, treasurer to the Spanish monarchs, was written by Columbus in Lisbon on March 14, 1493, shortly after returning from his first voyage across the Atlantic. In this excerpt, he describes the native people he encountered.

> **Consider:** *How Columbus viewed the natives; what Columbus was most concerned with; how this letter reflects Columbus' motives.*

The inhabitants of both sexes in this island, and in all the others which I have seen, or of which I have received information, go always naked as they were born, with the exception of some of the women, who use the covering of leaf, or small bough, or an apron of cotton which they prepare for that purpose. None of them, as I have already said, are possessed of any iron, neither have they weapons, being unacquainted with, and indeed incompetent to use them, not from any deformity of body (for they are well-formed), but because they are timid and full of fear. They carry however in lieu of arms, canes dried in the sun, on the ends of which they fix heads of dried wood sharpened to a point, and even these they dare not use habitually; for it has often occurred when I have sent two or three of my men to any of the villages to speak with the natives, that they have come out in a disorderly troop, and have fled in such haste at the approach of our men, that the fathers forsook their children and the children their fathers. This timidity did not arise from any loss or injury that they had received from us; for, on the contrary, I gave to all I approached whatever articles I had about me, such as cloth and many other things, taking nothing of theirs in return: but they are naturally timid and fearful. As soon however as they see that they are safe, and have laid aside all fear, they are very simple and honest, and exceedingly liberal with all they have; none of them refusing any thing he may possess when he is asked for it, but on the contrary inviting us to ask them. They exhibit great love towards all others in preference to themselves: they also give objects of great value for trifles, and content themselves with very little or nothing in return. I however forbad that these trifles and articles of no value (such as pieces of dishes, plates, and glass, keys, and leather straps) should be given to them, although if they could obtain them, they imagined themselves to be possessed of the most beautiful trinkets in the world. It even happened that a sailor received for a leather strap as much gold as was worth three golden nobles, and for things of more trifling value offered by our men, especially newly coined blancas, or any gold coins, the Indians would give whatever the seller required; as, for instance, an ounce and a half or two ounces of gold, or thirty or forty pounds of cotton, with which commodity they were already acquainted. Thus they bartered, like idiots, cotton and gold for fragments of bows, glasses, bottles, and jars; which I forbad as being unjust, and myself gave them many beautiful and acceptable articles which I had brought with me, taking nothing from them in return; I did this in order that I might the more easily conciliate them, that they might be led to become Christians, and be inclined to entertain a regard for the King and Queen, our Princes and all Spaniards, and that I might induce them to take an interest in seeking out, and collecting, and delivering to us such things as they possessed in abundance, but which we greatly needed. They practise no kind of idolatry, but have a firm belief that all strength and power, and indeed all good things, are in heaven, and that I had descended from thence with these ships and sailors, and under this impression was I received after they had thrown aside their fears. Nor are they slow or stupid, but of very clear understanding; and those men who have crossed to the neighbouring islands give an admirable description of everything they observed; but they never saw any people clothed, nor any ships like ours. On my arrival at that sea, I had taken some Indians by force from the first island that I came to, in order that they might learn our language, and communicate to us what they knew respecting the country; which plan succeeded excellently, and was a great advantage to us, for in a short time, either by gestures and signs, or by words, we were enabled to understand each other. These men are still travelling with me, and although they have been with us now a long time, they continue to entertain the idea that I have descended from heaven; and on our arrival at any new place they published this, crying out immediately with a loud voice to the other Indians, "Come, come and look upon beings of a celestial race": upon which both women and men, children and adults, young men and old, when they got rid of the fear they at first entertained, would come out in throngs, crowding the roads to see us, some bringing food, others drink, with astonishing affection and kindness. . . . In all these islands there is no difference of physiognomy, of manners, or of language, but they all clearly understand each other, a circumstance very propitious for the realization of what I conceive to be the principal wish of our most serene King, namely, the conversion of these people to the holy faith of Christ, to which indeed, as far as I can judge, they are very favourable and well-disposed.

Memoirs: The Aztecs

Bernal Diaz del Castillo

While many Europeans who first came into contact with non-Western peoples viewed them with arrogance, others were quite impressed with what they saw. This was particularly true of some Spanish observers in Mexico. Before Cortez's conquest of Mexico in 1519, the Aztecs dominated much of the "middle American" world. This selection, written a half-century later by Bernal Diaz (1492–1581), a member of Cortez's conquering army, gives a sense of the Aztec's highly developed civilization and the splendor of their capital.

> **Consider:** *What most impressed Diaz; why Diaz was astonished at the wealth of this civilization; how this account compares with that of Columbus.*

When we gazed upon all this splendour . . . we scarcely knew what to think, and we doubted whether all that we beheld was real. A series of large towns stretched themselves along the banks of the lake, out of which still larger ones rose magnificently above the waters. Innumerable crowds of canoes were plying everywhere around us; at regular distances we continually passed over new bridges, and before us lay the great city of Mexico in all its splendour. . . .

SOURCE: I. I. Lockhart, trans., *The Memoirs of the Conquistador Bernal de Castillo* (London: J. Hatchard and Son, 1844), pp. 220–21, 235–38.

Motecusuma himself, according to his custom, was sumptuously attired, had on a species of half boot, richly set with jewels, and whose soles were made of solid gold. The four grandees who supported him were also richly attired, which they must have put on somewhere on the road, in order to wait upon Motecusuma; they were not so sumptuously dressed when they first came out to meet us. Besides these distinguished caziques, there were many other grandees around the monarch, some of whom held the canopy over his head, while others again occupied the road before him, and spread cotton cloths on the ground that his feet might not touch the bare earth. No one of his suite ever looked at him full in the face; every one in his presence stood with eyes downcast, and it was only his four nephews and cousins who supported him that durst look up. . . .

Our commander, attended by the greater part of our cavalry and foot, all well armed, as, indeed, we were at all times, had proceeded to the Tlatelulco. . . . The moment we arrived in this immense market, we were perfectly astonished at the vast numbers of people, the profusion of merchandise which was there exposed for sale, and at the good police and order that reigned throughout. The grandees who accompanied us drew our attention to the smallest circumstance, and gave us full explanation of all we saw. Every species of merchandise had a separate spot for its sale. We first of all visited those divisions of the market appropriated for the sale of gold and silver wares, of jewels, of cloths interwoven with feathers, and of other manufactured goods; besides slaves of both sexes. . . . Next to these came the dealers in coarser wares—cotton, twisted thread, and cacao. . . . In one place were sold the stuffs manufactured of nequen; ropes, and sandals; in another place, the sweet maguey root, ready cooked, and various other things made from this plant. In another division of the market were exposed the skins of tigers, lions, jackals, otters, red deer, wild cats, and of other beasts of prey, some of which were tanned. In another place were sold beans and sage, with other herbs and vegetables. A particular market was assigned for the merchants in fowls, turkeys, ducks, rabbits, hares, deer, and dogs; also for fruit-sellers, pastry-cooks, and tripe-sellers. Not far from these were exposed all manner of earthenware, from the large earthen cauldron to the smaller pitchers. Then came the dealers in honey and honey-cakes, and other sweetmeats. Next to these, the timber-merchants, furniture-dealers, with their stores of tables, benches, cradles, and all sorts of wooden implements, all separately arranged. . . .

In this market-place there were also courts of justice, to which three judges and several constables were appointed, who inspected the goods exposed for sale. . . . I wish I had completed the enumeration of all this profusion of merchandise. The variety was so great that it would occupy more space than I can well spare to note them down in; besides which, the market was so crowded with people, and the thronging so excessive in the porticoes, that it was quite impossible to see all in one day. . . .

Indeed, this infernal temple, from its great height, commanded a view of the whole surrounding neighbourhood. From this place we could likewise see the three causeways which led into Mexico. . . . We also observed the aqueduct which ran from Chapultepec, and provided the whole town with sweet water. We could also distinctly see the bridges across the openings, by which these causeways were intersected, and through which the waters of the lake ebbed and flowed. The lake itself was crowded with canoes, which were bringing provisions, manufactures, and other merchandise to the city. From here we also discovered that the only communication of the houses in this city, and of all the other towns built in the lake, was by means of drawbridge or canoes. In all these towns the beautiful white plastered temples rose above the smaller ones, . . . and this, it may be imagined, was a splendid sight.

After we had sufficiently gazed upon this magnificent picture, we again turned our eyes toward the great market, and beheld the vast numbers of buyers and sellers who thronged them. The bustle and noise occasioned by this multitude of human beings was so great that it could be heard at a distance of more than four miles.

Letter to Charles V: Finance and Politics

Jacob Fugger

The explorations and conquests of the fifteenth and sixteenth centuries were connected with the commercial expansion occurring in Europe at the same time. Central to this expansion was the rise of great international financial houses, such as the House of Fugger. The House of Fugger originated in Augsburg, Germany, and the Fuggers established branches throughout Europe and became directly tied not only to the growth of commerce but also to political developments as financiers to royal families. The extent of the Fuggers' political influence is suggested by the tone and content of the following letter, written in 1523, by Jacob Fugger, head of the firm, to Charles V, head of the House of Hapsburg, Holy Roman Emperor, King of Spain, and the most powerful ruler in Europe. The letter refers to the financial support provided by the Fuggers that enabled Charles, rather than his competitor Francis I of France, to be elected Holy Roman Emperor in 1519 by the electoral princes of Germany.

> **Consider:** *The tone of this letter; the interests the Fuggers might have in establishing a relationship with Charles V; Jacob Fugger's options had Charles rejected this request for repayment of the loan.*

Your Imperial Majesty doubtless knows how I and my kinsmen have ever hitherto been disposed to serve the House of Austria in all loyalty to the furtherance of its well-being and prosperity; wherefore, in order to be pleasing to Your Majesty's Grandsire, the late Emperor Maximilian, and to gain for Your Majesty the Roman Crown, we have held ourselves bounden to engage ourselves towards divers princes who placed their Trust and Reliance upon myself and perchance on No Man besides. We have, moreover, advanced to Your Majesty's Agents for the same end a Great Sum of Money, of which we ourselves have had to raise a large part from our Friends. It is well known that Your Imperial Majesty could not have gained the Roman Crown save with mine aid, and I can prove the same by the writings of Your Majesty's Agents given by their own hands. In this matter I have not studied mine own Profit. For had I left the House of Austria and had been minded to further France, I had obtained much money and property, such as was then offered to me. How grave a Disadvantage had in this case accrued to Your Majesty and the House of Austria, Your Majesty's Royal Mind well knoweth.

SOURCE: From Richard Ehrenberg, *Capital and Finance in the Age of the Renaissance: A Study of the Fuggers and Their Connections*, trans. H. M. Lucas (New York: Augustus M. Kelley, 1963), p. 80. Reprinted by permission.

VISUAL SOURCES

The Assets and Liabilities of Empire

Frans Fracken II

This painting by Frans Fracken II (photo 14-1) represents the abdication of Emperor Charles V in 1555. In the center sits Charles V with outstretched hands, symbolically giving Spain and the Netherlands to his son Philip on his left and the Empire to his brother Ferdinand on his right. Next to Philip stand various political figures, and below them are banners representing the provinces. In the foreground is an allegorical scene representing Spain's dominance of the sea and the New World. On the left is the bearded Neptune with a globe and his court; on the right is an Indian and other exotic figures and animals offering homage (in the form of gold treasure). The

Photo 14-1

Rijksmuseum, Amsterdam

event occurred in Brussels on October 25, 1555, shortly after Charles assented to the Peace of Augsburg, which has been interpreted as a double defeat for him: a recognition of Lutheranism and a political victory for German princes over imperial authority. There Charles made a speech, which included the following statements:

> *I had no inordinate ambition to rule a multitude of kingdoms, but merely sought to secure the welfare of Germany, to provide for the defense of Flanders, to consecrate my forces to the safety of Christianity against the Turk, and to labor for the extension of the Christian religion. But although such zeal was mine, I was unable to show so much of it as I might have wished, on account of the troubles raised by the heresies of Luther and other innovators of Germany, and on account of serious war into which the hostility and envy of neighboring princes had driven men, and from which I have safely emerged, thanks to the favor of God. . . . I am determined then to retire to Spain, to yield to my son Philip the possession of all my states, and to my brother, the king of the Romans, the Empire. . . . Above all, beware of infection from the sects of neighboring lands. Extirpate at once the germs, if they appear in your midst, for fear lest they may spread abroad and utterly overthrow your state, and lest you may fall into the direst calamities.*

Consider: *How this picture and speech reflect the position and predicament of the Hapsburgs during this period.*

Exploration, Expansion, and Politics

Aside from the various motivations for the voyages of discovery during the fifteenth and sixteenth centuries, a number of factors combined to make those voyages physically possible when earlier they were not. Technological discoveries significantly improved shipbuilding and navigation. But also important was the understanding and mapping of prevailing ocean currents and winds in relation to land masses. It was much easier to sail with, rather than against, currents and winds, and sailors counted on finding land masses for supplies along the way.

The early voyages tended to take advantage of currents and winds as shown in this map. Thus, for example, early voyages to North America usually took a more southerly route westward across the Atlantic and returned on a more northerly route, while Portuguese ships headed east to the Indian Ocean by following winds and currents to Brazil and then crossed the Atlantic farther south. Prevailing currents and winds also explain the difficulty of westward voyages around the tip of South America. These patterns of voyages also shed light on some of the geopolitical results of expansion. For example, even though Portugal's efforts were directed toward an eastern route to the Far East, she acquired Brazil (her only territory in the New World) to the west since it was on a route favored by winds and currents.

Consider: *How map 14-1 helps explain the pattern of exploration and colonization by the various European powers.*

Map 14-2 shows some of the geopolitical connections of international finance during the sixteenth century. First, it shows the extent of Fugger agencies throughout Europe, thus indicating how much international finance had grown by this time. Second, it reveals some of the direct connections between industry and finance, for the Fuggers were involved in both and often took mineral

Map 14-1 Overseas Explorations

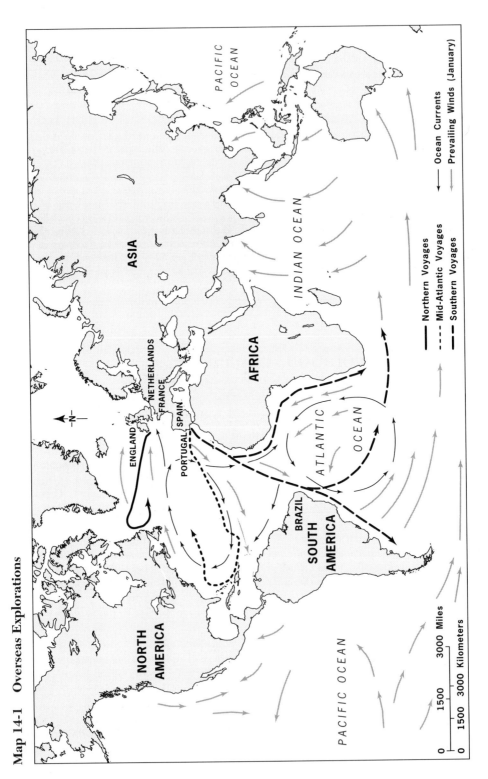

concessions or rights in mines as security or repayment for loans. Third, it suggests some of the political connections between the Fuggers and the House of Hapsburg; most of the firm's branches and mines were within Hapsburg lands, and not surprisingly the Fuggers became tied to the Hapsburgs by a series of loans.

Consider: *How the following map relates to the letter of Jacob Fugger to Charles V.*

Map 14-2   Commercial Expansion and Politics

SECONDARY SOURCES

The Expansion of Europe

Richard B. Reed

In analyzing the overseas expansion of the fifteenth and sixteenth centuries, historians typically emphasize a combination of economic and religious factors to explain the motivation behind expansion while focusing on the establishment of adequate knowledge and technology as key conditions for its occurrence. In the following selection Richard B. Reed argues that European expansion was a nationalistic phenomenon, and because of this Portugal was able to become the early leader.

> **Consider:** *Why Italy and Germany did not participate in overseas expansion; how one might attack Reed's argument that Portugal was in a better position to initiate expansion than any other country; other factors that might help explain why Portugal led in overseas expansion.*

The expansion of Europe was an intensely nationalistic phenomenon. It was an aspect of the trend, most evident in the late fifteenth and early sixteenth centuries, toward the establishment of strong centralized authority in the "new monarchies," as they have been called, and the emergence of the nation-state. A policy of overseas expansion required a degree of internal stability and national consciousness that only a powerful central government could command. Portugal achieved this position long before her eventual competitors, and under the leadership of the dynamic house of Avis became a consolidated kingdom comparatively free from feudal divisions before the end of the fifteenth century. While Spain was still divided into a number of conflicting political jurisdictions, England and France were preoccupied with their own and each other's affairs, and the Dutch were still an appendage of the Empire, the Portuguese combined the advantages of their natural geographic situation with their political and economic stability to initiate the age of discovery. Spain in the sixteenth century, and England, France, and the Netherlands in the seventeenth century, became active colonial powers only after each had matured into strong national entities, independent of feudal political and economic restrictions. . . .

The importance of the nation-state in Renaissance expansion is particularly apparent when the Italian city-states are considered. Venice and Genoa, cities that had contributed so many of the medieval travelers and early Renaissance geographers and mapmakers, did not participate directly in Europe's overseas expansion. Yet Italian names dominated the rolls of the early voyagers. Prince Henry employed Venetians and Florentines in his naval establishment, while Columbus, Vespucci, Verrazano, the Cabots,

---

SOURCE: Richard B. Reed, "The Expansion of Europe," in *The Meaning of the Renaissance and Reformation,* ed. Richard L. DeMolen (Boston: Houghton Mifflin, 1974), p. 299. Reprinted by permission.

and many others sailed for Spain, France, and England. Italian cartography was the best in Europe until the second half of the sixteenth century, and a high proportion of the books and pamphlets that chronicled new discoveries emanated from the presses of Vicenza, Venice, Rome, and Florence. Italian bankers and merchants were also very active in the commercial life of the principal Iberian cities. A divided Italy was instrumental in making Renaissance expansion possible, but it could not take full advantage of its own endowments. Germans, too, figured prominently in the expansion of the sixteenth century, as the names of Federmann, Staden, Welser, and Fugger attest. But Germany, like Italy, was not united, and the emergence of these two nations as colonial powers had to wait until their respective consolidations in the nineteenth century.

While every nationality in Western Europe was represented in Renaissance expansion, it was by no means an international venture. On the contrary, it was very much an expression of that nationalistic fervor that characterized political developments in the fifteenth and sixteenth centuries. It was primarily a state enterprise, often financed privately but controlled and protected by the governments of the concerned powers. There was no cooperation between nations, and even after the upheaval of the Protestant Reformation, when political loyalties and alignments were conditioned by religious sympathies, there were no colonial alliances that provided for mutual Protestant or Catholic overseas policies.

The Effects of Expansion on the Non-European World

M. L. Bush

While the expansion of Europe was of great significance for European history, it was of even greater consequence for the non-European world touched by the explorers. However, its effects differed greatly in the New World, where the Spanish dominated, and the East, where the Portuguese were the leaders. In the following selection M. L. Bush analyzes these differences.

> **Consider:** *Internal factors in non-Western societies that help explain these differences; contrasts between Portugal and Spain that help explain the different consequences for non-Western societies.*

The Castilian Empire in the West and the Portuguese Empire in the East had very different effects upon the world outside of Europe. In the first place, the Castilian expansion westwards precipitated a series of overseas migrations which were unparalleled in earlier times. For most of the sixteenth century, 1,000 or 2,000 Spaniards settled in the New World each year. Later this was followed by a large wave of emigrants from northwestern Europe, fleeing from persecution at home to the Atlantic sea-board of North

SOURCE: M. L. Bush, *Renaissance, Reformation and the Outer World* (New York: Harper & Row, 1967), pp. 143–145.

America and the Caribbean, and a final wave of Africans forced into slavery in the West Indies and in Brazil. On the other hand, in the East, there was virtually no settlement in the sixteenth century. Europe impressed itself only by fort, factory and church, by colonial official, trader and missionary.

In the second place, the settlement of the New World had a severe effect upon native peoples, whereas in the East, European influence was very slight until much later times.

In the early 1520s, the conquistadors brought with them smallpox and typhoid. Between them these European diseases soon decimated the Indian population, particularly in the great epidemics of the 1520s, 1540s and 1570s. In central Mexico, for example, an Indian population which numbered 11,000,000 in 1519 numbered no more than 2,500,000 by the end of the century. In addition, the Indian was beset by enormous grazing herds of horned cattle which the white settler introduced. He escaped the herds by working for the white settler, but if this led him to the crowded labour settlements, as it quite often did, he stood less chance of escaping infection. Either through falling hopelessly in debt as a result of desiring the goods of the white man, or through entering the labour settlements on a permanent basis to avoid the herds and also the system of obligatory labour introduced by the Spaniard,[1] there was a strong tendency for the Indian to become europeanised. He became a wage-earner, a debtor and a Christian. The Indian was exploited. But in the law he remained free. Enslavement was practised, but it was not officially tolerated. Moreover, the Franciscan order, a powerful missionary force in the New World, did its best to save the Indian from the evil ways of the white man. In Bartholomew de Las Casas and Francisco de Vitoria, the Indian found influential defenders; and through their schemes for separate Indian Christian communities, he found a partial escape from the white man. But the Indian mission towns, which were permitted by Charles V, were objected to by his successor, Philip II, and they only survived in remote areas.

With few exceptions, the way of life of the surviving Indians was basically changed by the coming of the white man. The outstanding exception was in Portuguese Brazil where the more primitive, nomadic Indians had a greater opportunity to retreat into the bush. There was also less settlement in Brazil, and generally less impression was made because of Portuguese preoccupations elsewhere, and also because of their lack of resources for empire-building on the Spanish scale. Furthermore, within the Spanish Empire, the European impressed himself less on the Incas in Peru than upon the Aztecs in Mexico. Because of the slow subjection of Peru, several Inca risings, the nature of the terrain, the smallness of the Spanish community, the process of europeanisation was much slower, and in the long run much less complete. The remnants of the Inca aristocracy became Spanish in their habits and Catholic in their religion, but the peasantry tended to remain pagan. In contrast to these developments, the westernisation of the East was a development of more modern times.

The West impinged upon the East in the sixteenth century mainly through the missionary. With the arrival of St. Francis Xavier in 1542 in India, an impressive process of conversion was begun. Concentrating upon the poor fishermen of the Cape Comorin

---

[1]This system depended upon every Indian village offering a proportion of its menfolk or labour service for a limited amount of time throughout the year.

coast, within ten years he had secured, it was said, 60,000 converts. The Jesuits fixed their attention on the East, choosing Goa as their main headquarters outside of Rome. Little was accomplished in Malaya, Sumatra and China in the sixteenth century, and Christianity soon suffered setbacks in the Moluccas after a promising start; but in Ceylon the conversion of the young king of Kotte in 1557 was a signal triumph, and so were the conversions in Japan. In the 1580s Jesuit missionaries in Japan claimed to have converted 150,000, most of whom, however, were inhabitants of the island of Kyushu.

Christianity was not a new religion in the East. There were extensive communities of Nestorian Christians, but they were regarded as alien as the Muslim by the Europeans. The new Christians by 1583 were supposed to number 600,000. But compared with the expansion of Islam in the East—a process which was taking place at the same time—the expansion of Christianity was a minute achievement.

Finally, the Portuguese sea empire did little to transport Portuguese habits abroad. Their empire was essentially formed in response to local conditions. On the other hand, the Spanish land empire was to a much greater extent reflective of Castilian ways.

In the New World a carefully developed and regulated system of government was established in which it was seen that the care taken to limit the independent power of feudal aristocrats in the Old World should also be applied to the New. There was a firm insistence upon government officials being royal servants. However, the government of the New World became much more regulated from the centre than that of the old. There was less respect for aristocratic privilege. Less power was unreservedly placed in the hands of the nobility. In the New World, in fact, the weaknesses of government, at first, did not lie in the powers and privileges of the nobility but rather in the cumbersome nature of the government machinery. Nevertheless, in spite of these precautions, the New World, by the early seventeenth century, had become a land of great feudal magnates enjoying, in practice, untrammelled power.

Red, White, and Black:
The Peoples of Early America

Gary Nash

Europeans often came into conflict with the peoples they encountered overseas. In the Americas, diverging understanding of the meaning of land ownership and, more broadly, private property, would lead to continual conflict. Europeans took for granted that people had the right to buy and sell land. Yet, this was not the case for Native Americans. In North America, European settlers would fence in land and hunt for private profit. This would undermine the entire livelihood of nomadic tribes that depended on freedom to move, hunt, and establish temporary communities. In the following selection, Gary Nash, a historian of early American history at UCLA, describes the clash of cultures and economic systems between white settlers and the native inhabitants of North America.

SOURCE: Gary B. Nash, *Red, White and Black: The Peoples of Early America*, 3d ed. (Englewood Cliffs, NJ: Prentice-Hall, 1982), pp. 25–27. Copyright © 1982, 1992. Reprinted by permission of Prentice-Hall.

Consider: *The differences between the Native American and European world views concerning land and personal identity; in light of what we now know regarding ecological destruction, how you might evaluate the Native American view of the symmetry of nature.*

While Native American and European cultures were not nearly so different as the concepts of "savagery" and "civilization" imply, societies on the eastern and western sides of the Atlantic had developed different systems of values in the centuries that preceded contact. Underlying the physical confrontations that would take place when European and Native American met were incompatible ways of looking at the world. These latent conflicts can be seen in contrasting European and Indian views of man's relationship to his environment, the concept of property, and personal identity.

In the European view the natural world was a resource for man to use. "Subdue the earth," it was said in Genesis, "and have dominion over every living thing that moves on the earth." The cosmos was still ruled by God, of course, and supernatural forces, manifesting themselves in earthquakes, hurricanes, drought, and flood, could not be controlled by man. But a scientific revolution was under way in the early modern period, which gave humans more confidence that they could comprehend the natural world—and thus eventually control it. For Europeans the secular and the sacred were distinct, and man's relationship to his natural environment fell into the secular sphere.

In the Indian ethos no such separation of secular and sacred existed. Every part of the natural world was sacred, for Native Americans believed the world was inhabited by a great variety of "beings," each possessing spiritual power and all linked together to form a sacred whole. "Plants, animals, rocks, and stars," explains Murray Wax, "are thus seen not as objects governed by laws of nature but as 'fellows' with whom the individual or band may have a more or less advantageous relationship." Consequently, if one offended the land by stripping it of its cover, the spiritual power in the land—called *manitou* by some woodlands tribes—would strike back. If one overfished or destroyed game beyond one's needs, the spiritual power inhering in fish and animals would take revenge because humans had broken the mutual trust and reciprocity that governed relations between all beings—human and nonhuman. To exploit the land or to treat with disrespect any part of the natural world was to cut oneself off from the spiritual power dwelling in all things and "was thus equivalent to repudiating the vital force in Nature."

Because Europeans regarded the land as a resource to be exploited for man's gain it was easier to regard it as a commodity to be privately held. Private ownership of property became one of the fundamental bases upon which European culture rested. Fences became the symbols of exclusively held property, inheritance became the mechanism for transmitting these "assets" from one generation to another within the same family, and courts provided the institutional apparatus for settling property disputes. In a largely agricultural society property became the basis of political power. In fact, political rights in England derived from the ownership of a specified quantity of land. In addition, the social structure was largely defined by the distribution of property, with those possessing great quantities of it standing at the apex of the social pyramid and the mass of propertyless individuals forming the broad base.

In the Indian world this view of land as a privately held asset was incomprehensible. Tribes recognized territorial boundaries, but within these limits the land was held in common. Land was not a commodity but a part of nature that was entrusted to the living by the Creator. . . . Thus, land was a gift of the Creator, to be used with care, and was not for the exclusive possession of particular human beings.

In the area of personal identity Indian and European values also differed sharply. Europeans were acquisitive, competitive, and over a long period of time had been enhancing the role of the individual. Wider choices and greater opportunities for the individual to improve his status—by industriousness, valor, or even personal sacrifice leading to martyrdom—were regarded as desirable. Personal ambition, in fact, played a large role in the migration of Europeans across the Atlantic in the sixteenth and seventeenth centuries. In contrast, the cultural traditions of Native Americans emphasized the collectivity rather than the individual. Because land and other natural resources were held in common and society was far less hierarchical than in Europe, the accumulative spirit and personal ambition were inappropriate. . . . Hence, individualism was more likely to lead to ostracism than admiration in Indian communities.

Charles V
G. R. Elton

Politically, much of the period between 1516 and 1556 swirls around Charles V. As head of the Hapsburg dynasty, he was King of Spain, Holy Roman Emperor, and ruler of numerous areas within Europe in addition to having control over expanding Spanish holdings overseas. He is best known for his competition with the dynamic Francis I of France and for his leadership of the Catholic cause against the Protestant Reformation. In the following selection from the authoritative The New Cambridge Modern History, *G. R. Elton, a prominent historian from Cambridge University, evaluates Charles V's rule and his significance.*

> **Consider:** *The ways in which Charles V was in his own times a figure more of the fading past; why the imperial title and authority may have been more of a liability than an asset; how this analysis fits with the painting of Charles V and his speech.*

The emperor ascended the throne of Spain a year before Luther's first public appearance as a danger to the papal government of the Church; he abdicated his many dominions shortly after the Peace of Augsburg. His empire was the last attempt at something like universal secular rule in the medieval manner; for, 'modern' as many parts of his territories were in their organisation and attitude, Charles himself looked upon his position in something of the spirit of Charlemagne—a Charlemagne whose stature is less manifestly heroic and whose dynastic preoccupations stand out rather more clearly. But the comparison is not totally absurd, for the virtue and ability of this greatest of the Habsburgs are becoming increasingly evident; nor is it unhistorical, because it describes a real

SOURCE: G. R. Elton, "Introduction: The Age of Reformation," in *The New Cambridge Modern History*, vol. II, ed. G. R. Elton (Cambridge, England: Cambridge University Press, 1958), pp. 6–7, 11. Reprinted by permission.

element in Charles's own thinking. If Germany and the imperial title defeated him, it is also worth notice that he preserved the ostensible existence of that massive anachronism at a critical time. If he was out of date in regarding himself as the champion of the Church, it must yet be conceded that his championship (readily reconciled with a high-handed attitude to popes as such) prevented the total lapse of central Europe to Protestantism and in Spain and elsewhere prepared for the revival of Roman Catholicism. Charles's reign was by no means all failure. He failed in his chief ambitions because they were extravagant: there was no prospect of making a reality out of those shadows of power and purpose which clung to the title of Holy Roman Emperor. But he gave some coherence to his vast conglomerate of lands and peoples; he assisted the economic hey-day of his Burgundian homeland; he saved the Papacy; and if he was the last of the me-dieval emperors, he was also the first king of Spain's golden age. . . .

Charles V did believe in his imperial mission. The fight with Protestantism was to him more than a struggle for dynastic ascendancy against disruption; it was a battle for the unity of Catholic Europe. The unity had long ceased to exist—if ever it had existed—and the centre of Charles's physical power, Spain, was the Catholic country least inclined to grant anything to the Papacy; but the emperor still envisaged his task in this grandiose, respectable and impossible light. Of all the many politicians who talked about the Turk-ish danger and vaguely appealed to Christendom to unite against it, he was the only one willing to translate words into action. Naturally, it may be said that he was also the only one likely to profit by such united action, but this is not altogether true—all Europe would have done well to push the Turk back into Asia—nor does it diminish the element of genuine idealism in Charles's attitude.

However, the days of his ascendancy saw the end of the dream. His imperial title and authority, so far from being an asset, proved an obstacle to the achievement of his more realistic ambitions. Instead of uniting Europe behind himself, he witnessed and in part caused the final disintegration of Germany and maintained a state of almost constant war among the powers. Worst of all, Francis I, by calling in the sultan to assist him, proved the utter emptiness of all that talk of crusades and Christendom. International politics had long (perhaps always) been at heart a matter of power and ambition; now their true character was revealed to the naked eye. But myths have a power to bind, and the myth of Christian unity had exercised a restraining influence which now vanished for good. The assertion of the national state, the rise of national armies, ended the legends of Christendom and chivalry.

Chapter Questions

1. What factors best explain the West's overseas expansion?

2. In what ways was overseas expansion tied to the political and economic developments of the fifteenth and sixteenth centuries?

3. What consequences flowed from this interaction of Western and non-Western civilizations?

IV

THE EARLY MODERN PERIOD

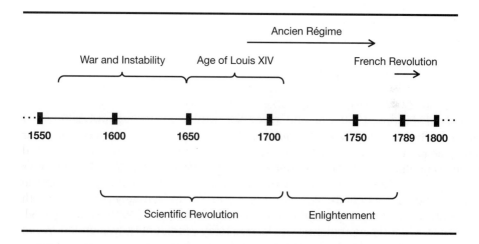

CHAPTER FIFTEEN

War and Revolution: 1560–1660

Between 1560 and 1660 war and revolution broke out throughout Europe. In France different political and religious factions struggled under a weak monarchy in what amounted at times to an extended civil war during the second half of the sixteenth century. Although stronger kings and ministers brought more stability during the seventeenth century, the nobility again rose at mid-century before the final assertion of French absolutism under Louis XIV. In Germany political and religious divisions contributed to the outbreak of a local war in 1618, which quickly turned into a bloody international war lasting thirty years, until it was ended by the Treaty of Westphalia in 1648. Few wars in history have been as devastating to Germany as this; perhaps a third of the people lost their lives. In England the growing conflict between king and Parliament, further fueled by religious and social divisions, led to a revolution and civil war during the 1640s and the extraordinary rule of Oliver Cromwell during the 1650s. In 1660 relative stability was restored under Charles II. Finally, in the Netherlands extended bloodshed marked the long effort by Spain to retain control over the Dutch, who finally succeeded in gaining complete independence in 1648.

The documents in this chapter deal with three of the upheavals—in France, in Central Europe, and in England—during the period from the mid-sixteenth to mid-seventeenth centuries. What was the nature of the civil wars in sixteenth-century France? In what ways was monarchical absolutism an answer to the political and religious struggles in France? Was the Thirty Years' War in Central Europe primarily a German conflict or a struggle against the predominance of Spain? How important were religious as compared with political causes of this war? Beyond the death and destruction involved, how decisive or significant was this war? What was the nature of the conflict between royal and parliamentary authority in England? How did political theory in England reflect these conflicts? What were some of several consequences of all these struggles?

The materials in this chapter characterize this century as one of extraordinary violence—sometimes directed at women in particular—and struggle for political and religious control. The violence diminishes and a new sense of stability is gained in the second half of the seventeenth century, as will be seen in the next chapter.

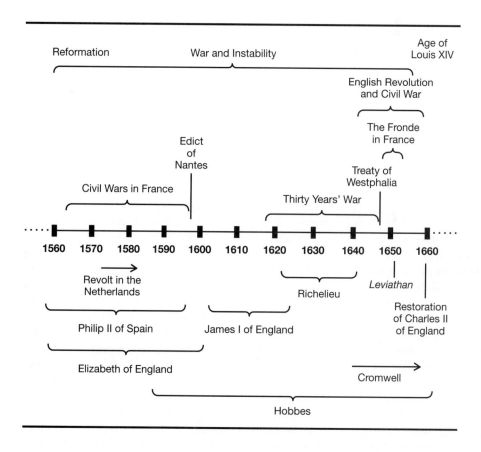

PRIMARY SOURCES

Civil War in France

Ogier Ghiselin de Busbecq

France was one of the first areas in which the turmoil, instability, and war characteristic of the period between 1560 and 1660 occurred. There, political and religious divisions combined to produce a long period of bloodshed and sporadic civil war. The nature and effects of this turmoil are described in the following selection from a letter written in 1575 by Ogier Ghiselin de Busbecq, the Holy Roman Emperor's ambassador to France.

Consider: *Busbecq's perception of the forces and grievances that were threatening to worsen the civil wars that had already broken out; the consequences of the civil wars for various segments of society.*

Ever since the commencement of the civil wars which are distracting the country, there has been a terrible change for the worse. So complete is the alteration, that those who knew France before would not recognise her again. Everywhere are to be seen shattered buildings, fallen churches, and towns in ruins; while the traveller gazes horror-stricken on spots which have but lately been the scenes of murderous deeds and inhuman cruelties. The fields are left untilled: the farmer's stock and tools have been carried off by the soldier as his booty, he is plundered alike by Frenchman and by foreigner. Commerce is crippled; the towns lately thronged with merchants and customers are now mourning their desolation in the midst of closed shops and silent manufactories. Meanwhile, the inhabitants, ground down by ceaseless exactions, are crying out at the immense sums which are being squandered for nought, or applied to purposes for which they were never intended. They demand a reckoning in tones which breathe a spirit of rebellion. Men of experience, members of the oldest families in France, are in many cases regarded with suspicion, and either not allowed to come to Court, or left to vegetate at home. Besides the two parties into which Frenchmen are divided by their religious differences, there are also feuds and quarrels which affect every grade of society.

In the first place, the feeling against the Italians who are in the French service is very strong; the high promotion they have received and the important duties with which they have been intrusted, arouse the jealousy of men who consider them ignorant of French business, and hold that they have neither merit, services, nor birth to justify their appointment. . . .

The feuds which separate the leading families of France are more bitter than those described in ancient tragedy; this is the state of feeling which exists between the Houses

SOURCE: From Charles Thornton Forster and F. H. Blackburne Daniell, *The Life and Letters of Ogier Ghiselin de Busbecq*, vol. II (London, 1881), pp. 38–40.

of Guise, Vendôme and Bourbon, not to mention that of Montmorency, which, through its alliances and connections, has a considerable party of its own.

Political Will and Testament

Richelieu

The civil wars in France were ended under the rule of Henry IV at the end of the sixteenth century. This strong king prevailed over rival factions and strengthened the French monarchy. But religious conflict and the competition with the nobility for authority were not over in France. Rather, the monarchy was built up toward a position of absolutism under a series of powerful figures, including Cardinal Richelieu (1585–1642), who served as principal adviser to the king between 1624 and 1642 and virtual ruler for most of that period. In the following selection from his Political Will and Testament, *Richelieu presents his view of monarchical power.*

> **Consider:** *How Richelieu justifies monarchical power; how Machiavelli might have responded to this view.*

Power being one of the most necessary ingredients towards the grandeur of kings, and the prosperity of their governments; those who have the chief management of affairs are particularly obliged not to omit anything which may contribute to authorize their master so far as to make all the world reject him.

As goodness is the object of love, power is the cause of dread: and it is most certain, that among all the princes who are capable to stir a state, fear grounded upon esteem and reverence has so much force, that it engages everyone to perform his duty.

If this principle is of great efficacy in respect to the internal part of states, it is to the full as prevailing abroad: subjects and strangers looking with the same eyes upon a formidable power, both the one and the other abstain from offending a prince, whom they are sensible is in a condition to hurt them, if he were so inclined.

I have observed by the by, that the ground of the power I am speaking of must be esteem and respect; . . . that when it is grounded upon any other principle, it is very dangerous; in the case instead of creating a reasonable fear, it inclines men to hate princes, who are never in a worse condition than when it turns to public aversion.

The power which induces men to respect and fear princes with love . . . is a tree which has five divers branches, which all draw their nutriment and substance from one and the same root.

The Prince must be powerful by his reputation.

By a reasonable army always kept on foot.

And by a notable sum of money in his coffers, to supply unexpected exigencies, which often come to pass when they are least expected.

Finally, by the possession of his subjects' hearts. . . .

SOURCE: Armand Jean du Plessis, Duc de Richelieu, *Political Will and Testament,* vol. II (London, 1695), pp. 45–46.

The Powers of the Monarch in England

James I

In England friction between the monarchy and Parliament increased under the Stuart kings, starting with James I. Already the Scottish monarch, James became King of England on the death of Elizabeth in 1603. James had a scholarly background and a reputation for his strong views about the monarchy. One of his clearest presentations of these views was in a speech to Parliament made in 1610. In it, he comments on the nature of the king's power, not simply in England but everywhere.

> **Consider:** *How James justifies the high position and vast powers he feels should rightly belong to kings; the limits to monarchical powers.*

The state of Monarchy is the supremest thing upon earth; for kings are not only God's lieutenants upon earth and sit upon God's throne, but even by God himself they are called gods. There be three principal similitudes that illustrate the state of Monarchy: one taken out of the Word of God and the two other out of the grounds of policy and philosophy. In the Scriptures kings are called gods, and so their power after a certain relation compared to the Divine power. Kings are also compared to the fathers of families, for a king is truly *parens patriae*, the politic father of his people. And lastly, kings are compared to the head of his microcosm of the body of man.

Kings are justly called gods for that they exercise a manner or resemblance of Divine power upon earth; for if you will consider the attributes to God you shall see how they agree in the person of a king. God hath power to create or destroy, make or unmake, at his pleasure; to give life or send death; to judge all, and to be judged nor accomptable to none; to raise low things and to make high things low at his pleasure; and to God are both soul and body due. And the like power have kings; they make and unmake their subjects; they have power of raising and casting down; of life and of death; judges over all their subjects and in all causes, and yet accomptable to none but God only. They have power to exalt low things and abase high things, and make of their subjects like men at the chess, a pawn to take a bishop or a knight, and to cry up or down any of their subjects as they do their money. And to the King is due both the affection of the soul and the service of the body of his subjects. . . .

As for the father of a family, they had of old under the Law of Nature *patriam potestatem*, which was *potestatem vitae et necis*, over their children or family, (I mean such fathers of families as were the lineal heirs of those families whereof kings did originally come), for kings had their first original from them who planted and spread themselves in colonies through the world. Now a father may dispose of his inheritance to his children at his pleasure, yea, even disinherit the eldest upon just occasions and prefer the

---

Source: From J. R. Tanner, *Constitutional Documents of the Reign of James I, A.D. 1603–1625* (Cambridge, England: Cambridge University Press, 1930), pp. 15–16. Reprinted by permission.

youngest, according to his liking; make them beggars or rich at his pleasure; restrain or banish out of his presence, as he finds them give cause of offence, or restore them in favour again with the penitent sinner. So may the King deal with his subjects.

And lastly, as for the head of the natural body, the head hath the power of directing all the members of the body to that use which the judgment in the head thinks most convenient. . . .

The Powers of Parliament in England

The House of Commons

James' views on monarchical powers were not accepted by members of Parliament. Indeed, from the beginning of his reign through the reign of his son Charles I, king and Parliament struggled over their relative powers. Along with other problems, this struggle culminated in the 1640s with the outbreak of civil war and the eventual beheading of Charles I. The nature of this struggle is partially revealed in the following statements issued by the House of Commons in 1604 to the new king, James I.

> **Consider:** *The powers over which the House of Commons and the king differed; the justifications used by James I and the House of Commons for their claims; any ways in which compromise was possible between these two positions.*

Now concerning the ancient rights of the subjects of this realm, chiefly consisting in the privileges of this House of Parliament, the misinformation openly delivered to your Majesty hath been in three things:

First, That we held not privileges of right, but of grace only, renewed every Parliament by way of donature upon petition, and so to be limited.

Secondly, That we are no Court of Record, nor yet a Court that can command view of records, but that our proceedings here are only to acts and memorials, and that the attendance with the records is courtesy, not duty.

Thirdly and lastly, That the examination of the return of writs for knights and burgesses is without our compass, and due to the Chancery.

Against which assertions, most gracious Sovereign, tending directly and apparently to the utter overthrow of the very fundamental privileges of our House, and therein of the rights and liberties of the whole Commons of your realm of England which they and their ancestors from time immemorable have undoubtedly enjoyed under your Majesty's most noble progenitors, we, the knights, citizens, and burgesses of the House of Commons assembled in Parliament, and in the name of the whole commons of the realm of England, with uniform consent for ourselves and our posterity, do expressly protest, as

SOURCE: From J. R. Tanner, *Constitutional Documents of the Reign of James I, A.D. 1603–1625* (Cambridge, England: Cambridge University Press, 1930), pp. 220–222. Reprinted by permission.

being derogatory in the highest degree to the true dignity, liberty, and authority of your Majesty's High Court of Parliament, and consequently to the rights of all your Majesty's said subjects and the whole body of this your kingdom: And desire that this our protestation may be recorded to all posterity.

And contrariwise, with all humble and due respect to your Majesty our Sovereign Lord and Head, against those misinformations we most truly avouch,

First, That our privileges and liberties are our right and due inheritance, no less than our very lands and goods.

Secondly, That they cannot be withheld from us, denied, or impaired, but with apparent wrong to the whole state of the realm.

Thirdly, And that our making of request in the entrance of Parliament to enjoy our privilege is an act only of manners, and doth weaken our right no more than our suing to the King for our lands by petition. . . .

Fourthly, We avouch also, That our House is a Court of Record, and so ever esteemed.

Fifthly, That there is not the highest standing Court in this land that ought to enter into competency, either for dignity or authority, with this High Court of Parliament, which with your Majesty's royal assent gives laws to other Courts but from other Courts receives neither laws nor orders.

Sixthly and lastly, We avouch that the House of Commons is the sole proper judge of return of all such writs and of the election of all such members as belong to it, without which the freedom of election were not entire: And that the Chancery, though a standing Court under your Majesty, be to send out those writs and receive the returns and to preserve them, yet the same is done only for the use of the Parliament, over which neither the Chancery nor any other Court ever had or ought to have any manner of jurisdiction.

From these misinformed positions, most gracious Sovereign, the greatest part of our troubles, distrusts, and jealousies have risen. . . .

The Hammer of Witches

Heinrich Krämer and Jacob Sprenger

The upheavals of the period between 1560 and 1660 included growing violence against women in the form of persecuting women as witches. While witch hunting was widespread, it was particularly prevalent in Germany, where both Catholics and Protestants took part in the hunts and prosecutions. Authorities often used witch-hunters' manuals as guides to beliefs about witches. The most influential of these manuals, the Malleus Maleficarum *(The Hammer of Witches), was written in 1486 by two Dominican Inquisitors. The following excerpt focuses on why most witches were women.*

SOURCE: Kors, Alan C. and Edward Peters, eds. *Witchcraft in Europe, 1100–1700, A Documentary History.* (Philadelphia: University of Pennsylvania Press, 1972), pp. 114, 119, 121, 123.

Consider: *Exactly why, according to these authors, women are more likely than men to be witches; what this reveals about attitudes toward women.*

As for the first question, why a greater number of witches is found in the fragile feminine sex than among men . . . the first reason is, that they are more credulous, and since the chief aim of the devil is to corrupt faith, therefore he rather attacks them . . . the second reason is, that women are naturally more impressionable, and . . . the third reason is that they have slippery tongues, and are unable to conceal from their fellow-women those things which by evil arts they know. . . . But the natural reason is that she is more carnal than a man, as is clear from her many carnal abominations. And it should be noted that there was a defect in the formation of the first woman, since she was formed from a bent rib, that is, a rib of the breast, which is bent as it were in a contrary direction to a man. And since through this defect she is an imperfect animal, she always deceives. . . . And this is indicated by the etymology of the world; for Femina comes from Fe and Minus, since she is ever weaker to hold and preserve the faith. . . . To conclude. All witchcraft comes from carnal lust, which is in women insatiable.

VISUAL SOURCES

War and Violence

Jan Brueghel and Sebastien Vrancx

This painting (photo 15-1), by the Flemish artists Jan Brueghel (1568–1625), and Sebastien Vrancx (1573–1647), is of marauding armies during the Thirty Years' War. This war was a disaster for Germany not only because of its length and viciousness, but because of the common use of mercenary soldiers. In this picture mercenaries, without common uniforms or banners, attack what appears to be a wagon train of civilians probably fleeing on hearing rumors of their approach. Women and children are being attacked by the mercenaries, as are men, whether armed or not. Johann Jakob Christoffel von Grimmelshausen, a contemporary observer of such mercenaries, described them as inflicting "nothing but hurting and harming and being in their turn hurt and harmed, this was their whole purpose and existence. From this nothing could divert them—not winter or summer, snow or ice, heat or cold, wind or rain, mountain or valley, . . . or the very fear of eternal damnation itself. At this task they laboured until at last, in battles, sieges, assaults, campaigns, or even in their winter quarters, which is the soldiers' paradise, one by one they died, perished and rotted." The picture conveys the sense of almost random, out-of-control violence that was so typical of this period.

Consider: *The ways in which this painting and this observation might be used to describe how the Thirty Years' War was experienced by those involved.*

Photo 15-1

Kunsthistorisches Museum, Vienna

Leviathan: Political Order and Political Theory

Thomas Hobbes

Although England avoided the Thirty Years' War, it had its own experiences with passionate war and disruption of authority. Between 1640 and 1660 England endured the civil war, the trial and execution of its king, Charles I, the rise to power of Oliver Cromwell, and the return to power of the Stuart king, Charles II. These events stimulated Thomas Hobbes (1588–1679) to formulate one of the most important statements of political theory in history.

Hobbes supported the royalist cause during the civil war and served as tutor to the future Charles II. Applying some of the new philosophical and scientific concepts being developed during the seventeenth century, he presented a theory for the origins and proper functioning of the state and political authority. His main ideas appear in Leviathan *(1651), the title page of which appears here (photo 15-2). It shows a giant monarchical figure, with symbols of power and authority, presiding over a well-ordered city and surrounding lands. On close examination one can see that the monarch's body is composed of the citizens of this commonwealth who, according to Hobbes' theory, have mutually agreed to give up their independence to an all-powerful sovereign who will keep order. This is explained in the following selection from Hobbes' book, in which he relates the reasons for the formation of a commonwealth to the nature of authority in that commonwealth.*

SOURCE: Thomas Hobbes, *Leviathan,* vol. III of *The English Works of Thomas Hobbes,* ed. Sir William Molesworth (London: John Bohn, 1889), pp. 113, 151–153, 157, 159.

Photo 15-2

Consider: *Why men form such a commonwealth and why they give such power to the sovereign; how Hobbes' argument compares with that of James I; why both those favoring more power for the House of Commons and those favoring increased monarchical power might criticize this argument.*

Whatsoever therefore is consequent to a time of war, where every man is enemy to every man; the same is consequent to the time, wherein men live without other security, than what their own strength, and their own invention shall furnish them withal. In such condition, there is no place for industry; because the fruit thereof is uncertain: and consequently no culture of the earth; no navigation, nor use of the commodities that may be imported by sea; no commodious building; no instruments of moving, and removing, such things as require much force; no knowledge of the face of the earth; no account of time; no arts; no letters; no society; and which is worst of all, continual fear, and danger of violent death; and the life of man, solitary, poor, nasty, brutish, and short. . . .

The final cause, end, or design of men who naturally love liberty, and dominion over others, in the introduction of that restraint upon themselves, in which we see them live in commonwealths, is the foresight of their own preservation, and of a more contented life thereby; that is to say, of getting themselves out from that miserable condition of war, which is necessarily consequent, as hath been shown in chapter XIII, to the natural passions of men, when there is no visible power to keep them in awe, and tie them by fear of punishment to the performance of their covenants, and observation of those laws of nature set down. . . .

For the laws of nature, as *justice, equity, modesty, mercy,* and, in sum, doing to others, as we would be done to, of themselves, without the terror of some power, to cause them to be observed, are contrary to our natural passions, that carry us to partiality, pride, revenge, and the like. And covenants, without the sword, are but words, and of no strength to secure a man at all. . . .

The only way to erect such a common power, as may be able to defend them from the invasion of foreigners, and the injuries of one another, and thereby to secure them in such sort, as that by their own industry, and by the fruits of the earth, they may nourish themselves and live contentedly; is, to confer all their power and strength upon one man, or upon one assembly of men, that may reduce all their wills, by plurality of voices, unto one will: which is as much as to say, to appoint one man, or assembly of men, to bear their person; and every one to own, and acknowledge himself to be author of whatsoever he that so beareth their person, shall act, or cause to be acted, in those things which concern the common peace and safety; and therein to submit their wills, every one to his will, and their judgments, to his judgment. This is more than consent, or concord; it is a real unity of them all, in one and the same person, made by covenant of every man with every man, in such manner, as if every man should say to every man, *I authorise and give up my right of governing myself, to this man, or to this assembly of men, on this condition, that thou give up thy right to him, and authorise all his actions in like manner.* This done, the multitude so united in one person, is called a COMMONWEALTH, . . . This is the generation of that great LEVIATHAN, or rather, to speak more reverently, of that *mortal god,* to which we owe under the *immortal God,* our peace and defence. For by this authority, given him by every particular man in the commonwealth, he hath the use of so much power and strength conferred on him, that by terror thereof, he is enabled to perform the wills of them all, to peace at home, and mutual aid against their enemies abroad. And in him consisteth the essence of the commonwealth; which to define it, is *one person, of whose acts a great multitude, by mutual covenants one with another, have made themselves every one the author, to the end he may use the strength and means of them all, as he shall think expedient, for their peace and common defence.*

And he that carrieth this person, is called SOVEREIGN, and said to have *sovereign power;* and every one besides, his subject.

Germany and the Thirty Years' War

These maps center on circumstances in Germany during the Thirty Years' War. The first (map 15-1) shows the approximate political and religious divisions at the beginning of the war. This

Map 15-1   Political and Religious Divisions

Map 15-2   Main War Zones

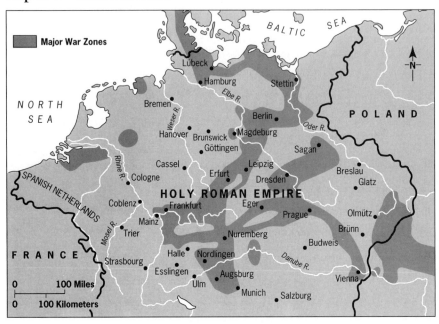

Map 15-3   Population Change: 1618–1648

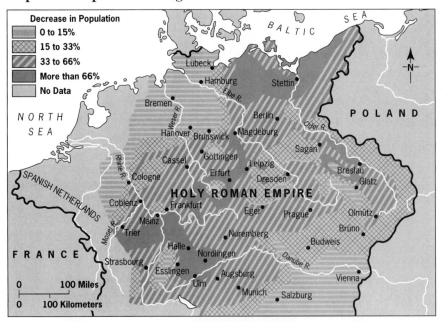

map is simplified for clarity in a number of ways. It does not show areas of minority religious allegiance or areas where Protestant sects other than Calvinists or Lutherans made up substantial proportions of the population. It denotes only some of the political divisions, which numbered close to three hundred in this area. The second map (map 15-2) shows the main areas of battle during the Thirty Years' War. Map 15-3 indicates the changes in population, primarily due to war and plague, between 1618 and 1648.

Together, these maps reveal some of the political and religious problems facing Germany. Despite the theoretical existence of the Holy Roman Empire, Germany was in reality the most politically and religiously divided area in seventeenth-century Europe. It is thus not surprising that historians find it difficult to determine the political and religious factors causing this war and the responsibility for its long continuation. Some of the demographic effects are indicated through a comparison of the main areas of battle and changes in population. Indeed, the continued political and religious division of Germany after this war, along with such massive destruction of the area and the population, helps explain Germany's weakness and inability to unify for the following two centuries.

> **Consider:** *In what ways the geopolitical and religious divisions of Germany explain the duration and extent of damages of the Thirty Years' War; how historians might use these maps to support their interpretations of the causes and significance of the Thirty Years' War.*

SECONDARY SOURCES

A Political Interpretation of the Thirty Years' War

Hajo Holborn

Historians have long disagreed about the essential causes of the Thirty Years' War. Some focus on a particular area, such as Germany or Spain; others emphasize a particular set of causes, such as religion or politics; and still others argue that it was only part of a general seventeenth-century crisis affecting all aspects of society. In the following selection Hajo Holborn, a historian known for his work on German history, argues that the war was primarily a political struggle in the German states of the Hapsburgs. He accepts the religious issue as at most a contributing cause.

> **Consider:** *The role religion played in the conflict even though it may not have been primary in causing the war; other factors that might have caused the war.*

SOURCE: Hajo Holborn, *A History of Modern Germany: The Reformation* (New York: Alfred A. Knopf, 1959), pp. 305–306.

It was not a conflict among European powers, not even an acute controversy between the emperor and the princes of the Empire or among these princes themselves that led to the outbreak of the long war that lived on in the memory of the German people as the "Great War" and in the books of the historians as the Thirty Years' War. Rather, it was a struggle between the estates and the monarchy in the territories of the Habsburg dynasty which set fire to all of Germany and to the European continent. Without the grave crisis in the constitutional life of the Empire, the weakness of the German states, and the ambitions of the great powers of Europe, the events that occurred in Bohemia could not have developed into a disaster from which Germany was to emerge crippled and mutilated.

It is difficult to determine to what extent differences in the interpretation of Christian faith were a direct cause of the catastrophe. There is no doubt but that religious motivation was strong in the lives of individuals and societies, and even in the relations among states and nations, in this age. But the confessional war started at a time when enthusiasm for the religious revivals, both Protestant and Catholic, had lost much of its original force and religious ideas had again become conventionalized. Frank skepticism was rare in Germany, but ever larger groups of people had ceased to find in religious ideals the full satisfaction of their human aspirations. Nevertheless, the reality of heaven and hell was nowhere questioned, nor was the necessity of basing the political and social order on principles that would keep Satan from undoing the work of God. Religious zeal found expression not only in the ghastly fury of witch trials, which reached its climax during these years, but also in the care with which all governments attended to the direction of church life in their dominions. Yet while on the one hand religion deteriorated into superstition, on the other it tended to become formalized and to lose genuineness. Every political action was publicly cloaked in religious terms, but religion seemed to be used more and more to rationalize actions motivated by secular interests.

A Religious Interpretation of the Thirty Years' War

Carl J. Friedrich

An older scholarly tradition attributes primary importance to religion in explaining the causes of the Thirty Years' War. This tradition has been revived by Carl J. Friedrich, a highly respected historian from Harvard. In The Age of the Baroque, 1610–1660, *Friedrich places the war in the context of the still strong religious assumptions of the time, arguing that historians who emphasize political causes overlook the importance of this religious context. The following is an excerpt from that work.*

> **Consider:** *The evidence Friedrich uses to support his argument; why, according to Friedrich, many historians have rejected the religious interpretation of the war; how Holborn might criticize this argument.*

Source: Excerpts from *The Age of the Baroque* by Carl J. Friedrich. Copyright 1952 by Harper & Row, Publishers, Inc. Reprinted by permission of HarperCollins Publishers, Inc.

It has been the fashion to minimize the religious aspect of the great wars which raged in the heart of Europe, over the territory of the Holy Roman Empire of the German Nation. Not only the calculating statecraft of Richelieu and Mazarin, but even Pope Urban VIII's own insistence lent support to such a view in a later age which had come to look upon religion and politics as fairly well separated fields of thought and action. Liberal historians found it difficult to perceive that for baroque man religion and politics were cut from the same cloth, indeed that the most intensely political issues were precisely the religious ones. Gone was the neopaganism of the renaissance, with its preoccupation with self-fulfillment here and now. Once again, and for the last time, life was seen as meaningful in religious, even theological, terms, and the greater insight into power which the renaissance had brought served merely to deepen the political passion brought to the struggle over religious faiths.

Without a full appreciation of the close links between secular and religious issues, it becomes impossible to comprehend the Thirty Years' War. Frederick, the unlucky Palatine, as well as Ferdinand, Tilly and Gustavus Adolphus, Maximilian of Bavaria and John George of Saxony, they all must be considered fools unless their religious motivation is understood as the quintessential core of their politics. Time and again, they appear to have done the "wrong thing," if their actions are viewed in a strictly secular perspective. To be sure, men became increasingly sophisticated as the war dragged on; but even after peace was finally concluded in 1648, the religious controversies continued. Ever since the Diet of Augsburg (1555) had adopted the callous position that a man must confess the religion of those who had authority over the territory he lived in—a view which came to be known under the slogan of *"cujus regio, ejus religio"*—the intimate tie of religion and government had been the basis of the Holy Empire's tenuous peace. Born of the spirit of its time—Lutheran otherworldliness combining with Humanistic indifferentism—this doctrine was no more than an unstable compromise between Catholics and Lutherans, the Calvinists being entirely outside its protective sphere. But in the seventeenth century not only the Calvinists, who by 1618 had become the fighting protagonists of Protestantism, but likewise the more ardent Catholics, inspired by the Council of Trent, by the Jesuits and Capuchins, backed by the power of Spain and filled with the ardor of the Counter Reformation, had come to look upon this doctrine as wicked and contrary to their deepest convictions.

When Ferdinand, after claiming the crown of Bohemia by heredity, proceeded to push the work of counter reformation, his strongest motivation was religious; so was the resistance offered by the Bohemian people, as well as Frederick's acceptance of the crown of Bohemia on the basis of an election. Dynastic and national sentiments played their part, surely, but they reinforced the basic religious urge. The same concurrence of religious with dynastic, political, even economic motives persisted throughout the protracted struggle, but the religious did not cease to be the all-pervasive feeling; baroque man, far from being bothered by the contradictions, experienced these polarities as inescapable.

If religion played a vital role in persuading Ferdinand II to dismiss his victorious general, it was even more decisive in inspiring Gustavus Adolphus to enter the war against both the emperor and the League. The nineteenth century, incapable of feeling the religious passions which stirred baroque humanity and much impressed with the solidified national states which the seventeenth century bequeathed to posterity, was prone to magnify the dynastic and often Machiavellian policies adopted by rulers who professed to be deeply religious, and the twentieth century has largely followed suit in denying the religious character of these wars. But it is precisely this capacity to regard the statesman as the champion of religion, to live and act the drama of man's dual dependence upon faith and power that constituted the quintessence of the baroque.

War and Peace in the Old Regime

M. S. Anderson

Western societies rarely went for long periods of time without becoming involved in wars. However, war was particularly prevalent and destructive in the period between 1618 and 1660. Historians have long debated the causes for these wars. In the following selection, M. S. Anderson, who has written extensively on the Early Modern period, analyzes what war meant to Europeans and the broader significance of war during the seventeenth century.

> **Consider:** *How Europeans perceived the causes, nature, and consequences of war; the distinctions between war and peace; the connections between war and politics.*

In early modern Europe almost everyone regarded war as a normal, perhaps even a necessary, part of human life. Events seemed to bear out this view; in the period 1618–60 every year saw serious armed conflict between states somewhere in Europe, and during a large proportion of it destructive struggles were being waged simultaneously in several parts of the continent. The ubiquity and apparent inevitability of war meant that serious discussion of its causes was rare. As an integral and unavoidable aspect of existence it was received like bad weather or epidemics, as something clearly beyond the power of the ordinary man to avert, something demanding acceptance rather than analysis. Luther's dictum that 'war is as necessary as eating, drinking or any other business' reflects in typically blunt terms this matter-of-fact and fatalistic attitude. Nor was there much grasp of the deeper and more lasting effects it might sometimes have. It was only too obvious that in the short term it meant for many death, destruction and loss. But against this was put the venerable and well-established argument that prolonged peace weakened the moral fibre of a society, making it lax, slothful, even corrupt, whereas war focused and mobilized energies, called forth many of the better qualities of man, and had a generally tonic and purifying effect. It was clear also that a successful war could heighten the personal prestige of a ruler; the vindication of claims put forward by monarchs to disputed territories, to alleged hereditary rights, even merely to precedence over rivals or to specific symbols of such precedence, were by far the most common ostensible causes of conflict.

SOURCE: M. S. Anderson. *War and Society in Europe of the Old Regime, 1618–1789.* New York: St. Martin's Press, 1988, pp. 13–15.

Occasionally it was realized that war might have important long-term economic results, that it might foster the trade of a victorious state against that of its defeated enemies and that economic rivalry might be one of its causes. Struggles inspired simply or even mainly by this kind of material rivalry were not frequent in this period but they did take place. . . . However the idea that war might, through the demands it made on societies and the impetus it gave to the growth of powerful central governments, help fundamentally to change these societies, was still a strange one. . . .

Finally, a clear-cut distinction between war and peace, a dividing line whose crossing was instantly recognizable, was something which was only beginning to emerge. The position of neutrals was still ambiguous, their status poorly guaranteed by embryonic international law and liable to frequent infringements. There was a general belief that a belligerent had some right to march its forces across neutral territory if it made good any damage they caused in the process (the right of *transitus innoxius*). Frontiers were still poorly defined, zones of contact between neighbouring powers rather than lines clearly demarcated. The hold of central governments over officials and commanders in border areas was often still incomplete, so that in these areas locally inspired acts of oppression and outright violence could frequently occur, though usually without involving the states concerned in formal conflict. In this violent age incidents of this kind formed a sort of grumbling undertone to international relations, seldom actively menacing peace between states but always a potential threat. . . .

Armed conflict in early seventeenth-century Europe, therefore, ramified into every aspect of life and was able to do this because it was still in many ways badly defined, because the boundary between peace and war was still fuzzy. But lack of clear definition did nothing to reduce its importance. Most of the governments of Europe were first and foremost, as they had been for generations, machines for waging war. Both the scale on which they fought and the effective control they could exert over their fighting forces were to increase markedly during the seventeenth and early eighteenth centuries.

The Causes of the English Civil War

Conrad Russell

The civil war in England, which broke out in the middle of the seventeenth century, is even more controversial among historians than the Thirty Years' War. At the heart of the controversy are two related issues: first, what the balance of religious, political, economic, and social forces was in causing the civil war; second, what groups or classes can be said to have supported each side. In the following selection Conrad Russell argues that the civil war resulted from a conjunction of three causes of instability: the problem of multiple kingdoms (England and Scotland), the problem of religious division, and the financial pressures on the crown.

SOURCE: From Conrad Russell, *The Causes of the English Civil War*, pp. 213–217. © Conrad Russell 1990. Reprinted by permission of Oxford University Press.

Consider: *How Russell's three causes worked together; why Charles' attempt to enforce English religion on Scotland in 1637 was so important.*

[The English Civil War] was the result of three long-term causes of instability, all of them well established before Charles came to the throne, and all of them ones which can be observed to have troubled European, as well as British, monarchies. There is nothing peculiarly British (still less English) about any of them: they were not even exceptionally acute in England. What is peculiar to the two cases of England and the Netherlands is that all of them came to a head at the same time. These three long-term causes were the problem of multiple kingdoms, the problem of religious division, and the breakdown of a financial and political system in the face of inflation and the rising cost of war.

The problem of multiple kingdoms was always a likely cause of instability from 1603 onwards. The temptation to press for greater harmonization was always there, and was always likely to produce serious troubles. In 1603 England encountered . . . the shock of subjection to a supra-national authority. . . . [T]he English . . . wished to treat both James and Charles as if they were only kings of a single nation-state called England. Since this was patently not the case, and the kings could not help knowing it, the English were always likely to misread royal actions, and in particular to press their kings to do things which, in British terms, they could not do. When, as in 1637, a British king fell victim to a similar misapprehension, and attempted to govern all Britain as king of England, he found this was something he could not do. . . .

England's basic error in 1603 was the failure to absorb that what had taken place was the union of two sovereign, and therefore legally equal, states. Not even James could really turn Scotland into 'North Britain'. It was a state with institutions, law, and culture of its own, and one determined to insist that any resulting relationship must be a legally equal partnership. . . .

[T]he problem of religious division . . . derived its explosive force from the belief that religion ought to be enforced. It was a problem of a society which had carried on the assumptions appropriate to a society with a single church into one which had many churches. . . .

But August 1640, when the Scottish army, by entering England, merged the religious problem with the British problem, was too early for it to have cooled enough. One might say of the English Calvinists what Machiavelli said of the Pope in Italy: they were too weak to unite the country, but too strong to allow anyone else to do so. When the Scots entered England, they were able to join forces with a large group of people who preferred Scottish religion to what was coming to be taken for their own.

The strains caused for monarchies by the combination of inflation with the massive increases in the cost of war known collectively as 'the military revolution' is also a European theme. The financial difficulties faced, after the conclusion of the long wars of the 1590s, by James VI and I, Philip III of Spain, and Henri IV of France have too much in common to be entirely coincidental. The changes following the regular use of gunpowder, especially the trend to larger-scale fortifications and to larger armies, much increased the economic drain of war. The resulting financial pressures put strain on the principle of consent to taxation everywhere in Europe, and perhaps only the Netherlands, with the advantage of a visible enemy at the gate, were able to combine consent with the levying of taxes on the scale needed. England, because the principle of consent to taxation was so particularly well entrenched, was perhaps put under more constitutional strain by this process than some other powers. . . .

No one, or even two, of these forces was in the event enough: it took the conjunction of all three to drive England into civil war. . . . Both the religious and the financial problem had been plainly visible by the 1550s, and they had not created civil war in ninety years since then. England in 1637 was, no doubt, a country with plenty of discontents, some of them potentially serious, but it was also still a very stable and peaceful one, and one which does not show many visible signs of being on the edge of a major upheaval. . . . The attempt which Charles made in 1637 to enforce English religion on Scotland, was thus by far the likeliest reason for a merging of these three long-term causes of instability. It is difficult to argue that Charles took this risk with his eyes open. It is equally difficult to see what action a king could have taken which would have been better designed to precipitate an English civil war.

The Devil's Handmaid: Women in the Age of Reformations

William Monter

As indicated by the document The Hammer of Witches, *beliefs in witchcraft were widespread during the sixteenth and seventeenth centuries, and authoritative sources supported the belief that most witches were women. Many people were also accused of killing their children (infanticide). For both witchcraft and infanticide, the vast majority of those accused were women. In this selection, William Monter, a historian specializing in the Reformation era, analyzes why witchcraft and infanticide seemed to grow in sixteenth- and seventeenth-century Europe.*

> **Consider:** *Which three developments best explain the growing prosecutions for witchcraft and infanticide during this period; which groups of women were most affected and why.*

Three key developments combined and interacted to shape the male hysteria about witchcraft and infanticide in Reformation Europe. First and foremost, public institutions—state and church alike—were increasingly interfering in daily life. Throughout Protestant and Catholic Europe, the state enforced attendance at church; church officials preached obedience to the state; and both increasingly tried to regulate everyone's behavior. Ecclesiastical courts such as Catholic inquisitions or Calvinist consistories depended heavily on state enforcement of their policies; states like England or France relied on clergymen to provide records of baptisms or to proclaim government edicts from the pulpit.

Source: William Monter, "Protestant Wives, Catholic Saints, and the Devil's Handmaid: Women in the Age of Reformations," in Renate Bridenthal, Claudia Koonz, and Susan Stuard, eds., *Becoming Visible: Women in European History,* First and Second Editions, copyright © 1977 & 1987 by Houghton Mifflin Company. Used with permission.

Secondly, these increasingly active public authorities inhabited a fear-ridden world. Most Protestant and Catholic Europeans still peered at their neighbors from walled towns and fortified castles; Luther's greatest hymn begins, "A Mighty Fortress is our God." We cannot find many material reasons for such pervasive fears at this time; bubonic plague, the great killer of pre-industrial Europe, did most of its damage either before or after the age of reformations. The reformers of Protestant and Catholic Europe, determined to attack all forms of "superstition" (including, of course, witchcraft), reduced the influence of benevolent magic, like exorcisms or special prayers, but provided nothing to replace them. Modern science did not yet exist; official medicine often had no explanations (and worse, no effective remedies) for many illnesses. Under such conditions, Protestant and Catholic reformers imposed the "Triumph of Lent" on unwed mothers of stillborns, and made old women with deviant dreams into scapegoats for sixteenth-century Christianity's obsession with the Devil.

Finally, the patriarchal theories of late-Renaissance Europe played an important role in determining which groups of women became victims of these obsessions. Accused witches were disproportionately widows, while infanticide defendants were single women; both groups lived outside direct male supervision in this age of reinforced patriarchal nuclear families. Their "unnatural" position aroused suspicion and sometimes fear; neighborhood enmities did the rest.

Chapter Questions

1.   Clearly, there were both political and religious aspects to the turmoil between 1560 and 1660. On balance, which do you think were most important? On what evidence have you based your answer? What argument can be formulated that admits the importance of both aspects?

2.   How might the themes in this chapter be related to the political and religious developments from the mid-fifteenth to the mid-sixteenth centuries that were the focus of the two preceding chapters?

CHAPTER SIXTEEN

Aristocracy and Absolutism in the Seventeenth Century

The second half of the seventeenth century was a period of relative political stability in Europe. Although wars still occurred, they lacked the intensity of the preceding period. In the ascendant states, such as France, Prussia, Austria, Russia, and England, central governments were gaining authority. The primary power, and for many states the model of political authority, was France. There, Louis XIV, supported by a strong standing army, a policy of mercantilism, and a growing bureaucracy, wielded absolute power. There were similar situations in Prussia, Austria, and Russia. A different pattern occurred in England, where the central government remained strong while the monarchy itself weakened. There, after the return to power of the Stuart kings between 1660 and 1688, a revolution furthered the authority of Parliament.

During this period, important social, political, and economic changes occurred unevenly and generally benefited those who were already prominent and well to do. Aristocrats lost some of their independence to kings in countries like France and Prussia, but they continued to staff most of the important government offices, to maintain their elevated prestige, and to influence cultural styles and tastes. For most people, the structure of society, the way of life, and the relevant institutions changed little throughout this period.

This chapter concentrates on two broad topics: the growth of central government and Early Modern society. The selections address a number of questions.

For the first topic, what was the nature of monarchical absolutism in France? How did it differ from Prussian monarchical absolutism? How did the pattern of monarchical absolutism compare with the growth of parliamentary power in England? What institutions and policies were developed to facilitate the growth of central governments? For the second topic, what was the nature of the family in Early Modern Europe? What were typical attitudes toward childhood? What were the traditional values and patterns of life for commoners during this period?

This dual focus should provide some broad insights into Europe during the seventeenth century and help establish a background for eighteenth-century developments.

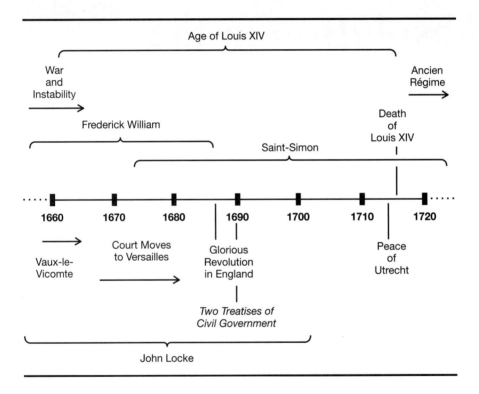

PRIMARY SOURCES

Austria Over All If She Only Will: Mercantilism

Philipp W. von Hornick

Mercantilism, a loose set of economic ideas and corresponding government policies, was a common component of political absolutism during the seventeenth century. Typical mercantilist goals were the acquisition of bullion, a positive balance of trade, and economic self-sufficiency. An unusually clear and influential statement of mercantilist policies was published in 1684 by Philipp Wilhelm von Hornick. A lawyer and later a government official, Hornick set down what he considered to be the nine principal rules for a proper economic policy. These are excerpted here.

> **Consider:** *The political and military purposes served by encouraging mercantilist policies; the foreign policy decisions such economic policies would support; the political and economic circumstances that would make it easiest for a country to adhere to and benefit from mercantilist policies.*

NINE PRINCIPAL RULES OF NATIONAL ECONOMY

If the might and eminence of a country consist in its surplus of gold, silver, and all other things necessary or convenient for its *subsistence*, derived, so far as possible, from its own resources, without *dependence* upon other countries, and in the proper fostering, use, and application of these, then it follows that a general national *economy (Landes-Oeconomie)* should consider how such a surplus, fostering, and enjoyment can be brought about, without *dependence* upon others, or where this is not feasible in every respect, with as little *dependence* as possible upon foreign countries, and sparing use of the country's own cash. For this purpose the following nine rules are especially serviceable.

First, to inspect the country's soil with the greatest care, and not to leave the agricultural possibilities or a single corner or clod of earth unconsidered. Every useful form of *plant* under the sun should be experimented with, to see whether it is adapted to the country, for the distance or nearness of the sun is not all that counts. Above all, no trouble or expense should be spared to discover gold and silver.

Second, all commodities found in a country, which cannot be used in their natural state, should be worked up within the country; since the payment for *manufacturing* generally exceeds the value of the raw material by two, three, ten, twenty, and even a hundred fold, and the neglect of this is an abomination to prudent managers.

Third, for carrying out the above two rules, there will be need of people, both for producing and cultivating the raw materials and for working them up. Therefore, attention should be given to the population, that it may be as large as the country can support, this

SOURCE: Philipp W. von Hornick, "Austria Over All If She Only Will," in Arthur Eli Monroe, ed., *Early Economic Thought.* Reprinted by permission of Harvard University Press (Cambridge, Mass., 1927), pp. 223–225. Copyright © 1924 by The President and Fellows of Harvard College.

being a well-ordered state's most important concern, but, unfortunately, one that is often neglected. And the people should be turned by all possible means from idleness to re-munerative *professions;* instructed and encouraged in all kinds of *inventions,* arts, and trades; and, if necessary, instructors should be brought in from foreign countries for this.

Fourth, gold and silver once in the country, whether from its own mines or obtained by *industry* from foreign countries, are under no circumstances to be taken out for any purpose, so far as possible, or allowed to be buried in chests or coffers, but must always remain in *circulation;* nor should much be permitted in uses where they are at once *de-stroyed* and cannot be utilized again. For under these conditions, it will be impossible for a country that has once acquired a considerable supply of cash, especially one that pos-sesses gold and silver mines, ever to sink into poverty; indeed, it is impossible that it should not continually increase in wealth and property. Therefore,

Fifth, the inhabitants of the country should make every effort to get along with their domestic products, to confine their luxury to these alone, and to do without foreign prod-ucts as far as possible (except where great need leaves no alternative, or if not need, wide-spread, unavoidable abuse, of which Indian spices are an example). And so on.

Sixth, in case the said purchases were indispensable because of necessity or *irremedi-able* abuse, they should be obtained from these foreigners at first hand, so far as possi-ble, and not for gold or silver, but in exchange for other domestic wares.

Seventh, such foreign commodities should in this case be imported in unfinished form, and worked up within the country, thus earning the wages of *manufacture* there.

Eighth, opportunities should be sought night and day for selling the country's super-fluous goods to these foreigners in manufactured form, so far as this is necessary, and for gold and silver; and to this end, *consumption,* so to speak, must be sought in the farthest ends of the earth, and developed in every possible way.

Ninth, except for important considerations, no importation should be allowed under any circumstances of commodities of which there is sufficient supply of suitable quality at home; and in this matter neither sympathy nor compassion should be shown foreign-ers, be they friends, kinsfolk, *allies,* or enemies. For all friendship ceases, when it in-volves my own weakness and ruin. And this holds good, even if the domestic commodities are of poorer quality, or even higher priced. For it would be better to pay for an article two dollars which remain in the country than only one which goes out, how-ever strange this may seem to the ill-informed.

A Secret Letter: Monarchical Authority in Prussia

Frederick William, The Great Elector

Seventeenth-century monarchs attained unprecedented authority within their realms, often through the skillful use of policies designed to enhance their power. The most dramatic consolidation of power was made by the head of the Hohenzollerns, Frederick William (1640–1688), known as the

SOURCE: From *Documents of German History,* edited by Louis Snyder. Copyright © 1958 by Rutgers, The State University.

"great elector" of Brandenburg-Prussia. He instituted new taxes, developed a trained bureaucracy staffed by members of the nobility, modernized his army, and asserted his own authority over competing claims from the nobility and representative institutions. In 1667 he wrote a secret letter of advice to his son, who was in line to inherit the throne. An excerpt of this letter appears here.

Consider: *The greatest threats to monarchical authority according to Frederick William; the policies Frederick William thought were most important for maintaining power; which of Frederick William's recommendations echo the attitudes expressed in mercantilist doctrines.*

It is necessary that you conduct yourself as a good father to your people, that you love your subjects regardless of their religious convictions, and that you try to promote their welfare at all times. Work to stimulate trade everywhere, and keep in mind the population increase of the Mark of Brandenburg. Take advantage of the advice of the clergy and nobility as much as you can; listen to them and be gracious to them all, as befits one of your position; recognize ability where you find it, so that you will increase the love and affection of your subjects toward you. But, it is essential that you always be moderate in your attitudes, in order not to endanger your position and lose respect. With those of your own station in life, be careful never to give way in matters of precedence and in all to which you are entitled; on the contrary, hold fast to the eminence of your superior position. Remember that one can lose one's superior position if one allows too great pomposity and too great a show upon the part of members of the court.

Be keenly interested in the administration of justice throughout your land. See to it that justice is maintained for the poor as well as for the rich without discrimination of any kind. See to it that lawsuits are carried out without delay, without procrastination, for in doing this, you will solidify your own position. . . .

Seek to maintain friendly relations with the princes and the nobility of the Empire. Correspond with them frequently and maintain your friendship with them. Be certain not to give them cause for ill-will; try not to arouse emotions of jealousy or enmity, but be sure that you are always in a strong position to maintain your weight in disputes that may arise. . . .

It is wise to have alliances, if necessary, but it is better to rely on your own strength. You are in a weak position if you do not have the means and do not possess the confidence of the people. These are the things, God be praised, which have made me powerful since the time I began to have them. I only regret that, in the beginning of my reign, I forsook these policies and followed the advice of others against my will.

Mémoires: The Aristocracy Undermined in France

Saint-Simon

Louis XIV of France was the most powerful ruler of his time. He had inherited the throne as a child in 1643. He took personal command by 1661, ruling France until his death in 1715.

SOURCE: Orest Ranum and Patricia Ranum, eds. and trans., *The Century of Louis XIV.* Reprinted by permission of Harper & Row (New York, 1972), pp. 81, 83, 87–88.

Contemporary rulers viewed him as a model ruler. One of the ways in which he reinforced his position was by conducting a magnificent court life at his palace of Versailles. There, nobles hoping for favors or appointments competed for his attention and increasingly became dependent upon royal whim. One of those nobles, the Duke of Saint-Simon (1675–1755), felt slighted and grew to resent the king. Saint-Simon chronicled life at Versailles in his Mémoires. *In the following excerpt, he shows how Louis XIV used this court life to his own ends.*

> **Consider:** *How the king's activities undermined the position of the nobility; the options available to a noble who wanted to maintain or increase his own power; how the king's activities compare with the great elector's recommendations to his son.*

Frequent fetes, private walks at Versailles, and excursions were means which the King seized upon in order to single out or to mortify [individuals] by naming the persons who should be there each time, and in order to keep each person assiduous and attentive to pleasing him. He sensed that he lacked by far enough favors to distribute in order to create a continuous effect. Therefore he substituted imaginary favors for real ones, through jealousy—little preferences which were shown daily, and one might say at each moment—[and] through his artfulness. The hopes to which these little preferences and these honors gave birth, and the deference which resulted from them—no one was more ingenious than he in unceasingly inventing these sorts of things. Marly, eventually, was of great use to him in this respect; and Trianon, where everyone, as a matter of fact, could go pay court to him, but where ladies had the honor of eating with him and where they were chosen at each meal; the candlestick which he had held for him each evening at bedtime by a courtier whom he wished to honor, and always from among the most worthy of those present, whom he named aloud upon coming out from saying his prayers.

Louis XIV carefully trained himself to be well informed about what was happening everywhere, in public places, in private homes, in public encounters, in the secrecy of families or of [amorous] liaisons. Spies and tell tales were countless. They existed in all forms: some who were unaware that their denunciations went as far as [the King], others who knew it; some who wrote him directly by having their letters delivered by routes which he had established for them, and those letters were seen only by him, and always before all other things; and lastly, some others who sometimes spoke to him secretly in his cabinets, by the back passageways. These secret communications broke the necks of an infinity of persons of all social positions, without their ever having been able to discover the cause, often very unjustly, and the King, once warned, never reconsidered, or so rarely that nothing was more [determined]. . . .

In everything he loved splendor, magnificence, profusion. He turned this taste into a maxim for political reasons, and instilled it into his court on all matters. One could please him by throwing oneself into fine food, clothes, retinue, buildings, gambling. These were occasions which enabled him to talk to people. The essence of it was that by this he attempted and succeeded in exhausting everyone by making luxury a virtue, and for certain persons a necessity, and thus he gradually reduced everyone to depending entirely upon his generosity in order to subsist. In this he also found satisfaction for his pride through a court which was superb in all respects, and through a greater confusion which increasingly destroyed natural distinctions. This is an evil which, once introduced, became the internal cancer which is devouring all individuals—because from the court it promptly spread to Paris and into the provinces and the armies, where persons, whatever their position, are considered important only in proportion to the table they lay and their magnificence ever since this unfortunate innovation—which is devouring all individuals, which forces those who are in a position to steal not to restrain themselves from doing so for the most part, in their need to keep up with their expenditures; [a cancer] which is nourished by the confusion of social positions, pride, and even decency, and which by a mad desire to grow keeps constantly increasing, whose consequences are infinite and lead to nothing less than ruin and general upheaval.

Second Treatise of Civil Government: Legislative Power

John Locke

In England royal absolutism had been under attack throughout the seventeenth century and finally was defeated by the Glorious Revolution of 1688–1689. At that point there was a definitive shift in power to Parliament, which was controlled by the upper classes. John Locke (1632–1704), in his Two Treatises of Civil Government *(1690), justified the revolution and the new political constitution of England and expounded political ideas that became influential during the eighteenth and nineteenth centuries. This work and other writings established Locke as a first-rate empirical philosopher and political theorist. In the following selection from his* Second Treatise of Civil Government, *Locke analyzes legislative power.*

> **Consider:** *The purposes for entering into society; the extent of and limitations on legislative power; how Locke justifies his argument; how these ideas are contrary to monarchical absolutism.*

134. The great end of men's entering into society being the enjoyment of their properties in peace and safety, and the great instrument and means of that being the laws established in that society, the first and fundamental positive law of all commonwealths is the establishing of the legislative power, as the first and fundamental natural law which is to govern even the legislative. Itself is the preservation of the society and (as far as will consist with the public good) of every person in it. This legislative is not only the supreme power of the commonwealth, but sacred and unalterable in the hands where the community have once placed it. Nor can any edict of anybody else, in what form soever conceived, or by what power soever backed, have the force and obligation of a law which has not its sanction from that legislative which the public has chosen and appointed; for without this the law could not have that which is absolutely necessary to its being a law, the consent of the society, over whom nobody can have a power to make laws

---

SOURCE: John Locke, *Two Treatises of Civil Government* (London: J. M. Dent, Everyman, 1924), pp. 183–184, 189–190.

but by their own consent and by authority received from them; and therefore all the obedience, which by the most solemn ties any one can be obliged to pay, ultimately terminates in this supreme power, and is directed by those laws which it enacts. Nor can any oaths to any foreign power whatsoever, or any domestic subordinate power, discharge any member of the society from his obedience to the legislative, acting pursuant to their trust, nor oblige him to any obedience contrary to the laws so enacted or farther than they do allow, it being ridiculous to imagine one can be tied ultimately to obey any power in the society which is not the supreme.

*

142. These are the bounds which the trust that is put in them by the society and the law of God and Nature have set to the legislative power of every commonwealth, in all forms of government. First: They are to govern by promulgated established laws, not to be varied in particular cases, but to have one rule for rich and poor, for the favourite at Court, and the countryman at plough. Secondly: These laws also ought to be designed for no other end ultimately but the good of the people. Thirdly: They must not raise taxes on the property of the people without the consent of the people given by themselves or their deputies. And this properly concerns only such governments where the legislative is always in being, or at least where the people have not reserved any part of the legislative to deputies, to be from time to time chosen by themselves. Fourthly: Legislative neither must nor can transfer the power of making laws to anybody else, or place it anywhere but where the people have.

VISUAL SOURCES

The Early Modern Château

The following picture of the château, grounds, and park of Vaux-le-Vicomte in France (photo 16-1) reveals both the wealth of France and certain trends of the seventeenth century. The château was built between 1657 and 1660 on the orders of France's superintendent of finance, Fouquet, and according to the plans of the architect Le Vau, the painter Lebrun, and the landscape gardener Le Nôtre. With its geometric orderliness and balance, it exemplifies the Classical style. In its conquest and manipulation of nature according to the rational plans of humans, it reflects the growing scientific spirit of the age. It also reflects a fundamentally stable society that was still dominated politically, socially, and economically by a small elite. It and buildings like it do not call out for military defense as did medieval castles. It later served as a model for Versailles, which itself became the model of monarchical splendor in seventeenth- and eighteenth-century Europe.

Consider: *Why such buildings and parks might have been built and how Saint-Simon might have viewed such projects.*

Photo 16-1

Alain Perceval

Maternal Care

Pieter de Hooch

This scene of domestic life (photo 16-2) is painted by the seventeenth-century Dutch artist Pieter de Hooch. Entitled Maternal Care, *it shows a girl kneeling while her mother examines and delouses her head. The scene takes place in Holland, the most urban and commercial European country. The moderate wealth of the rooms, revealed particularly by the paintings and the quality of the drapes, and the emphasis on cleanliness, privacy, and relative austerity, indicate that this is a middle-class home.*

Consider: *What the painter intended to communicate to the viewer of this painting.*

Photo 16-2

Fotocommissie Rijksmuseum Amsterdam

SECONDARY SOURCES

Absolutism: Myth and Reality
G. Durand

During the seventeenth century, several monarchs attained such unprecedented power and authority that historians have used the term "absolutism" to describe these political systems. Other historians have argued that the term is misleading, that neither the ambitions of the monarchs nor the results constituted political absolutism. In the following selection G. Durand analyzes the myth and the reality of absolutism.

> **Consider:** *Why Durand prefers to view absolutism as a tendency; how Durand evaluates the goals and attitudes of the monarchs; whether the primary sources by Frederick William and Saint-Simon support Durand's analysis.*

Viewed as a tendency rather than as a political system, absolutism is an undeniable reality. In every state the sovereign sought to free himself from pressure and control. The means were everywhere the same; the monarch tried to rule through councillors whom he chose rather than nobles who claimed such positions as their right. He also tried to recover control of the administration of justice which had been taken over by the feudal nobility and the church. These tendencies produced two institutions common to every state.

First a small, inner or secret council, a cabinet ('Conseil des Affaires'), distinct from the traditional councils which had grown from the division of the functions of the old *Curia Regis*. There is great similarity between, for instance, the *Consejo de Estado* in Castile, the inner circle of the privy council in England, the Austrian Council of State of 1748 and the Imperial council set up by Catherine the Great in 1769.

Second, a system of unifying and centralising judicial institutions. In France the drafting of customary law in the sixteenth century and the publication of the Codes and Great Ordinances in the seventeenth, formed the basis for royal intervention in the judicial process. The procedures of *évocation* to a higher court, or judgement by special commissioners named by the king, were specifically French; but an institution like the *conseil des parties* had its counterpart in the Royal Council of Castile, the English Star Chamber, or the Austrian *Hofrat*.

From this we may infer the existence of a general climate of absolutism, more or less pervasive, which offered the monarch no more than the opportunity to deliberate on matters of state without being affected by intrigue and pressure, and to ensure that the judicial process followed his wishes and directives.

SOURCE: From George Durand, "What Is Absolutism?" in *Louis XIV and Absolutism*, pp. 23–24, ed. by Ragnhild Hatton, copyright © 1976 The Macmillan Press, Ltd. Reprinted by permission of the publisher.

As an actual political system, absolutism is a myth. The monarchs themselves never regarded themselves as absolute, except in the case of the autocrats of Russia, where the lack of fundamental laws, of established customs and corporate orders within the state allowed the growth of a dictatorial form of government. In France, however, even Louis XIV never planned to abolish the Parlement, but merely curbed its pretensions and in December 1655 limited its right of remonstrance; nor did he try to abolish the estates. Monarchs did not try to create a system of institutions which would destroy any possibility of resistance through inertia. They merely sought to restrict the activities of persons who might cause trouble and to set up a new administrative structure parallel to the old; a handful of commissioners directed, urged on and controlled the system inherited from a time when counsel, remonstrance and shared power were the rule. Sovereigns also continued to delegate their administrative powers through the sale of offices, or to farm them out to financial potentates who became virtual states within the state. The kings of Spain suffered the tyranny of their own councils. In practice absolutism seems much more the result of circumstances and personalities than of a deliberate intention to revolutionise the whole structure of the state.

The English Revolution, 1688–1689

George Macaulay Trevelyan

In England two blows to monarchical authority proved to be turning points. The first was the civil war and the execution of Charles I in the 1640s. But although this was a victory for Parliament, the Cromwellian period that followed and the return from exile of Charles II in 1660 cast doubt on the permanence of Parliament's victory. The second was the "Glorious Revolution" of 1688, which removed James II from power without the turmoil of the first revolution. In the following selection Cambridge historian George Macaulay Trevelyan compares the two revolutions and analyzes the significance of the second one. Following the Whig tradition, Trevelyan views these trends in British history as constructive and progressive. More than most historians, he sees this revolution as an admirable triumph for Parliament.

Consider: *Why the second revolution was a more clear-cut victory for Parliament than the first; factors that contributed to the victory of Parliament.*

The fundamental question at issue in 1688 had been this—Is the law above the King, or is the King above the law? The interest of Parliament was identified with that of the law, because, undoubtedly, Parliament could alter the law. It followed that, if law stood above the King's will, yet remained alterable by Parliament, Parliament would be the supreme power in the State.

James II attempted to make the law alterable wholesale by the King. This, if it had been permitted, must have made the King supreme over Parliament, and, in fact, a

SOURCE: George Macaulay Trevelyan, *The English Revolution, 1688–1689*. Reprinted by permission of Oxford University Press (Oxford, England, 1938), pp. 164–166.

despot. The events of the winter of 1688–9 gave the victory to the opposite idea, which Chief Justice Coke and Selden had enunciated early in the century, that the King was the chief servant of the law, but not its master; the executant of the law, not its source; the laws should only be alterable by Parliament—Kings, Lords and Commons together. It is this that makes the Revolution the decisive event in the history of the English Constitution. It was decisive because it was never undone, as most of the work of the Cromwellian Revolution had been undone.

It is true that the first Civil War had been fought partly on this same issue:—the Common Law in league with Parliament had, on the field of Naseby, triumphed over the King in the struggle for the supreme place in the Constitution. But the victory of Law and Parliament had, on that occasion, been won only because Puritanism, the strongest religious passion of the hour, had supplied the fighting force. And religious passion very soon confused the Constitutional issue. Puritanism burst the legal bounds and, coupled with militarism, overthrew law and Parliament as well as King. Hence the necessity of the restoration in 1660 of King, law and Parliament together, without any clear definition of their ultimate mutual relations.

Now, in this second crisis of 1688, law and Parliament had on their side not only the Puritan passion, which had greatly declined, but the whole force of Protestant-Anglicanism, which was then at its height, and the rising influence of Latitudinarian scepticism—all arrayed against the weak Roman Catholic interest to which James had attached the political fortunes of the royal cause. The ultimate victor of the seventeenth-century struggle was not Pym or Cromwell, with their Puritan ideals, but Coke and Selden with their secular idea of the supremacy of law. In 1689 the Puritans had to be content with a bare toleration. But law triumphed, and therefore the law-making Parliament triumphed finally over the King.

Centuries of Childhood

Philippe Ariès

Through analysis of paintings such as Maternal Care *by Pieter de Hooch as well as other kinds of evidence, historians have changed our assumptions about attitudes toward childhood in Early Modern times. The most important of these historians is Philippe Ariès. The following is a selection from his* Centuries of Childhood.

> **Consider:** *How this reading relates to Hooch's painting; the differences between the seventeenth-century family, the medieval family, and the modern family according to Ariès.*

Between the end of the Middle Ages and the seventeenth century, the child had won a place beside his parents to which he could not lay claim at a time when it was customary to entrust him to strangers. This return of the children to the home was a great event: it gave the seventeenth-century family its principal characteristic, which distinguished it

---

SOURCE: Philippe Ariès, *Centuries of Childhood,* trans. Robert Baldick. Reprinted by permission of Alfred A. Knopf, Inc. (New York, 1962), pp. 403–404. Copyright © 1962 by Alfred A. Knopf, Inc.

from the medieval family. The child became an indispensable element of everyday life, and his parents worried about his education, his career, his future. He was not yet the pivot of the whole system, but he had become a much more important character. Yet this seventeenth-century family was not the modern family: it was distinguished from the latter by the enormous mass of sociability which it retained. Where the family existed, that is to say in the big houses, it was a centre of social relations, the capital of a little complex and graduated society under the command of the paterfamilias.

The modern family, on the contrary, cuts itself off from the world and opposes to society the isolated group of parents and children. All the energy of the group is expended on helping the children to rise in the world, individually and without any collective ambition: the children rather than the family.

The World We Have Lost: The Early Modern Family

Peter Laslett

The family is a tremendously important institution in any society. Changes in its structure and functions occur very slowly and gradually. With the passage of centuries since Early Modern times, we can see some sharp differences between the family of that period and the family of today. In the following selection Peter Laslett, a social historian from Cambridge who has written extensively on the Early Modern period, points out these differences.

> **Consider:** *The economic and social functions of the family revealed in this selection; what this document adds to the image of the family provided in the painting by Hooch and the document by Ariès; how the structure of this family differs from that of a typical twentieth-century family.*

In the year 1619 the bakers of London applied to the authorities for an increase in the price of bread. They sent in support of their claim a complete description of a bakery and an account of its weekly costs. There were thirteen or fourteen people in such an establishment: the baker and his wife, four paid employees who were called journeymen, two apprentices, two maidservants and the three or four children of the master baker himself. . . .

The only word used at that time to describe such a group of people was "family." The man at the head of the group, the entrepreneur, the employer, or the manager, was then known as the master or head of the family. He was father to some of its members and in place of father to the rest. There was no sharp distinction between his domestic and his economic functions. His wife was both his partner and his subordinate, a partner because she ran the family, took charge of the food and managed the women-servants, a subordinate because she was woman and wife, mother and in place of mother to the rest.

SOURCE: Excerpt from *The World We Have Lost* by Peter Laslett. Copyright © 1965 by Peter Laslett. Reprinted by permission of Charles Scribner's Sons.

The paid servants of both sexes had their specified and familiar position in the family, as much part of it as the children but not quite in the same position. At that time the family was not one society only but three societies fused together: the society of man and wife, of parents and children and of master and servant. But when they were young, and servants were, for the most part, young, unmarried people, they were very close to children in their status and their function. . . .

Apprentices, therefore, were workers who were also children, extra sons or extra daughters (for girls could be apprenticed too), clothed and educated as well as fed, obliged to obedience and forbidden to marry, unpaid and absolutely dependent until the age of twenty-one. If apprentices were workers in the position of sons and daughters, the sons and daughters of the house were workers too. John Locke laid it down in 1697 that the children of the poor must work for some part of the day when they reached the age of three. The sons and daughters of a London baker were not free to go to school for many years of their young lives, or even to play as they wished when they came back home. Soon they would find themselves doing what they could in *bolting*, that is sieving flour, or in helping the maidservant with her panniers of loaves on the way to the market stall, or in playing their small parts in preparing the never-ending succession of meals for the whole household.

We may see at once, therefore, that the world we have lost, as I have chosen to call it, was no paradise or golden age of equality, tolerance or loving kindness. It is so important that I should not be misunderstood on this point that I will say at once that the coming of industry cannot be shown to have brought economic oppression and exploitation along with it. It was there already. The patriarchal arrangements which we have begun to explore were not new in the England of Shakespeare and Elizabeth. They were as old as the Greeks, as old as European history, and not confined to Europe. And it may well be that they abused and enslaved people quite as remorselessly as the economic arrangements which had replaced them in the England of Blake and Victoria. When people could expect to live for only thirty years in all, how must a man have felt when he realized that so much of his adult life, perhaps all, must go in working for his keep and very little more in someone else's family?

Chapter Questions

1. What conditions facilitated the development of monarchical absolutism in the seventeenth century? What policies were used by kings to this end?
2. Why might mercantilist doctrines be particularly appealing to seventeenth-century monarchs?
3. How does family life reflect broader social, economic, and political aspects of the seventeenth century?

CHAPTER SEVENTEEN

The Scientific Revolution

One of the most important intellectual revolutions in Western civilization occurred in the seventeenth century. Building on some sixteenth-century breakthroughs and a more deeply rooted interest in the workings of the natural world, a small elite of thinkers and scientists—Descartes, Galileo, Newton, Kepler, Bacon, and Boyle—established the foundations for the modern sciences of astronomy, mathematics, physics, and chemistry. Although at first their work was known to only a few, their ideas spread widely during the eighteenth century.

In the process of developing the modern sciences, these thinkers challenged the established conception of the universe as well as previous assumptions about knowledge. This ultimately successful challenge, now known as the Scientific Revolution, had a number of key elements. First, the view of the universe as being stable, fixed, and finite, with the earth at its center, gave way to a view of the universe as moving and almost infinite, with the earth merely one of millions of bodies, all subject to the laws of nature. Second, earlier methods for ascertaining the truth, which primarily involved referring to traditional authorities such as Aristotle, Ptolemy, and the Church, were replaced by methods that emphasized scepticism, rationalism, and rigorous reasoning based on observed facts and mathematical laws. Third, although these thinkers remained concerned with their own deeply held religious beliefs, the general scientific orientation shifted from theological questions to secular questions that focused on how things worked.

The primary documents in this chapter emphasize two broad questions that faced these seventeenth-century scientists. First, how can one ascertain the truth? The answers of Descartes, Galileo, and Newton are examined. Second, what is the proper line between science and scriptural authority? Galileo, who came most directly into conflict with Church authorities, provides us with clues.

The secondary documents concentrate on the nature and causes of the Scientific Revolution. In what ways was seventeenth-century science different from the science of earlier centuries? What explains these differences? What were the motives of seventeenth-century scientists?

Most of these intellectual developments were known to only a few throughout Europe. In the eighteenth century these scientific ideas and methods became popularized as part of the intellectual ferment of the Enlightenment.

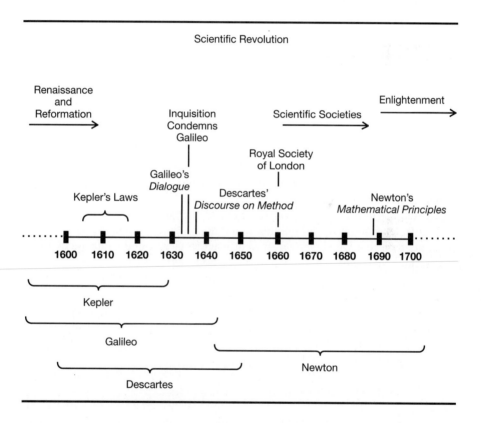

PRIMARY SOURCES

The Discourse on Method

René Descartes

Seventeenth-century science needed new philosophical and methodological standards for truth to replace those traditionally used to support scientific assumptions. These were forcefully provided by René Descartes (1596–1650) in his Discourse on Method *(1637). Born and educated in France, but spending his most productive years in Holland, Descartes gained fame as a mathematician, physicist, and metaphysical philosopher. The following excerpt from his* Discourse *contains the best-known statement of his approach to discovering truth.*

> **Consider:** *The ways in which Descartes' approach constitutes a break with traditional ways of ascertaining the truth; the weaknesses of this approach and how a modern scientist might criticize this method; how this approach reflects Descartes' background as a mathematician.*

In place of the multitude of precepts of which logic is composed, I believed I should find the four following rules quite sufficient, provided I should firmly and steadfastly resolve not to fail of observing them in a single instance.

The first rule was never to receive anything as a truth which I did not clearly know to be such; that is, to avoid haste and prejudice, and not to comprehend anything more in my judgments than that which should present itself so clearly and so distinctly to my mind that I should have no occasion to entertain a doubt of it.

The second rule was to divide every difficulty which I should examine into as many parts as possible, or as might be required for resolving it.

The third rule was to conduct my thoughts in an orderly manner, beginning with objects the most simple and the easiest to understand, in order to ascend as it were by steps to the knowledge of the most composite, assuming some order to exist even in things which did not appear to be naturally connected.

The last rule was to make enumerations so complete, and reviews so comprehensive, that I should be certain of omitting nothing.

Those long chains of reasoning, quite simple and easy, which geometers are wont to employ in the accomplishment of their most difficult demonstrations, led me to think that everything which might fall under the cognizance of the human mind might be connected together in a similar manner, and that, provided only one should take care not to receive anything as true which was not so, and if one were always careful to preserve the order necessary for deducing one truth from another, there would be none so remote at which he might not at last arrive, nor so concealed which he might not discover. And I had no great difficulty in finding those with which to make a beginning, for I knew

SOURCE: René Descartes, *The Discourse on Method*, in *The Philosophy of Descartes*, ed. and trans. Henry A. P. Torrey (New York: Henry Holt, 1982), pp. 46–48.

already that these must be the simplest and easiest to apprehend; and considering that, among all those who had up to this time made discoveries in the sciences, it was the mathematicians alone who had been able to arrive at demonstrations—that is to say, at proofs certain and evident—I did not doubt that I should begin with the same truths which they investigated.

Letter to Christina of Tuscany: Science and Scripture

Galileo Galilei

The most renowned scientist at the beginning of the seventeenth century was the Italian astronomer, mathematician, and physicist Galileo Galilei (1564–1642). His discoveries about gravity, velocity, and the movement of astronomical bodies were grounded in a scientific method that ran contrary to the accepted standards for truth and authority. In the following excerpt from a letter to the Grand Duchess Christina of Tuscany (1615), Galileo defends his ideas and delineates his view of the correct line between science and scriptural authority.

> **Consider:** *According to Galileo's view, the kinds of topics or questions that are appropriately scientific and those that are appropriately theological; how Galileo's views compare with those of Descartes; why Galileo's views are so crucial to the Scientific Revolution.*

I think that in discussions of physical problems we ought to begin not from the authority of scriptural passages, but from sense-experiences and necessary demonstrations; for the holy Bible and the phenomena of nature proceed alike from the divine Word, the former as the dictate of the Holy Ghost and the latter as the observant executrix of God's commands. It is necessary for the Bible, in order to be accommodated to the understanding of every man, to speak many things which appear to differ from the absolute truth so far as the bare meaning of the words is concerned. But Nature, on the other hand, is inexorable and immutable; she never transgresses the laws imposed upon her, or cares a whit whether her abstruse reasons and methods of operation are understandable to men. For that reason it appears that nothing physical which sense-experience sets before our eyes, or which necessary demonstrations prove to us, ought to be called in question (much less condemned) upon the testimony of biblical passages which may have some different meaning beneath their words. For the Bible is not chained in every expression to conditions as strict as those which govern all physical effects; nor is God any less excellently revealed in Nature's actions than in the sacred statements of the Bible. . . .

From this I do not mean to infer that we need not have an extraordinary esteem for the passages of holy Scripture. On the contrary, having arrived at any certainties in physics, we ought to utilize these as the most appropriate aids in the true exposition of

SOURCE: From Galileo Galilei, *Discoveries and Opinions of Galileo*, Stillman Drake, ed. and trans. Reprinted by permission of Doubleday & Company, Inc. (New York, 1957), pp. 182–183. Copyright © 1957 by Stillman Drake.

the Bible and in the investigation of those meanings which are necessarily contained therein, for these must be concordant with demonstrated truths. I should judge that the authority of the Bible was designed to persuade men of those articles and propositions which, surpassing all human reasoning, could not be made credible by science, or by any other means than through the very mouth of the Holy Spirit.

Yet even in those propositions which are not matters of faith, this authority ought to be preferred over that of all human writings which are supported only by bare assertions or probable arguments, and not set forth in a demonstrative way. This I hold to be necessary and proper to the same extent that divine wisdom surpasses all human judgment and conjecture.

But I do not feel obliged to believe that that same God who has endowed us with senses, reason, and intellect has intended to forgo their use and by some other means to give us knowledge which we can attain by them.

The Papal Inquisition of 1633: Galileo Condemned

Not surprisingly, Galileo found his views under attack from a variety of corners, including important groups within the Church. Ultimately his defense of Copernicanism, which held that the earth was not the center of the universe, was formally condemned by the Church. When he argumentatively summarized these ideas again in his Dialogue Concerning the Two Chief World Systems *(1632), he was brought before the Papal Inquisition, forced to recant his views, and confined to a villa on the outskirts of Florence. The following are some of the main charges against Galileo during his trial for heresy before the Inquisition in 1633.*

Consider: *Why Galileo's views were so threatening to the Church; some of the long-range consequences of such a stance by the Church toward these views.*

We say, pronounce, sentence, and declare that you, the said Galileo, by reason of the matters adduced in trial, and by you confessed as above, have rendered yourself in the judgment of this Holy Office vehemently suspected of heresy, namely, of having believed and held the doctrine—which is false and contrary to the sacred and divine Scriptures—that the Sun is the center of the world and does not move from east to west and that the Earth moves and is not the center of the world; and that an opinion may be held and defended as probable after it has been declared and defined to be contrary to the Holy Scripture; and that consequently you have incurred all the censures and penalties imposed and promulgated in the sacred canons and other constitutions, general and particular, against such delinquents. From which we are content that you be absolved, provided that, first, with a sincere heart and unfeigned faith, you abjure, curse, and detest before us the aforesaid errors and heresies and every other error and heresy contrary to the Catholic and Apostolic Roman Church in the form to be prescribed by us for you.

Source: Excerpt from George Santillana, *The Crime of Galileo*, p. 310. Reprinted by permission of The University of Chicago Press (Chicago, 1955). Copyright © 1955.

Mathematical Principles of Natural Philosophy

Sir Isaac Newton

The greatest scientific synthesis of the seventeenth century was made by Isaac Newton (1642–1727), who was born in England and attained a post as professor of mathematics at Cambridge University. Newton made his most important discoveries early in life. By the beginning of the eighteenth century he was the most admired scientific figure in Europe. He made fundamental discoveries concerning gravity, light, and differential calculus. Most important, he synthesized various scientific findings and methods into a description of the universe as working according to measurable, predictable mechanical laws. Newton's most famous work, Mathematical Principles of Natural Philosophy *(1687), contains his theory of universal gravitation. In the following selection from that work, Newton describes his four rules for arriving at knowledge.*

Consider: *Why Newton's rules might be particularly useful for the experimental sciences; ways these rules differ from those of Descartes.*

RULE I

We are to admit no more causes of natural things than such as are both true and sufficient to explain their appearances.

To this purpose the philosophers say that Nature does nothing in vain, and more is in vain when less will serve; for Nature is pleased with simplicity, and affects not the pomp of superfluous causes.

RULE II

Therefore to the same natural effects we must, as far as possible, assign the same causes.

As to respiration in a man and in a beast; the descent of stones in *Europe* and in *America;* the light of our culinary fire and of the sun; the reflection of light in the earth, and in the planets.

RULE III

The qualities of bodies, which admit neither intensification nor remission of degrees, and which are found to belong to all bodies within the reach of our experiments, are to be esteemed the universal qualities of all bodies whatsoever.

For since the qualities of bodies are only known to us by experiments, we are to hold for universal all such as universally agree with experiments; and such as are not liable to diminution can never be quite taken away.

SOURCE: Sir Isaac Newton, *Mathematical Principles of Natural Philosophy,* trans. Andrew Motte, rev. Florian Cajori (Berkeley, Calif.: University of California Press, 1947), pp. 398, 400. Reprinted by permission of the University of California Press.

RULE IV

In experimental philosophy we are to look upon propositions inferred by general induction from phenomena as accurately or very nearly true, notwithstanding any contrary hypotheses that may be imagined, till such time as other phenomena occur, by which they may either be made more accurate, or liable to exceptions.

This rule we must follow, that the argument of induction may not be evaded by hypotheses.

VISUAL SOURCES

A Vision of the New Science

One of the most important figures of the Scientific Revolution was the astronomer and mathematician Johannes Kepler (1571–1630). Photo 17-1 shows a page from the front of one of his works, first printed in Nuremberg in 1627, in which the "edifice" of astronomy is presented allegorically. The older but still respectable pillars of astronomy of Hipparchus and Ptolemy give way to the new, sturdy pillars of Kepler's immediate predecessors, Copernicus and Tycho Brahe. In the lower left panel Kepler is pictured in his study; in the center panel is a map of the island where Brahe's observatory was located; in the right-hand panel is a picture of two people working on a printing press. Throughout are various instruments used in astronomy.

The picture reveals much about the Scientific Revolution. The instruments emphasize how important measurement and observation were to the new science. The depiction of the old and new pillars suggests that the new scientists were replacing if not necessarily challenging the old, accepted scientific authorities by building on the work of their immediate predecessors—here Brahe on Copernicus, and Kepler on Brahe and Copernicus. The importance of communication among scientists is indicated by tribute to the printing press.

Consider: *How this picture illustrates the ways in which seventeenth-century scientists were breaking with earlier scientific assumptions.*

Photo 17-1

SECONDARY SOURCES

Why Was Science Backward in the Middle Ages?

Michael Postan

The scientific advances of the seventeenth century are commonly considered revolutionary because of their contrast with the previous state of science. One way to gain insight into the origins of the seventeenth-century developments is to look at earlier periods to see whether something was missing then that explains this contrast. In the following selection Michael Postan takes this approach, focusing specifically on the lack of scientific incentives in the Middle Ages.

> **Consider:** *Why scientific incentives were lacking in the Middle Ages; the typically medieval traits that discouraged the men of the Middle Ages from scientific exploration; how the concerns and problems faced by Galileo relate to this argument.*

It is generally agreed that the Middle Ages preserved for the use of later times the science of the ancients. Therein lies both the scientific achievement and the scientific failure of the medieval civilization. . . . What the Middle Ages took over they did not very much enrich. Indeed so small was their own contribution that historians of science are apt to regard the Middle Ages as something of a pause. . . .

Thus some advance on planes both purely intellectual and technical there was; yet taken together and placed against the vast panorama of medieval life, or indeed against the achievements of Greek and Hellenistic science in the fourth century B.C., or with the scientific activity of the seventeenth century, all these achievements are bound to appear very poor. Why then this poverty?

To this question many answers can be and have been given. But what most of them boil down to is the absence in medieval life of what I should be inclined to call scientific incentives. Students of science sometimes differ about the true inspiration of scientific progress. Some seek and find it in man's intellectual curiosity, in his desire to understand the workings of nature. Others believe that scientific knowledge grew and still grows out of man's attempts to improve his tools and his methods of production; that, in short, scientific truth is a by-product of technical progress. I do not want here to take sides in this particular controversy; what I want to suggest is that the Middle Ages were doubly unfortunate in that both the inspirations, the intellectual as well as the practical, failed more or less.

The easiest to account for is the intellectual. The Middle Ages were the age of faith, and to that extent they were unfavourable to scientific speculation. It is not that scientists as such were proscribed. For on the whole the persecution of men for their scientific ideas was very rare: rare because men with dangerous ideas, or indeed with any scientific

SOURCE: Michael Postan, "Why Was Science Backward in the Middle Ages?" in *A Short History of Science: Origins and Results of the Scientific Revolution* (London: Routledge and Kegan Paul), pp. 10–17. Reprinted by permission of Routledge and Kegan Paul, Ltd.

ideas at all, were themselves very rare; and it is indeed surprising that there were any at all. This does not mean that there were no intellectual giants. All it means is that in an age which was one of faith, men of intellect and spirit found the calls of faith itself—its elucidation, its controversies, and its conquests—a task sufficient to absorb them. To put it simply, they had no time for occupations like science.

In fact they had neither the time nor the inclination. For even if there had been enough men to engage in activities as mundane as science, there would still be very little reason for them to do so. In times when medieval religious dogma stood whole and unshaken the intellectual objects and the methods of science were, to say the least, superfluous. The purpose of scientific enquiry is to build up piecemeal a unified theory of the universe, of its origin and of its working. But in the Middle Ages was that process really necessary? Did not medieval man already possess in God, in the story of Creation and in the doctrine of Omnipotent Will, a complete explanation of how the world came about and of how, by what means and to what purpose, it was being conducted? Why build up in laborious and painstaking mosaic a design, which was already there from the outset, clear and visible to all?

So much for intellectual incentive. The practical incentive was almost equally feeble. Greater understanding of nature could not come from technical improvements, chiefly because technical improvements were so few. Medieval occupations continued for centuries without appreciable change of method. After the great period of initial development, i.e., after the late eleventh century, the routine of medieval farming in the greater part of Europe became as fixed as the landscape itself. In the history of the smithies, the weaving shops, or the potteries, there were occasional periods of innovation, but taking the Middle Ages as a whole technical improvement was very rare and very slow. For this medieval economic policy was largely to blame. In the course of centuries economic activities got surrounded with a vast structure of bye-laws and regulations. . . . For bye-laws were as a rule based on the technical methods in existence when they were framed; and once framed they were to stand in the way of all subsequent change.

What is more, so deeply ingrained was the spirit of protection that in every local trade the technical methods were treated as a secret. . . . The men of the Middle Ages were unable to do more than they did because they were lacking in scientific incentive. What they achieved in advancing the practical arts of humanity or in preserving and transmitting ancient learning, they did in so far and as long as they were not typically medieval.

Early Modern Europe: Motives for the Scientific Revolution

Sir George Clark

By the seventeenth century, certain broad historical developments had set the stage for individuals to make the discoveries we associate with the Scientific Revolution. In addition, these individuals

---

SOURCE: Sir George Clark, *Early Modern Europe.* Reprinted by permission of The Oxford University Press (Oxford, England, 1957), pp. 164–165.

were motivated in ways that medieval people were not and used the new and growing body of techniques, materials, and knowledge to make their discoveries. In the following selection, British historian Sir George Clark, a recognized authority on the seventeenth century, examines some of the motives that led people to engage in scientific work.

> **Consider:** *The distinctions Clark makes among different people engaged in scientific work; why, more than thirteenth- or fourteenth-century people, these seventeenth-century people had a "disinterested desire to know."*

There were an infinite number of motives which led men to engage in scientific work and to clear the scientific point of view from encumbrances; but we may group together some of the most important under general headings, always remembering that in actual life each of them was compounded with the others. There were economic motives. The Portuguese explorers wanted their new instrument for navigation; the German mine-owners asked questions about metallurgy and about machines for lifting and carrying heavy loads; Italian engineers improved their canals and locks and harbours by applying the principles of hydrostatics; English trading companies employed experts who used new methods of drawing charts. Not far removed from the economic motives were those of the physicians and surgeons, who revolutionized anatomy and physiology, and did much more good than harm with their new medicines and new operations, though some of them now seem absurd. Like the doctors, the soldiers called science to their aid in designing and aiming artillery or in planning fortifications. But there were other motives far removed from the economic sphere. Jewellers learnt much about precious and semi-precious stones, but so did magicians. Musicians learnt the mathematics of harmony; painters and architects studied light and colour, substances and proportions, not only as craftsmen but as artists. For a number of reasons religion impelled men to scientific study. The most definite and old-established was the desire to reach absolute correctness in calculating the dates for the annual fixed and movable festivals of the Church: it was a pope who presided over the astronomical researchers by which the calendar was reformed in the sixteenth century. Deeper and stronger was the desire to study the wonders of science, and the order which it unravelled in the universe, as manifestations of the Creator's will. This was closer than any of the other motives to the central impulse which actuated them all, the disinterested desire to know.

No Scientific Revolution for Women

Bonnie S. Anderson and Judith P. Zinsser

The Scientific Revolution was generally carried out by men. A few women participated directly in the Scientific Revolution, but they were the exception rather than the rule. The Scientific

---

SOURCE: Excerpts from *A History of Their Own*, vol. II, by Bonnie Anderson and Judith Zinsser. Copyright © 1988 by Bonnie Anderson and Judith Zinsser. Reprinted by permission of HarperCollins Publishers, Inc.

Revolution was based on principles such as observing, measuring, experimenting, and coming to reasoned conclusions. Were these principles applied by men to change assumptions about women, particularly about female physiology? Bonnie S. Anderson and Judith P. Zinsser address this question in their interpretive survey of women in European history, A History of Their Own.

> **Consider:** *According to Anderson and Zinsser, why there was no Scientific Revolution for women; how perceptions of female physiology relate to broader assumptions about women and men.*

In the sixteenth and seventeenth centuries Europe's learned men questioned, altered, and dismissed some of the most hallowed precepts of Europe's inherited wisdom. The intellectual upheaval of the Scientific Revolution caused them to examine and describe anew the nature of the universe and its forces, the nature of the human body and its functions. Men used telescopes and rejected the traditional insistence on the smooth surface of the moon. Galileo, Leibnitz, and Newton studied and charted the movement of the planets, discovered gravity and the true relationship between the earth and the sun. Fallopio dissected the human body, Harvey discovered the circulation of the blood, and Leeuwenhoek found spermatozoa with his microscope.

For women, however, there was no Scientific Revolution. When men studied female anatomy, when they spoke of female physiology, of women's reproductive organs, of the female role in procreation, they ceased to be scientific. They suspended reason and did not accept the evidence of their senses. Tradition, prejudice, and imagination, not scientific observation, governed their conclusions about women. The writings of the classical authors like Aristotle and Galen continued to carry the same authority as they had when first written, long after they had been discarded in other areas. Men spoke in the name of the new "science" but mouthed words and phrases from the old misogyny. In the name of "science" they gave a supposed physiological basis to the traditional views of women's nature, function, and role. Science affirmed what men had always known, what custom, law, and religion had postulated and justified. With the authority of their "objective," "rational" inquiry they restated ancient premises and arrived at the same traditional conclusions: the innate superiority of the male and the justifiable subordination of the female.

Chapter Questions

1. What were the main ways in which the science of the seventeenth century constituted a break from the past? What were some of the main problems facing seventeenth-century scientists in making this break? How did they handle these problems?

2. How would you explain the occurrence of the Scientific Revolution in the seventeenth century rather than in the sixteenth or eighteenth century?